C000227693

THE SPIR

MERIDIAN

Crossing Aesthetics

Werner Hamacher

& David E. Wellbery

Editors

Translated by
Anthony A. Nassar

Stanford
University
Press

Stanford
California
2000

THE SPIRIT OF UTOPIA

Ernst Bloch

Assistance for the translation has been provided
by Inter Nationes, Bonn.

The Spirit of Utopia follows the second edition
of the original German text, published in 1964 as
Geist der Utopie: Bearbeitete Neuauflage der zweiten Fassung von 1923
© dieser Fassung Suhrkamp Verlag Frankfurt am Main 1964.

Stanford University Press
Stanford, California

Printed in the United States of America

CIP data are at the end of the book

In Everlasting Memory of
Else Bloch-von Stritzky
† *2 January 1921*

Contents

THE SPIRIT OF UTOPIA

OBJECTIVE (1918, 1923)

I am. We are.

That is enough. Now we have to begin. Life has been put in our hands. For itself it became empty already long ago. It pitches senselessly back and forth, but we stand firm, and so we want to be its initiative and we want to be its ends.

What just was will probably soon be forgotten. Only an empty, awful memory hangs in the air. Who was defended? Foul, wretched profiteers. What was young had to fall, was forced to die for ends so alien and inimical to the spirit, but the despicable ones were saved, and now they sit there in their comfortable drawing rooms.[1] Not one of them was lost, but those who waved other flags, so much bloom, so much dream, so much hope for the spirit, are dead. The artists defended the middlemen and kept the home front warm for the instigators. There has never been a more dismal military objective than Imperial Germany's: a suffocating coercion imposed by mediocrities and tolerated by mediocrities; a triumph of stupidity, guarded by the gendarme, acclaimed by the intellectuals who did not have enough brains to provide slogans.

So of course it has remained, even up to today, as though we had not been burned badly enough. The War ended, the Revolution began, and along with the Revolution, doors opened. But of course, they soon shut. The black marketeer moved, sat back down, and everything obsolete drifted back into place. The profiteering farmer, the mighty *grand bourgeois* truly put out the fire in places, and the panicked *petit bourgeois* helps to enfeeble and encrust, as always. Nonproletarian youth itself is more coarse and stupid than youth has ever been; the universities have truly become the spirit's burial mounds, filled with the stink of corruption and immovable gloom. So those who apparently have been restored completely reenact what the reaction of a century ago auditioned: the slogans about native soil, the traditionalism of *Vaterland,* and that oblivious Romanticism that forgot the Peasant's War and saw only knights' castles rising into enchanted, moonlit nights. Once again, predictably, the writer helps to apply the brake; indeed, Expressionism's former votaries—incinerating what they had just recently exalted—rush to help incompetent literary homesteaders patch together misrepresentations from the tasteful ruins of the past, in order to bar the way for the vitally formative consciousness of the future, of the city, of the collective; in order to transform profiteers' lies into ideology; in order to make their lamentable hygiene, their doubly imitative Romanticism absolute. Meanwhile the West with its millions of proletarians has not yet spoken; meanwhile there is a Marxist republic in Russia; meanwhile the eternal questions of our souls, of our religious conscience, still burn, undiminished, unbowed, their absolute claims unredeemed. More than that: we have at least learned from the same outlook on reality that came a century ago. Marx thoroughly purified socialist logic of all simple, false, disengaged and abstract enthusiasm, mere Jacobinism, and we will certainly not forget the spirit of Kant and Baader above all *Realpolitik*—whereas the Romanticism of the latest reaction has inherited absolutely nothing real, is neither objective nor enthusiastic nor universalistic, but simply stupid, isolated, without spirit and without Christ, in its pathos of the "autochthonous" capable only of eliciting the decline of Western Civilization into animalistic insensibility and irreligious obliteration: faded bud, faded blossom, and for today just a civilized enervation, a large fleet, and merely the pessimistic registration of the continuing passage of history as the only goal, but for Europe only imminent, eternal death.

This is how bad things could, had to get with us. Certainly, I would sing for my supper. But this dance around the golden calf, better, the calfskin with nothing underneath: this still came as a surprise. It means we have no idea of socialism. Instead we have become the poorest of vertebrates; whoever among us does not worship his belly worships the state; everything else has sunk to the level of a joke, of entertainment. We have longing, and brief knowledge, but little deed, and—which also explains this lack—no breadth, no outlook, no ends, no inner threshold, presentiently crossed, no kernel, and at the center no gathering conscience of the Absolute.[2] Here, however, in this book, a new beginning is posited, and the unlost heritage takes possession of itself; that glow deep inside, over there, is no cowardly "as if," no pointless commentary; rather, what rises above all the masquerades and the expired civilizations is the one, the eternal goal, the one presentiment, the one conscience, the one salvation: rises from our hearts, unbroken in spite of everything, from the deepest part, that is, the realest part of our waking dreams: that is, from the last thing remaining to us, the only thing worthy to remain. This book offers an introduction to our figure, our blossoming gathering: it already begins to ring out through our interpretation of a simple pitcher; then as the *a priori* latent theme of all the plastic arts, though it is really central to all the magic of music; then, finally, in the ultimate self-encounter, in the comprehended darkness of the lived moment, as this one thing leaps up and hears itself in the inconstruable, absolute question, the problem of the We in itself. This is as far as the *internal* path can at first go, namely toward what we call a self-encounter, the preparation of the inner word, without which every gaze outward remains empty, instead of being the magnet, the force that draws forth the inner word and helps it break through the falseness of this world. In the end, however, *after* this *internal* vertical movement: may a new expanse appear, the *world* of the soul, the *external, cosmic* function of utopia, maintained against misery, death, the husk-realm of mere physical nature. Only in us does this light still burn, and we are beginning a fantastic journey toward it, a journey toward the interpretation of our waking dream, toward the implementation of the central concept of utopia. To find it, to find the right thing, for which it is worthy to live, to be organized, and to have time: that is why we go, why we cut new, metaphysically constitutive paths, summon what is not, build into the blue, and build ourselves into the blue, and there seek the true, the real, where the merely factual disappears—*incipit vita nova.*

The Self-Encounter

An Old Pitcher

Too Near

I am by my self.[1]

That I move, that I speak: is not there. Only immediately afterward can I hold it up in front of me. Ourselves within: while we live, we do not see it; we trickle away. What really happened there, then, what we really were there, refuses to coincide with what we can really experience.[2] It is not what one is, and certainly not what one means.

Slightly Beneath

I want to occupy my self, however.

Yet, I am still beneath the glass from which I drink. Insofar as I move it, and finally carry it to my mouth, I am above it: the glass serves me. But I do not keep myself in such an immaculate place as the glass, which I can at least see completely. While I stand so near to myself, whether I am drinking or not, that I have always just been experienced, not yet seen.

THE GLASS AND THE PITCHER

I am by the pitcher. Thus it leads inside, stands before the wall in the room.[3] The wall is green, the mirror is golden, the window is black, the lamp burns brightly. But the pitcher is not simply warm, let alone so indisputably beautiful as other fine old artifacts.

Such pitchers are now often imitated. There is no harm in that, but there are expensive "bearded man" pitchers, beautifully preserved, delib-

7

erately sculpted and elaborately fluted, with narrow necks, a neatly coifed head on the neck and a heraldic shield on the belly, and they overshadow the simple pitcher. Who loves the pitcher, however, knows how superficial the expensive pitchers are, and prefers the clumsy, brown implement, with almost no neck, a wild man's bearded face, and a significant, snail-shaped solar emblem on the curvature.

They come mainly from the Rhine-Franconian area. Perhaps they are even Roman: at least the clay of which they are fired reminds one of inexpensive Roman pieces. They also echo the Italic sense of form, if much more muscular, even soldierly, and then Nordic, coarsened. And so they wandered from the *taverna* into the public houses of the German Imperial cities, where now they stand, filled with wine, on the shelves along every wall; here and there, farmers such as one sees in Tenier's paintings, with broad noses, still wrap their hands around them. Soon they had to disappear, as everything hand-crafted has disappeared. What one most notices is the bearded wild man on the belly of this solid, Northern artifact. With him, a strange thread weaves back to us. For the dead are thirsty and weary, and the little pitcher buried with them soon runs dry. Elsewhere, however, wild men keep new pitchers, magical pitchers filled with the water of life.[4] One usually meets them on lonely hillsides, and even now, mostly in Low German areas, such places are still disreputably called "Nobiskrug," and the inn of the dead is supposed to lie close by.[5] The men tend a herd not far from Urd's well from which the golden water flows, and no doubt they direct the souls of the dead so that they will not miss the way home.[6] Hence the wild man holding an uprooted pine tree in his hand can still be seen on signs outside inns, and similarly, for he knows and guards the secrets of the eternal treasure, on coins and paper currency. Most often, however, one sees him in allegorical form, bearing the coats of arms of Low German as well as Prussian nobility. Here, however, on our pitcher, the bearded aspect of the forest spirit still peers out at us; the dark, moist, primordial forests have suddenly drawn very near, and this gigantic troll's head radiates his faunish, amulet-like, alchemical image. They speak to us, these old pitchers, from a time when they say the long-eared hare could still be seen dancing with the fiery man on Hessian fields before nightfall, and they preserve the old things, like farmers: literally.

It is hard to find out what it looks like inside the dark, spacious belly of these pitchers. One would no doubt like to occupy that space here.

The endless, curious children's question arises again. For the pitcher is close kin to the child-like. And additionally, here the interior goes along; the pitcher holds and has its measure. But only the sense of smell can still deduce, rather than perceive, its faint aroma of long-forgotten beverages. And yet whoever looks long enough at the pitcher soon begins to carry its color and form with him. Not every puddle I step in makes me gray; not every railroad track bends me around a corner. But I could probably be formed like the pitcher, see myself as something brown, something peculiarly organic, some Nordic amphora, and not just mimetically or simply empathetically, but so that I thus become for my part richer, more present, cultivated further toward myself by this artifact that participates in me. That is true of all things that have grown, and here, in drinking pitchers, the people labored to express their pleasure and their deeper sense of contentment, to affix themselves to these implements of the household and the public house. Everything that was ever made in this way, out of love and necessity, leads a life of its own, leads into a strange, new territory, and returns with us formed as we could not be in life, adorned with a certain, however weak sign, the seal of our self. Here, too, one feels oneself looking down a long, sunlit corridor with a door at the far end, as in a work of art. The pitcher is not one, it has nothing of the work of art about it, but a work of art should at least be like this in order really to be one, and that alone would certainly already be a lot.

The Production of the Ornament

We, however, start from the beginning.

We are poor, we have unlearned how to play. We have forgotten it, our hands have unlearned how to dabble.

This is also more or less how flint was smoothed. All around us it looks as though no one had ever known a craft and been capable of passing it down. But in return, we paint like savages again, in the best sense, in the sense of the primordial, the restless, unconcerned, concerned. For this is more or less how the mask was carved. This is more or less how primitive man shaped his fetishes, if only the simple need to express oneself should again be the same. Thus the two clearly and immediately separate, which helps us, forces us, to really kill the cold machinery, so one can see what still remains to be generously warmed up again.

TECHNOLOGICAL COLD

At first, certainly, almost everything just looks back at us hollowly.

How could it be otherwise, and where would a vital, beautifully made implement come from, now that no one knows living in one place to make his house warm and sturdy?

Yet that alone is not to blame for the lowlier things. Their basis is not only that the client has become unfamiliar or anonymous. For if we consider the problem of the office: then in the working man, who only uses his room in the evening, to relax, to read or to receive male guests, and in the writer or scholar, as the born occupant of the workroom and library, conceivable in so to speak Faustian terms, we are given at least two parallel sets of needs, demands, and design problems. Meanwhile what the market as well as every design offers, already anticipating the middle class, remains irredeemably predetermined by the lowest common denominator, the so-called smoking room. One could certainly claim, therefore, that customers are ready for something that the inanity of the available selection cannot provide. It is accordingly not so much the consumer but the producer who bears the blame for all this ugly stuff—and not even he alone; rather, the machine which he operates also has this misery and this pervasive destruction of the imagination on its conscience—this man who has forced every museum's applied art collection to end with the 1840s.

It knew, the machine, how to make everything as lifeless and subhuman on a small scale as our newer urban developments are on a larger scale. Its real objective is the bathroom and the toilet, these most indisputable and original accomplishments of our time, just as Rococo furniture and Gothic cathedrals represent structures that define every other art object of their respective epochs. Now *lavatoriality* dominates; somehow, water runs from every wall, and even the most expensive products of our age's industrial diligence now partake of the wizardry of modern sanitation, the *a priori* of the finished industrial product.

One should certainly think *busily* and economically for a while. All the more so as we no longer have a choice, for the old craftsmen will not return. And we would certainly not choose the new ones; the sight of them is so horrible that nothing more could still be grafted onto them. Often it is precisely the dirtiest *petit bourgeois* scoundrels, with all the bad qualities of a *Mittelstand* in decline, greedy, duplicitous, undependable, shameless, and sloppy, who as producers of handicrafts now occupy the role of the master craftsmen. But if this battle is already lost, then a so to speak humanly *warm* industrial mode of manufacture must also fail. For progress and capitalism have till now constructed technology, at least in its industrial application, solely for purposes of fast turnover and high profits, and certainly not, as is so often claimed, in order to alleviate our labor, let alone improve the results. We could not say where the alleviation was in the humming of the modern loom, in the night shift, in the terrible coercion of its invariant rotations per minute, in the prevention of a human being's pleasure in work who has only pieces to work on and never at any point experiences the joy of seeing the whole, finished product—we would not know what the alleviation was, let alone the improvement in comparison to the older, more comfortable mode of manufacture (here a house, and there, not far away, a workshop) of a small quantum of honestly made, artful wares. An entirely different, in other words, a humanistic technology would have to come, and not for profit, and would have to be invented for entirely different, for purely functional ends, without any amateurishness in the production of commodities or in the replacement of goods once made with artistic intention: if relief is to come, but the limit as well, the transformation of the mechanical spirit's functional form, the appearance of free, purely expressive color and fullness liberated from adornment, from the old luxury. All honor to the Industrial Revolution, but everything it brought which is not purely serviceable and *functional* (such as the locomotive or the steel factory): all the *static* junk which it vomited up as replacements will be packed away one morning, and the exploitative, culturally ruinous means by which these replacements were produced will be put into the same peculiar museum as the cannon, in order to clarify the allusions in certain ancient sagas. Again, we must surely think *busily*, industrially, for in this breathless pace, in this acceleration, disquiet, and expansion of our sphere of activity, great spiritual and intellectual works are latent. But as far as technology goes, that applies only to the machine as a functional alleviation, and not to the factories' craven mass junk, let alone to the frightful desolation of a *total* automation of the world.

Then, of course, when one isolates it in this fashion, the cold appliance no longer remains everywhere problematic. Then there will certainly be opportunities to turn against the machine in anger; where Marx will be proved right against the syndicalists; where on behalf of expression finally freed from toil and stylistic necessity one can at least give thanks to the immovable cold, to the however joyless comfort, to serviceability and functionality as the machine's honorable future, sole vocation. Even if the end of good taste, the intended beginning of primitive, purely objective function will not lead us back into the aesthetically traditional good old days, nonetheless, consciously functional technology can, under certain conditions, lead to a significant emancipation of *art* from stylization, from obsolete style, and, on the other hand, from bare functional form. For in the end the machine is no more the decisive *movens* of a monstrous transformation of civilized visibility than is the consumer or the producer. Rather the machine is likewise just a link in a chain; decline like hope are here really just the counterparts of Spirit in retreat, endangered, but perhaps also escaped into larger domains; the machine's conditions of possibility, as well as of its pure application, belong ultimately to the philosophy of history, closely connected to the conditions of the possibility of an antiluxurious Expressionism.

FUNCTIONAL FORM AND EXPRESSIVE EXUBERANCE

Certainly, people are already striving here and there on a lower level to escape from the hardness, regrettably. It's true as far as it goes: obstetric tongs must be smooth, sugar cube tongs never. So one tries to ease things with *color*: nothing may just be pasted on, nothing may be embellished with the same mangy or ulcerous abominations as before, and yet all this bare rectilinearity looks as though it were about to disappear, glazed bricks try to conciliate us, pleasant vistas try to appear here and there, the factory goods are garlanded. But all that happens rarely now, and certainly not at the right end. Depleted soil is being planted that will bloom sparsely if at all, will yield little more than stones.

For what precisely remains doubtful is whether artful craft objects, each individually, luxuriously decorated, can ever appear around us again. Even if they could—after every organic transmission of tradition has broken off, after the force with which the machine installed itself and awaits its consequence—even if a crafted object, a commodity object, a static implement could be produced beautifully: this still hardly goes much beyond the beauty of brightly painted concrete; it seems that even at the theoretical extreme, only the *stylistic minimum* is sporadically attainable that was displayed by the very first frame chairs, prior to any stylistic beauty, and which, accordingly, last appeared a century ago, as Biedermeier. It is no accident that almost none of our many sober and unimaginative draftsmen can ever go any further that that. Concrete cannot be set on fire; it is healthy in an entirely other sense, and without concrete we would have no usably modern houses. Even the prudent machine has a certain, for its part justifiable ambition to abbreviate the processes which were aesthetically honorable precisely for their laboriousness, for their— this is Ruskin's enchantingly sentimental doctrine—organicity, their humanly *freighted* expressivity. One cannot—if on the other hand one still gives weight to unity of conception—one cannot possibly build an Expressionistic house; it would be impossible to make airtight windows, elevators, desks, telephones, and the entire rectangularly flashing world of functional forms excessively ornamental, to break or outfit them with Lehmbruck's, with Archipenko's curves. The only point of contact, and here again an illusory one, is offered by the banquet hall, the concert hall, and the theater, particularly where, as with Pölzig, the building radiates onto the stage, and into the discrete magic of its illusionism; may the cupola also remain a permanently discrete structure, already a link to sacral architecture. Otherwise, however, the more recent art, in spite of its temporary Cubistic auxiliary forms, is in no position to redraw functional devices or buildings, let alone "decoratively" to cloak them; it would contradict such art to realize in emotional terms equipment whose value and postulated essence consists precisely in the imperceptibility, the unemotional practice, the purely utilitarian objectives, the happily obvious sobriety of the *inessential.* The greatest aesthetic attainment still possible with the machine, and with the pure, functional forms it has brought— as long as not every device has disappeared and become purely functional, socializable equipment—is thus precisely the return to the Biedermeier, the stylistic minimum at the base and after the expiry of every style. But even this final remainder, which after all does not need to be *petit bourgeois* or bucolic, nonetheless, as one can recognize, represents something ultimately superfluous, an emblem not set by the neat manner of the mechanical spirit. The achievement of new styles by functional form thus becomes impossible; the constructions of engineers, as well as the Biedermeier that may still abruptly expand them, must avoid the kind of constructional similarity which the skyscraper attempts to display to the Birs Nimrud, and the festive cinema façade to the oldest geometrical architecture, which of course depends on an entirely different geometry. For no opposition is more irreconcilable than the one between these constructions pretending to be art by sliding over into the monumental or Egyptian, and something entirely different coming due in our time: purely spiritual, musical expression that aspires to be *ornament.*

Only when functional form is content to fulfill its modest duty will expression emerge, without a care, freed from style. A comprehended unburdening, a comprehended release, purifying what had been contaminated by work, by handicraft, by eudaemonist stylistics: marching separately, attacking together. The birth of integral technology and the birth of integral expression, the two held carefully apart, will occur by means of the same magic: the most thorough lack of decoration on the one side, the most fundamental exuberance, ornamentalism on the other, and both of them variables of the same exodus. So let us honestly get to work, and let life go only where it alone should. It has been said that an oppressed Russian peasant would have to have been a saint in order to become a decent person at all. Or, following Lukács, that a modern architect would need at least the talent of a Michelangelo just in order to design a handsomely solid table. One must add, however, that, like children or farmers, a needy amateur afflicted by the pressures of life, whose skill does not compare to even the least of the old masters, can still, in the strange atmosphere of these times, create inartistic, unstylish, but expressive and sigillary artifacts that have nothing in common with the *objets d'art* of competent interior decoration or even so-called connoisseurship. This is the way that Klee and Marc wanted to point out, and it is the same goddess who in craft grants the need, in technology a tremendously successful alleviation, in expression a surplus: a flash of fiery and enigmatic signs, a sudden convergence of every road on an overgrown, insignificant side road that becomes the main road to human progress. That was already the secret tendency, as the Renaissance began to secularize style, that let Karlstadt, Savonarola, and the other iconoclasts rage and flare up against eudaemonist art: undiscriminating, but for reasons of pure light, forthright expression, the demolition of compromise, spiritual directness. May art henceforth stay far from utility, and renounce the lower vocation of taste, of the luxurious stylization of the lower life; may *great technique* dominate, an unburdening, cool, ingenious, democratic "luxury" for all, a reconstruction of this star the earth with the goal of the abolition of poverty, delegation of toil to machines, centralized automation of the inessential, and thereby the possibility of idleness; and may *great expression* rule, moving ornamentation into the depths again and granting pure signs of understanding, pure ornaments of resolution to the sounding of our inner care above the silence of the outer.

This is the place, after the aesthetic has been secured emphatically enough against confusions, compromises, and slippages into the practical sphere, to call attention to a correlation within *historical* handicraft, one already in its time irritating to every utility, a still latent, salvageable, decidedly spiritual meaning. Of course even in this instance, a chair is still only there in order to be sat on; it simply refers to the person at rest. And a statue is there in order to be seen, or rather—since it is just as indifferent to every other correlation slipping into the life surrounding it—it rests within itself, turned toward its own glory. The psycho-socially embedded difference between applied and pure, high art is immediately defined by this changed angle of vision, by the observer's own rotational process. For everything that is to be used, everything that remains floor and armchair, that is occupied by an individual *presently* experiencing himself, falls into the category of craft; whereas creations that elicit the gaze, that rise up as entablature, as a sculpture extending over us, in other words become the armchair, the shrine for the body of the higher, the godly, are occupied solely by the individual experiencing himself *symbolically* therein, and hence belong to high art. And because craft objects helpfully surround us, it was always desirable that they be comfortably luxurious, maintain an elegant perfection, and wear style as a concept as much of taste as of the deliberate construction appropriate to *objets d'art*. It has always been the characteristic of applied art that it arrests certain elements of ornamentation and construction from the expressive movement that would overshoot it, and stabilizes them as rhythm or measure; just as the entire Greek middle period and half of the modern age, that is, the modern age of art "classically" framed by the Renaissance and the Empire, leaving aside the Baroque, has after all supplied art as an agreeable but unspiritual accompaniment to life, not as the allaying of the soul's need, not as the consolatory song of individual expression unconcerned with beauty or ugliness, not as the portrayal of the higher story of redemption brought down to a human level. There is thus a powerful difference between tastefully appointed functionality and high art: it is not diminished when the subject of consumption can linger in different places, when what the cavalier employs as a practical object appears to the peasant as high art, when much of what the Sun King owned as the most exquisite decrees of his personal absoluteness and readily emphasized as such, became and was seen to become high art, art merely to be gazed upon as meaningful in itself, for later eras for which the social, the as it were already now theologically emphatic point of the individual, has submerged. What we have to add here, what is decisive, is this: There is something about and above the old chair which lives, which does not remain simply comfortable, and lets us look across at something more than the person who happens to be resting there. *Tertium datur*: there are Baroque armchairs too significant for practical use, that make something new out of the strange attitude, out of the removed mask, so to speak, of "sitting down": something casually spectral, fabulous, the most remarkable line. No longer taste; no longer deliberate, laboriously stylized, autonomously immanent form; rather what emerges here—and extends into a sphere in which stands only the ultimacy of pure art—an impression from life, indeed, an already indicatively descriptive formal sign, a seal of the depth and of the waking dream: painted as if to copy the skin, and carved as if to copy the skeleton of a wraith, a spirit, an inner figure. In other words the project of Baroque insignia, now merely luxurious instead of mystical, was only possible in eras where the throne commingled with the altar, where persons of state sealed a blasphemous bond with the metaphysical, where solar kings and the Holy Roman emperor's theological majesty emphasized, godlike, an entirely differently meaningful ornamental art. If with socialism and reformation in our hearts we dissolve this bond in order to rethink the past as well as the present, we destroy this sacrilege: whereupon it immediately becomes clear that *truly great historical applied art* least of all supports secular implements and secular purposes as wealthy, feudal, theocratic, pontifical luxury; rather it all the more—with this exemplary benefit for Expression: not having to lose all architecture—points to a spiritual *a priori* of construction, of architecture, to a mundanely useless construction for the sake of a great seal to another world. A third element thus lives between chair and statue, perhaps even above the statue: a higher-order "applied art" in which, instead of a comfortable, as it were stagnant carpet, assembled from moments of stabilization, a purely luxurious carpet for use, a true carpet extends, pointing beyond, a carpet of pure, abstract form.[1] In this other kind of "applied art," whose adaptation would be, precisely, Expressionistic, linear, arabesque ornament appears as a prelude, meaning precisely: as true carpet and pure form, as the more easily accomplished but thereby exemplary corrective to the transcendent form, to the seal, to the erupted, multidimensional, transcending ornament of recent painting, sculpture and architecture. Here there is no longer any danger that dryness, the Egyptian world of stone that nevertheless remains part of the constructional intention, will affect Expression's so completely different seriousness, its tentatively extramundane abstraction. Rather, a new exuberance will appear, finally to grant the Baroque profaned by luxury—even, further back—the *ceremonial masks*, the *totems*, the *carved roofbeams*, the *Gothic sacristies*—a decisive share in the rerememberance of metapsychological and nonetheless outward ornament.

We have never really wanted anything but to see ourselves openly. So we have always whittled since early times, worked in wood. One did not need to be skilled; whatever impressed or deeply pained someone was banished with a few strokes, or by just the angularity of the wood.[2]

But the weak flesh cannot survive alone, and reaches for a husk. Thus the tool appeared, which had to be handy and comfortable. The flint was smoothed jaggedly, in other words functionally; the clay vessel was turned to be easily gripped; the material itself and its intended function alone set the conditions. This is a particular world, and it led us increasingly outside, from the expression of something inward toward the subjectively alien material. In the earliest carvings, our inner dimensions still interfere, magnifying the legs, the eyes according to the importance which we had given them, and the magical volition pushing upward already lent these masks our remote countenance. In contrast, the earliest, materially consistent functional forms leave the path from a human being to what is human; stone, structural clarity, in other words something incipiently Egyptian and then again natural, forces itself into the labor of shaping.

The Appeal of the Greek

Nevertheless, this artistic vitality, the only thing one aimed at, will not cease moving. So weavings, pitchers began to be covered in stripes and cheerfully clear lines, at least; a sort of sparingly decorative life sprang up again, a playfully geometrizing regularity. Above all, however, there appears, in a truly vital empathy, suffusing the functional proportions of the construction, the *Greek* style, whose traces can be found everywhere even where there was no actual cultural transmission. Of course, the Greek smile is still sociable and restrained, and does not yet take up the inner luxuriance against the stone; instead it wants to be both living and subdued, empathetic and symmetrical, painterly and architectonic at once, thus becoming pure "plasticity." In its amphitheaters, Greek art becomes simply a harmonized landscape, in its temples simply an urbane façade, a eudaemonistic balance between life and rigor staged *before* the depths of either, and which thus attains neither inward expressivity nor the power of an outward space.

Hence one simply enjoys the beauty here, and takes and uses what one likes. The vine, the acanthus blooms; tree stumps hold up the figure; a soft, elastic Ionic cushion is still laid between the column and the entablature. But also: ovolo and meander extend their stricter line through it all, their as it were inorganic character, and the spirit of the stone triumphs at the very least as symmetry, as a harmless, finely decorative sort of geometry. On the one hand, then, Greek form has such life that Pygmalion can desire it as his beloved, such that the form is indifferent to whether it is fashioned in ivory, silver, bronze, clay, marble or even flesh. On the other hand, however, the figure is here so well balanced again, so full of *euphrosyne* and measure, that she meets the unity of the slab at least halfway; for this reason, the Hellenic torsi from which has been broken off that which had to be broken off in accordance with the spirit of the material, seem better than the originals. The Venus de Milo is first "perfected" as a torso; in contrast, the damaged statue of Khefre, which had already ceded everything to the stone, or, for entirely different reasons, namely its fullness of life, fullness of expression, one of the Apostles' statues at Reims that seems to have escaped its material, seem like shards in their condition as torsi, and do not even permit the extra-artistic, elegiac associations that ruins do. In short: Greece as well as the Renaissance occupy the same impious, eudaemonistic, unserious and indecisive place; what so grievously disturbs us in the profound, Italian-influenced Dürer, the combination of creased folds, angled outlines with right-angled doors and walls: that the Greek style attained by means of a most remarkable attenuation of both fullness and angularity, became frictionless, a harmonious symmetry *ante rem.* In this way the Greeks escaped, fashioned a world for themselves where they could live, where at any moment they could evade the terror of chaos, but also the seriousness of decision. Here everything is muted, in such an Apollonian mixture of the vegetal and the inert, that the mild weather of mere beauty could appear, a shapely façade. Perhaps only in the very distant refinement that frames the Chinese artist's naturally so much more digressive, decisive lifelines does Greek *sophrosyne* have a relative, as she composes herself into form, into a flawless cosmos. For Chinese culture, to which wisdom in its highest form appears as loveliness, is also discreet, measured, and Taoist, and reduced the incandescence of its early heroic-Orphic phase into a luxurious, basically just aesthetic style. Indeed, a Greek element survived even into the Christian Middle Ages, beneath all the Gothic fervor, in the middle of the most pervasive transcendentalism: for soon equally beautiful curves appeared, and as arduous as the paths may be, they nonetheless all come to a pleasantly festive end; the congregation becomes a secure, autonomous, secular-sacred *poleis*, the cathedrals of the South excel each other in crystalline tracery, in towers without turrets, in their broad, almost pleasant horizontal; Thomism is eminently aesthetic, balances the world, and only gives up the Hellenic unisubstantiality of being, the contiguously integrated, concentric order, in order to replace it with the more delightful construct of a heterogeneous harmony; and so the Christian leap is all too often, in the varied architecture of the official Middle Ages, transformed merely into a rather Classical hierarchy within a spiritual cosmos. Of course, if we may return to the Greek column and peristyle that reversed the colonnade of the Egyptian inner temple into a mere showpiece: one cannot evade seriousness, neither in art nor anywhere else, and since construction above all dominates both functional form and the deliberate, stylizing artistic volition, Egyptian immobility, as the danger of unbroken constructedness, awaits every "style" at its limit, in the *moment of crisis* when it stabilizes or comes to rest.

The Egyptian Volition to Become Like Stone

For as soon as we begin to build, this structural regularity reimposes itself. Nothing seems inscribed in plaster as irreversibly as the power to make its worlds "Egyptian." And in just this way, even when life weakly ruffles and warms the material, Egyptian rigor lies continuously near to Greek measure. This means: construction forms the *tertium comparationis* between functional form, style and Egypt, albeit the depth of its relation to the respective terms differs greatly; in construction a complete externality emerges, the recurrence of functional form, form as such, the absolute spirit of stone, an ultimately hostile geometry, figuring objectively as *Egypt*, as the total dominance of inorganic nature over life. Man also sees his future here, but sees himself dying, hides himself in the grave. After death he arrives in the underworld, the land where the sun shines at night, or at best, if the judges find his life to have been virtuous, reaches paradise, to live with the murdered and reborn Osiris, Lord of the Dead. Nowhere however does the departed, or his gaze into the beyond, leave this world; even where such profound figures as *ba*, the soul-bird, or *ka*, the personal guardian spirit or *genius*, distantly appear: always, a nameless fear of death dominates every Egyptian image and every Egyptian face, and no other means of rescue but the affirmation of death and the suppression of the inner life, the volition to become like stone. The famous path that leads past rows of rams, sphinxes, or columns to the holy of holies is truly just a "guide" and thus as it were a purely pedagogical affair; what remains characteristic, as the total impression, as the total essence of Egyptian sacral art, is lifeless, gaping silence. Only the columns take up vegetal motifs, as a whole they are geometrical bundles of papyrus or lotus stems, and the capital even clearly shows the buds or flowers of this mystical flora, the symbol and the vehicle of rebirth. The pyramids, the pylons, the Egyptian temples, these houses of God, extend the inorganic landscape within themselves, life-negating, rectilinear, cubic, with a monstrous fanaticism of immobility. The insides of such structures abandon the blossoming, transient, yet also interior kingdom of life all the more: a pyramid, as Hegel said, is a shrine where a dead man lives; the holy of holies within the deepest room of the temple is nothing but a grave, between whose walls the barque, the colossal statue of the god of the universe, weighs us down and crushes us. Even where the gaze penetrates through ever smaller and darker spaces into the most uncanny chamber, this narrowness is not the interiority of the soul, after all, but merely provides the contrast, or the paradox, to the thereby more absolutely immense and colossal sun god Ra: Ra, always visible through every animal and human form and every local god of Egypt, in the spirit of an absolute astral mythos. The mystery of the Christian sanctuary is of an entirely different nature, and far from accommodating itself to inorganic rigidity, to a life-negating, macrocosmic cubism; even the immense Christos Pantokrator of the Byzantine *apsis* bows down over us, is in the most central aspect of his representation a servant, the lord of the human kingdom, while the most sublime symbol, only still visible as the tiny, distant shape of the dove of the Holy Spirit, soars away.

We had said that function and style, however falsely lifelike they may try to seem, lead back in the same way to stony essence. Or, rather, to be consistent in our terms: perhaps not functional form as a still completely inartistic, purely negative, incidental artifact of meticulousness, but the *next* thing after it in practical terms, which represents it after a single leap within the artistic sphere: namely the Biedermeier style, just like the *highest* thing after it in terms of constructional stylistics: namely the rigor and cubicity of Egypt, both always remain near to Greek style, style as such, which remains between Biedermeier and Egypt at a eudaemonistic median. Something like the Biedermeier is already noticeable in the earliest stone sculptures, and draws its neat, practical lines in Renaissance, Regency, Louis XVI and Empire, to finally remain so to speak at the base after every style is dismantled at the beginning of the nineteenth century; as we said: as the absolute stylistic (but for that reason capable of being combined with any or every style) minimum. The Egyptian element first imposed itself among the Aeginetans, and finally under the Empire, where the expedition to the pyramids made a formal influence possible, and, just as the Biedermeier represents the lower boundary against the condition of sheer entertainment, forms the upper space of the transcendent correlation of the Greek style and thus of style as such. But what appears beyond functional form that has forgotten its place, and especially beyond style, is the continuing betrayal to Egypt, avoidable only as long as life is retained, and the austere triangle of the gable, the pure arc of the arch—chosen out of worldly piety, certainly, but shaped as well by the severity of death—and absolutely the entire antagonistic symmetry of Greek and Classical style is confined in that imprecise, homeless, shallow, nonobjective immanence, which only out of indecisiveness fails to go over to Egypt, the land of winter, of death, the winter of the world, as it is called in ancient occult writings, and to the place of the purely inorganic sphere of value. For Egypt remains the ideal as well as the fulfillment of unbroken constructedness, of a *meaningful* constructedness no longer dictated by the effort of stylization but by the spirit of the material and by stone-immanence as such. Only Christian life truly breaks through the stone; here even *external space* can become Gothic, and the Annunciation in the choir of the Church of St. Lorenz in Nuremberg was created just in order to sing the space where it hangs, in order to make this space sing, and by hanging in the middle, to concentrate in itself the inner song of this spatial complex. Whereas even in Romanesque or Byzantine style, even in the horizontal Gothic, everywhere where gravity and order appear as the essence of figuration, in other words, a final, singular potential of Egypt reappears, transposed from astrology into overt mysticism.

The Gothic Volition to Become Like the Resurrection

But the inner life, moving toward itself, only flares up again more strongly. It makes its forms tangled, angular, sets one in front of another and piles them all up. Here one should keep early man in mind, and think in terms of whittling. Wood is the medium; the inner essence, no longer to be flattened, no longer walled up in stone, breaks free; and the fanciful, the effervescently animated, the flourish becomes its plainest expression.

Indeed, this vital trace already bends upward toward us from that place where no one yet is. It is the same force expressed in lava, in hot lead thrown into cold water, in the veining of wood and above all in the twitching, bleeding, ragged or peculiarly compacted form of internal organs. The Negroes have until now kept their gods of life carved according to the wood, transmitting its vitality through handles, rattles, beams, thrones, and idols. Their magical volition, their need to transform themselves, to push into the upper circles of procreation, brought about the mask above all, which elevates them demonically to the animal ancestor, to the always abstractly organic totem and taboo; it bears the likeness of our remote countenance, but Christ does not yet shine; only the blazing demon of life dominates these dream progeny, these dark, plastic systems of fertility and power, and then only indefinitely. But Nordic man in particular, like the Oriental, remembered the *absolutum* of carving, of wood, of the spirit of life; in the art of the mass migrations, and most deeply in the *Gothic*, there occurred a Nordic-Oriental symbiosis; there, organic-psychological longing was truly attained in the form of ornament. We are familiar with the twining snakes and seahorses, the twinned dragons of Nordic line work, and nothing can compare to this uncanny pathos, which is incorrectly attributed to an animation of the inorganic. If salvation is now even possible beyond the discarded, obsolete styles, it can occur only through the resumption of these almost completely forgotten organic lines. Everything that would blossom and be abundant must learn from such pre-Gothic artifacts, and there is no spiral, no digression, and no architectural power with the deeply organic laws of this digressiveness that does not also breathe with its head in the wild, cloudy atmosphere of this organicity, so filled with flutterings, musical intimations, infinities. Since Worringer's felicitous and suggestive presentation, there can be no doubt that here in this ornamentalism of interwoven bands and animals is given the secret Gothic within the Baroque and after.

Here, however, in a fashion not at all Greek, the foliage closes in, the most peculiar decoration covers every surface, and crawls over the walls to break them up. We have seen: *Greek* line captured life only in its outward manifestation, as that organicity visible to everyone, without mystery, epidermal, and its light, tasteful rhythm, determined by an inner, animated equilibrium. We have seen: the *Egyptian* line knows absolutely only rigor, and *sophrosyne* suddenly becomes geometry, insofar as only stone and not flesh is being thought within the stone, consistent with the spirit of the material, which is the spirit of the desert or the alpine landscape, and of inorganic nature's monstrous mausoleum. For the Egyptians, guided by the form of the stone, the way leads outward, mysterious without mystery: here, in this eternal model for every absolute architecture of construction, a long-forgotten groundwater rises, folding back the leaves, uncoiling itself so to speak, a granite and astral faith, such that a sort of higher-order mineralogy crystallizes in the realm of art, a sort of natural philosophy suspended above the soul. *Gothic* line, on the other hand, contains all this agitation within itself; this line is restless and uncanny like its forms: the protuberances, the snakes, the animal heads, the streams, a chaotic intertwining and twitching where a warm amniotic fluid and the heat of incubation stands, and the womb of all suffering, all delight, all births and all organic images begins to speak; only the Gothic has this fire at the center, over which the deepest organic and the deeper spiritual essences bring themselves to fruition. Such a thing could not be more foreign to the feeble Greek life, and at the same time the most complete contrast to Egypt as the mastery of death, as the gaze to which God appears as a wall rather than as hand, as the land into which Joseph was sold as a slave, as the spirit of the depopulated astral mythology which the Jews left behind in order to see the great vineyard of Canaan. Egypt stratifies, the Gothic brings forth; Egypt models the world's structure, the Gothic is symbolically productive in the direction of the embrace, the angular world of the soul. Egypt, stone comprehended, is the spirit of the tomb, the spirit of complete form, complete constructedness for material reasons; is the consummately descriptive formal sign for a consummate alien clarity, the clarity of oppression and death, the artistic equivalent of the world of the dead, of astral myth. The Gothic, in contrast, comprehended life, is the spirit of the resurrection, the spirit of the helpful formula, reduced, fragmentary constructedness as a still merely lower objective determination; is the unconsummatedly *expressive*-descriptive *sigillary sign* for the unconsummated mystery of the We and of the ground, for a spontaneously animated, unconsummated, functional, in itself still symbolic ornamentalism and symbolism; is the artistic suggestion of living space [*Lebensraum*], of the problem of the We flashing like lightning as of every approximation of the mythos of the logos. Not the brightly and evenly articulated Greek line, but the essentially adventurous, farsighted, functional Gothic line alone is complete life, the finally pure kingdom above functional form, *the free spirit of the very movement of expression*, and only in alliance with this line could Egypt, constructed stone, be broken through in those epochs that were above style. Whereby the Romanesque, Byzantine, Arabic-Indian, Gothic, and, ignoring its actually improper stylization for the moment, the Baroque represent this organic exuberance's progressive triumph over the crystal.

In other words: the inner human being can want nothing but the endless line, without cheating himself of himself. The forest wanders into the desert through this line, into the crystal, reducing it to merely a long extinguished auxiliary. The endless line, in its first Nordic manifestation, blossomed and grew everywhere without knowing where to go; only as Gothic line did it become true, not merely organic but organic-spiritual transcendence, in the sense that above its surging tide the star of the Son of Man could rise that fully determines it. The medium of the stone has burst, the completely formal, the meaningfully, absolutely constructional element has been demoted, is now merely a reinforcing, technically supporting formula (vestment, clustered columns, crossvault), or at most a form, as the *prius* of the foreground in the observed Gothic object (ecstatic distention, denaturalization of the model, angular filigree). The deepest object dominates, expressed foremost in organically abstract sigillary signs, with the meaning that Gothic art (and everything remotely connected with it) makes an exodus expressive within external material, as otherwise only music can.

In other words something stirs and seethes here in these stones, trying to blossom as we do, to have the life we do. For one simply cannot omit oneself when one is building with the energies of the Son of Man inside oneself. The law has never yet made a great man, but freedom breeds the true colossi and the true extremities. Thus even Egypt, in particular—as the model for the secret stockpiling of the false god—leads to those constructs where, finally, the once again organic, the organically abstract recurs. In no other way can externalized interiority occur, and therefore a higher-level organicity, the ornament in excess and the I's quiet reunion with the I who I will be: *only as the Gothic entelechy of all fine art.* Man, and not the sun, not geomancy or astrology, but man in his very deepest inwardness, as Christ, here became the alchemical standard of everything that is built. If one just gazes into this flowering and its development, one can see one's inmost soul flowing there, changing, transforming itself toward itself. Here dominates that beautiful *warmth* where the living soul does not suffocate, the warmth of the beloved and the light that radiates

from the flower, from the lucerne of every maiden, the beautiful warmth
in which the living soul is vanquished by humility and devotion and taken
into the arms of the Gothic Virgin like the very Christ child himself. The
Gothic will to render the choir and indeed the entire interior ever more
transfigured, the Gothic's upward tendency in its fullness dematerializes
all mass: now the obsessive illustrations have room; the laces and tendrils
of an unprecedented mason's art shoot up into the crockets and capitals,
and mingle filigree and rose into the glowing windows; vaulting, and not
simply vaults, rises into the nave and into the choir's depths; sin and
atonement, a glittering satanic beauty and the kingdom of the mild, humble, and patient soul all meet most closely in these vast cathedrals of figures, making them a fossilized procession on the Christian quest. But in
these stones *light* also races and proliferates and burns, in this statue, this
house of the human heart; nowhere are we disavowed, the tribute to the
enclosing power of the material remains no more than reflexive, the wall
has been broken through, the brightly colored windows lead into un-
mapped domains, we stand in the midst of love, surrounded by the heavenly host, even the robes and the countenances of the saints assume all
power to enclose space, it is a ship of stone, a second Noah's ark flying to
God, the tower's spire transforms into the finial as the mystical larynx that
receives the word of the Son: and above all these wonders—"How far I'm
led with every stride!"—"That is the deepest mystery, / What once was
time, is space instead!"[3]—above all this endless chaos of line smiles the
Virgin, so sweet, so wise, as if the graves were lighting up, as if the distant
mystical chambers were being prepared and the *restitutio in integrum*
stood illuminated before the lowliest of us. Certainly much is dispropor-
tionate about these cathedrals, these domed structures in human form,
but it is the disproportion between our heart and our world. Here, in
other words, the breakthrough will also succeed: the constructs of the
only, the organically, the metaphysically eidetic art still to come present
themselves and culminate together in the lineaments of the secret human
form; the now still loose and flowing ornamentation and signature of the
immediate human being is its sole, foundationally *a priori* object.

THE IMAGE OF THE INNERMOST SHAPE

This may be the direction home, and just for that reason it seemed desirable not to formalistically obscure the point where the new, colorful seriousness is to take effect. May it also not be further obscured by another

kind of rigor, by an all too indiscriminate neglect of the agitation within our own, Impressionist heritage—its impatience and its nevertheless already achieved loosening of formal totality, its at any rate already available even if often inferior and still reflexive, inexpressive subjectivation of the image of the world. Modernity's paths, the irreversible eruption of its mystical nominalism, have to be followed through to the end, or Egypt, or perhaps the equally obsolete coherence of the historical as opposed to the aprioristic Gothic, will again be enthroned.

For there is one thing that separates us from it, powerfully and precisely. We have become more individual, searching, homeless; we are formed more *flowingly*, the self of us all rises up close by. Thus the lifeblood of the new artistic statements springs much less than before from the medium's sources, from the formal energy. Form is no longer the only means one requires to speak, to draw attention; in fact, it is no longer even a means that one especially needs.

Thus even *color*, painting's proper ambition—to create with color, transpose into color, model through color—has retracted somewhat. Certainly one would like to see clearly, and, if possible, airlessly. Still, that is not decisive, since Kokoschka paints with gray, brown, dark violet, and every other earth tone. And when Marc and Kandinsky take up purer colors, the latter indeed aiming at a theory of color harmony, and if in general the fashion is to revel in clear, skinless local colors instead of an atmospheric blur, then here one is no longer taking pleasure in color as such; rather, it is the capacity for excitement for whose sake here only the purest, crassest luminosity is selected and assembled. It is that peculiar emotional value accruing as much to the individual colors as to their composition: hate, fervor, anger, love, mystery, in order that the entire aura in which this psychological landscape lies can be rendered. Thus Däubler can say of such colors: "Thrusts of intense yellow reach into blue inevitabilities."[4] That is the power of color, and at the same time the limit of its appointment, for here color must serve as never before. Color can be broken any number of times in its own pleasure, its own formal energy, and the purely painterly, which many Impressionists are vaguely proud of having rediscovered, retreats before the drive toward expression.

On the other hand *drawing* certainly drives us powerfully forward again as well. No more visual devotion to inferior, cursory impressions. And it cannot be denied that this is more than just a consolidation, that since Marées, thinking in terms of drawing, the new being-thought-of in terms of surfaces, seems to strive even more deeply. What is being sought is not line in itself, any more than color in itself, unless the line does not smoothly outline, and is dense, and expressively compacted. As when in Rousseau or Kandinsky trembling or riding appears as a short, striking curve, or the desire for revenge as a jagged, arrow-shaped formation, or benevolence as a blossoming flower. The outline sharpens and charges to the same degree in Archipenko or in Boccioni's striding statue as Däubler translated it into words, that is, no longer the person at rest, who incidentally can stride forth, but striding as such, which dominates the body, takes shape as corporeality: "The ankles want to break out, the soles drag space behind them, the breasts symbolize microcosmic man slipping himself between the constellations, in our heads we roll an entire world through our orbits: an overabundance is man, but by our movements we break continuously into animated geometries, on our shoulders and shanks we convey as yet unexpressed crystallizations of space into the rhythm of our stride." Beyond this logic, a planar logic, this new being-thought-of in terms of cubes and curves also seems to tend most immediately deeper mimetically, and Cubism is the consistent expression of this new, new-old spatial magic. It began by simply disassembling things, folding their unseen surfaces into the visual plane. Thus an early painting by Picasso still bears the telltale title: "Dismantled Violin": but soon such games, such experiments became actual experience; the strange charm offered by the divided plane, such as one can sense in site plans and architectural blueprints, became apparent. The appeal of the active, mysterious partitioning, the way the weights are equilibrated as on a scale, and the bare, active creature of line itself; the deliberate volition to reinstate, even against the slightly subdued surface arabesque, the awareness of mass, volume, and weight, the awareness of that secret gravitation, order and statics that regulates space as an assemblage of quadratic and cubic equilibrations. Still other, more fruitful possibilities appear—far from mere functional form, from engineering, or from the ultimate false reminder of the Egyptian hall of the dead—and directs us upward: not only Marées, not only Cézanne in his famous dictum about sphere, cone and cylinder in the construction of form, already suggest artists who think in spatial terms; indeed even the Sistine Madonna—who seems surrounded by distantly sounding spatial relationships, along with so to speak heavenly spatialities that are partly conveyed to us—leads something of a Cubistic life within space, as Paul Fechter boldly and rightly pointed out. And certainly it is not simply effective placement that makes something Cubist, since every image from the past, and especially from absolute epochs of style, could then be represented as Cubist; rather, it is the remarkably heterogeneous Raphael who clarifies this issue far more than the otherwise so much more significant Leonardo. Now things do not merely exist in space, but space exists within things, and space can certainly build a foundation without equal, as in the Roman Pantheon or even in Gothic cathedrals.

But of course much else lags behind, and besides, *drawing* must still be *broken*. Drawing can and must reinforce, so that the fugitive aspect of a great feeling, going beyond the gaze to resound far and wide, will have a physical support. It can also signify a lower objective determination, like any other meaningful formalization. But all too often something, already obvious has quadratically moved in, walled itself up, and obstructed its banal world with boxes, chests and cubes from which little can be unpacked, no matter how deeply they seem to pile up. Moreover, while Kokoschka or Picasso break through the earlier faith in mere color, the Futurist movement, with its addiction to ecstasy, dynamism, and all-pervading contemporaneity, and, particularly in the Cubist work, disturbs the circles of a vacuous or sterile structuration.[5] Movement, but even more: the most unexpected allegorical meaning rises up within drawing, within line, and, as the strongest reaction against every kind of painting seeming to rest within itself, seems mimetic in itself, against every "absolute" painting, reduces even Cubist or any other useful statuary to a mediating, stabilizing formula, or at best to a form of lower objective determinacy in the series of Expressionist self-shapings, self-projections. In addition, if one otherwise has the impression that certain familiar remnants, an eye, a violin's tuning peg, or even just a numeral, have been caught so to speak against their will in the Cubist painting, then Braque, Dérain, and other, younger painters from the Picasso school are just the ones to show that one wants to encounter these objective allusions throughout all Cubism's misdirections, that is, not only at the beginning, as the final witnesses of an emotional goodbye to the world, not only in artwork's subject, but precisely in its most abstract predicate: so that these peculiar images can be comprehended as the most tortuous auxiliary constructions, whose concentrated abstraction will in turn resolve itself into a newly achieved objective corrrelation and objective symbolism. So if one should want to make a more deeply mimetic form out of such painting inward, painting into the spatial stillness, which the Cu-

bists have cultivated against Impressionism's agitation and naturalism, the
attempt will be completely impossible by Cubism's definition as pure,
pictorial composition in terms of surfaces and weights, and in a larger
sense conceivable only insofar as a cube as ornament is no ornament at
all, that is, no broken one, but is rather the one which most helpfully
reaches across toward the *figure of meaning*. In accordance with a formal
transparency that only ensues with the formal actualization, without co-
inciding with it or being even somewhat continuously accompanied by
its stylization, by the constructional pleasure still available in Impressionism and once again totally geometrically hypertrophied in Cubism.

But is it even still possible to build, to vault upward? Here our introduction of a higher artisanal logic must prove itself, as was shown by our
earlier example of the Baroque chair. It is probable that, in accordance
with the extraordinary search for expression, certain artisanal and then
sculptural and architectonic realizations will triumph over the till now
purely painterly element. Whereby in other words, under the aspect of
the future, beyond applied art in its narrower, socially subservient sense,
in the stylistic sense, beyond ornament in its unilinear, untranscendent
sense, a Sheraton chair or the unearthly curve of certain Baroque cabi-
netry could contain more aesthetic character and significance than the
loveliest Perugino or even more famous historicist illusionisms. Much already points in this direction, and much that had long been forgotten or
never understood at all is now reemerging: thus the ceremonial masks,
the totems, the carved beams, the banding, the sacristies; thus the notion
of a sculpture carved from the inside out as well, whether of Negro,
Nordic, Gothic, Baroque type, the nameless body of a sculpture as architecture. Because of all this, the architecture now so threatened by barren-
ness and functionalism, by which it may indeed even have been lost, can
always be explored as the interior of the space of home, which art must
furnish and approximate well. With painting, sculpture in an increasingly anthropomorphic space of construction that must repeatedly, and
today more than ever, be broken as the anticipatory expression of a *tat
twam asi*, "Thou art it too."[6] As the self-encounter within painted objects
and with them; and music, no longer frozen, nearby.[7]

OUR SECRET SIGNATURE IN ART

So we seek the artist who lets us approach ourselves purely, encounter
ourselves. His novel gaze molds unrecognizable new shapes and moves

like a swimmer, like a cyclone through the given. There is something beautiful about flowing water, an old tree, even a dark, elevated alpine lake. It suffices to possess all this in nature, however, where one can also enjoy what art cannot represent, such as air, calculable physical distances, and so on, better than any of the pleasures of art appreciation ever could do. In any case the cinema now provides an exemplary substitute; one can even say that for anyone who would like the impression of nature without any deformations through the medium of the image, the cinematograph is the best portrait gallery, the substitute for all the world's great general art exhibitions. Everyone should keep this in mind who demands to know of an Expressionist image what it represents: by what means, in other words, hell can shrivel down to a street corner before their eyes which resemble mere photographic plates. For things have been different ever since van Gogh; we are also present in the painting, and precisely this presence is what is being painted; true, there is still visible turmoil, still railings, subways, girders, brick walls, but it suddenly, peculiarly undercuts itself, the rejected cornerstone strikes sparks all at once, and the element within all appearance which was already drawn, which is incomprehensibly akin to us, lost to us, near, far, the Sais-like quality of the world, suddenly emerges into the light in van Gogh's paintings as it otherwise does only in Strindberg.[8] In Cézanne as well, though more latently, and concealed somewhat under the more powerful, purely painterly façade that makes Cézanne the last great modern stylist, but perhaps even more deeply than in van Gogh, the Expressionist revolution is evident: for this is no longer fruit, nor is it fruit modeled in paint; instead all imaginable life is in them, and if they were to fall, a universal conflagration would ensue, to such an extent are these still lifes already heroic landscapes, so loaded are these paintings with mystical gravity and a yet unknown, nameless mythology. The still life does not appear groundless here, for the major events of this world, as well as the world presented by self-enclosed cultures, are past, and cannot properly be adapted again to some Romantic model or zodiacal theosophy; whereas the "still life" not only persists as painting's almost sole object, but in its having-escaped, its intensity in small things, is or can be higher than any culture. Precise in this new tableau, then—be it nevertheless and at best only a seal at first, like the conceivably ultimate music and conceivably final metaphysics, and not ideogrammatically equivalent to our inmost intensity, the mystery of the We and of the ground—even in the new tableau the thing becomes a

mask, a "concept," the deformed, denaturalized manner of secret teleotro-
pisms; the human interior and the world's shift together. Suddenly I see
my eyes, my ears, my state: I myself am this drawer and these fish, I am
these fish of a kind that lies in drawers; for the difference vanishes, the
distance lifts between the artistic subject and the artistically represented
object that is to be reborn to a different materiality than a mere thing's,
reborn to its essence as the inmost principle of its potentiality, of all our
potentiality. My dance, my morning stars sing, and everything so trans-
parently formed attains the same individual structural horizon as well as
the same subjective ornament of its entelechy—a trace, a sign of the *macanthropos*, the seal of its mysterious figure—to be of the soul's Jerusalem
concealed from itself.[9]

Here there is nothing more to be borrowed from outside; the soul need
no longer accept alien dictates. Rather, its own need is strong enough to
attract whatever husks and markers it needs for support, and images
become just our *own* reemergence, but at another place. If van Gogh
guided us out of ourselves, if things still speak in his work, however emphatically, apparently just of themselves and not as echoes of man, then
we suddenly hear only ourselves echo back from them; then, conversely,
after Expressionism man has only a Kaspar Hauser kind of nature that
uses objects solely as keepsakes of its ineradicable lineage or as pointing
marks for keeping and conserving its progressive anamnesis.[10] Things
thus become like the inhabitants of one's own interior, and if the visible
world seems to be crumbling anyway, to be increasingly emptying itself
of its own soul, becoming uncategorial, then in it and through it the
sounds of the invisible world correspondingly want to become pictoriality: vanishing obverse, intensifying fullness, a becoming-the-forest, an influx and reflux of things into the self's crystalline forest, creative, deepest
outburst, pansubjectivism within the object, beyond the object, as object
itself, so that the external object disappears to the extent that it returns
like one of the 500 deities in the forbidden temple of Canton. Here the
pictures, strangely familiar, can appear like magical mirrors where we
glimpse our future, like the masked ornaments of our inmost shape, like
the finally perceived, adequate fulfillment, self-presence of what has eternally been meant, of the I, of the We, of the *tat twam asi*, of our glory vibrating within mystery, of our secret divine existence. This is the same as
the longing to finally see the human countenance, and the only remaining dream streets, even for the magical picture, will be like those where

Sesenheim's experience of riding toward himself could occur, and no other objective correlation but one that mirrors throughout the world the mysterious outline of the human countenance, and thus connects the most abstract organicity with the longing for our own heart, for the fullness of the manifestation to oneself.[11]

The Philosophy of Music

Dream

We hear only ourselves.

For we are gradually becoming blind to the outside.

Whatever else we still shape leads back around us. It is not exactly as readily individual, not exactly as hazy, hovering, warm, dark, and incorporeal as my feeling of always being just by myself, always just conscious. It is a stuff, an alien experience. But we walk in the forest and we feel we are or could be what the forest dreams. We walk between the tree trunks, small, incorporeal, and imperceptible to ourselves, as their sound, as what could never again become forest or external day and perceptibility. We do not have it—all that this moss, these strange flowers, roots, stems and shafts of light are or signify—because we ourselves are it, and stand too near to it, this ghostly and ever so nameless quality of consciousness or of becoming-inward. But the note flares out of us, the *heard* note, not the note itself or its forms. Yet it shows us our way without alien means, shows us our historically inner path as a flame in which not the vibrating air but we ourselves begin to tremble, and throw off our coats.

On the History of Music

How do we hear ourselves at first?

As an endless singing-to-oneself, and in the dance.

Both are still nameless. They have no life in themselves, and no one personally gave them form. Where one encounters them, they possess the appeal of every originary beginning. But one had to go through something else in order that expression be amply and securely equipped.

BEGINNINGS

This only began gradually. Of the earliest melodies, very little is known even now. Not even the Greek songs have been preserved to any extent.

What has come down to us is mostly charmless and empty. One can just as little form a favorable image of the sound of Greek or early medieval ensembles. All the players had to confine themselves to the same melody. The most that was permitted was to sound the root and the fifth, like the bagpipe's drone, and to let them sustain. Hymnody also remained within the straits of monophony. To be sure, it began quite early to be structured by the congregation's responsorial. Thus in its insistent psalmodizing, its numerous articulations and jubilations of the Ambrosian and Gregorian psalter, its ornamentation of a simple, fine melodic line, and not least in these chorales' truly basilican solidity, hymnody may have meant more to the congregation than one can still relive outside of religious ecstasies.

For as a whole these assets have entirely depreciated. It is not much different for the later, polyphonic music of the Middle Ages. Only the traveling minstrels begin to innovate. They are untrained, in the additional sense that they are the very first to dare to devise polyphonic settings. At least a stroke on the harp was permitted to a troubadour even in eras of the strictest monophony. In addition, because the harp is unsuited to free embellishment as a discretely audible figuration of the melody, it leads by nature toward chordal blending. Thus not only freer movement and expressive need dwell here, but also, independently and far more decisively than in the merely rational attempts of the harmonists who had banished the troubadours from the schools, a clearly recognizable approximation of major, minor, and the modulations to come. Nonetheless these benefits have been lost, or were obviated by the later, related, but in all respects more magnificent Italian masters of *cantilena*. As for the contemporary attempts at polyphony, on the other hand (and they occurred only in European music), even in the music of the late Middle Ages these essentially do not go beyond a merely theoretical groundwork outside of the properly artistic attitude toward technique. Even if learned monks discovered all kinds of things—Hucbald and the first intuition that different notes could be sounded together,

Guido of Arezzo and the beginning of exact notation, Franco of Cologne and the mensural notation derived from the custom of singing several notes in the descant against one—this all remains academic stuff, whose intrinsic merit can no longer be assessed, as empathy into the objective problems of that time is impossible, and in any case its actual artistry, even in a theoretical sense, was far exceeded by the succeeding, already modern epoch of the Flemings.

But with them, too, the outlook is still dismal. One thinks here primarily of the significant Josquin. There are certainly smaller pieces by him that are full of surprisingly heartfelt effects, completely reliant on vocal animation. But how dry becomes the bread whenever it becomes more determined to nourish us; how severe remains the voice leading, how unsongful, inexpressive and unmelodic Dufay's and Ockeghem's artful and impressive settings still are! The text is simply there, without any influence, and the massive intellectual effort remains barrenly closed in on itself. It is a pencil that would perform calculations on its own, and a sinuous figure 8 leading nowhere. It is a study score of unprecedented rank, which might not have lacked a certain laborious power on hearing, but essentially represents only the technical provisions for the entirely different Baroque. Here a push from below was needed for things to become simple, and guide the score's pointless calculations back to the site of spiritual and textual necessity. Only thus could Luther's judgment: "The others had to do what the notes wanted, but *Josquin* is master over the notes; they had to do what he wanted"—be fulfilled in the beautiful, antiformal sense.

The new influence came from folk song. Where it was sung in three to six voices, it appeared as the madrigal. Since it remained slight, mostly erotic in content, the originally songful element shifted strongly into the melodious upper voice. Shortly thereafter, the ancient modes begin to be chromatically embroidered. It was the Fleming Willaert, under Italian influence, significantly, who first wrote chromatically and within the new distinction between major and minor chord. In place of the once delicately interweaving voices, he put a chord clearly defined as sounding simultaneously, and thus discovered what the Venetians called the *aurum potabile*, that is, the new potential for a harmonic music in the middle of a still purely contrapuntal age. Soon after, Haßler brought the new harmonic sound to Germany, in order to adapt its splendor to the polyphonic treatment of Protestant hymns. Here the song moved decisively to the surface; that is, the *cantus firmus*, which had previously been sung by the tenor, a middle voice, shifted to the uppermost voice, thus subordinating the remaining voices, which became inner voices, ever more decisively to the descant as the songful principal melody's vehicle. At first this occurred in the most expedient way, as the accompanying voices moved as regularly as possible in step with the upper voice in simultaneous harmony, instead of every voice, *ex cantus firmi una voce plures faciens*, going its own way as demanded by imitation, inversion, retrogression and the other canonical and contrapuntal rules. And so, beginning with *Orlando di Lasso*, complete freedom has been won. He is the master of the drinking song no less than the solemnity of his deeply affecting *Penitential Psalms*; everything is ready for expression to the broadest extent, the tonal edifice has been built, the range, the perspective, the transcendence of the tonal space, all truly and properly "musical" for the first time, are there in prototype. The contrary melodic Italian and contrapuntal Flemish styles fuse together, providing the resulting expression, only attained with passion and deliberate subjectivity, the desired means. Now all the harshness, imbalance, and indecision is gone: the subject Orlando has settled the conflict between *trouver* and *construer* for a long time, so completely and decisively that from now on every voice sings, and troubadour and academy are united. Thus both the first element, melody (which here comes preponderantly from the scale and not from the chordal energy, and so once again demands not so much harmony as the multilinearity of contrapuntal writing), as well as the second element, counterpoint itself, this ancient combinatorial calculus, once so unconcerned with the beauty of its melismatic and thematic material, undergo their complete unification in the joy of making music. If by the way Orlando had a Rembrandtian nature, then *Palestrina* was Raphaelian. In his work the notes have become quieter, and move with the most glorious inclination toward greater chordal convergence and repose. The way that a small number of human voices are grouped together, now, in the Roman chorales, leading back to the most intimate harmonic simplicity; then again, as his *Stabat Mater* and even more his famous *Missa Papae Marcelli* show, into the spatial power of the notes' movement, each imbuing itself homophonically: all this is already so extraordinarily harmonic, not harmonic-dramatic, but rather harmonic in a still arrhythmic, seraphic sense (a carpet for Bruckner and the late Wagner) such that now only chordal listening is valid for an adequate grasp of these compositions, in other words, a kind of hearing that coordinates vertically below and horizontally only above, where the total melodic effect occurs. Thus did Orlando di Lasso and Palestrina, as the first musical geniuses, refute academicist construction for its own sake. The melodic expression, the melody, has been elevated to the sole content of counterpoint: in Orlando advancing passionately, predominantly linearly; in Palestrina more pious, held together predominantly chordally.

THE PROCEDURE

From now on one may no longer be narrow. For everything technical moves into the second rank. The sound stands firm, the forge has been built. What is to come will not be accomplished just by technical mastery. One may be a diligent composer, and nonetheless everything remains lifeless, because the mere craftsman gets confused by precisely what first makes craft worthwhile.

Progress in Craft

There is also something else forcing us to become very vital. Clearly nothing detracts from even the more important artists as badly as inserting or fixing them into some succession of developments in craft, into a history of merely mediating, reinforcing, technical formulae. How boring Hoffmann's *Undine* has become to anyone who does not know this, and perhaps even more so to anyone who does, since Weber did the same thing so much better in the *Freischütz*, however much he may have learned instrumentally from the earlier work! Yet how disagreeable Weber's harmonies, the most novel of their time, can sound, particularly in *Euryanthe*, to the extent that the listener fails to repress the nagging but absurd suspicion that here is a plagiarism from *Lohengrin*! Once something has been discovered, later periods have no interest in it or empathy for it as a technical problem or a fresh innovation, if it really was no more than a technical problem; the true particularity [*Sosein*] of the great composers is thus not defined by the history of musical technique. Otherwise predecessors would be that main idea that they do not contain, that they only prefigure in terms of formal analysis, but fail to explore fully. The more that great masters owe to existing rules, the less new is their craft as opposed to its highly particular application. Should one specifically say that Mozart is inconceivable without the Mannheim orchestra and *opera buffa*?

Is it the rules that make Gluck so superior to Florentine and French opera, or is it not far more what he makes of the rules? Must one still add how Bach clung to the old ways, how clearly he turns away from the ever more mannerly Neapolitan harmonies in order to study the old Flemish and Italian composers instead of Scarlatti? In any case this also occurred alongside the preservation of a certain *bel canto*; the dances and chansons play a large role formally; and when it comes to the other issue, thematic technique, where Bach returns to the past in a kind of reaction almost reminiscent of Brahms, he exceeds the old masters' contrapuntal erudition only in the manner of application and hardly in thematic technique. With Beethoven, whose new manner is not at all new technically, things look even more peculiar. For many influences converged in the sonata, and though Haydn may have invented this multithematic structure as a work, it remains after all most instructive that precisely this objectively tranquil composer lives on as the father of the revolution, to the precise extent that he loved technical experiments far more than Beethoven did. Whereas Beethoven himself, Haydn's student, encountered nothing technical against which he would have had to revolt on the grounds of his particular musical manner.

There is thus nothing here to classify or to assemble somehow "progressively." Great individuals are incomparable, and truly born to something better than the leash of technique. One has only to recall Hanslick's spiteful chatter about Gluck, against whom he plays off Mozart, or about Mozart, against whom he plays off Rossini, or about Rossini, against whom he plays off Meyerbeer. Then one will comprehend how this way of playing one composer off against another just in technical terms provides the formula for baseness and the most shallow kind of disrespect, particularly where, as in Hanslick, the critic suddenly hits the brake at that point where everything becomes the most decidedly modern, violates the principle of banal progress, and remaining consistent only with his own baseness, reaches outside of history in order to win his game. If no two characters sing at the same time in the *Rheingold*, there are reasons for it that occur nowhere else, and *Tristan* in its essential aspects no more goes back to the old Florentine homophony than *Don Giovanni* is a middling musical drama. Others were not much better, and when one sees how the shabbier Wagnerians liked to rank all the old masters of recitative and *arioso* opera as more or less untalented predecessors of a Wagnerian style that made even and especially the Ninth Symphony superfluous, then one will recognize by one's disgust that a historical classification in terms of craft or technique breaks down before everything essential in the story of music, indeed that it even makes the incomparability of the individual life mediating itself through technique even more forcefully obvious than would have been possible without the attempt at a purely technical-formal "theory of progress."

The Sociological Context

What is far more important here is to construct for every truly great composer an individual house where he can live for himself as a particular "state" even beyond his talents. In here he is free, brings in only his own soul. This is self-evidently something different again from what circulates among people, what unites them in mere contemporaneity. Here, after the technical approach has failed, it is hopeless to try to advance by constructing links, by former similarities, or other comparative tactics. Only composers of the lower and middle ranks have certain artistic or poetic colleagues, who live alongside them as such and say the same thing in other ways. Perhaps Nicola Piccini is Rococo, but it would be superficial to claim that Gluck coexists with Louis Seize, or Mozart with the Austrian Rococo, or Beethoven with the Empire, or Wagner—now who or what could fully coexist with Wagner? Nietzsche sensed this at least partly when he taught: "Of all the arts that grow on a particular cultural soil . . . music appears as the last plant. Indeed, sometimes music rings like the language of a vanished age into an astonished, modern world, and comes too late. Only in the art of the Flemish composers did the soul of medieval Christianity achieve its complete resonance. . . . Only in the music of Handel did what was best in the soul of Luther and his kind finally resound, that mighty, Jewish-heroic tendency that created the entire Reformation. Only Mozart repaid the age of Louis XIV and Claude Lorrain in *ringing* gold. Only in the music of Beethoven and Rossini did the eighteenth century sing out: the century of enthusiasm, of ruined ideals and fleeting joys."[1] External circumstances may certainly have supported such deep historical nonsynchronisms: for Bach is certainly to be "sociologically" comprehended on some lower level in terms of a Germany "delayed" in comparison to the West, for example, and even the bindings of his volumes, with elegant Renaissance and even Rococo formats all around, retain their medieval, folio-like appearance; and so, despite the triumph of the *concertante*, homophonically individual, emancipated single voice, for a long time voice leading, organic articulation, a compressed, inconspicuous linearity, and late Gothic piety persisted as the light of Germany. Meanwhile, precisely, all this "explaining" from the outside in remains ultimately superficial, and does not make Bach's total manifestation, his profound historical isolation, his sociologically uninvolvable level of existence comprehensible, not to mention that even where Nietzsche grasps music's historical nonsynchronism, music becomes far too much a mere revenant, related all too historically to the past, instead of being illuminated from the direction of the future: as Spirit *in utopian degree*, which accordingly, in the middle of history and sociology, builds only its own house, the framework for its own discoveries of inner levels of existence, albeit with countless elective affinities and free adaptations. It remains a strange enough fact here, and the real anomaly within the philosophy of history, that the Greeks and the medievals remained nearly mute, and then suddenly Bach appeared in the days of Watteau and Tiepolo as the legatee of 700 years of history, a somber, opulent, bewildering, in many places Gothic master; and that music, so very young, a persistent syncope even in modern history, quite clearly obeys another rhythm than that of its corresponding morphologically, sociologically given cultural whole. As Beethoven evolves only out of himself, just as Mahler, even superficially, created his Eighth Symphony to a certain extent for another society, so also did Wagner invent Eva and the people on the Festival meadow, a self-appointed Bayreuth, posited by the artist himself as an inspiration and a utopia, remote from all of contemporary sociology, its contents and its volition to form. In other words, if a composer can feel so independent of the will of his epoch (and there is something great and mysterious in the fact that the nineteenth century's two greatest composers were revolutionaries), then it is surely not the essence of the music—what lies beyond Schumann, Mendelssohn, and the merely formal—which can be economically and sociologically categorized. However beneficial an economic perspective might be in all other cases, or any such perspective, whoever would totalize it in respect of music, errs. Water will not fuel a fire; it can even be the same force that drives everything upward in the economy, in politics, which wreaks one disaster after another in technique as such. Whoever disagrees, and would like to harness the greatest variety to the same historical-sociological pace, in order to be able to drive a larger team, and to harness nonsynchronous, indeed spherically incomparable elements

within one epochal unity, will become more superficial, and the more
God forsaken, the more energetically the subject matter responds to its
internal impulses and the more surprisingly those movements seem to
reciprocally elucidate each other that had passed so homogeneously into
the genetic-polyhistorical, universal-historical, or morphologico-synoptic
concept. We thus assert that neither the single, negative, that is, incon-
clusive and with respect to content causally ineffectual economic contexts
of determination, nor the interpersonal relationships objectified only in
politics and restricted to all those incessant "sociologies of—": none of
these can offer any periodization or sociology of music that expresses
something about the actual development and objectivity of music, understood as a discrete sphere. It is only possible to explain something in
social terms, let alone completely encompass it, where the interpersonal,
that is, the socially interested point of view, coincides with its object,
such as morality as an ongoing relation between persons, or economy,
law, and the state as forms of relations between persons. Where things are
not so, where it is impossible to conclude with the state and homogenize
other values such as art, religion, science and philosophy as its fairest
flowers, what is essentially intended remains different, articulated as a
surplus, living only so to speak before its *a priori* audience, and for its
great representatives, themes, and works, demands *the solitary, historically
eccentric* typification according to *a priori* effective and material problems. Certainly not even the isolated activity of genius is fully unde-
ducible: but that is something different than the sensibility of a group of
people unified by more than just contemporaneity, when, as occasionally
happened in Greece and the Middle Ages, the will of the age and the will
of genius accord as though by secret compact; when great individuals
suddenly find themselves following the peculiar rise and fall of the same
line; when above them a whispering is perceptible, which their inner self
obeys, and transindividual dispatches that determine their work's design;
when genius's determination thus and not otherwise transforms into a
sign for a suprahistorical canonical *diapason*; when in other words a correlative series appears, in the true sense of the "philosophy of history," remote from any economic-social pragmatics or morphological synoptics,
in which great individuals become categories, and the entire sequence of
geniuses, foremost those of music, begins to pass into a system of categories having to do with our consciousness of ourselves, God's consciousness of himself.

Music's Explosive Youth

Here, however, we have nevertheless repeatedly grown younger. And it is neither the skill nor the maturity that have disappeared, but only the academicism. So it is certain from this standpoint, too, that the usual acclamation for the past in all musical matters must end in disaster. Of course even the most novel images tend to be judged more indulgently than the most modern kinds of composition. But the shock soon passes, and the ears that one wanted in all seriousness to have lined with sheet metal the first time one heard *Figaro* learn new habits; the battle over the principles of the beautiful and the melodic is settled as soon as one leaves one's own rut and seeks out and understands the rules of these new constructs. Technique went deeper, small forms shattered, an expressively more deeply grounded form arose, and expressivity increased, so clearly that the decline of painterly ability and then its powerful resurgence in the nineteenth century does not even offer a parallel. How little mere age signifies in music, two cases will sufficiently demonstrate. When a young man is supposed to find the spell that will prevent his suicide, and restore all his lost vital powers, Balzac requires an entire antiquities shop glutted with the past's fashions, inventions, furniture, artifacts and relics as the setting for his miraculous *Donkeyskin*. When on the other hand the plot concerns three libertines who have joined up with a crowd of desperate rabble, in order to violate the nuns and then smash the icons as well, whereupon St. Cecilia herself appears, to rescue her cloister, it seems rather senseless, indeed musically amateurish that at this moment, and quite deliberately, Kleist would let an ancient Italian mass be conducted where a contemporary piece by Palestrina would have been more adequate, and in fact, disregarding the anachronism, a movement from a symphony by Bruckner would have performed even more magical service.[2] Just this is the essential thing: that one naturally has to abandon every visual artifact of Balzac's time to create a backdrop for a significant event, or at least pile them up to the point of suffocation, whereas the sonorous present given by music can be closely affiliated to any imaginable adventure or miracle. In this sense there flows through music a single current of born equals— not only in the self-evident aspect of their craft, but also in terms of their power of personal expression—which remains unaffected by all the ups and downs that made Bach, and, in a completely different and more amazing fashion, even Wagner anachronisms in their time, and which as a whole enables for all contemporary music at least the same high degree of fantasy otherwise found only in the past.

But does this innovation, this improvement to the sound, now continue aimlessly? Is not the flourishing sonorous whole, playing more than ever within itself, perhaps the expression of the loss of the upper band attached to objectivity, whose fluttering and falling ends we can of course still observe for a time within subjectivity? Which indeed can be more clearly seen the farther they fall, in other words the closer fall, life, and end are associated? Is there in the completely enigmatic fact that music is becoming ever younger, ever more unbound, ever more spacious, a guarantee of its inexhaustibility and immunity to the *Zeitgeist*? Many factors converge to suggest an affirmative answer, but of course only at the price of introducing an entire set of reservations, which, even if they in no way justify the customary acclamation for the past in musical matters, nonetheless problematize music's merely empty, unsystematic youthfulness. We had already said that an artist's ability here partakes thoroughly of the care inherent in craft; indeed one can even claim that the power of melodic invention and the devotion to detail in chamber-musical voice leading has risen since Beethoven. Meanwhile all this depends on one set of eyes, empty eyes; we have neither an academy nor the secure, intellectual beauty of a musical style, the only style still possible for us, and music refuses to begin. There are only artists here and no art, but individual artists do not simply have the right already to be categorial for themselves, or when they do, then only in this way: that the historical great individuals who stand as categories have built a categorial context providing the latecomers, irrespective of all their glorious youthfulness, with the checks and balances of a sphere to substantially ground every youthfulness, futurity, subjectivity. Because they go deeper, sonic constructs do not simply possess youth as an attribute: they become younger precisely by becoming older, and resting on themselves, and attaining the new-old quality of what is concealed in this repose. They thus advance as artists and as artworks, not senselessly, within time's empty, formalistic advance; rather, what is new rounds itself off, in order to find its measure and its rigor; it becomes a dignity, ultimately a homecoming, and in the end it is exactly what is most reckless, painful, what lets itself go, what is most paradoxical to itself, which also stands closest to what is old, most primordially basic, simplest, given, immemorially longed-for, lost to the adult world. This loosening of the inessential, which is essential to almost the entire history of music, and the increasing subjectivation, the adequation of the search and the adventure of the modern spirit in itself, toward itself, even in its *imprévu*, and particularly in the impressionality of this *imprévu*, belongs to an expressionistic idea directed toward the essential, an idea repeatedly making the *trouver* triumph over the *construer*. So the youth who never dies, never renounces, the youth who perpetually rejuvenates himself, first provides maturity in the genius, but precisely that *maturity* as which "youth" first acquires substance, and the vagrant dissonances, the freely proliferating intensifications, indeed even the seeming anarchy of atonal music, in truth form just the lower countermovement to a higher Expressionism asserting itself therein, and the manifestation, barely even attained in the beginnings, of its Gothic exuberance. Yet all of that is what it is precisely by means of its direction, its anamnesis, its secret *system* of revolutionary youth emerging, emerging ever further, revolutionary out of a final orthodoxy. If the new sound is thus already the better one, it is so certainly not because of its smooth complexion or because of the surprises with which it stimulates only the need for variety, but because time, self-developing modernity, Advent defined as a concept, needs and loves the composer.

The Problem of a Historical Philosophy of Music

That is why musicians must nonetheless be held together, in order that nothing may dissipate. This bond perhaps draws, directs, is perhaps fashioned progressively, but defined spatially far more than just chronologically. It is fashioned so that the single points that it touches as form are absolutely fixed as existent. The point here is to define particular inspired individual states, which become canonical for everyone with a Mozartian, Beethovenian, or Bachian gift. But just for this purpose, everything that has been assembled merely historically must be most thoroughly disassembled for the sake of a new totality of overview. The givens and then apparently so different givens have become comprehensive enough that just as the great masters freely used the different forms of song, fugue or sonata insofar as the "spirit" of the relevant passage required it—just in this way we can set Mozart before Bach, or derive from Mozart's, Bach's, Wagner's forms a sequence of composition and its objects, historically unsurpassable, but always to be repostulated. In terms of time, in other words of mere, brutal successiveness, the differences are of course quite immense. Nowhere does change penetrate as deeply, and most of all nowhere does the timespan in which this change takes place have the same vehement tempo and brevity as in music, and nowhere is the road as hopelessly linear, or if one prefers, as hopefully linear as in this art. Everywhere else there are models arching over the distantly, diffusely affiliated: unique ways to comprehend the absolute and adaptive. The Greek column but also the Gothic column, the Homeric epic but also the Old Testament are such basic forms, and Plato's philosophy is one no less, just like Kantian philosophy; that means it suffices to have been the first to have meaningfully explored this region, thus providing an initial model that is at the same time indestructible, exhaustive at least in the fashion of a carpet, a certain perimeter or encirclement, an inventory of all possible content. Only recently, however, in spite of the achieved, always operative landmarks of Mozart, Beethoven, even Bach, has such a new totality, a superior overview, arisen in music. The composer may feel like the wheel rolling automatically, now as before, but the senseless turbulence of sheer progress has disappeared; out of the vanity and the most anarchic possible competition with the past rises a structure, a location within the structure, so that every idea in the formal complex given by history can find its particular position, which certainly does not need to be depleted even at the moment of its historical occurrence, and very likely requires further improvement, more fervent fantasy and the utopian elaboration of its substance. Only recently, in other words, since Brahms and particularly since Bruckner, does the final start seem to have been made; unremitting novelty, complete with all the bad infinity of its straight line, seems to want to go over into a parabola of shapes, into an *open system* and into the occupied or (when genius is new like a metaphysical breakthrough is new) the projected fields within this periodic system of forms, or, better: of sigillary musical categories.

There is a clear intention here, and it also separates, orders, purely cumulatively. To describe what is taking shape there we introduce an auxiliary concept first used by Lukács, the "carpet" as pure, corrective form, where reality is fulfilled, correlated, constitutive form.[3] In this way we can distinguish three schemata according to the momentum of the applied force, in part as clarifications, in part to be complemented anamnestically. The *first* includes the endless singing-to-oneself, dance and finally chamber music, the last having declined from something higher, become a carpet in large part inauthentically. The *second* takes a longer approach: it is the self-enclosed *Lied*, Mozart or the *Spieloper*, with their brief secular ex-

citation, the oratorio, Bach or the *Passions*, with their brief spiritual excitation, and above all the fugue, which of course with respect to its endless
melody already passes into dramatic form, from which its purely architectonic, undramatic counterpoint decisively distinguishes it, however.
Here, invariably, live compositions with a self-enclosed or at least a tran-
quilly unfolding, monothematic melody. This *second* schema has no
longer declined into complete inobjectivity, but has its object in a somewhat easier, more easily attainable, lower-lying region of the self, but only
such that next to every more forceful movement, that is, next to its corresponding dramatic form, it appears like a prelude, like a carpet, albeit a
true one, like pure form, like a corrective, which with its beautiful, immobile unity—motivated purely lyrically and otherwise only assembled—
shall radiate into the *third* schema, *event-form*, into the turmoil of the
heavy, more chaotic, dynamically symbolic opera, the great choral work,
and Beethoven-Bruckner or the symphony, as the liberated, secularly even
if not yet spiritually great, entirely dramatically motivated, entirely transcendentally objective event-forms, which incorporate everything authentically or inauthentically carpet-like and fulfill it in their movement toward the tempo, toward the thunder and lightning in the upper regions
of the self. One is reminded here of the tripartite, syllogistic progression
of forms in the other arts. The still life, the portrait, the large landscape;
the linear ornament, the sculpture and the multidimensional ornamentation of eidetic figural composition and of architecture; the novella, the
lyric, and beyond them the great epics and dramas; indeed, if one wants
to extend the syllogism of mere composition even further, even religion's
characteristic formal sequence of the ecstatic craving for miracles, then
Protestantism, and finally structured, mediated institutional faith—all
these abstract beginnings, individual medians and concrete fulfillments of
abstraction obey a rhythm like that of musical forms, and a related syllogism: from the pleasantly beautiful game as the stage of the heart, to full
individuality transforming within itself as the stage of sincerity and of the
soul, up to the luminous solidity of the system as the stage of power, of
depth, and of spirit. The still more central development, which assuredly
explodes the merely formal play of dialectical arrangement: that is the correlation, which we can only just indicate here, of the Greek Mozart, the
Gothic Bach, the Baroque Beethoven and Wagner and the unknown seraphic composer to the corresponding status indicators of a philosophy of
history of the inwardness uplifted in the world.

FULLNESS AND ITS SCHEMA

I.

How did we first hear ourselves, then?

As an endless singing-to-oneself, and in the dance.

Both of these, we had said, are still anonymous. They have no life in themselves, and no one personally gave them form. They possess, where one comes across them, the charm of a first beginning. But first one simply had to go through something else that deliberately brought the original tune out of its mere immediacy. That in particular let expression be extensively and securely equipped. Then of course we can see the cry again, the dance, when an artist reflects on them.

They are remainders or promises, either way. They might remain lying here along with chamber music, half the time the most stagnant exercise form, half the time the most fruitful contrapuntal subtlety and the deliverance of the sonata from its all too sloppy, all too headlong plunge. So it will still retrospectively have to be recognized what significance that endless singing, and then dance above all, attain in Bach and Wagner.

II.

Song

But everything here still takes place very quietly.

So one rounds one's singing delicately. It may have rung true in the open air, but with Silcher it begins to ring false.[4] It is the stillborn character of the false folk song or popular song. Singing abandoned the cry, the dance, and the incantation quite early. At least the *Minnesänger* already seem to have composed out of a quite muted midpoint. But it is astonishing that even such modern artists as Schumann—the early Schumann—indeed even Brahms, effected significant work there. Through them the self-enclosed song was established as a soft, homophonically melodious form with the most simple tempi. They revel, one is carried along by these songs; they die out only as moods; they are German and nevertheless, in contradictory fashion, finite and well-mannered, especially when each strophe is melodically closed. It may be that the Biedermeier's quiet love of singing, soon so degraded by the amateur choral society, contributed greatly to this triumph of the bourgeois in the middle of an age that had sought quite other goals, if not in Zelter then most assuredly in Schubert. The aria is clear, and especially the easily learned Italian *cantilena*, pleasantly closed, truly popular and still perfectly attuned to the lute. It survives in opera, survives because every showpiece begins and ends, and so, from Pergolesi to Offenbach, has its complete, carpet-like pattern, as understandable from the singer's standpoint as from the opera's.

On Mozart

Mozart is at the head of this splendid line.

He is capable of singing gently and enchantingly, of self-enclosed singing. There he knows quite singularly how to speak of himself, of us, insofar as we can be reached there. In Mozart things become quiet in a different way; night falls and lovely figures draw us into their ranks. Then again, it is not yet that night when everything is transformed, when the light is extinguished and the hill fairy appears, and a shimmer like a red dawn, as when the sun will soon rise, spreads across every wall. Rather, the candles burn on, everything remains lit up by them, more lovely and more transfiguring than daylight can do, here and there abutting the beyond in Rococo fashion, but otherwise pearlescent, and luminous only by reflection. The motion of such colorful sonorous shapes is highly buoyant, winged, but there is no delirium and no eruption, not even in the more excited scenes in *Figaro*; above all, the only action is intended and proffered merely as recitative, passing into, going through, and passing through song again. So each scene quickly issues into an aria, as gathering emotion, the gathering feeling of a situation, as the duration of an expression of an emotion without any tendency tempestuously to abandon both the punctual corporeal self and its moderate space. Whether delicate, sorrowful, or cheerful, this last courtly music is calm and plastic to such an extent that the melody, charmingly taking up and letting off, neatly answering, entwining itself in neat answers, feels no need to distinguish between even the cheerful banquet and Don Juan's mystical destruction, in view of its invariable closure and plasticity of line and form. Thus nearly everything in this moderately sustained action, in the melancholically sweet composure and poise of this aria, remains silvery, porcelain; even the excited, free, clattering march dresses up in chinoiserie; and as the recitative closes itself off more or less like a carpet, the depiction of the inner life—of its actions presented here only in recitative, of the outpourings of its fullness here expended only lyrically—does not go so deeply into the more turbulent, real self, into the dramatically eruptive or even mystically recognized self, that Mozartian opera could ever leave behind the sphere of puppet show, *Spieloper*, fairy-tale opera, or in the highest instance, the carpet for the musical drama of redemption. Certainly there are unforgettable moments nevertheless: the dialogue with the priest and the solemnity with which the priestly melody suddenly breaks in, or the fugal writing, and how above it the stony *cantus firmus* of the two armored men before the temple gate rises erect like a baptismal or nummular stamp; both these enormous sonorous shapes from the *Magic Flute* are second sight, they tear the carpet like a tremendous, gaping, gorgonic vision recollecting itself above the otherwise pure form's playful, playlike, and evenly paradisiacal element. But even this is childhood, at bottom an unproven dream; it is the music of being 17 years old, beyond which adulthood's decline threatens, and which at other moments does not make this art, immanent like a carpet, decisively real, does not force the crisis.

Hence Mozart remains the king of a musical South, almost always still reshapable into visibility and plastic delight. Thus he did not want to be disrupted by melody during his longer strides or motions, nor be led into the distance. One begins to understand how quickly the soul is encapsulated here, even in the broad and atmospheric work of his *sonata*. One experiences these works with melodic and often, as in the incomparable Overture to the *Magic Flute* or in the Finale of the *Jupiter Symphony*, with chamber-musical reward, but seldom or never with symphonic reward. They are quite gracefully devised, often with an incredibly great arc of the most splendid intervals, and on the level of detail always so efflorescent and lavish that only Schubert approaches such melodic wealth: but nothing has happened when the theme reemerges, nothing charges, nothing discharges, there are no snowy roads, no fog, no forests, no going astray and no warm light in the distance; it is a melodious getting-carried-away and a drifting-past strung like pearls, and the counter-subject creates neither light nor heat, nor that music of the confusion which after all otherwise reigns masterfully over the *opera buffa*. So much stays at rest in the small secular self's small sequence of moods, motionless among themselves, and the mere, spatially as much as chronologically brief dynamism of its corporeal soul.[5] On this subject it must also be said, with no sanctimony and out of devotion to the carpet: the development here neither wants to nor can maintain the kind of tension or will to the long line that ought to proceed from the expansive, out of necessity expansive fire of its thematic oppositions. The whole in Mozart displays an arithmetical tendency, which fundamentally contradicts the Beethovenian symphony as a deliberate formation joining together visibly to itself and organically. This is exactly what led Wagner to the justified observation that in Mozart were combined the most delicate grace and an astonishing mathematical talent, from which the value-character of this captivating but not shattering music, this mundanely clarifying but spiritually almost unproblematic Hellenism within music, precisely results.

The Passions

One did not even immediately wish to be moved beyond here.

Longing in *Bach* was no raging wildfire, but a depth of spirit remaining within itself.

Just for this reason it had no desire to immediately show itself as excited and open. In Bach, too, the narration takes place mainly in unvarying recitative. Only where the voice chokes up, so to speak, and for crying cannot continue narrating the sacred events to itself, do the more excited tones of *lyrical* reflection break free. These lyrical constructs, however, without leaving their accepted place, are placed under the voice's equally deeply submerged authority, or even—as it was customary for Keiser and the Hamburg school to digress into the operatic—placed under the continuous domination of the chorale. In the *chorale*, then, the agitated element returns to a self-enclosed, lyrical and therefore undramatic context, of course always already with the ultimate purpose of breaking across to this also supradramatic context. For when Jesus says: "Einer unter euch wird mich verraten" [I say unto you that one of you shall betray me], and the apostles, in the most vehement allegro anxiously cry in confusion, "Herr, bin ich's?" [Lord, is it I?], and then, after a marvelous pause, the congregation sings the chorale, "Ich bin's, ich sollte büßen" [It is I, I should atone], the inmost element resounds at this moment of the St. Matthew Passion, and Kierkegaard himself could have found no more powerful sermon for this way of speaking *ad hominem*, for Christian conduct and the subjectivation of what is Christian. In other words, then, the lyrical attunement of the chorale disregards the merely private lyricism of individuals as well as the outer drama of the actual choruses, to be discussed presently. For like some arias dedicated to reflection, the chorale is essentially the expressive form of a higher congregation, a Zion dwelling so to speak beyond events; in the overriding carpet of its no longer private, or no longer—this would be impossible as such anyway—excited, processual, and dramatic, but rather truly supra-dramatic, *ontological* lyricism, it corresponds to that highest stage that the medieval mystery plays erected as Heaven over Earth and Hell. Completely different, certainly, is the way the actual *choruses* present themselves where Bach, like the vigorous, epic Handel, no longer counterpoints in the homophonic form of the old Protestant chorales, but rather wildly, jaggedly, in rhythmic sections. Here at least there is action, and we see right into the passionate agitation. As with the "Kreuzige!" [Crucify!] and the furiously bellowed demand for Barabbas, the raving chorus: "Sind Blitze, sind Donner in Wolken verschwunden" [Have thunder, have lightning, vanished into the clouds?], in fact every Jewish or secular congregational chorus where a crowd demands or accuses in order to intervene in the action differently than the narrative recitative, indeed to create a more passionate action than even the biblical one.[6] Nevertheless, the text is not only thereby abandoned, just as the quiet and self-enclosed type of form in the narrower sense is finally burst. The human voice can only still serve as a musical instrument in this chorus, just as the more developed vocal music by itself indeed drove toward transmitting its animation onto the at once richer as well as more stable coloration of the instruments, in fact to disperse in that direction, or at least to remain only the highest, most powerfully expressive section of the orchestra. When Bach carried the old vocalism over to organ and orchestra, the inevitable result, in other words, was that the "voices" that had already lost everything specifically lyrical within their intricate choral deployment would here truly be subject to the rhythm of a new style resulting from their coordination and contrapuntal development. And this style, as a kind of melodic or rather melismatic invention under disadvantaged conditions, had to considerably weaken the melody's untroubled, self-enclosed, previously just accompanied even if more or less filigranely accompanied solo; after which the fugues of Bach, and soon after Bach something unsuspected, the sonata up to Beethoven, resulted from the breakup of self-enclosed melody.

Bach, His Form and His Object

Song, in other words, becomes extensive, infinite, but so to speak internally infinite, in the fugue.

Here everything must be played thoroughly songfully, and be clearly filigreed. But should Bach therefore be regarded in purely scalar terms, with a reticence about chordal combinations? This is what is most easily accessible to the superficial, academic mind, certainly. So of course there is no better sort of vicar who does not think of himself as Bach's trumpet, and endeavor to transform these inconceivably lofty works into proper sexton's music. But it has been said, however, and correctly, that the harpsichord's sharp, short sound fulfills not a single one of Bach's requirements. Similarly, it is also not at all completely true that only the organ, the vocal organ, the orchestral organ, represented the proper sonic image to Bach. And there can be no doubt that only our own pianos, the incomparable Steinways that were born for the modern Bach, clear, booming, edged with silver, have revealed how the master should now be played, how one should conceive of the many ornaments, but also of the seemingly unwavering consistency, and where, into what kind of songful, in other words not simply harmonic, but certainly not extraharmonic flower the well-tempered clavier has to open. Bach adopted the endless song as well as the old dances with their multiple rhythmic sections; the recovery of the oldest carpet thus begins. What is dearest to this master of inner reanimation is the thematic germ within this singing dividedness; he loves his theme, into which, like no one else, he has compressed what is to follow—conflict and the sharpest delineation of conflict—and he lovingly considers this theme from every angle and every aspiration until it blossoms and in the fugue's great variations becomes an unlocked shrine, an internally limited—meaning, in other words, limited precisely by the theme's life-span—an internally infinite melody, a melismatic universe with respect to the developed individuality of its theme. Just for this reason Bach is not set purely on diatonicism, however clearly everything may be filigreed. Obviously, the harmonic element as such becomes indifferent in Bach, where it appears as the incidental, pleasantly meaningful simultaneity of the voices. Then again not indifferent in the sense that the movements toward such incidents, and their whole, in other words the counterpoint, would now also be the overarching and quintessentially accentuated element. Certainly, insofar as counterpoint signifies a complete horizontal clarity, it is more the essence of Bach than of Beethoven and Wagner. Yet there is in the disposition of the elements in Bach, too, a willing, and the richly interrelated flood of a thematic succession streaming all the way through, of a double, in itself already richly conflictual thematics dependent on transitions, turning points and corners, but foremost on the harmony's rhythmically emphasized anchor points—as one can see, no simple, homophonic harmony, but rather a different, deliberate, underlining harmony, accentuating by means of its mass—far more strongly than on the irresolute voice leading of continuous polyphony. And the volition radiates into the disposition, even if Bach remains the master of the single voice, doubling or quintupling the old homophony; the inner master of spinning out lines into the latter's seemingly unlyrical, superlyrical space. The fusing, harmonic-rhythmic element nonetheless maintains an influence and prevents an indulgence in contrapuntal technique and form even there in Bach where the separation of the voices fundamentally contributes to preventing a vertical blending, in other words the existence and evolution of entire sonic columns or chordal forces, however they may be rhythmically subdivided, or entwined and then released by the dominant. Foremost, however, because it is only the song, the theme which wants to become extensive, infinite within the so to speak internally infinite melody of the fugue, it is precisely the diatonic contrapuntality which declines to a mere means, to something reflexive, permitted only because the forever songfully flourishing melismata more sharply profile themselves against the juxtaposition, and because they can best represent their sheltered, unriven simultaneity, their *lyricism* that no longer concerns anything particular, but signifies simply soul, developed soul—the central element of Bach's church music, notwithstanding all the dramatic congregational choruses—in the contrapuntal, or, better: the bilinear system of equilibrium. Where this equilibrium acquires independence, it becomes a simple matter—just as in the uneven surface of a bas-relief's ground we perceive air, the disposition of figures in the landscape, indeed an entire landscape submerged in the rise and fall of the uneven ground—to recognize in the framework of Bach's counterpoint the submerged, assembled, stratified lyricism of the *Passions* built into the niches of the three-dimensional contrapuntality.

The necessary result here is that the vitally, melismatically played fugue is also a carpet or corrective. The fugue may be designated as the carpet *prior* to all the complications of the agitated, chaotic, melodically disrupted symphony, in other words as the carpet of fulfillment, of corrective-fulfillment, valid alongside the *Spieloper* and the chorales of the congregation of Zion. It seems appropriate here, though—in order not to be forced against our principles to glide over something—to pause at two points, to emphasize as prototypical two features in Bach: first the *inner soul* (only with the difference that now, in the works for keyboard, organ and orchestra, the shape like the limit of this lyricism becomes clearer than in the *Passions* through recourse to an essentially architectonically contrapuntal topography); and *further* the *space* of this lyrical element, that is, the fusion and balance of the lyrical and the structured in an essentially *architectonic*, Gothically architectonic harmony and counterpoint, which acts as the particular house, the so to speak spatially constitutive system of this lyricism. Accordingly one may well speak of a reverse correlation within this circle, when the lyrical closure in which, into which the whole of Bach's harmony, his symphony ultimately builds itself up or installs itself, also clearly restricts the constitutive object of this circle to the more easily consummated carpet or corrective of something more difficult, real, absolute.

In Mozart it is the mundane self, in Bach the spiritual self which becomes objective. As Mozart in his excited way, lightly, freely, elatedly and brilliantly makes feelings sonorous, so does Bach display, in a more measured way, heavily, urgently, firmly, with hard rhythms and somber profundity, the self and its emotional inventory. Therefore in Mozart it is the (still small) mundanely Luciferan self, with Bach the (likewise still small) spiritually Christian self, the self of goodness or of the redeemed Adam, still attainable through the more self-immediate, more subjective, Protestant sensibility, in other words not yet the self concealed beyond an entirely different dynamic, the self of the gathering, the glory, or the redeemed Lucifer. It is the inwardly illuminated enclosure of the Christian volition to act, in the sense that Bach's music expresses the struggle for the soul's salvation, the stage of Charity and Hope, beyond which—parallel but inaccessible to Bach—rise the three higher living essences: the stages of Faith, of the Illumination and of the Apocalypse, within a not more sublime, but more difficult and more definitive religious phenomenology.

III.

But what do we finally hear ourselves for? Now we soon feel freer. For the note also wants to push toward action.

It sits more loosely; it tenses and charges. The third schema, completely adventurous, arises. The old cloister breaks; the chaotic world, the external dream before the genuine cloister, shines in.

Carmen

So we move on more easily now. That does not yet mean that individual songs ramble into the distance without lines or demarcations. If we take *Carmen*, for example, each wild, colorful song is still self-enclosed. But it is characteristic of them that they are not simply set in a row, but rather, without being broken, appear open and mobile, at least insofar as they are able to momentarily follow the course of the action instead of lyrically decorating and arresting it. Thus the sound moves out into the wide world in order to make room for not only the enthusiastic, playful human being, but also the abrupt, mobile human being losing and proving himself in fast-paced adventure, though not yet actually "finding" himself, of course. One need only recall the exemplary way that a tempo shift changes the expressivity of the *Carmen* motif. The way that Escamillo and Don José sing to each other before and after the duel, in its passionately various succession—which because of the simple melodies can nevertheless aim at rounded, very trimly turned forms—also provides a good example of animatedly self-enclosed ideas.

Open Song and 'Fidelio'

Of course things are different with the open song. It truly began foremost with the late Schubert. Nothing remains conventional, or bound to the strophe; the lower voices are amply relaxed, supple and ready to accompany anything, the vocal line is expressively true to the meaning, and the flow of the intensification becomes the essential nature of the whole. This applies above all to Hugo Wolf, less so to Strauß, who becomes shallow, Biedermeieresque and trivial everywhere he wants to move us with soft tones; but where astringent writing is called for, to set the long arc of passionate, serious texts to music, Klopstock and the like, Strauß becomes the better composer. But where action is called for, open-ended song also saves the day. Particularly after it became increasingly richly filigrane, carefully filled out. The sound had been too drab in the recitative, and too longwinded at lyrical moments. Now the ringing exclamations go along with the singing, and transform it into an abbreviated melodic incident variable enough to also convey the sensations and outbursts of people in action, the atmosphere's entire charge of immediacy, fate, decision. Wherever a person intervenes more earnestly in the action, and the action in the person, it therefore becomes necessary more decisively to break up the lyrical form, and leave it open. So it is in Weber, and even more in Marschner's highly significant *Hans Heiling* with its magnificent aria and singular melodrama; above all, however, in Beethoven's *Fidelio* and its enigmatic melody. Over time, of course, it has become so widespread, and hence a means to embellish the inconsequential and provide some melismatically compounded substitute in place of melodically self-enclosed ideas, that the *Spieloper* no longer exists, and instead everything is dragged onto terrain that should remain reserved for the most vehement passion and action. For here alone is such excitement permitted: formally still an opera of action, but one that knows how to bring things to a boil, thus distinguished by its symphonic character from the *Carmen* type. Even *Der fliegende Holländer, Tannhäuser, Lohengrin* and above all *Die Meistersinger*—which moreover maintains a complete operatic structure—as well as large parts of the *Ring* count as operas of action, which have dramatic opera as their essential goal. But just as anything songful in Beethoven becomes so to speak pregnant with an endless, erupting movement, so also in *Fidelio*, as the *a priori* generic model of the symphonic drama, does no single song and certainly not the raging of the ensemble scenes remain contained in the secure space of the melody, however excited. The digressively deployed sound, the surge of sounds and the continued accretion of tension, chaos and fate boils over into an overwhelmingly unmelodic, recitatively melismatic, motivically thematic and as a whole purely symphonically developing type of music, which—in itself already making a mockery of any well-considered text—not only follows the action, but itself generates action, a still indeterminate, nameless action, into which the theatrical application and a textual "justification" now have to be installed.

'Missa Solemnis'

All of this escalates further in Beethoven's use of the chorus. To sing in communion, that was once the need: to confess in communion. They were solitary voices that called in the darkness, that answered one another, and thus attained a unison in the deeper sense. Of course we saw how human voices in chorus can now only be used as an instrument, but at the same time we realized that the voice is saved as the uppermost, most powerfully expressive part of the orchestra. The text, previously so important, thereby retreats; it becomes like a mesh or backing into which the notes are embroidered, and which can certainly no longer be suggested or traced by their entwining. Certainly the four, even eight voices prohibit too much mobility, but they are human voices, and especially since Beethoven they not only know how to develop intensifications with the most fearsome seriousness, but are now also truly able, when it comes to force, calm, spirituality, mystery, in other words the climaxes and denouements of the dramatically symphonic style, to propagate the full supradramatic, enigmatic shimmer of the cry of a community's prayer, if not yet the acknowledgment. So the ancient congregation has been smashed, and we can only delight in the chorus and its work, and certainly only create it, as the desired but no longer existing power and unity of faith. A different kind of gathering has come, a different kind of searching and finding of the souls standing firmly together there, a different kind of longing for organization and above all for the meaning of organization, a global breadth that leads people together, that gives them, in the chorus, a thousand voices to demand one thing, to proclaim to the heights the awakening, to summon salvation with a thousand-fold cry become musically transcendent. The chorus is a means; it offers itself for these purposes, tempestuous and cathedralic, with the ascending line of the new devotion that extends in an ever more passionate Baroque from Bach's B minor Mass to the "pater omnipotens" of the *Missa solemnis*, to Bruckner's sacred music, above all his F minor Mass. To an ever more resolute awareness, and one no less to be pursued philosophically, that the congregation has less to praise the Holy Spirit than to testify it.

The Birth of the Sonata

Much else has already appeared, and brought new life. Now animated, operatic thought contributes its most characteristic fruit, the sonata. We know how decisively compositional style changed shortly after Bach. He himself had stood like a strange forest giant among the *galant* composers, after all. Light and strong, the individually *concertante* solo voice of violin and song had already risen. No longer subordinate to voice leading, freely digressive, ever further from the corporative configuration of the medieval *a capella* style. Bach's son C. P. E. had already helped to found the new style, the liberation of homophonic individuality; and *Haydn* is his greater successor in the sonata form, just as Scarlatti's tripartite operatic prelude was his significant model. Here the song, within a now fully mobile compositional method, freely runs its own course, which dominates the entire sonata. The other parts are there to surround the melody from all sides, to let it submerge and seemingly dissolve itself in them, in order to then more readily retreat into a subordinate, merely decorative, developmental state. There are thus no longer exclusively developed voices; rather, Haydn employs inner voices and in particular groups of instruments to enable the desired orchestral effect and harmonic color. So the theme becomes indifferent, even on superficial observation; it no longer wants to generate the development, but rather, conversely, to be trained by the development to ever greater life and brilliance—a lighter fabric with a trace of impatience impossible for the fugue, such that it has been rightly observed that a bad measure ruins a fugue, but a single good measure saves a sonata. Nonetheless there is no going back now that a voice can enter freely, and one simply cannot, after the great cost of this positive accomplishment, turn back the pages now sadly become so "poetic," or even just skip over them in order measure by measure to reclaim a thoughtfully, listlessly good fugal style. Here it remains the case, completely so, even for those who do not love this new way of being taken by surprise, that with the *Eroica* we have our marching orders, by command of the veritable *Zeit-Geist*. Whereby it may incidentally become a simple matter, even for more cautious tastes, to give themselves up to Beethoven's sonatas—which are really just as full of demagogic artifices as of promises, true climaxes and the wide oscillations of dominant tensions— all the way to their conclusion, differently, but just as completely, as to Bach's fugues. What unsettles us so deeply here: the lightning-quick dynamics, the miraculous horns, the way the sound fills out with a blossoming, a suffusing and a reverberating until it compares to a pedal, the bitter cold—the changing of the guard and storytelling by night—belief and unbelief—the star—and then it appears, the ghost or perhaps the Spirit, with all the devices of percussion, trombones, organ and full orchestra maintained at the most extreme *fortissimo*: it is a new mode of existence for instrumental and dynamic expression, permitting invention from color and illumination, so to speak, out of the harmonic drama, and forcing a new rushing of the wind, a Venetian glow, into the initially so thin and insubstantial character of the thematic transformation. Of course at first Haydn uses the exhilarating succession of colors only insofar as one no longer simply sings here, but rather a battle rages in the upper melody filigreed repeatedly by melisma from below: in other words, insofar as a second melody, a countersubject, and the developmental as well as unifying impetus of this countersubject comes along. That seems like very little, particularly as the bithematic form was not actually invented by Haydn. Bach also, particularly in the introductions to his *Partitas*, makes clearly apparent the principle of a countersubject, expressed in a second theme, as the archetype of the sonata. But what emerged here in closed form, Haydn will continuously uphold and make the basis of a formalized, compositional, polythematic *Weltanschauung* directly predestining the adventurous totality of the loosened, dramatically symphonic style of the absolute sonata, Beethoven's sonata.

Brahms and Chamber Music

Here those composers became false who loved to murmur, at the same time quite cheaply making themselves clear. Once again the demure songwriters emerged here, became "symphonic," and spread oil on the newly surging waters. Only one man dissents, sought Beethoven's true trail: the late Schubert, who hated his older homophonic *Lieder*, and died at almost exactly the moment when he understood his true, proper gift for reveling in long passages and structure at the same time, which sets him next to Bruckner. But the others, as diverse as they may be as "symphonists"—the pathetic Mendelssohn, ever more cheerful and skillful; Schumann the unfortunate would-be; Chopin the *ancien régime's* piano star; and the virile, incomparably greater Brahms, a giant in comparison—nonetheless have the same fatally decorous and moderate streak that leaves only Chopin occasionally free, as in his very interesting chromaticism, related to Wagner's, but then condemns him elsewhere to the vacuous contrasts of salon brilliance, the splendid but mostly meaningless art of *fiorituri*. A streak that lets Brahms, fiery, somber, deep Brahms, be misunderstood again and again as the speaker and party leader of a prim, Central German bourgeoisie. So the kind of upright composers appeared who were until recently propagated in musical academies, as the unworthy if not entirely unmerited successors of the malign majority backing Brahms. Music was then in serious danger of declining from a universal concern to an academic affair of the German sitting room, the educated class with all its inhibitions and its barren sentimentality. But it is very lamentable that Brahms of all people withdrew so cozily into an aversion to all fire. He has color: his sonic image has quite aptly been compared with the North German heath, which from the distance appears as a wide, monotonous plain, but one sets foot in it and all of a sudden the gray dissolves into a profusion of little flowers and colors. Of course

Brahms does not want to paint or compose mood music, rather, he wants to force the melismatic substance together with the pleasure of organic construction, by the meticulous old polyphonic methods, and with a goal of organically plastic articulation, impeded by a dense warp and woof of scalar lines. Still, one cannot, however high-mindedly, expand the arrangement and revel in plasticity precisely where good construction really becomes less important than emotionally effective rhythmic placement. Nothing can thus be more inauthentic, and a worse discipleship toward Beethoven, than to reduce the master, in accordance with Brahms's conservatorial impetus, from the world-spirit of music who smashed the pianos, in whose music the boulders rain down, who transformed even the most powerful orchestras into fragile junk by the *a priori* immoderacy of his scores, to a well-bred piano and chamber music.

This is why we have in all seriousness already presented such art as being like a carpet. One can see by it what someone was capable of or had learned, but a few parts bring everything to light. Much perhaps is unstable besides, and searches acutely for transitions to something real. It is possible that there could be a particular movement of four, five, or six voices that needed no more voices, and that for itself maintained that autonomy which it denies to other constructs, such as the octet, which clearly slide toward the symphonic. But all that is nothing in and of itself, until it undergoes the application of its neatness and transparency in a larger context. No good listener would or could concede a string quartet its own soul in some expressive statement, no matter how illuminated by its insistent structuration. Where things are different, as in Beethoven's late quartets, it is a small matter to place the light in back instead of in front, as the extension inward and backward of the great composition's enigmatic structure absolutely demands. Here one may not illuminate the painted windowpane from the front and by day, where of course it could not even survive next to the genuine, the plastic arts of form; rather, in Wagner's outstanding metaphor, Beethoven places the magical stained glass into the nocturnal silence, between the phenomenal world and the deeply inner, hermetically radiant world of the essence of all things, whereby the hidden portrait first comes to life and testifies to a world to which not ordered but only molded, vitally developing form, that is, only music's organically eidetic transparency, has access. But everywhere else there remains only the cold, academic pleasure in the weaving of the themes, their entry, their meeting, their greeting one another, waning, waxing, going side by side and uniting, as if and not even as if they were real people who meet and thereby let drama's destinies commence. If they should even survive, all these joys and self-affirmations of the connoisseur whose politics after all have all too often been the snobbish or pedantic politics of the *Mittelstand*, then only to the extent that chamber music withdraws to the place of pure form, the preserve of neatness and the melismatic beauty of detail, of an inventive, flourishing solo playing by every instrument, from which, after Beethoven, the Brucknerian symphony that truly ventured into the active, the "effective," real symphony drew sustenance for its details. To that extent, then—and this has now become definite—the quartet style was a carpet and a corrective: not in the worse pieces, of course, which are simply regressive, but all the more so in the better ones where chamber music blossoms anew in counterpoint, where almost everything transparent remains to be regained, in order to impart its *sophrosyne* to the not only more democratic but also more transcendent construct of the symphony.

Beethoven, His Form, His Object and the Spirit of the Sonata

But now everything false and stale falls away. The leadenness disperses, the distortion vanishes, and Beethoven follows through to the unknown end. How one's heart leaps up at the thought of you, infinite one![7] We certainly sense that even greater glories will appear, but that is wish and not fact, and so our soul froths up to the stars in this music's first, rough, storm-driven, eloquent sea. Beethoven is Lucifer's good son, the psychopomp to the last things.

In other words we breathe easily for the first time here. Singing that rounds itself off has almost come to an end, of course. In its thematic concision, too, at least in the great movements. Excepted is only the variation, still constantly flourishing melodically around the theme. Obviously the drawn-out adagio, which already no longer suffers or rests, of course, but becomes persuasively sentimental. Variation, as Bekker aptly defined it, is the unraveling, or the inward, unconflicted unfolding, in other words the predominantly passive expansion of the theme, still given here as a song and as a melody, and laid out as a sequence of feelings. It is joined by the almost equally still melodic rondo, basically distinguished by presenting several ideas rather than one. The rondo is fashioned such that in it the loose contiguity of moods, avoiding the stricter sonata form, increases to an almost rhapsodic diversity of moods, to a certain extent as intermediate elements between feeling and thematic idea. Thus the rondo represents a hybrid form of the elements of lyrical variation and the elements of the dramatic sonata. The connections already become more excited and at the same time stricter in the scherzo, Beethoven's most characteristic form, insofar as it adapts the old minuet in the light of an enigmatic joy combined of laughter and mockery, their furiously exuberant or ironically hovering dance rhythms. To get to the essence, however, to the sonata's great utilizing movements themselves: passion, pain, cheer and ease remain the components of the sonata as the proper and cumulative Beethovenian form. To these movements generally correspond, of course with occasional strong changes in significance, the pedagogical designations *allegro, adagio, scherzo* and *finale.* The first movement in particular is usually anything but an allegro, and the last, the finale, includes the rondo as well, in fact sometimes even the variation as well, which is otherwise supposed to be completely opposed to the strict, antithetical development, and which nonetheless, because it expands arbitrarily, loosely, more freely, now forms the sonata's most significant section next to the first movement. Perhaps one should still mention Beethoven's piano concerto as a particular form. It reflects to a certain extent the conventional order of gloomier labyrinths and free, easy play on the plateau. For in Mozart the piano was still integrated, striking up the theme, but otherwise figuring only below the orchestral writing; in contrast there is for Beethoven no movement which the piano will not take up and no path which the orchestra must not finally abandon in order to find in the piano, always rushing upward, culminating in panoply, its complete glory. The remaining piano sonatas as such, primarily the later ones, are not so unambiguous. Particular sonatas, above all the *Hammerklavier,* suggest an orchestration, and then one would have a symphony. The two are closely related; the sonata like the symphony is inhabited by the same organically articulated action, of which contemporaries, after all, also believed that here was a disguised opera, and in fact one cannot deny the dramatic structuring principle of Beethoven's symphonies. With all this completely operative, suprathematic activity it becomes dramatically productive to ask what it is that leads into the depths of the whole if it is no longer the singing theme. For the theme, since the moment when Beethoven realized his talent to lead, to command, and to carry us off, has wholly retreated before the rushing, the urge to persuade, and the tendency toward dramatic form. It is just the theme in Beethoven that shows itself far removed from counting as a living individuality; there is no greater distance in these symphonic works than between the fury of the particular and the powerful stability of the whole. One simply cannot, for just this reason, deduce every benefit from the often-praised distinctness of Beethoven's themes, which often—as Halm showed precisely for the scenic *D minor Sonata*, where a turn forms the upper voice, a scale the theme of the *allegro* and a chord the theme of the *largo*—rest on the primordial facts of triad, dominant, and tonic. That the themes are so sharply outlined is due above all to the *rhythm*, which first makes them precisely identifiable at all, and then, after the long developmental divagations, the immediacy, the sudden return of the old integrative tonic and identity. Here the fog is cast onto the fire, there are dark shafts, one traverses the development as through a mine and out again, toward the light of the first theme, which looks at first like a distant arc lamp until it swells into the open under full daylight, the tonic of the initial theme, longingly striven for and only now, after being taken away, regained with benefit. But all this germinates out of something other than the theme; it derives from less or from more, from the ebb and flow of the excitement, from wavering and hesitating, subsiding, waning, doubting, embarking and the new, dynamic, expressive means of an affect wildly hurling itself, unreservedly abandoning itself, singing out, venturing out, its illumination and the worldly spectacle of its development. It derives from a *harmonic-rhythmic* logic, from the correctly chosen, well-prepared chord's arrival at the correct moment, from the comprehended power of the cadence, from the now regained tonic chord and the *organization* of its entry, which as a question of power is just as much a question of rhythm. It comes from the abstract tension between the two themes, as the two different witnesses of a dynamic state, as the two opposed principles, and so in Beethoven the treasures of the development as well as the power of the climaxes are born of a new, richly interrelated *succession*, hence of a *horizontalism* no longer of *lines*, but of *complexes* that first become present in memory, each vertically built; of a *dramatically formative counterpoint* developed for the goal, whose reward has yet to be spent.

Thus one sees directly into the excited, generative interior breaking out into the world. The self strikes the little tents, the hero drives out in the full strength of his synthetically expanding character. His voice in itself already becomes cries for help and of outrage into a night where the drowning soul barely still feels illuminated; indeed, where every stellar and every angelic space, however distant, is gradually sunk in oblivion. Loudly and recklessly rises the cry of the Beethovenian subject whom nothing in this illusory life satisfies, who stands above even the highest level of what the real world can encompass, who like the genius of music itself is exemplified or welcomed nowhere in the world. Who travels through every gradation of passion and fantasy, only to be driven back on himself in the end, on the longing for the brother and for the visionary father. There is here a passion for leaving behind the merely inner life, the self-enclosed stillness of interiority, one that transforms the self into a true cosmic structure so high and so deep that suns, moons and stars could rise and set without colliding, that the entire circuit of humanity has a place. Though greater glories may yet come, these are the waves of the exterior mystical sea, crashing even onto the stars, and this is the great Roman Empire of inwardness, with its discoveries of event, magic and the philosophy of history, where Wagner and Bruckner were born and where alone the prophet of music may one day appear. Or in other words: though Beethoven may be essentially only the outline, as yet without fullness; though one may already, listening to the then as now wholly improbable overture to the Parisian *Tannhäuser*, as the ear peers into the glowing mist of the underworld, and from the gigantic columns of the Pilgrim's Chorus the Church's victorious temple finally rises against it, over it—though one may already then be tempted to believe that Beethoven is essentially only a dying Moses, with a strategic eye only for appropriation, but that here, in Wagner, the promised land, lyrical melisma within a nevertheless dramatic counterpoint, beckons in the distance: this could all be disregarded, but Beethoven can never be disregarded, and he lies no less far above Wagner than Kant does above Hegel, than the restless *a priori* within man lies above every sort of all too prematurely fulfilled objectivism. For only in Beethoven does the self advance further toward the discovery of that certain ground that perhaps extends all the way into the final God, and Beethoven's symphony, the hand-wringing, the turmoil of primordial feelings lived in this symphony, through it, the *macanthropos* and his eloquent sea, this sea framed within one single, discrete structure, this erupting, external dream of humanity, throws the strongest beam of a heroic-mystical atheism, of a desperation that will not be permanent, toward a diffident Heaven. Here the We and the Absolute finally meet in the spirit of music, a throng of faces such as are depicted on carvings of the *majestas Christi*, and that truly symphonically expanded space where the We hears itself, where the fraternally shared ground of the world echoes and the It of this musical event becomes definable as the individual multiverse. All this appears only in Beethoven, the great chosen one of the dynamic, Luciferan spirit, still completely at a remove, as mere expectant, heroic, synthetic, spiritually Luciferan vision and not in an assured Christian ontology. But whereas Bach speaks out of the lyrically attained self of hoping, albeit intricately-consummately, and as the eternal corrective to all beyond within the dramatic form, Beethoven stirs up the debris and the magic of the End in a wholly different way, with a power that can certainly enter the three upper stages, Faith, Illumination and Apocalypse, as the stages of the complete I, in exactly that proportion as Beethoven's lord and object is no longer the first and not yet the second Jesus, but rather Lucifer, the pioneer, the *seed* of the paraclete, active human essentiality itself.

Strauß, Mahler, Bruckner

But before it, everyone still feels far too weak. Of course everyone also dreams of speaking differently, broods about it.

Perhaps not so certainly in the case of those living now. Pfitzner, a subtle, colorful flower; Reger, an empty, dangerous aptitude, and a lie as well. He just does not know, ignorant as he already is, whether he should write waltzes or passacaglias, whether he should set the "Isle of Death" or the Hundredth Psalm to music. Music and language do not look like this when one kneels by their fountainhead every morning. How empty everything remains when Reger, the least Bachian manifestation imaginable, claims to be religious as well, because this born follower and composer of variations just happens formally to be on this track. He is nothing, he has nothing but a dexterity of a higher order, and the outrage remains that he really is not just nothing, but rather a source of chronic, unproductive irritation.

We feel completely differently with *Mahler*, this vehement, severe Jewish man. Our ears are still inadequate to empathize with this great man, or understand him. He is essentially still valued only as an important conductor, and many a wretched reviewer unabashedly dares to ask if Mahler was even destined to be a composer, as if it were a matter of some music student's five or six tentative accomplishments. Almost none of the symphonic works are performed, and when it happens, the result usually remains an embarrassed silence or that unbelievably base gossip about

Mahler's Judaizing or his pseudotitanism to which the nonentities who enjoy everything else resort when faced with the purity of the real thing, which is of course alien to them. Certainly he is not effortless, nor do we want to claim that the studied simplicity and chauvinistically sentimental clutter of many of Mahler's *Lieder*, foremost those of *Des Knaben Wunderhorn*, are pleasant or easily bearable. But that is one issue, a minor issue in itself, unrelated to the other Mahler, the decisive preponderance of Mahler's works: there appear the *Kindertotenlieder*, the last canto from the *Lied von der Erde*, the Second, Third, and Seventh Symphonies and the most solemn introduction imaginable to the conclusion of *Faust* in the Eighth, which no one will forget whom this music has led to the lofty, terraced mountain landscape of the anchorites. However often the axle on the wagon, mere talent, may bend under this enormous burden: no one had ever been carried closer to heaven under the power of soulful, surging, visionary music than this yearning, holy, hymnic man. One's heart bursts at the "Ewig, ewig," at the primordial light deep inside; like a messenger from afar this artist came into his empty, weary, skeptical age, noble of temperament, unprecedented in the power and virile fervor of his emotion, and truly on the verge of bestowing music's final mystery on the world and over every grave.

It is as though their blood had been switched. Mahler is German, or at least wants to count absolutely as a German composer, which fails, for this is truly Judaism in music, Jewish grief and Jewish fervor: and then *Strauß* has to put up with comparisons to Meyerbeer. It is not easy to sort him out. He is conventional, and one can see in him the industrious man who knows how to enjoy life and take it for what it is. But just for this reason, and in spite of it, Strauß is good company. Even where he is the merely clever composer of seasonal hits, in the middle of the most revolting kitsch, he is upper class through and through, with easy, playful, sovereign, cosmopolitan manners from which every trace of the old German *Kleinbürger* has disappeared. He is furthermore unprincipled, and takes his material wherever he finds it, but now and then he finds something good by trusting in his effortless, harmless and in itself completely naïve love of making music: here a new, tender song, there the most intervallically rich arc, here a new way of interspersing pulverized motifs like metallic dust (where Liszt's model protects Strauß from Debussy's mere, spineless chordal vibrato), here strength and brilliance of thematic modeling, of a gale blowing between the thematic blocks and of a rhythmic uplift to which his teacher Liszt offers nothing comparable. By such means, however vulgar, frantic and sensational, and however lurid, mawkish and eudamonistic his orchestral fireworks, Strauß gains an expressive pliancy that assuredly represents an artistic plus against the threatening Wagnerian school's addiction to endless ceremony and Pilotyesque sublimity.[8] Of course Strauß surprises us in large part only because he basically does not develop, and repeatedly comes to a standstill in different ways. He has no kernel that needs to ripen in some other direction than from the serenade arbitrarily upward to *Elektra* and then back down again to satisfy the new plutocracy's need for self-enclosed melody, then to the *Rosenkavalier*, in order finally to attempt salvation in a very euphonious, very erotic fairy-tale mysticism. Strauß triumphs predominantly with just verve and sensuality, the legacy of an early, rustically energetic, colorful cabaret style, which he made fruitful in his way thanks to his extraordinary intellect. Thus everything sounds quite splendid, and there is often a wonderful jubilation in this music; the verve intensifies into a contrasting joviality, the sensuality into a certain *soi-disant* mysticism, albeit inferior and eudaemonist: and certainly when Eulenspiegel jingles, when the light in the Sendlingergasse goes out, when the dances in *Zarathustra* pipe, when the staggering Narraboth is seduced, when Don Juan's hubris breaks through all the themes of tarrying, when Transfiguration, ascending with such ineffable beauty out of Death, is led through the three-fold suspension to the blessedness of its tonic, when the silver rose gleams, when the dark chords of Orestes are counterposed to all the preceding unrest in the women's voices, when the recognition scene in *Elektra* rises from the messenger of death's motif, when the god descends on Ariadne: all that is accomplished, even supratechnically accomplished, and one would need a powerful aesthetic understanding of how to incite and exploit in order so brilliantly to realize a profit. But what is being capitalized on here are really essentially just cerebral gifts; soul is missing, as exclusively lyrical-erotic as the mood may always be, the dreadfully Mendelssohnian Jochanaan motif alone already exposes the religious shallowness, the lack of a kernel—and Strauß's music in its deepest moments bears at best the melancholy of inspired emptiness in its eyes. It is animated enough to convey conflict and the most excitable subject matter, but never so moved with seriousness that real expanse or a multimovement event could arise from it. None of it ventures forward, in spite of the forceful, jubilant gesture; it remains a colorful shadow behind all the program's details, in fact it follows these the most insistently; the love for the soft, flowery, atmospheric Viennese libretto has a basis in conviviality, and where the thing is to write dramatically, Straußian incense consumes every *true* reality in its perfume and the merely mimetic fantasy of its shallow characterizations. What is thus continuously operative, the compositional principle, and moreover the lifeblood of system and method in Strauß, lies in the extraordinarily descriptive power of this music that demands the painterly expression of even the smallest thing, certainly also the most trivial, unmusical, but in the meantime even here and there the façade of deeper things, and moreover with a sweep that melds all the details, creates the miracle of purely lyrical, "paganly" lyrically descriptive, undramatic symphonicism. It is therefore no accident that Strauß prefers Berlioz and Liszt's single-movement form, whereas not only Schumann and Brahms but, more importantly, Schubert, Mahler and Bruckner, the true inheritors of the Beethovenian spirit, retained the symphony's multimovement form, the form of dramatic expanse, the Beethovenian prototype. So it can appear even now as if much has dissipated out of Strauß that had seemed on first listening different, stronger, less virtuosic. And indeed not as the consequence of a changed evaluation, but precisely by virtue of the transient, brief, fashionable content. One thinks of Simmel: here, too, only and always the vivid, nervous, purely responsive margins of life are portrayed; and Rodin and Bergson are this condition's most gifted reagents. The suggestion would be to grant Strauß the same place in this uncentral, novelty-loving age as is occupied by the three refuted esoteric philosophers in the Spanish Chapel in Florence, at the feet of Saint Thomas, whereupon we are free to venerate Bruckner, who dedicated his Ninth Symphony "to the dear Lord," as at least the precursor of St. Thomas.

~

With *Bruckner* song finally returned to the world, singing with a clear conscience. He learned from Wagner, but the overheated character, the "blood-soaked" score has vanished. An active mobility appears and a radiance of an intellectual nature, an intellectual essentiality, transforming itself within itself: a hovering serenity, albeit drawn by Bruckner even more from the "cosmic" realm than the "intelligible."

But he is as conscientious as he is variable and deep. What we love about him is his warmth, his conviviality, and the joy of the wayfaring, which had been lost.[9]

Whereby the extrinsic, merely nervous febrility has disappeared. But we have had enough overly agitated variety, of bluff and of the misconceived Faustianism that wants to absolutize the wild gesture because that is the most easily copied aspect of skill. One can also become too brief or too empty in these gaps, and did not Wagner himself commend the adagio as the specifically German tempo? Bruckner additionally demands absolutely no sacrifice of genuine temperament, after all, nor even of true, contentual, objective intensification. Quite on the contrary, the latter is much too powerful for that in his devout upward impulse, and moreover grounded for all to hear in the flamboyant South German Baroque splendor of his orchestral language.

The work here is painstaking and neat, with an eye to good voice leading. *The first carpet, that of chamber music, has thereby been regained.* What Bruckner accomplishes is, to be brief, the reintroduction of a melismatic, chamber-musical cultivation of the parts, and thereby to be sure decontaminated the symphonic body, that is, freed it from every extrinsic fever, or those arising from the will and not the work. Here, as Grunsky rightly emphasizes, every sonorous intensification is the legitimate expression of rigorously prepared and maintained suspensions, not only in predominantly rhythmic form as in Beethoven, but in a form worked out, thought through, in terms of modulation and counterpoint. Just for this reason, of course, Bruckner has been maliciously reproached for all sorts of things: ponderous and disparate diction, longeurs and then fits and starts again, at least in the terminal movements. Where such a reproach is not simply due to the listener's ear (for Brahms it is naturally easier to be coherent, and no less for the Liszt school, where the mood or simply the program's descriptively directive power replaces every more strictly musical development) one can nonetheless effortlessly restrict this reproach, disregarding a few inconsiderable sins of omission, to the problem, the problematic, of the Brucknerian finale.

The way it weaves together is certainly often enough peculiarly wide and formless, sketchy. But the ending is already a difficult chapter in itself, even in Beethoven. Whereas in the first movement the ideas are thoroughly bridled, and one is succeeded by the next according to exactly observed rules, the end of the symphony is the blithe old last dance, the received form of spontaneity, much more loosely formed, bent on leaping and flying, with arbitrarily colliding countersubjects and extravagant fantasy in the development, regulated by nothing but the requirement that the initial theme have as brilliantly or shatteringly triumphal a return as possible. That was so for Beethoven, and more so for Bruckner, who allows the finale to remain unresolved, and like a synthesis carried out only extensively. For precisely the finale is usually fashioned such that it noisily, laxly and formlessly dismisses the listener back into the quotidian. He may return to the entrance, but the intensification itself has bowed down to the world outside, which alone ultimately concludes the concert. Here the conclusion is perhaps superficially connected to the end of the adagio, but it only confirms the scherzo, this rediscovered equilibrium, and the most worldly part of the symphony. Because the triumph stands at the end of the symphony, even the finale of Beethoven's C minor Symphony awakens the impression that the storms that passed by, the sweetness, even the so insatiably savored triumph itself were not to be taken as entirely real; at least the music makes the end all too obvious and personally detracts from itself by insistently proclaiming its cessation. At any rate, Bruckner advances past even Beethoven and the Classical phase of the finale in one respect. In Bruckner the finale is not supposed to scatter the audience; it has much more been developed as a musical ecstasy, as an admission to the most spatial and objective part of music generally. One watches these memory images and is freed from the compulsion of temporality, sees beyond the passions, the provinces, and the declared ground color of the whole performance, in the expectation of visionary moments and as a whole in the awareness of standing at the birthplace of the symphony's lyrically ontological element. That is certainly no longer dramatic after having sunk so strongly back into epic, but it is probably in the order of things that the dramatic element only engenders itself in the first movement, and that the final movement, the finale, now no longer introduces any new discharges, for which there was time and exposition enough before anyway, but instead posits another heightening, a new adagio (already in the lyrical form the most difficult music to compose, as is well known), in other words adds a spiritual, Brucknerian epic element in the highest serenity and eucharistic completion.

Here, even in Bruckner, only the deeper, and in the current state of compositional technique irresolvable, difficulty of the musical finale as *joyful final chapter* still impedes us. It is necessary to intensify and to resolve, but for that reason the jubilation often simply stands there, neatly contrived. That is so in Beethoven and of course in Bruckner as well: a formally posited but unproven brushing against the edge of heaven. The jubilation certainly comes from Beethoven's final experience, and is here no mere appendix to the intensification, no conventionally assured climax, but it does not emerge from the musical necessity itself. And so the appended jubilation can signify nothing purely musically, and if one cannot be satisfied with the idioms: how could it be any different? There is a light at the end of the tunnel! Or, Beethoven be not the man who—well, who endured gloom, unheroic depression, unless one numbers among the cheerful panlogicians for whom everything has to end well, and to whom suffering signifies only the spice of life, a splendidly engaging ceremony of the prolongation of our wayfaring: then, purely musically, nothing could be more indifferent than this only biographically suitable jubilation, which, though formally well placed, and located at the end with the effect of the tonic, procures no additional, properly musically-metaphysically compelling dignity. Joy is always paradoxical in any great thing; in music, too, joy is not actually engendered by the development, the intensification of the dominant, is in other words not brought about in the deeper sense, necessarily brought about; rather, there should be a particular kind of speaking, a "productive" development, a music of longing, calling, believing, a birth of faith out of music that could finally strike up the "Sed signifer sanctus Michael" from the quietest, inmost, farthest depths of music—a goal that up until now even the greatest composers have seldom been able to attain, and then usually such that the productive vision tended to arrive in the adagio rather than the finale, with its fantastically epic formations. Insofar as the latter lies too far from the burning kernel of the soul, from the pure self-vision working toward one single point, from the properly lyrical ontologism.

Recently Bruckner found in August Halm a devoted exegete of his ability and his situation. Halm has shown that Bruckner offers what Beethoven did not give him, for the latter sacrificed song for the great achievement, the energized motif and the power to manage large masses. Through Bruckner's accomplishment, the impure goad of a poetic rationale becomes forever superfluous; rather, it was this composer's feat to have finally released the Wagnerian style's accomplishment, music that "speaks," from the need for a subvention through a program or musical drama, and so—at the same time, significantly, as Brahms's entirely different feat—internalized it as form and content in one, even as a path to other seas than those of poetry. Thus Bruckner, the heir of Schubert, the elucidation of Wagner, connects himself at the same time to Bach and

Beethoven, each of whom he connects to the other, insofar as here the well-articulated individuality of the particular and of the theme in Bach is maintained simultaneously and most lovingly in the form of Beethovenian strategy and social organization.

On Wagner

But all this only began to flourish because of one man. Certainly no one began as badly as Wagner. He was questionable and tasteless, and some of that never entirely receded. And yet: what had come before him was quite extensively regained by Wagner. He churns and froths together so much that had already been shaped, so that it would really be present: there to begin.

Predecessors

A short time before, the self-enclosed song had still thoroughly predominated popularly. But now singing-to-oneself came back into favor. Wagner brought an entirely new sort of melody, or to be exact, a new path into the forest and the long-forgotten mountains. Before him, only the simple, homophonically composed tune with a modest beat was still known as melody. The lesser Italian songs, or better yet, since we are speaking here of the German tradition, Mendelssohn's *Songs Without Words* or Meyerbeer's arias make evident the poverty of this style, which confines the homophonic accompaniment below and whose stable, unsyncopated rhythm represses nearly every differently self-enclosed polyphony. Though this may have been necessary for the lyrical *Spieloper*'s gentle solemnity, it is no different in Mozart, the greatest master of a predominantly homophonically embellished lyricism. Only Schubert presents a different case. Here it seems to have become possible that the old self-enclosed vocal melody might persist within symphonic practice. But if one looks more closely—this is also true here and there in Schumann's more accomplished songs, for example in the astonishing "Zwielicht"— two things are notable about Schubert, the contemporary of the grossest fanaticism of the *Lied*. It is a long way from the melodies of "Wohin?" to the "Erlkönig" or "Die Nonne" that depend absolutely on the melody, to those other, no less luxuriant and extended melodies of the instrumental works, which no longer have anything to do with the all too soft, sentimentally melodious homophony. All of this is conceived quite melismatically and polyphonically, though, like Weber, in spite of his ghost scenes, or even the fantastic Berlioz and the early Wagner himself, it may lack the energy and conflict of the countermelodies, and the once again distantly ranging melody breaking through the meter's regular divisions. Soon thereafter came something new, remarkable, and yet unexpected only because of the miserable prevailing condition of the music: *sprechgesang* and infinite melody.

False Polemics

In fact it was no longer so easy to remember. One could neither hum along, nor even transport it discretely. The bourgeois of the time was in any case accustomed to amuse himself with the readily and basically trivializable stuff of the homophonic *Lied*-mongering of that time as the "melody" as such. Only thus was it possible that the connections to Bach could be so maliciously misjudged, which after all span the Rome Narrative, in the middle of the still so intolerably, consistently homophonic *Tannhäuser*. What were people not willing to say against it, and what sorts of meanness would they not unearth! And today we have again reached a point when the most mendacious gossips appoint themselves moral-aesthetic judges where Beethoven himself would have criticized with hat in hand. What were people not willing to say, from the petty, oblivious scoundrels who learn nothing from anything significant that appears to them, only their own meanness, and next by the lovers of the Florentine landscape and everything else that favors the garden over the Gothic forest—against the continuous modulation, against Wagner's lack of invention and weakness of design, against the melody that wears itself down in endless false endings, against the extreme irritability without any punctuation, and the tiresomely austere psalmody into which the singers are forced, above a formlessly surging or at best realistically pictorial orchestra. Truly, if ever anything was simple and ancient, and conserved and multiplied its rightful inheritance, it was this overthrow of the self-enclosed melody and birth of the endless melody. And certainly not as though the connections here had been merely superficial, for what could already have been broken? Would it be, perhaps because he "could" not make them to order, the old operatic pieces? Wagner surely did not smash them in order then, with coldly calculated pell-mell, with an anxious avoidance of every partial and full cadence, to reassemble them into infinity. How or where, as it might appear from Weber's example, could one have detected a mere conglomeration, when there is no single note in these "preludes," so close to Bach in particular, that could or would want to dissent from the constant dominant tension? This is the new melismatic-polyphonic form as such, so much so that after the appearance of Weber, the manifestation of Beethoven's symphonies, and the incorporation of Bach's polyphony a composer could have halted before this immanent line of development only through force. Certainly, as we said, all this is no longer so easy to remember, and that it succeeds in the upper voice is not always a benefit, above all when it is just a matter of a merely narrative recitative. Further, the form of the delayed resolution, in its literal sense, is only recognizable at the end as shape, synopsis and "form," with all the virtue of its gigantic arcs, its sparse cadences, and the dominant tension of an act gathering itself seemingly only poetically. But that does not yet grant us the right to mention the wide and justified movements of the infinite melody in the same breath as the *Gesamtkunstwerk*'s entirely distinct and in any case practically dubious fusion, and to reject them both. The liberation of the old operatic schema's small structures from entirely different kinds of continuities by means of a new, larger form is one thing; it is manifestly another thing if halfway related elements persist next to each other, in order mutually to renounce their respective structures and spheres and thereby, in the exchange of musical and poetic components, produce this mixed construct, the *Gesamtkunstwerk*, which could have become a viable if fundamentally uncanonical category only through Wagner's genius. Technically, of course, Wagner needed them both against any kind of sphere or plasticity—the loose disposition of *sprechgesang* and the newly arioso recitative, as well as the tremendously problematic auxiliary construction of the *Gesamtkunstwerk*—in order thus, by means of such immoderate totalization, to gain a corresponding music of destiny.

'Sprechgesang', Syncopation, and Chordal Polyphony

Now the singing becomes merely one voice among many. It can be pliant, brief, and merely narrative. The song can also flower into an aria, with breadth and all the release one could want, elevated, sonorous and emotional. Naturally it is often ponderous and exhausting, the way Wagner through-composes in the upper voices; a give and take is lacking, and now and then one would like to have back the old distinction between pastry and filling. Nevertheless all the voices now sound, and the song often submerges at will, abundantly flooded by the other voices when they have more to give, in a reciprocally intertwining play. One can thus say that in Wagner the human voice, which had previously carried everything and has already ceded its entire evolution into vocal polyphony to the orchestra, now relinquishes its meager remnant in order to preside over the course only melodically, and, having become completely free and unburdened, again withdraws back to a *singing-to-oneself,* to its inception and its initial wandering, psalmodizing state.

~

The next element was facilitated by dance and the syncopic effect. Syncope was essentially invented by Beethoven, and then so completely elaborated by Wagner that one can learn all its inflections from him, as in the almost continuously syncopated *Tristan.* It is a dragging or a pushing forward, a retarding or an anticipating of the melodic trend, or, as Grunsky first correctly defined the syncope, contrary to Riemann, a new way of drawing out and newly emphasizing rhythmically unaccented spots, the accent stretching and measuring itself against the unaccented beat, and the other way around, whereby the friction that develops from the coincidence of different divisions of time makes it possible to develop several rhythms at once, even if they can only be felt in the jolt at the end of the measure. In this way, though of course not only in this way, the beat is variously broken up; indeed, exaggerating to make a point, one could say that the beat is transformed into a thousand beats, and the unstable, richly syncopated polyrhythms make room for every polyphony. Every one of the many voices ringing out simultaneously again has something to play, a solo; melisma binds itself to harmony, harmony to rhythm and rhythm to the totality of syncope's new chronological structure, now no longer just empty, unblended, extraharmonic, but purely harmonic, and, additionally, audible as musical drama.

This can no longer be understood as a gentle hovering, in other words. Here the old rustic dances are more likely to have preserved the more forceful movements. Even today every savage tribe has its changefully mysterious whirling, and from there to the dancing of dervishes and David's dance before the Ark of the Covenant takes perhaps less than a step. This gyration is not only physically intoxicating, as an image of pursuit, desire, and various convulsions, but is in addition completely determined by the stars. The dancing dervishes, for their part, take part in the dance of the *houris,* indeed of the angels, as they dance in circles and whirl about their own axes until fits, coma, and sidereal ecstasies ensue. For the *houri* are considered the stellar spirits who guide our destinies; when the dervish mimetically propels himself into this rotation, he seeks to become conformal with the stars, to receive and call down onto himself the out-pouring of the *primus agens* around which the heavenly bodies revolve, and whose eternal glory the stars most immediately contemplate. Hence the dervish takes on the different kinds of circular movement as a duty, as ibn Tufayl[10] explains; even Dionysus the Areopagite praised the circular movement of the soul as its withdrawal into itself, no longer of course to imitate the circuits of the stellar spirits, their sidereal rotation, but rather—already beginning to distance himself from every Dionysian or Mithraic ecstasy—because of the cyclical occurrence of the soul's reflection on the beautiful and good of its *own* ground. Thus every outward convulsion was finally rejected by the early Christian congregations as heathen. That means that the singing that had accompanied the dance remained as a religious stimulus, but as the seductive sound of the instruments was execrated, even the robustly and variably divided beat of the ancient dances seemed to conflict with the Christian temperament's oceanic tranquillity. Thus arose the merely harmonic suggestion of a change of meter within the chorale—devoutly free of every tension, unless one sees tension even in the most placid movement toward the tonic. It is also probable that the conception of the stress before the rest as a rhythmically articulating fermata in the chorale is not old, as unavoidable as it has become for us. This picture only changed with the emergence of the Italian and French *galant* composers. In their craving for more lively movement, however, they did not fall back on the old peasant dances. Rather, just as rigidified people recently could no longer dance to anything but waltzes, they devised (they were actually a graceful kind, and as the gigue proves, the leap from the village fair to the ball does not automatically mean a loss of every more refined tempo) a certain light, flexible, and then again quite delightfully restrained hovering within regularity, which maintains the musical pace just as it still forbids the further consequence, the polyphonic chaos of the syncope. Indeed, the earlier introduction of mensural notation had opened the way to a more divided beat. But all that extended too far over into impracticability, sonic and artistic irrelevance, into the study score and mere theory. Hence the situation would only change through the incorporation of the old folk dance, by Bach above all, which after all reaches far back into the past, has faithfully preserved many primitive elements, and, as the music of the Hungarian Gypsies still shows, is not too far removed from polyphonic music's more diverse rhythm. So Bach rhythmized in a way—let us here recall only the aria "Erbarme dich

mein" from the *St. Matthew Passion*, or the numerous "reworkings" of
French dance forms in the Partitas—that act like the obviously involun-
tarily and unwittingly reclaimed primitive, pagan cultic rhythms of rocks
and drums. But then just that strange, unsought intoxication also returned, which was not only spiritual. We know how aptly Wagner explained Beethoven in terms of dance, of seizing, breathing, the curve of
the pulse. Of course that did not prevent Wagner, in inconsistent fashion,
from ultimately proscribing dance forms from the musical totality, because he keeps only dance's social, banally eurhythmic manifestations in
mind. It is odd enough that Wagner, after coining the well-known phrase
that Beethoven's Eighth Symphony is the apotheosis of the dance, then
turns around and denies Beethoven's music, just because it is so tied to
dance, the ability to overstep certain limits of musical expression. Most
likely the dance rhythm, insofar as Wagner defined it as just an acoustic
ballet, as a kaleidoscope for the ears, also lowered the passionate and tragic
tendency so badly in this form that the question of a "why," of an empirical, causal conjunction utterly foreign to the tonal event in itself becomes
unavoidable. Though Wagner tirelessly posed rhythmic problems for himself, and was a declared lover of the sonorous gesture and of every theatrical symbolization, he was therefore never inclined to assess the rhythmic
aspect very highly, inasmuch as he saw in it only a contact, a *tertium comparationis* with the legible plastic world by means of which, like light
against a solid body, music would first become perceptible, in accordance
with the inferior sense of an empirical reality. Nevertheless, the one important thing, the definitive thing here is that Wagner, in spite of all his
antisocial, indeed antimundane reservations, could be defined as the one
who would invoke and restore the orgiastic Dionysos, when the latter appears in a completely idealized form as dramatic action, and accordingly
becomes capable of a correlation to the passionate, tragic, and transcendent tendencies of music. Thus along with *singing-to-oneself, with the incorporation of dance and with chamber-musical subtlety*, which in Wagner-
Bruckner found its orchestra, *the entire first, as yet nameless, genuine carpet
of primitive and correct abundance has been regained*. But exactly because
the syncopic effect receives support from the new-old dance, this fiery
rhythm does not merely lie at the feet of Wagnerian polyphony like a carpet with a corrective value that practically and objectively commits one to
nothing; rather precisely in a practical sense, a primordially incarnate heathenism also goes along, not only to impart its Dionysian character, but

to prescribe for music every sort of ecstatic self-annihilation, the tyranny of the lower body, and physiologically earth-bound, even star-bound, Dionysian-Mithraic astral transcendences.

～

The *third* and most important element leading to the colorful, polyphonic, and thereby dramatic fabric of infinite melody was harmony. Already in the song every note is excited and active. That means that a note in a monodic sequence is already active in the direction of the tonic. The musical pace everywhere comes from the feeling of the dominant and the cadence, is guided and melodically drawn by it. Hence during all the time one perhaps sang in ignorance of harmony, the scale—and then the abrupt relationships within it, in other words ultimately the harmony—was nevertheless always the decisive motive and hidden cause. "The surprising effect that many ascribe only to the composer's natural genius is often simply attained by the correct use and resolution of diminished seventh chords": these are Beethoven's own words, and, as we will show, undoubtedly capable, in league with a differently rhythmic harmony, of illuminating vast stretches of his work, among them the entire first movement of his last sonata. At any rate, all the notes move and stir, they advance, they lead and are led, until the scale imposes its will and consonance appears in the form of a conclusion. But even the latter is not really there: where a consonance sounds without having been harmonically anticipated it is the most indifferent thing imaginable; and where it finally, even after the shudder of the most grandiose general rest, truly "appears," there remain, as Bruckner showed most brilliantly, foremost in the first movement of his Seventh Symphony, such infinite tensions, and such endless climaxes on the dominant and on dominant effects are possible before the final consonance, that Halm could justifiably say: it never happens, consonance exists only as a challenge, the history of music is the history of dissonance. Where then but in the chord, in harmony, could an opportunity, a compulsion or a directive for the search be demonstrated? Bach is great, and his fugues are an unforgettable admonition: but he maintains his influence, on Beethoven as well as on Wagner, essentially as a richly filigrane harmonist. Despite the astonishing forgetting of his works, he himself had to recall himself to memory, to the extent that one had given up the homophonically melodic kind of composition and returned to a polyphonic eventfulness, which now became rigorous, and needed every voice in order to attain polyphonic chordal energy. Certainly the homophonically melodious composers are far removed from the extraordinarily richly graded voice leading of an early time, but one look at certain of Haydn's creations—who can often become enigmatically serious and profound, as for example in the chorus depicting the fall of Hell's demons, or the overture to the *Creation*—already reveals such a surprisingly bold, already quite Romantic harmony, though one drawn at the same time, without exception, from Bach's harmonic "coincidences," that one might be inclined to consider everything that follows, all of Classical and Romantic chromaticism and polyphony, as the mobile, newly interesting, independent activity of a spring that Bach had set over a quieter space. One thing is true about it, certainly: that after some initial homophonic privation an ever richer solo playing, an inward-individual music-making and a chamber-musically linear melisma could again take shape in Haydn's and Beethoven's sonatas, and that the, please note, harmonic-rhythmic Bachian counterpoint, employed with a chordal aim, clearly persists in Wagnerian polyphony, in a higher-order polyphony, no longer as architectonic but as dramatic contrapuntality. It is not just that the new orchestral coloration sets itself off, differentiates itself and again sensuously counterpoints itself; the development in Wagner also assumes the primary role, and through the restlessness of its harmony—now erected over everything only temporarily, and never, as in Beethoven, over every motif or theme which has been fixed as the goal—attains a form of polyphony that incorporates Bach's covert verticalism, that is, a form of rising dramatic polyphony turned more toward the chord than away from it. In other words: the chordal energy is not a product but a *prius*, and in no way only theoretically. Compared to harmony, counterpoint, at least the kind designed for playing or composing *fugues*, is a second-order working method, surpassed in the meantime by *harmony* and *symphony*, which within the discrete melodic stratification must at every step take into consideration the chordal "results," the dissonances and the chordal-rhythmic accents, junctures. It may thus signify the same thing, only expressed differently, to consider the structure of one of Wagner's compositions from the viewpoint of harmonic economy, which of course still very much needs to be complemented by a rhythmics, as to seek to draw up the still pending structural theory of Wagner's style from the viewpoint of a new counterpoint developed not so much from the juxtaposition, the superimposition, as rather from the *succession* stripping everything harmonically "incidental" from the fugue, and thus additionally gaining a surplus of harmonic suspensions, rhythmic contrasts, thematic developments, in short every complex-relation of the "symphony." What thus first revives in Beethoven and culminates in Wagner, at least to date, is primarily Bach as the richly filigrane, polyphonic, vertical harmonist, whereas it is certainly ultimately the *linear* handiwork that still far more powerfully influences Wagner through the *chamber-musical carpet*, and the *ontological* element that still far more obviously influences him through Palestrina's seraphic chordal carpet than through Bach's fugal carpet, through a lyrically con-trapuntal *equilibrium or repose*. This of course is the carpet and the cor-rective whose recapture, as music's final possible, conceivable adaptation, will come only at the still unforeseeable end of music. There are two ways of singing and storming—within the scale and within the chordal energy, in other words the linear Bach's and the inclusive, vertical Bach's way—that are guided into the symphony's contrastive sequences; and Wagner, as vehemently or as ceremoniously as he may have mastered the scale, had still already helped filigrane chordal energy to the first rank over linear counterpoint. Insofar as it most of all reciprocally intensifies, fuses and guards the fire of the melismata, and so at the same time allows the most fruitful articulation of the *richly interrelated succession of the new harmonic counterpoint*.

Thus did the tempestuous sonata become heavy and redolent again. Thus are the three modes—the cry, or the regained carpet of singing-to-oneself; the syncope, or the regained carpet of primitive dance; dramati-cally applied harmony, or the regained carpets of chamber-musical sub-tlety and seraphic chordal luminosity—ultimately secured for symphonic-dramatic practice. It is astonishing how much the symphonic tends to first murder what is songful, then to bestow it again, newly flowing and intri-cate; how much it was the joy of melisma that first led to a truly active music, to the *true* animation and humanization of its mechanism. Only when Wagner wanted to write no note that could not serve as a sign of Bachian lyricism within his dramatic, metadramatic sonata form, did the process begin, as Nietzsche says, of opening up the unknown musical do-main not only with ethos, but with transcendental pathos, that is, with mystical reward.

Transcendent Opera and Its Object

But Mozart still awaits his fulfillment.

Even he, the tender one, with his soft movements, here froths over completely. We are not speaking here of *Der fliegende Holländer, Tann-häuser* or *Lohengrin*, nor of the miraculous edifice of the *Meistersinger*, all of which, in spite of certain transitional features, represent operas along the lines of Beethoven's *Fidelio*. Even less do we have the *Ring* in mind, which is subservient to the pagan dance and so often drifts into vacuity or dreary animality. Rather *Tristan* and *Parsifal* above all, *as the reward-fulfillments of Mozartian fairy-tale opera*, come under consideration here, as the intensification of the tender, softly moving element, which needed no people of the kind who challenge destiny in order to achieve the great secular self and to its transformation in the act of redemption. Here, however, human beings again step forward out of the realm of destiny, in order that, in the musical space that forms the homeland and the mythos, the metadramatic lyricism of redemption may appear as the proper object of transcendent opera: it begins in *Tristan*.

~

Now we advance into ourselves, just as quietly as deeply. The others are agitated and always lead back out again. Tristan and Isolde have fled the bustling day, they do not act. It is our own inmost dreaming, to be found where words and steps no longer hasten. It is we who go along, we obscure ourselves chromatically, we move in a state of yearning and float toward the dream taking shape in the advancing night.

One can already see it in the prelude, as it abducts us from time. For it spins out only the same ahistorical, abstract *Sehnsucht* motif, touching nothing, floating freely, but ready to descend and be incarnated. Its place becomes bright, but just beyond it everything remains distant and still. Only the first act acquires a charge, leads these two people away from the day. Here everything is still shrill and mocking, all too conscious, and the love potion leads us to the wrong gate. But neither Isolde nor Tristan would need this drink to find the other. They pass each other by only in appearance, superficially, in the uncertain shimmer of the day that still veils from them, with their night vision, what has always already appeared. Isolde thinks she hates, when all she does betrays her love, and Tristan is so inflexible, so immoderately intent on decorum, so strangely soft, and thus ungainly and maladept, that the potion gives them both only what they have long had, which is fate and now breaks into time, becomes destiny, conveyed by a symbol of the leap. Here nothing simply doubles back again as in the *Ring*, when Hagen prepares the opposite potion for Siegfried so that what is remote from him will not slip his mind:

as something remote within the action, which can be reiterated and only recollected because the Siegfried of the action knows the place where the birds, Brünhild's stone and the magical fire have power. What happens because of or beyond the Irish potion, however, is never action; it is not even a key, not even a catalyst, not even the sort of accident which is really not one and which tragic necessity involves as its accomplice; instead, just as a place one has never been can nonetheless be home, it is only a temporal glimpse, a temporal derivate of what happens within eternity, within the supratemporality, mythicality of love. Here two human beings advance into the night; they go from one world over into another, and otherwise nothing happens, as one should be able to recognize from the first act and certainly the two last acts, and nothing sounds but the music of their advance and their ultimate disappearance. This is what Wagner wanted us to recognize when he called Tristan a mere "action" [*Handlung*]; it is a nameless trend, a tremendous adagio into which almost nothing antithetical penetrates from the outside such that Tristan or Isolde could even become aware of it as conflict, catastrophe; and just this is the meaning of the word "action" on the title page, not as though it really were one, but only to contrast it to a properly dramatic movement and meaningfulness, to the diurnal fate in an antithetical kind of symphonic movement or musical drama.

Only the final scenes are still animated, or bring themselves to an end in a superficially visible way. Perhaps that is necessary in terms of stage technique, but like Pfitzner one cannot avoid the impression that the day thereby intrudes again, just where one has become the most sensitive to it. It should be additionally clear after what has been said that the recapitulation does not exert the same effect assured for it within symphonies. One feels how it begins to decline here, how the pure path of soul, to which no one may return, is being abandoned, and that one has already heard all this in the great final duet of Act Two, so much more beautifully than in the orchestral movement at the end of the third act, which simply *cannot* have experienced anything underway, insofar as any actual forward movement is lacking, and which would therefore be incapable of figuring as the regained now, the reprise and the conclusion of a symphonic development. It must be said, with all due respect, that the so very deliberately inserted and seemingly discrete final orchestral piece "Isoldens Liebestod" begins to decline into insufferable softness, into unmystical sweetness, which—as with the arpeggiated triads, with the sixtyfold celebration at the conclusion of *Parsifal* that refuses to end—threatens to drop all the more steeply from its tremendous height as a proper, theatrical ending tries to ally itself with the entirely different definitiveness of the birth of redemption from the spirit of music. So much less was spoken, and in the second act the night of love overtook us with such world-redeeming profundity, that we no longer want to see the death itself on the stage, which would give us corpses and bystanders and emotional benedictions to marvel at just where the naturally more unrepresentable encounter by universal night should have its place. When Siegfried dies, and the vassals slowly carry his remains away over the cliffs, the funeral music sounds as long as the procession is still visible. But soon fog rises off the Rhine to veil the scene from us, whereupon rings out the peculiar, exuberant rejoicing of the intermezzo, which has nothing whatever in common with a conventional song of consolation or any other funereal category. Only when the fog lifts, when it comes back to us, to those left behind, to our world, does the funeral music return, more terrible and oppressive than before, precisely insofar as it is the mere, lower, visible world around Siegfried's corpse which appears, rather than the unrepresentable paradoxicality that can quintessentially be preserved only in music. Of course the fog only rises so that the act will not be interrupted by the change of scenery, but just because Wagner veils our eyes from the rejoicing, though not our ears or our hearts, a kind of reticence is operating here that precisely corresponds, better than *Tristan*'s conclusion, to Wagner's demand for an increasing depotentiation of the sense of sight in proportion to the musical intensification.

Nevertheless, the sound here has already become distant and nocturnal. Certainly, but significantly not everywhere, Melot, Brangäne, and Kurwenal, even Marke sing differently. Brangäne remains foolish and trivial, without suspecting what is happening; Melot, the antagonist, becomes a myopically judgmental traitor; and only Kurwenal and Marke, two decent men, stand cautiously, humbled in the face of the entirely inscrutable—Kurwenal will not even ask, or permit the shepherd's curiosity—before the unfathomably mysterious logic that has made Tristan a criminal and which is expressed only very inadequately even in the *Sehnsucht* motif. One can sense the change in tone when the daytime people speak, these stupid wakeful adults as such, and when the two who are consecrated to the night speak. Less so at first, where one still hears about Isolde's shame and Tristan's honor in jagged or stiff rhythms, but how infinitely powerful in the second act: the anchor is lifted, the wheel has been handed over to the storm and the sails to the winds, the world, power, fame, eminence, honor, chivalry, friendship, every daytime asset has scattered like an insubstantial dream; preparations are being made for a trip to the most mysterious land, and the flashy *Tag* motif over which the despicable Melot first sings, harmonically related to the "Wer wagt mich zu höhnen?" [Who dares to deride me?] of the first act, with its abrupt interval and its lashing, hard, and strongly evident plastic rhythms, cuts perceptibly into the slow motion, into the predominantly chordal, rhythmically hesitant Adagio of the Night. Indeed, even there one has the irresistible impression that there could not even be such an extremely quiet music if Tristan and Isolde could really die, if in that other world a longing did not still bind them to this one, which is why after all Wagner in his first draft wanted to have the wandering Parsifal appear at the mortally wounded Tristan's deathbed. The light had still not gone out, it was still not completely dark in the house: otherwise there would have been nothing to perceive, but the urge, desire, the Will eternally giving birth to itself again, if no longer the will to propagate on this earth, no longer the will of the species, the convulsive mother who will not die, though she must if her spiritual child would live—all these remain, and the ancient, solemn shepherd's air sounds, to yearn, dyingly to yearn, not to die out of sheer yearning: for Isolde, who still lives in the day, for Tristan who in the realm before which he trembles could not encounter Isolde, because the night throws him back onto the day, and so that very deepest but still somehow exoteric music that dwells at this final crossing also becomes audible again. It need not be this way, of course, for sound has no limits. It is strange enough that Tristan and Isolde could even vanish from us, that even in sound, where they are so profoundly supplied, they have nothing to say to us. For never before was music so much designed to convey all of night as a condition and a concept, extending through the entire work and forming Tristan's proper terminology. But then it only seems to be the dusk, of course a faraway one, and not the night to which the music of *Tristan*, still earthly, processual, relates. As palpably as here and there the end of the illusion seems to flash—soundless dreams of colored shadows, a spiritual life, the *Liebestod*, the space of love, the *passio* flooded over with miracles, the lyrically enduring, metadramatic glory—it all retreats, inadequate, within the wide and imprecise perspective of the Absolute, of love as such, and similar formless centers. Certainly the self had never been so thoroughly exploded and so decisively ceded to the other. "You stepped out of my dream, and I stepped forth from yours"[11]: to thus achieve in the other, after having changed places, and with the other's image at heart, the lyricism of the other's feelings, the sense of oneself dwelling in the other. But the one essentiality, And, that binds Tristan and Isolde's love, really cannot at the same time distance them; it converts each soul into the other, makes their countenances and their figures finally unrecognizable and thus, consistent with Schopenhauer's Hindu theory of the musical object, expels everything that is of the self, everything Luciferan, from the human subject, with the cost that in its place—into the universal breath's wafting cosmos, drowning, going under, dead to the world—the heathen, unsubjective and Asiatic universality of a Brahms can expand. That is why even Wagner's nocturnal sound stands there with empty hands, that is why *Tristan* and also *Parsifal* offer us total lyrical brilliance, the total, supradramatic flaring of the lyrical self, consequently the objective, ontological fulfillment of Mozartian fairy-tale opera, indeed even of Bach's *Passions* and their passionately Adamic-Christian lyricism; but as pervasively as the quieter, more deeply Christian brilliance of the adagio may everywhere always already lie above it: what lies beyond the trial of yearning is peace, complete soul, Bach's fugue as *musica sacra*, the metaphysical adagio, music as "space," music of the Paracletan self, architectonic contrapuntality of the highest order: all of this remains unachieved because of the deeply un-Christian mysticism of Wagner's universality and absoluteness.

Who has truly been to the other side does not return unscathed. He is way off course, as though his feet were bleeding, or—it depends—he can see further. Tristan has also forgotten everything and has become completely alien after five hundred thousand years of gazing into the night. "Welcher König?" [What king?] he asks Kurwenal, who has to point overboard at Marke, as though there had ever even been another king for Tristan. "Bin ich in Kornwall?" [Am I in Cornwall?] he finally asks, as he no longer recognizes Kareol, the castle of his forefathers. And again: "O König, das kann ich dir nicht sagen, / Und was du fragst, das kannst du nie erfahren" [O King, that I cannot tell you, and what you ask, you can never know]: indeed, as he abruptly wakes, staring in bewilderment at Melot and the men swarming in, as he slowly seems to understand Marke's words and his own immeasurable shame and mortal sin, Tristan shows no understanding, but only pity and growing sorrow for Marke. For Tristan the world of appearances, where others live, has become as incomprehensible as his nighttime world is to them. Daytime phantoms, waking dreams, deceptive, coarse and utterly senseless in their acute banality. Here no light still burns that could resolve things with expanse and chromatically mythological history; the first man to enter the invisible realm, the truth, saw nothing; the second went mad, and Rabbi Akiba encountered no one there but himself; and the night where Tristan has been will never be followed by a morning on this earth.

But there is another hero and his journey. There is still another sun to be found, not opposed to but beyond the night. Toward this sun journey the four human beings in *Parsifal*, filled with a different longing. Kundry survives in fairy tales as the ogre's slyly good-natured wife or the devil's grandmother.[12] Even now the fairy tale "The Magic Table" preserves the entire Grail myth, with its thieving innkeeper, the cudgel in the sack or the holy lance, the donkey Bricklebrit or the lunar grail, and the table itself, the true, the highest solar grail itself.[13] We also know that Klingsor and Amfortas were originally one person, namely the cloud demon who blocks the sun. Parsifal himself, the hero who first brings fertility and then completely abstains, can not so clearly be disentangled. Early on he assumes the role of Thor the thunder god, who must repeatedly snatch the solar cauldron from the control of the giant Hymir, who lives in the East, the land of the primordial waters. In Indian and medieval sagas— which, as Schröder first and most felicitously pointed out, all go back to these ancient astral motifs—Parsifal also remained basically the one who steals back the cauldron, who seeks the grail, the hero who conquers the sun, the lord of the rain and above all of the magical light.[14] Only complete purity, innocence of heart, has been added as a Christian feature; otherwise astral myth still gleams through, insofar as Parsifal must either first seek the lance, or at once kill the cloud giant with the lance as the thunder weapon, in order to win the lunar dew as the drink *soma* or nectar, but foremost as the urn of light, *ambrosia*, meaning precisely that he must win the grail with the solar food, the dish in which Joseph of Arimathea later caught the solar blood, the Savior's blood. Here Wagner strengthened and deepened every aspect, adding the consecration through love. Kundry, sinful, confused, living a double live, divided between good and evil by a sleep like death, the womb of lust and endless birth, forever mocking, forever unbelieving, but also the healing, herb-gathering, most humble servant. Klingsor the thief, the wizard of the false day; Amfortas the defeated one, sick in his boundlessly desirous heart, an immemorially intensified Tristan who wants to die, a thief after a fashion, but full of holy desire for what has been promised, for the Orphic renewer of salvation; Parsifal, poor, inexperienced, the innocent fool, through pity knowingly become the innocent fool, far-sighted, whose eyes are opened by tremendous suffering, who slays the dragon, that other symbol of woman and of rebirth, and finally a different, higher Siegfried who understands not so much the language of birds as of that which cannot speak, the creature's anxious expectation of the revelation of the children of God. In him, chastity and purity have become absolute: Parsifal is thus no longer the exuberantly gushing youth of astral myth who splits the clouds and brings a purely natural fecundity; quite the contrary, he transforms the magic garden into a wasteland, and the fallow land of the grail territory is blessed with a quite different sun than the day's, and a quite deeper daybreak than that of the earth's merely natural summer. But nevertheless: onward to the sun, the secret footpath is clearly there, where the sun will rise over the mountains. Where the night of love did not succeed, the holy night did: at its fountainhead was won the beautiful meadow, the enigmatic light of Good Friday morning. Outward brightness already forsakes the day: "As the sun departs in gladness from the empty show of day,"[15] wrote Wagner's lover in the third of five poems of a strange dialectic: to be night-mystical and yet also save the day-star; and the music of *Parsifal*, at least where it is not mere action, that is, only traverses the paths of errancy and suffering, but becomes still, and makes an effort to pay the heavenly dawning the fixed, metadramatic, ontological interpretation which is its due: at the last midday, at the exequies, as dawn swells down below and the beam of light from on high grows, at the pious, enigmatic blasphemy of "Erlösung dem Erloser!" [Redemption to the Redeemer]—this ontological music in *Parsifal* wants nothing but on that inmost day to guide us into the word "soul," which is no longer of this world and hardly still of the other, hardly still attached to the ages-old light-pageantry of thrones, dominions, and powers.[16] That is a light, now beyond all the words that just die away, or directed only toward that one word that shatters the locks, a word which nothing approaches as nearly as music's new apprehension and anamnesis of itself, which Hebbel anticipated in the unforgettable verses on the deaf and the mute, and God entrusted to him a word:

. . . he cannot even grasp it,
nor may he proclaim it
but to one he's never seen.

But then the dumb man shall speak,
And the deaf man hear the word
And right away decipher
The dark and godly symbols;
Then they will journey toward the dawn.

If they are to find each other,
Then all of you must pray.
If they who wander lonely
Should ever find each other
All the world will be at its goal.[17]

Of course for now trying to convey even the faintest shimmer of this day will succeed even less than the music of the night. Even if the sound in *Parsifal* points completely upward, that is, it does not drag the universal so deeply into broad, oceanic mysticism as in *Tristan*, it could not really see into the sun, here the music is even less able to "speak," let alone provide clear contact with the higher world, not just emotional, or formally mythical, but contentual, constitutively mythical contact. And that it cannot do this, that it does not express but at best only discloses, that the metaphysical adagio still remains mere, imprecisely ceremonious musical *sphere* without any category, proves again, in this rising polemic of admiration, against an absolute measure, how far Wagner's music is still separated from the final, holy state, from the fulfillment of music as annunciation, as the release of our secret nature beginning beyond all words, which his music was the first after Beethoven to explore so deeply.

Likewise, it can ultimately not be concealed that Wagner's work encroaches on other domains than might be desired on a deeper musical level. Just as an accursed ring brings all its owners to the same ruin, so did Wagner's altogether too extensive resumption of the ancient heathen-cultic action—instead of the pure fulfillment of the fairy-tale Mozart, the Christian Bach—irredeemably deliver him over to the dream of the mere natural Will as its musical object, particularly in the *Nibelungen* trilogy.

For no one acts here as the human being he could or would be. Is this man, so boastful, a hero? Is this other a god? Neither is what he so verbosely claims. Siegfried suffers, and with feeling and farcical blasts of the horn pursues his meaningless impulses. Wotan's damaged eye and the shade over it hinder him from being a god even theatrically, and there is nothing overpowering, mysterious about this tiresome figure. Mystery is shoved back on the Norns and Erda, whose authority is unconvincing. As we have said, the music here goes almost completely over into vacuity and dismal animality. Any prospect within this work that could lead out of the narrowness of personhood does so only by serving up a world of cardboard, greasepaint, and irredeemable heroic posturing. Feeling, acting human beings become almost entirely painted marionettes, against which the violations, indignities, impersonality and superficial universality and abstraction of this delusion plays itself out. It all acts on us with a seething, ostentatious display, with inert *sprechgesang* and endless, emotionally tedious, superfluous conversation, with embarrassing overtones of Wilhelm Jordan and Felix Dahn, and in verse which, in spite of many magnificent and inspired details that one might prefer to see elsewhere, cannot make one forget the tortuous quality of this saga that lay there too long before being taken up again, its artificiality and pedantry, its appearance of having been welded together with a torch.[18] Certainly the music in itself is incomparably purer than that new thing combined of music and text, all too sanctimoniously intruding but never comprehensible in performance. Wagner not only devises numerous details, indeed even entire figures, from the sonority—one thinks of Loge, who only commences in the flickering, or the sinking *Vergessenheit* motif that takes us down with it, or the somber grandeur and solitude, the *true* music of the end and of death in Brünhild's final song—rather, the composer discovers, even within his orchestra placed diagonally through the world of consciousness, and again diagonally under this world, essential means of animation and motivation, that is, leitmotifs in the polyvalent sense, which the wakeful libretto cannot contain. Thus there is often a clairvoyantly anticipatory activity at work here, quite capable of illuminating the nameless and conceptless dawning of the active forces of the will in the powerful downward and upward expansion of consciousness, in melismatic polyphony's multi-story structure, since the will's drives, joined as they are, can almost never fall into the upper voice's more complete consciousness, that is, into explicit human motivation. All of this does not abolish their mere drivenness, and the music just as often recoils into its almost military drumroll, or into its wide, basely, low-lyingly general *espressivo* as the fitting place for this strangely subjective animal lyricism. One can see that the sonority, for all its wide-ranging frenzy, gives rise only to passion, but no true action, and still less personally compelling, metaphysically significant destiny. That this happens to Brünhild and that to Siegfried is accidental; their fate is sad but not necessary, not tragic, and the gods who impose it are called gods without being so. If it has been rightly observed that Wagner's romantic heroines never become mothers, Sieglinde alone excepted, and then only so that love's fervent radiance will be repeated without further correction in Brünhild and Siegfried, then the whole—in spite of all its breadth, the encounters between gods and human beings; in spite of all the final softness, a fantastically animated nature, the gigantism of the destinies, the eschatologisms of the background, of *Ragnarök*—has no character, no forward or upward continuation, no true plot of a dramatic let alone a metadramatic nature. As a whole and in its essence it is subhuman; it can use its magical roots and herbs only to disclose a helpless, purely natural narcosis instead of redemption, and—instead of the billowing human heart, instead of the finally explicit, musically explicit Baroque abiding continuously with man—install underground trapdoors, generalities, intrigues and nature myths. It is untrue, and remains "art" in the bad sense, with no place in the philosophy of history or in metaphysics; decadent barbarians and decadent gods are the *dramatis personae*, and not the longing for Siegfried, the Germanic Messiah, not the distant, final God invoked by ontological music, the God of the Apocalypse and the apocalyptic "drama of grace."

Thus every conscious volition has been given up here, before a different desire, a volition toward the new, can be achieved. Everything thunders and flashes, the fog speaks, and yet it does not speak, for everything blurs together, and the predetermined word interferes. It must be achieved, however, this other volition; it is only now gathering the strength to open the inner door, if not break it down. Beethoven was on this path, with his virile, bold, morally objective strength, and this strength alone can make things mystical again, rightfully mystical. Wagner wanted to be lucent like this, but then he did not let his sensuous sound have its say, so that it would reveal to him his inborn spiritual language, but rather overcompensated for the gloom in the most illusory way, precisely through the intelligibility of the word. Of course the result was not the revealed Word, poetic or otherwise; the tonal haze was compressed only more densely, and the superficial adaptation of a Gluckian and Classicist explicitness against the constantly inundating, uncompleted sound just becomes the expression of a "confused representation" of inadequate fervor. Wagner would not wait until his *very own, the sound-word* [*Tonwort*] came, but it is precisely the gifted composer who must ultimately be able to remain fully detached, absolute, and to see where his art leads that he at first only partly knows, and can explore only through resoluteness, and into which immeasurable interior of his realm radical expression takes him; without any influence by the poetic, which, even in transcendental opera, must far more remain just a variable, and in the end loses every correlate in the face of music's suprarational, different correlate. Otherwise everything is dragged so far down that we do not even enter into consideration, and the unconscious, pathological Will reigns alone. The sound, hemmed in, takes revenge by damming itself up, by hypertrophying within its primitive, maenadic, chthonic, subluminous instead of superluminous and anamnestic warmth, and thus—after the poetry that will not let the sound have its say has already encamped here—relegates the dramatic agents back into a region where they can be only the flowers on a tree, which is the tree of the soul, indeed only tossing ships that unrestingly comply with the suffering, the struggle, the love and the longing for redemption of their subhuman ocean and over which, in every decisive moment, instead of the encounter toward one another and toward the depth of an individual fate, breaks only the universal wave of Schopenhauer's Will. Certainly individual souls put up a certain resistance, but not that of the *principium individuationis*, only the minimum basis generally needed for a theatrical realization, even an undramatic one. This is not the new, solitary persona that can speak only of itself and must let others decide if they can find themselves therein, nor is it the persona of the folk song or *minnesang* that speaks of the lover or the old man as such, as a collective type. Indeed, individual souls can not even still be regarded as mere stages where the abstract forces of sensuality and reason—which of course still refer back to the human beings—fight it out; rather, the lower fissures open, what is low takes the place of what is high, the ocean usurps the inheritance of heaven, and the self recoils, even here and there in the *Meistersinger*, so far back into urges, delusions, and the firefly simile, into midsummer night, midsummer day and unconsciousness as such, into swells, vaporous clouds and an inferior kind of deep sleep, that it no longer speaks for itself and certainly not for Beethoven and Comte's *grand être* as the socially mystical entity of humanity, but rather from the ancient nature god's belly, though utterly without his sidereal clarity or ancient plastic mathematics. Thus involuntary submission replaces the powerful testimony, the toughness and rigor, the awareness of sin, and the strictly individual postulates of Christian belief. It is all heathen, what Wagner's music for the *Nibelungen*, so strangely streaked with filth, gold, and narcosis, provided in the way of breadth, false ecstasy and anonymous glory in the service of a nature principle that Christianity has shaken but not exploded. That it could happen, that the exposition of transcendental opera's object, measured by its most dangerous and least successful type, could go so astonishingly far in respect of the feverishly inessential and deeply undramatic: it is repeatedly evident that this results not only from the dance rhythms motivated by the wrong object, but rather finally, precisely, absolutely from the poetic prefabrication deposited above the music, insofar as it wants to suppress the tonal energies and force the music, deposed though never really deposable in Wagner's genius, to unfold within the sole invariant, the unconscious, with such complete, inborn absoluteness that it forfeits its sight, forfeits the not-yet-conscious, the supraconscious, the heroic-mystical phantom of Man, and the *true* infinity of the inwardly real and ontological. Of course there are demands that cannot be fulfilled historically, according to the position of the higher clock. But to a certain extent Wagner cheated himself of his appointed hour, which was a great and holy hour, and where the tremendous impulses within his *Tristan*- and *Parsifal*-mystery became operative. What was therefore not achieved was that still pending fulfillment of Bach's ontological lyricism and of the fugue, of Bach's melismatic-contrapuntal equilibrium, the objective of purification, of the quintessential present, of the Virgin's unfaded rose, of the Son's unriven heart, of the subdual of all agency into spatiality, and of the homecoming of our weary, nameless Kaspar Hauser nature to the throne room of heavenly glory. To that extent one can say that Wagner diverged from the self's Luciferan orientation, to which music since Beethoven has been born; and Wagner's sonic motion, the born illuminator of the soul's higher realms, along with and because of the utterly mistaken, Schopenhauerian-Hindu definition of music, there veered off into the delusory and the poisonously, pathologically mysterious, where in the complete freedom and resoluteness of objective music the burgeoning glossolalia, that is, the Luciferan-Paracletan willing of the human music-spirit itself, could have proclaimed the mystery, the mystery of the intelligible Kingdom. But still, without Wagner as forerunner, the sense of a lack, which brings us to these realms as *realms of sound*, would never have chimed; *Tristan* is their beginning, the celeste in *Parsifal* their invocation.

~

Thus a long line ends. It brought us immeasurable glories, and yet the same bitter feeling remains that tormented Mozart, Schubert and Beethoven before their deaths—namely the feeling that they really should begin now, that they had not written a single note yet—a feeling in force for the concept as well, only with the difference that the bitterness is transformed into rejoicing and hope. Sound does not yet "speak"; it is lucid enough, but as yet no one entirely understands it; it is a fervent stammering, like a child's, and the presumptive, on its own authority prescriptive or even just conspicuous "poetry," at least in the musical drama, disrupts the sound as much as itself, its own equally subordinate, indeed subjugated power. Only the carpets are complete, these boundary stakes and future correctives, and then, minus Bach's fugues, their replenishment-fulfillment in an ever more concrete sphere, whereas it is just the symphony that Wagner raised to the highest expressive determinacy which still awaits its object—born absolutely in music, born absolutely through the symphony—awaits precisely the arrival of Bach's music, the music of space, a melismatic-contrapuntal equilibrium beyond every chordal-polyphonic drama, the music of the completely Christ-suffused soul and its true, sonorous ground-figure. There is much to hope for, and a great moment has now ripened; the days are at hand when the life that continuously gushes forth, the breakthrough and the presentiment of the most immediate, most extreme latency, can absolutely no longer express itself except within the musical, the ethical, and the metaphysical, when it will also no longer be necessary to content oneself with the Areopagite's dictum—that the divine darkness is the inapproachability where God lives—as the highest conception of all the associative as of all the transcendental factors of art.[19]

On the Theory of Music

But we hear only ourselves.

It is and certainly will remain weak enough. For too many, hearing would come more easily if they only knew how they ought to talk about it. That has to do with the highly insecure and derivative way people feel together. For they are made such that they feel at home absolutely only on the basis of communication. They must have some means to arrange their feelings, insofar as far slighter participation and far slighter personal commitment then become necessary, and the comprehension that is lacking can additionally be exchanged, replaced, or abstractly substituted. If this were not so, musical listening would be less distracted and nervous. Then the question could not even be raised, why it is precisely the latecomers to the concert who attract all the attention, nor would the answer be so uncomfortable for all concerned parties. Then it could easily be explained why it is, when every human being brings to music a great natural inclination, that one so seldom encounters a declared love for this art form in the *haute volée.* The middle class lives with music because it loves sociability and reads the concert reviews, whereas the inaccessibility of the discourse of painting makes it appear quite remote, as a field where one cannot help but miss the target. There were nevertheless times when the situation *vis à vis* painting was the same for the intellectual elite, until Winckelmann and more recently Riegl broke the fatal spell of individual noninvolvement and irresolution by some logical detours. The ability to hear is and will remain weak in comparison. For in music there never were any Winckelmanns, and the new ones are only Leopold Schmidt. Even August Halm remains a lone swallow; he does not a summer make. Paul Bekker is a very clever man, but he often makes us forget that, and his anecdotal book on Beethoven does not always do him honor. Grunsky, Hausegger also are to be recommended; also extraordinarily important—though far outside of this group—is Richard Wagner's essay on Beethoven; to be extensively trained in theoretical matters one will turn to Riemann, and of course Moritz Hauptmann's profound works do even more fundamental service here. The question of opera has come under discussion again thanks to Busoni above all, as well as to Pfitzner's critical stimulus. August Halm himself, to whom we owe much and who is distinguished by a great and learned clarity, is regrettable insofar as he evaluates too much just in terms of craft, criticizes all too literally and all too consistently analyzes only in terms of well-conceived themes and their dynamic movement. The tenor of his treatment of Beethoven also leaves something to be desired. Of course he succeeds in such significant and vital accomplishments as the critical analysis of the first movement of Beethoven's D minor Sonata, but he neither understands nor acknowledges the naïve, formalistically inaccessible, expressive musicality that mirrors a human being and not a technical category, and that can well sound unlike Bekker's psychodramatic reading. Even eternal life becomes only a world of stricter and higher laws within Halm's overextended formal concept of the musical as such, which an appended Spittelerian mythologizing neither clarifies nor deepens. It is nonetheless to be hoped that intellectuals will more readily be encouraged to enjoy music when secure, practically useful concepts are finally put in their acquiescent hands.

APPLICATION AND COMPOSITION

Inflection

But we need to bring ourselves to it.

Then we grasp immediately what is being called out to us. A glance, but far more an inflection, is clear in itself, without detours. We feel: this is us, this is about us, we too would call out like this, behave like this. The larynx, always quietly innervated, lets us see and understand, from the inside as it were, what is being called out to us and speaks.

Moreover, we also know no better way to express ourselves than through inflection. It goes deep, and where a glance would coarsen or allow a drawing back, where silence becomes more eloquent than speech, there especially can singing amplify even the quietest and most indistinct stirring. One might say that song, in order to be presentient, releases inflection, as the most fleeting and yet most powerful thing, from a human being, and gathers it into a continuous, compact construct. So much depends on the tone we strike, then. What circulates within it, in other words, what the singer or player "puts into" the sound, is more important than what the song contains purely tonally. For in itself the latter sets only a very general mood, strongly subject to the user's whim.

Attack

Far too little would ever be clear without it. It remains crucial to see the one who is musically calling or striking here.

Just for this reason, then, the same thing can be sung so very differently. We know how often a song can have changed masters without any listener becoming aware of how very incredible such a change often is. How could the most diverse strophes otherwise be set to the same music? One tries to avoid that nowadays, of course, but Schubert's "Lindenbaum" has such a defect, so it cannot be absolutely injurious to the sense. Besides, who could want to remain only formalistic after finding out that

it is the same melody from the old folk song "Mein Gemüt ist mir ver-
wirrt / Das macht eine Jungfrau zart" [My heart is all confused / A tender
maiden charms me] that later joined with the text "Herzlich tut mich ver-
langen nach einem sel'gen End" [My heart is desirous of a blessed end],
and now lives on in the melody of the chorale "O Haupt voll Blut and
Wunden" [O sacred head sore wounded]? The same b*b*-f#-g that stands
for "longingly" in Susanne's concluding aria accompanies, with no rhythmic displacement whatever, the radiance of the midsummer day in
Pogner's intonation, and therefore a total, jubilant state of fulfillment:
and neither, even taking into account the intended effect, is preferable.
One might of course object that such a thing does not happen with the
same composer. Or that Mozart, in accordance with his partly Italianate
nature, is hardly the perfect model of the meaningful allocation of notes
to words. But then Bach is an utterly German composer, and the richest,
most powerfully expressive melodist as well. Nonetheless, even in Bach,
in other words even within a unified *oeuvre*, the same song that in the
179th Cantata accompanies hypocrisy is used in the Kyrie of the G major
Mass as a plea for mercy, and the same aria that in *Die Wahl des Herkules*
[Hercules' Decision], a *dramma per musica*, expresses lust and its repulsion ("Ich will dich nicht hören, ich will dich nicht wissen, verworfene
Wollust, ich kenne dich nicht" [I will not hear you, nor will I know of
you, infamous craving, I know you not] is the setting for Maria's lullaby
in the *Christmas Oratorio*. Whereby the rejection of temptation, set a
third lower and accompanied by the woodwinds and the organ in addition to the strings as in the operatic version, but in no other way transposed, is transformed into the most avid counsel ("Bereite dich, Zion, mit
zärtlichen Trieben, den Schönsten, den Liebsten bald bei dir zu sehen"
[Make ready, O Zion, now gently prepare to take to your bosom the most
lovely, the dearest]). But insofar as it is sung differently, there is a perceptibly different kind of signification in it, obedient to the "sense," and just
as one no more thinks of "prey" when one hears "pray" or of the "sextant"
when hearing "sexton," as in the pun's empty moment of surprise, one
need not become aware of the melodic unity within these changes of significance, even when attending to the relevant passages in quicker succession. It means little on the other hand that vocal declamation, if it is
good, as it nearly always is in Wagner, pursues a certain, naturally always
identical doubling of the intervals within speech, within sense, or that
particular melismatic turns within absolute music—above all falling mo-

tifs of sighing, or motifs of longing, with a suspension—possess certain meanings that occur everywhere and are contentually identical.

So we always have it only from within ourselves, and not out of the sonic motion, what this motion means. Without a performance, sound remains blind. Certainly *sprechgesang* faithfully coexists with the spoken word's sonorous life. But the former is only understandable when seen from above, and not even the most detailed recitative could tell us what kind of weather prevails in the upper regions of the text. Matters stand no better, in fact far less favorably, with the language of melismatic excitation within both accompanying and absolute music. The sound may just rise up, and then it sinks back, short of breath, a seemingly clear case but actually just as ambiguous. In one instance this can mean that there is some real resignation, as for example in the simply beautiful accompanying figure to Sachs's "Schön Dank, mein Jung" after the *Wahnmonolog*; but it can also mean that the musical line is charging, and then, having arrived at the summit, turns to discharge its superabundance, as in Strauß's joyful accompanying melody to "Und die belohnende Lust" from Schiller's *Hymnus*, with no difference but a certain, in itself quite indeterminate breadth of the intervallic framework where the ascent and the incandescent return occur. Of course one could also reply that neither of these two related examples is melodically very pregnant; but where they are, the animated composer, the inner clavichord becomes even more important, and his own movements of sorrow or jubilation even directly, disproportionally oppose the given notation. Often a falling line is completely irrelevant to the mood, as in the adagio of Beethoven's Fifth Piano Concerto, where the line descends twice in succession through two and a half octaves, and activates, instead of the melancholy of the score, only a certain calm and confidence in aiming and striking. Just as often, as in the "Huldreichster Tag" motif from the *Meistersinger*, which with a small barb in the middle descends an octave through a triad, the expression is exactly contrary to the descent: and when in the overture the ascending march theme in the horns infringes on the jubilant "Huldreichster Tag" theme descending in the strings, it is truly not this countermovement within the orchestra that decides the success or failure of this music. Admittedly further interpretations might support convention, support it in terms of convention. Perhaps they will only allow tone painting: then lower notes are always dark, heavy, burdensome, massive, and the high notes always bright, light, airy, as well as the heavens, the angels, the stellar realm;

then, besides, what is dynamically weak as such is always incorporeal, shadowy, ghostly, what is dynamically strong is powerful, gigantic, tremendous; and finally we have more or less flowing, tempestuous, jagged, or brazen rhythms. Perhaps the interpretations also become more thorough, and ascribe to the sequence of notes a certain evaluative narrative of development, whereby the descending movement into the bass represents a stopping and an initial fading, whereas, as in Köstlin's sincere account in terms of Vischer's aesthetics, ascending movement, as the actually sonically generative movement, displays the living, creative principle within music, the squeezing of sound from matter mute in itself. But the same applies to such naturalism as to *sprechgesang*: without any prior human application there could be no such equivalencies, and that even the most analogous formal qualities could not by themselves point us to the spirits hiding in their uppermost logical regions.

So it is the touch, the delivery alone that make the speaker's fortune, that makes him a speaker; sound wants to turn toward a human being.[20] Everywhere it becomes important to observe the *expression*, which only the fact of being sung, the bowing of the violins, the touch on the piano, but foremost the artistic application add to the score, and without which neither dynamics nor rhythm could be struck in the manner intended by the composer. This attack combines in conducting, and indeed such that the latter first combines out of sonorous magic, volume, intensification, tempo changes, an emotionally coloring or draftsmanlike shaping counterpoint, as the individual elements of the communicated will. Nevertheless conducting contains something else, which rediscovers the creator's original vision still accessible in the "work" as the vision's only approximate suggestion and the mere cipher of actualization. It is the power of the born conductor—in contrast to the pedants who lifelessly, traditionally, but actually disrespectfully play just what is written, in contrast of course to the subjective swindlers who degrade the work into an aphrodisiac against their own impotence—it is the power of the born conductor to remain suggestible until everything suddenly plays itself, until the miracle of transformation, the lordly and blessed feeling of the transmission of genius has taken place within him, and the air around him—the work's atmosphere, the application and the soul of work—combines in a Beethovenian blaze. Then that mysterious place has been reached where the lifeless melismatic or harmonic or contrapuntal components fuse together into the original vision, and Bach or Beethoven become intelligible: not this or that apparent typism of the musical allocation, then, but the relevant composers themselves, as both the essential ciphers and objects. Thus in the end one obviously depends even more strongly than before on the inflection, the manner of speaking and the performer's sonorous gesture, which as such is alone able to amplify the only weak affective or otherwise significant determinacy of the formally given elements or any other analogously demonstrable typisms. Nowhere else does it appear so necessary to demand participation, and in addition a good interpreter, who can not only rescue or destroy the music, but whose receptively spontaneous intermediate form underlines and lays open music's particular experiential character, the musical object's only approximate, conceptually undeterminable and continuously processual aspect.

For it is still empty and uncertain, what is happening sonically. It is hopeless to allocate the music to already definite emotions. Not even whether a melody even *can* unequivocally express anger, longing, love *as such*—that is, if it is these emotional contents, already experienced by us anyway, at which music aims, and where it could easily excel a statue—is so easy to identify, once its upheavals begin to slur together. It is due to something other than the sonority if the horns sound like hunters and the trumpets like kings, indeed even when certain rhythms, here gently soaring, there with an oppressive *grave*, introduce into music humor, majesty or similar, externally associative categories subregional to music. The sound is neither isolated, it is too whorish for that from the standpoint of poetry, which is reflexive, and compared to which music does not even aspire to be better than whorish; neither is the sound simply just general, on the other hand, for it is too strong, too unabstract, too moving, too ontologically charged; it surges, "From airy tones wells up a mystery"[21]; all demanding here is at first only approximate. And indeed because in music, which everyone understands without knowing what it means, no tangibly clear, discrete life has as yet roused itself that could provide already precisely defined categories instead of the dramatic constraints we will discuss presently, in other words instead of the mere *outline* of symphonic drama and of ascending spheres of the self. If one considers a musical piece in its technical aspect, everything is correct but means nothing, like an algebraic equation; if on the other hand one considers it in its poetic aspect, then it says everything and defines nothing—a strange conflict still lacking any median or any equilibration accessible to the understanding, in spite of its agitated content. Here it does no good to keep to the technical, which remains lifeless and a mere template if one does not interpret it through its creator; and it also does no good to keep to the poetic, in order to force the "music's infinitely blurring character," as Wagner said, into categories which are not its categories. The only thing that helps here is to listen well, and presentiently await what kind of language and what kind of extreme, supraformal as well as supraprogrammatic determinacy might yet take shape within music, this pealing of bells in an invisible tower on high. Beethoven is already an initiative, and his art does not lack the clearest moral will, that is, the moral Will *sui generis* appertaining to music: but the future is still open, and to Schopenhauer's utterly false definition of music as "Will generally," which does apply to Wagner here and there, but which essentially eternalizes a temporary condition of uncertainty, it will let us counterpose a *non liquet* corresponding to the uncompleted quality of the material at hand.

Artistic Musicalization

Only what first sounds with us, then, can bring us *any closer here.*

First, applied sound makes every event more acute, penetrating, sensuous.

For as listeners we can also still get in close touch, so to speak. The ear is slightly more deeply embedded in the skin than even the eye.

It is not as if sound dragged us down, but it fills in well, and so lets us sense something as real. Therefore we bristle at having to watch a silent film, not without reason. For here only the monochrome optical impression has been excerpted, and since it is simply given as it is, there arises in accordance with the ear's exclusion the disagreeable impression of a solar eclipse, a mute and sensuously diminished life. But then the ear assumes a peculiar function: it serves as the proxy of the remaining senses; from things it removes alive their crackling, their friction, and from people their speech, and so the film's musical accompaniment, however vague or precise it may finally be, thus comes to be felt as the exact complement in its way to the photography. It can just as well be asserted that the sonorous frieze with which the opera supplements the libretto does not in itself detract, but makes things immediate, urgent, intelligible, and that all more grippingly the more the music ventures out into full extent of the action, into dramatic excitement and finally, especially, into what is otherwise remote, suprasensory.

Second, however, the applied sound actualizes in noticeably different ways, depending on whether it leads into the merely intelligible or into the meaningful.

Everything underneath must therefore already begin appropriately, and provide a certain density. The singing, the sound must be nuanced, and not only actualize by removing, but also by committing a more fervent human being, by calling out.

Consequently the sound must be able to save itself up; at every place where merely simple if also animated life speaks, it must be restrained as dispassionately as possible. Who shows too much, shows nothing; and it was just the self-contained opera's distinction, however easily attainable, to accompany with recitative, and to first place the aria, sovereign music, where the plot becomes denser, "realer," where the plot tightens and human beings must therefore sing. In open opera, on the other hand, everything that happens can be clearly marked; not only does this leave much of the plot unintelligible, but the music very often foregoes the freshest and most beautiful effects of a sudden emergence of heterogeneity, of a clear stratification of the real. Only in order not to lose this multiplicity does Wagner, does the open opera of the time seek to tirelessly rise, fall, and rise again, thereby inserting different levels into the uniformly mountainous landscape of the through-composed style. But that often makes everything insufferably overheated and melodramatic, where the word, the compulsion to reality, does not at all require it. How in fact an intensification might contrast itself and yet still flow is shown by Verdi's *Otello*; certainly here, in this completely singular work of genius, with such calm, depth, maturity and fullness of the speaking pitch (entire phrases along the same note) and then of the song, the lyrical dialogue, the wildest outbursts, the thunderclap of imminent catastrophe, the chord at the end of the heroic trajectory, one can certainly recognize the unification of the graduated with the through-composed dramatic-operatic style. Here merely the same thing again needs to be accomplished, paradoxically, at the end of the symphony's development, that at its inception the Mannheim school had accomplished by 1750: the brightening, darkening, soft-pedaling, diminuendo, crescendo, in sum the shaping of a relief within the orchestra. Precisely to the extent that polyphonic accompaniment has gradually become monotonous and, out of sheer exaggeration, a new *continuo* without any economy of musical actualization.

Only at the very top, where the upper register is sparingly applied, does the power to initiate and to actualize by means of intensification even seem to subside. And just at the place where sound makes things flowery, dulls the edges, and clothes every reverie in pleasant reality, meaning in this case by musically reversing the inside outward. This can turn out well or badly: the effect is poorly and flatly realized when the mood is simply trumpeted; when the hero, as Schlegel says, goes trilling to his death; when, as in Schiller's reproach to *Egmont*'s partly melodramatic conclusion, "we are transferred from the truest and most moving situation into an operatic world, in order to be shown a dream." We get an entirely different feeling, however, in those instances where the composer speaks of a better reality, where one forgets the *primadonna* and the languishing *Heldentenor*'s inferior intensity, where Wagner's music perhaps paints in "lyrical" terms again, and in its adagio converges on Mozartian fairy-tale opera, this first carpet of the ontological. This nevertheless hardly means, even then, that the amplifying, intensifying, actualizing power of music, its uncanny method of actualizing into sonorous silence, as depth, has waned. Just the reverse: only its object has shifted more deeply; it is the quieter, deeper kernel, some last decisive reversal and substantiation of destiny arrested in the illusion [*Schein*] of a musical "reality," in the manifestation [*Schein*] of a unchanging, characteristic intensification that brings meaning instead of intelligibility, makes it mythical, that is, reveals precisely the other, deeper stratum of reality, and instead of the veristic reality of *Spieloper*, adventure opera, action opera, stages the utopian reality of transcendental opera: ghosts and masquerades, the funhouse mirror for comic and the magic mirror for serious opera; the music that must ring out as soon as the suprasensory element enters the plot, in order that, according to Busoni's good operatic theory, musical impossibility will join the impossibility, the visionary element within the plot, and thus both become possible. In this way, then, the "aria" of self-contained opera, and more deeply of Bachian composure, of a supradramatic "lyricism," also returns by *a priori* demand, inevitably weighed down and on a very high level of reality, corresponding to the always just penultimate aspect of any excitement, to the absolute hierarchical surplus and telic content of intervening, of going into action, of faltering, mystical self-apprehension. Wherever the hardness and translucence of the mere verbal construct disappears, wherever just the light of the deeply penetrating musical awakening, realizing, emphasizing *suo modo* generates the miraculous atmosphere of untragic drama, there also arises that mythical music-space of the highest reality, which transcendent opera shares with the drama of grace, and which, as the mythos of love or of sanctity, depletes the spiritual ontologies beyond any possible world-destiny, any continuing world-epic.

Third, however, the music innervated through us quietly sets a constraint on our activity; the dramatic sound "composes" further and even involves *an automatic dramatic outline*.

Of course it has been hotly disputed that sound can go that far. Pfitzner for example completely separates isolated melodic elaboration from the total and substantiating tendency, which is of a poetic nature.

It undoubtedly sounds irresistible to say: If I want to communicate the essence of some musical work, I simply whistle the first theme. If on the other hand I want to narrate the essence of a literary work, then I will certainly not cite the first sentence, but rather report the basic features of the plot or the layout of the whole. Just as a composer would appear absurd to us if he claimed to carry a sonata or symphony around in his head, without a single theme, so would a poet who wrote down verses or sentences and claimed that here was a drama, although he did not yet know what would happen in it, although, in other words, its great, overriding idea had not yet occurred to him. The particular, then, is held to be the composer's special concern: this tiny, tangible unit, this inspired invention already beautiful and fully developed at birth, not needing to be stretched out into a symphony, its effect never changing through changes of context, is, according to Pfitzner, music's proper source of value. So inversely, the pervasive, the omnipresent is the poet's proper project: as what must first be achieved, as the great intangible unity or the inspired poetic idea, as it gradually, instead of being "composed," gradually precipitates and "condenses" and yet has value only as the binding element, an intuition of the whole *substantiating* the particular. If these two so totally different modes of operation are thus to be successfully combined, what is fundamental about one art form must be emphasized and complementarily balanced out. Bad scores, then, would be those that already tried to be extensively narrative or even intellectual, and bad libretti those that either excessively articulated the details or neglected to objectively ground the plot, in favor of a mere scaffolding in which to suspend duets, arias, and ensemble passages. The proper mission of music, then, according to Pfitzner, is to be accidental: music must relinquish the cultivation of autonomous forms, the skillfully distributed filler of the symphonic work, which has abolished the former separation of invention and conventional *tutti* passages in favor of a uniformity of the whole, combined indistinguishably out of invention and reflection. Not for nothing has the history of musical forms had a chronic difficulty in accommodating the material of musical inspiration. Poetry's mission would then be, to be contentual: it must relinquish sensuous particularity, that is, make room for music, and provide it, as concisely as possible, often by displacing the plot into symbols, the fundamental moods as well as the dramatic substantiation, the necessity, and destiny from the realm, accessible only to poetry, of a logic of forms and complexes. Thus Pfitzner loves himself and Schumann, and plays the latter off against Liszt; thus *Der Freischütz* and above all its Wolf's Glen music provide the archetype of the perfect opera: the basic problem of operatic composition has been solved, and Pfitzner believes that his idea of an as much musical as poetically elementary, that is, specifically musico-dramatic conception, avoids the dangerous complications of a music that itself wants to generate drama.

Much of this is as correct as it is astute, and it is interesting how astute something incorrect can often be. For if it were as Pfitzner says, then exactly the lesser and middling composers would have had the surest instincts, the best ideas. There is certainly an empty, calculated kind of work, and a fraudulence that acts Beethovenian when nothing but vacuity is apparent, where the thematic fabric is not even reflection, but rather has become just what the *tutti* passages used to be, namely patterning. There are no less weighty objections even to Beethoven's arias: they become unsonorous, unlyrical, all too poor in voices, and hard to organically counterpoint despite all their drive. Pfitzner equally has a point when he notes certain lifeless passages in Wagner where the recitative has nothing to say, because the text also has no drive, and where the leitmotif is inserted into the music not out of the purely symphonic necessity of a recapitulation, but only conceptually, as a sort of pedagogical point of orientation. However, if one would like to see this as confirmation of the perils of the border between music and drama, there should be this correction: that neither Schumann, nor Pfitzner, nor any other ingenuous, if highly reputable kind of composer who trusts in inspiration only to work up his brief moments of invention into the invention of the brief moment *pro domo*, but only Bruckner and Wagner made good "the sonata's responsibility to the ideal of music." One simply cannot somehow pass over Beethoven, and moreover there are precisely in Beethoven inventions which engender such movement, and especially expositions of these inventions, whose dialectical drama, commencing in the tension of these thematic "inventions," appertains purely to this music's dramatic element itself. As music that needs symphonic space, and remove, in order to be this kind of music, and to which time, which bears it forward and is involved in it, already suggests a generative total vision of at least the individual movement if not the entire symphony. Indeed, even the composer of the *Freischütz* and particularly the Wolf's Glen music praised by Pfitzner as especially individually and determinedly melodic—even Weber feels so little in accord with Pfitzner's theory that he can remark in an aphorism, quite symphonically: "While reading a poem, everything presses by the soul more quickly; a few words suffice to change the emotions, to define them. The composer cannot work the same way; his language needs longer accents, and the passage from one feeling into another puts many obstacles in his way." One could likewise say: if the antipathy to longer forms is really to be emphatically musical, then symphonic prolongation has still shattered more forms than the accretion of musical invention. One must finally reply to Pfitzner's nominalism that the sonata and the corresponding birth of Wagnerian drama from the spirit of the symphony represent not only a husk, one of the belated, interesting, chronic difficulties in accommodating the material of musical invention, but rather the totally legitimate body of a particular *melos* and its equally generative, inspiriting, dramatically definitive counterpoint.

In other words, to try to find the right words for music's power of action: here the sound truly *draws*, growing in flight, while the word just falls. If one merely observes how just a good song originates, one notices how little the mere particularities are enlivened. Thus in Pfitzner himself, in Hugo Wolf, in Bach and Wagner, the music is adapted only superficially to the text, with no intention of occurring only atomistically, as it were. An utter focus on the essential is at work here, such that, in Rudolf Louis's apt observation about Hugo Wolf, the whole piece is spun out in an overridingly absolutely musical development, as it does not so much take up the particularities of the text and its emotional immediacies, but rather keeps to a basic mood from the beginning or from the course of the text, which is then realized as music and laid out as the accompanying polyphony of this essential, basic mood. This mood is a limit, of course, but a limit precisely against the particular, and therefore a clear relationship to the whole, into which the poetry of a song or even an opera must now, conversely, introduce its particularity. For there need not always dominate, as in Pfitzner's *Palestrina*, such a stylistic difference between the lyrical visions of the first act and the merely querulous counterpoint of the council scene of the second; there is temperament, but above that there is also a mysticism of the *journey* and of *time*. As little as one should contentually overestimate symphonic accompaniment's power to set the plot, there is just as certainly, beginning with *Fidelio*, a purely musical compulsion that not only follows the plot by means of melismatic-symphonic animation, but itself produces plot, as yet undefined, nameless plot, the air, the tempo, the mood, the ground, the level, the dark, flickering, supraconscious, magical, mythical background to the plot, arbitrary in its particulars but constrained as a whole, into which the theatrically meaningful application and the as it were textual "grounding" that mimics it only on a lower level now have to be inserted. It goes without saying that here a concise, conspicuous action, often made legible through symbols, is worth more than a drama shaped in complete disregard for the music; that Schiller's *Kabale und Liebe*, in other words, provides a more questionable libretto than a Strauß-Hofmannsthal consultative project or the dramas that Wagner developed completely *secundum rem musicalem*, precisely insofar as neither the particular fullness, nor theoretically the more mysterious depth of the musical drama, can tolerate no prefabricated, no purely poetically formed drama.

Fourth, however, even the verbal totality of the plot is thus latently overtaken by the note that first sounds with us, the subjectively suffused note.

A poor text is already easy to disrupt in itself. It is superfluous, and wherever it appears it makes itself laughable next to the music which it wants to clarify, whose mood it wants to breathe out.

It is especially not groundless that nearly everything becomes too lofty when sung, that in opera even the poorest boatman rows with a golden oar. No one understands all that stuff about the poisonous ring or Emma's ghost, but Weber's music almost makes meaningful literature out of *Euryanthe*. Elsewhere the illusion goes so far that Pamina begins to seem like Beatrice, that all the *Magic Flute*'s cheap stage tricks appear as occult visions, just because Mozart's music deepens the mere theatricality and the superficial antagonisms, and traces them back to those theosophical actualities which in Schikaneder's text had become even more confusing, if not entirely nonsensical. It is also not groundless that one should be startled at a students' drinking song, which is how the truly hellishly driving and stomping opening chorus to *Tales of Hoffmann* seems to appear; music and text seem to "agree" absolutely nowhere in this unique masterpiece, nothing feels quite right. Or differently again, when a journeyman and then the students break off in the middle of the dance and announce the Meistersinger in fourths in a harmonically marvelous succession, as though the subject were not these complacent dignitaries but rather the entrance of the heavenly host. The voice of every great song, every deep word-music, is like the voice of that ghostly traveler from Hoffman's *Kreisleriana*, who tells of distant, unknown lands and peoples and strange destinies he has seen in his long travels, and whose speech finally "fades into a wonderful ringing, in which he spoke of unknown, most mysterious things, wordlessly but unmistakably."[22] But such a thing requires that the music overtake the text, and so in terms of the whole, the level that has been set, can ultimately not intrude into the text's continuously visible element, because this whole lies beyond the literary whole. In terms of just this whole, one really cannot say that any literature could be inserted into music's dramatic space other than arbitrarily, could do more than approximate its indefinite demands; in a broader context the text certainly follows the music's mysterious, immoderate power of action, but with its demystifying, more "logical" means, it cannot readily prove worthy of the musically required level. Even where the fourths might sound less distinctive, even where the scenic grounding has been placed higher than at the mere opening of the *Meistersinger*, the available transcendent drama is always poorer in implications than the music that prepares its own destinies, its mythos; and just this is the *true* boundary between the symphonic and the dramatic correlation.

Consequently the drive to translate something so remote back into everyday language can supply no meaning, not even in a hermeneutic respect. Here, above all, the silliest things are said about some sonic item. They remind one—even Bekker, Beethoven's biographer, was justly reproached for it—of the worst commentaries on "the picture of the month" from the old *Gartenlaube*. Here the prattle about the expressive pleading of the 32nd notes, the merry laughter of the violin's trill, the unison g# ringing out three times after the scherzo of the C# minor Quartet as if to ask: "Where am I going in this world?"—celebrates its widespread triumph. Here, with his explanatory chatter, lodges the smug philistine who believes not only to have said something, but to have settled the issue, when he summarizes the A major Symphony, in the magical language of some *Guide to Music*, as "the Song of Songs of Dionysian heroism." Bekker raised the device by which piano teachers attempt to improve their students' feeble imaginations to the exegetical discipline of musical poetics: and all this can supposedly be found in Beethoven, worse, this is supposed to be the interpreted, conceptually clarified Beethoven, this offensive stuff, where for every measure a little phrase is at the ready, next to which the most banal newspaper serialization reads like the *Aeneid*. One can say it this way or that, and if Adolf Bernhard Marx, Beethoven's other biographer, explicates the course of action in the *Eroica* as an idealized battle—the first movement depicts the battle itself, the funeral march depicts the night march across the battlefield, the scherzo is the cheerful and bawdy music of the camp, and the final movement depicts the eager, delighted homecoming to peacetime's joys and celebrations—then this is not such a bad thing, since the music has absolutely nothing to do with it, and makes its profundity accessible to such supplementary pictorial games according to popular preconceptions, though neither confirming nor denying them. On the other hand it remains irrelevant whether this or that composer necessarily thought he was depicting a jolly plowman. It does not help to investigate how much Beethoven personally, whether inspired or subsequently appreciating his own work, seems to have encouraged such inept fabulating. Certainly he would claim in later years that an earlier time had been more "poetic": "Everyone used to feel that the two sonatas of Opus no. 14 represented a dialog between two persons, because it just seems so obvious"; and we know how badly Beethoven wanted to give the earlier works poetic titles, in connection with just this complaint about the waning fantasy of music lovers. No less *non licet bovi* if Jupiter Wagner, poetry's fool, often put together the most arguable interpretations: thus, according to him, the andante of Mozart's G minor Symphony closes with a final testimonial to the bliss of a death through love, thus the surprising sweetness of the finale of the *Eroica* "symbolizes" the hero's consummation in love, whereas in the Prelude to *Lohengrin* a band of angels audibly bears the grail downward—all interpretations of the most incidental, arbitrary sort belied by the totality of Wagner's genius itself. Consequently if Beethoven insisted that his Overture to *Die Namensfeier* were not a composition but a poem, then this confusion of genres has to do first with the urge to be "intellectual," closer to science (the same urge that led Goethe to value his poetry less than his *Theory of Color*); and then Beethoven surely imagined the poetic as nothing but that digression among moods and enthusiasms, that "poetry" to which one always opposes prose, the prose of philistine, dreamless, unsymbolic life. However, Beethoven is no poet, he is less and more than a poet, and what the program symphony that apparently succeeded him has really added in terms of bleating sheep, sweltering sickrooms, ticking clocks, roaring waterfalls, cool forests and other narrowly circumscribed, banal photographic captions, all now lets us identify the programmatic poetry as merely a springboard to the inner, imageless pathos, to the inmost wordlessness of music. So one must—without wanting to number among those who want to remain nothing but formal and regard their epigonally received or produced formal residues as "absolute" music, while Hanslick and Herbart patrol the border against the indirect tradition—one must most decisively protest those program-musical essays that bestow fake flesh and bone insofar as they issue interpolations of a sort incidental, regionally inferior to music, as a language above music, or as the translation into adequate categories of an art with which we can be intimate only as foreigners.[23]

But even a good text, the poetically valuable one, will necessarily fall short of the music. Thus it matters little if Wagner represents things, even historically, as if one had to proceed from the sound back to the text again, and not the other way. He will not let the sound have its say, neither in the *Ring* nor in general fundamentally, theoretically, but rather resorts unconditionally to textual crutches instead of trusting in the not yet intuited, "eloquent," expressive future of music. According to Wagner, music would have to seek to dissolve itself in drama at any price, just as instrumental music arose from the chorus, just as if absolute instrumental music were a fallen woman who, after the dialectical differentiation of the merely metallic sonorities, now longed for the word's return and synthesis, the dissolution of its mere logogryph in a dramatically reinstated "chorus."[24] But then Wagner himself, who finds it so extraordinary when on the ruins of the librettist's art the composer should appear as the proper, true poet, says, disavowing his own theory: if one considers Beethoven's musical and Shakespeare's dramatic treatment of *Coriolanus*, then Shakespeare appears as just awaking though still dreaming Beethoven, and above him still this glow, this unbearable abundance, as the manifestation of the truly musical vision. But apart from that Wagner is also caught in a historical error; he overlooks the fact that the earliest operas were already taking shape during the orchestra's exclusive flowering, and what was later freed from the chorus and developed further within a particular instrumental form is no historical median, whose choric beginning is supposed to return, after a dialectical reversal, as the dramatic ending; rather the chorus, notwithstanding the Florentine opera or any other, notwithstanding the musical drama and in spite of the brilliant development of the orchestra that serves it, has absolutely remained the highest, most expressively powerful part of the orchestra, increasingly relinquishing any textual, program-musical, dramatic "logic," and remaining the mightiest climax of the pure symphony flourishing alongside it. It is and will remain the destiny even of the better text, however, even the poetically most valuable one, even the most musically involved one, to be completely caught up in the music, to go begging before the sound. "O namen-namelose Freude" [O name-nameless joy!], sing Leonore and Floristan; already in its simplest and crudest stages music quietly subdues literature and turns it into a reflection. Even the plainest note, even the most misused, is incapable of simply illustrating a text: music's dark elemental cry dissolves every word, every drama into itself, and inmost transformation, a fullness of the most mysterious visions, of the most mysterious immediacy and latency presses by us in the singing flames of great music. There is therefore no *great* music, certainly, which could *in the very end* leave room for something differently shaped or dramatically spoken, or whose prerequisites did not lie beyond the limits of even the most masterful and accomplished poetry; just as the awaited clairaudience, the legacy of our vanished clairvoyance, differs as much from the merely poetically mythical, in both formal and objective terms, as Apostolic glossolalia differed from Julian intellectuals' mere desire to believe in belief. Of course Nietzsche asks if we can imagine someone who could take in *Tristan's* Act 3 without any help from words or images and yet not expire before this echoing of numberless cries of joy and sorrow. But why should he not? one should ask; music is not there in order to protect us from mysticism, or to be protected from it, and the image of Apollo that *The Birth of Tragedy* would like to project over the Dionysian ocean remains, in Wagner as in Nietzsche, an admitted illusion, a lovely illusion in form and measure and *universalibus post rem* rather than *ante rem*, beyond which the primordial reality of Dionysos, or seen more deeply, of Christ, at once crashes shut again, so that the logical goal of the Nietzschean *quid pro quo* remains completely incomprehensible. Music quite simply dominates, and wants to be absolute; there is fundamentally no

other music but absolute music, music which speaks *per se* in its absoluteness, music now explicable only, purely speculatively. What has truly
been musically designed and musically thought through to its conclusion
will in the long term acknowledge no gaps between its worlds, where, like
Epicurus' real gods, the gods of poetics can lead whatever hermeneuti-
cally superfluous existence.

INTERPRETATION, OR, ON THE RELATIONSHIP BETWEEN
ABSOLUTE AND SPECULATIVE MUSIC

Of course none of this means that any discussion of music is useless. Certainly good listeners are rare. And something else must already be very
decisively emphasized here before we proceed to the particulars of the
tonal, harmonic, rhythmic and contrapuntal nexus. Everything always
depends on one set of eyes; it will never be possible directly with such
means, and without committing a new self, to decide or disclose what is
accessible to the receptive person and alone motivates the artist: soul, expression, and content.

The What of Expression Generally

What am I really seeking when I hear? I seek, when I listen, to become
richer and increase in content. Nothing is given to me if I just comfortably and easily resonate to it. Unless I fetch it myself, going further, contentually, beyond enjoyment. Even an artist will not stir us, will not signify, insofar as during his labor he truly wants nothing but the means.

For one can also proclaim and prophesy in art. More important than
whether the crowd outside hears song when a man is screaming inside
the red-hot belly of the Pharsalian bull, and certainly more important
than the mechanism through which cries are transformed into song,
communicated, are the cries themselves, their undiverted authenticity
and depth. One will not always be able to locate the shaping sensibility
in its merely formal precipitate. Such that everything would be dilettantish which did not push outward, and did not feel itself so completely
satisfied within the technical element; such that vision can only attain
full growth and active reality in the extratechnical element. Nothing
could be more false, incidental and art-historically restrictive; it is equally
alien to everyone who must testify, no farther from the child who draws,
the peasant who whittles, than from the great artist. Indeed one can find
in Lukács' *Soul and Form* the complete expression of this almost purely

formal-objectivist attitude, with a Neoclassical emphasis, but there it comes from an approach that keeps to the works and forms, though ultimately intending them only ironically, indirectly, essayistically, using them as the opportunity for the most esoteric, most singularly exquisite kind of profundity. A procedure which in some instances can doubtless be extraordinarily fruitful, but which as a whole, as the method within a system, as the divination of the work's homeland on the basis of a thorough formal analysis, finally overburdens the insignificant detail, cannot establish the inner limits of the cryptographic formal correlation without arbitrariness, and perpetuates the labored, inauthentic, Flaubertian element in the modern, merely stylistic, alienated compulsion to produce. One possesses a fully particular artistic "what" far more by who one is than by how one does it, apart from the fact that the austere, purely technical atelier definition is incapable of doing justice to the need, the exuberance of the artistic will and its object. Comic, ugly, beautiful, significant—all these are the short feelers and exclamations of a still superficial listenership. Green with red, free leg and engaged leg, *contrapposto*, cross-relations and Neapolitan sixths—these are likewise short-winded things, formulae, which certainly have a basic role, though not for long, as the prerequisites of communication, as the pedagogical *horos* of the fundamentally unconcluded artwork: trees that indicate the forest without being the forest, and coincide at best as auxiliary constructions with the forest's spirit, with the meaning [*Gehalt*] of the sphere of technique, which is already artistic just as content [*Inhalt*]. One should also not believe that one can give each particular mode of representation its respective, self-evident background by serving it up historically; by regarding the forms of the novel, the dialogue or the other expedients of talent as fixed onto a revolving firmament of intelligence within the philosophy of history, where particular forms of expression then just come and go; in sum, by reinterpreting the history of the artistic whos and their whats into a history of medieval-realist hows. At issue here are not color, stone, and language as the materials, already distracting enough, but rather precisely the shaping, the concerns of meticulousness, the questions of the operative, the communicative impulse, all of which can interpose themselves, even for the artist himself, before the perspective on the sole consideration, the *sphere of meaning*. The artist, however, need not always be so purely technical as such that his experiences have to enter into an unshakable alliance with the techniques of the work's specific art form in order just to attain that prestabilized harmony between vision, form, and a materiality first achieved in form.

Listeners already get home by a different route. Precisely from here and from now on, artistry may again appear as a displaced prophetic gift. Of course what has not been said does not exist, but it is the will, the content, that commands the means. And these days it seems that one no longer so rigorously, so technically needs to keep at a remove from what is said in order to hear it as a statement. Individually, collectively, then, it has again become possible for the most modern artist—even without our being surrounded by the rainbows and clouds that have already come too close—to grant us an artwork, the essential aspect of the artwork, without a constraining, distancing conception of form. Thus something inexpert can often become strangely profound; no good author, says Jean Paul, ever appears in his shirtsleeves; what we take to be his shirt is his vestment; the means themselves are catalytic, they come to light only as some particular means of realization left to the artist's discretion, without this forming determining the content in the least.[25] Elpore begins to remain Elpore, and to be completely recognized as such, even when she treads too near to the sleeping Prometheus; gradually something begins to glow that is significant to us as such, that other self and that other object that defines the artist and everything appropriate to art, and not a form collecting the beyond into artistic immanence.[26] When the essential will increases, its formalization of its objects of course increases; euphony calls forth many and true images. But here it is beheld *essence* which constructs its own body, and when this body, the form of the realization, the external reality of the work, appears denaturalized or to a high degree abstractive, then this is a retrospective impression, and moreover primarily abstract only in relation to the natural occurrence of the represented object. For in itself the new Expressionistic formulation of essence is just as "naturalistic" and merely descriptive, if not so completely descriptive of astral perfection as the gravestones bearing the name of Horus, the relief at Bel Merodach or the winged bulls of Assyria and of Ezekiel. Here a new directness and absoluteness are at work that possess the kind of architectonics of form that seems to rise up automatically—the solid construction, the Flaubertian labor of equalizing the levels—as a lower objective determination, as the beheld object's foreground-*prius*; but not as though here, as in times of style, the work were just as long as the statement, or, as in astral times, the consummately descriptive formal sign had overwhelmed the imperfectly expressive-descriptive sigillary sign. Rather, wherever any great, personally expressive work appears, it is only the will, the subject and its content, which is ultimately discernible in the means, the forms, the worthless, backgroundless ones; it is the authentic aspect of the abstraction, above the means and also above the reinforcement and the formally inferior object, it is the indicative seal or even the incipiently self-equivalent mystery of the We, the *ideogram*. Only in one way, then, can one speak objectively about form: there, namely, where the formal, constructive, objectivating element is no mediation, but an objective component itself, such as above all in the theatrical effects, in the rhythm, above all too in the various types of counterpoint that determine the shaping subjects as categories of their true particularity [*Sosein*], and generally in all art's temporal or spatially anamnestic problems. Here the shaping subject has truly advanced into a "form," as its own deeper aggregate condition, which accordingly represents the inferior, the so to speak epistemological, the metaphysically solidifying skeletal part of the object-series itself, *of course still separated from actual life, content, and the profundity of the aesthetic sphere of meaning by a leap into self and truth, into the power of the seal and into expression, into the ideogram of revealed inwardness, of the figure of life, of humanity.* It is the strange power of these times that one can hold the reins seemingly more loosely, or to be exact, more unconsciously, and yet steer toward our true home. Our artists are so astonishingly barbarous that when there is an inner necessity, the purely painterly element for example can arbitrarily be disregarded or become purely musical, and other similar signs of "decadence," scandalous from a meticulous standpoint, just as earlier, when one began to make plaster castings and collect ornamental trivia, one was likely to reproach this or that old artifact for lack of "purity of style." This is the kind of boldness being attempted here, not at all like the *Sturm und Drang* (it is far too troubled for that, takes far too little pleasure in its mere surplus of strength, feels much too severe a responsibility toward the object)—that utmost directness that up to now only and precisely the very greatest stylists, penitent and clairvoyant, carried out in their mature work: to be subjective, supraformal, the description of essence. Hence the "work" also is transitional; our eyes have grown stronger, one no longer needs the work's salutary attenuations or various deflections to disperse the superliminal stimuli to transcendence onto a large surface so that they will not all suddenly push toward us, or however else one prefers to make out of artistic weakness an Olympian pedagogy in accordance with the Classicist idolatry of form. In other words a new, more direct, archetypal emphasis on having something to say is emerging, which hardly fears the charge of dilettantism, indeed in which the dilettantish, the *a priori* dilettantish, the pure "content-aesthetic" element—insofar as the actual incompetence of individual wretchedness, of the negative kind of expression, is held at a distance—attains a metaphysical degree: the degree of the elimination of indulgence, the achievement of the work's statement of the self, a moral nominalism against any indirection that has become independent, a descriptive "naturalism" or, better, an Expressionistic realism of the "subject"; attains, finally, the power of proclamation, or how it was and how it could have, should have been; the dignity of knowledge, of the specific knowledge of an "aesthetic" reality and of its sphere's utopian-potential idea-imperative.

Precisely for this reason, then, art can from now on appear as a displaced prophetic gift again. How far everything in art's first heyday was from the intention to display and to have a beautiful effect: it was forbidden to approach the masks out of season; indeed, there were idols that could only be venerated in a completely darkened room, which realized a different world than our visual world. The primitive as well as the Gothic artistic volition, like all of the music, has not the least in common with the volition toward art as a deliberate effective concept, as a slight, insubstantial stylistic excerpt from a world without disappointment. The issue for such art, for all great art, is absolutely not any of the objective or normative formal problems of aesthetic "pleasure," which are the least important things in the world, insofar as the concept of *aisthesis* already means not an emotionalized sensation, but absolutely the same as perception, phenomenology, adequate realization. The issue, every time, is the content-"what" of what is upper-case Human, and of the pure ground, held open but still mysterious.

Today the last things are no longer given as easily to listeners as in the blessed times when God was near, but at least artists are again letting their arrows, their slower arrows of expression, fly in the esoteric direction, and just as art is the lowest level to which the sacred can decline, the colorfully obscured clairsentience of Expressionist art, with its utopian orientation to the content, to the object, may conversely be admired as the most immediate space before the dwelling of a coming *parousia*.[27] But it should be said in conclusion that the artist, even the one who in art would most eruptively preach, recognize, be contentual, always remains within the phenomenal realm. The aesthetic depictions available here and there are exciting, but for the present they are only virtually gleaming glass paintings, which point to human beings, point them further, but then finally dismiss them. And so this is the criterion of purely *aesthetic* illumination, considered in terms of its ultimate categories: *how could things be consummated, without apocalyptically ceasing to be*; how could everything and everyone be pushed to his upper limit, toward the leap; how could they be represented—still, in other words, mirrored, even if with Expressionistic brevity and directness, and yet, what above that is most important, perfectly illuminated—as long as the inner-higher light is still hidden, and the leap of its utterly differently transformative commitment of Jesus' heart into things, into human beings, and into the world, is still pending. Where this final aesthetic effort does not flag, and thus block us, blind us, turn heathenishly immanent, the great artwork becomes a dim reflection, a star of anticipation and a song of solace on the way home through the dark; and yet precisely just distance, shining, reflection, explicit contradiction to any consummation on this earth, unable already to make the needy human being himself at home in the so despairingly anticipated glory. Earlier, when we were closer—that is, before our eyes sealed up, before there were modern styles, stylizations —we had winged bulls, upper column placings, the mystery of the transept, legends, the transcendent connections of *epopoeia*, divine life itself according to its bright side it turned toward the world, all in our artistic-descriptive field of vision: *the same thing which should now—but differently, more gloomy, hazy and crepuscular, glowing more warmly, beyond a defunct secular and divine logic, as the incipient mystery of the We and of the ground*—take shape as the Dostoevskyan and Strindbergian sphere of a pure soul-reality, a purely moral "transcendence" of encounters, of the vaults and panoramas of something which is human suprasocially as well. By its colors, by its colorful reflection we also possess this life, this sermon; but if one gazes into the hidden sun itself, then that is no longer art, a still intramundanely virtual perfection, but rather it's me, an inner, image-less, indeed quite properly work-less God-seeking, in which what is objective so little still appears as auxiliary construction that only the rebirth, the appointment of the heart as work, may still appear.[28] This would then be—beyond all art—the morality and metaphysics of inwardness and its world, a new medium-less *standing-with-oneself-in-existence* of subjectivity and its non-world, that clearly divides the immanence of the artistic object from the transcendence of such a direct or religious object.

The Philosophical Theory of Music

Nevertheless this also does not mean that any discussion of music must end in disaster just when it tries to go deeper. One need not be afraid of slipping; the good listener has his definite, still artistic place. The only thing is to find a point from which one can cast a gaze into the utopian realms of significance seen through the work's windows, so to speak. The question here of course remains whether one even considers such an expansion necessary, even one carried out only predicatively. For the arc of a great work, in purely aesthetic terms, is completely self-contained, or rather—a closer inspection leaves no doubt—possesses in its artistic formal totality as well as its sigillary totality itself the aesthetically sufficient keystone, without leaving more than immanent room for a transcending interpretive construction. But then we stand here, and the work stands there; it is an easy thing for us to move away from the work again, as much as we may have been temporarily captivated, in order to be free for new contexts lying below or above it, and so it ought to be permitted to a sensibility that still lets nothing stabilize in itself, to which systematization in any sphere means misery, to consider even musical constructions as mere fixed wayfarings, and to trace them as mere *vestigia anabaseos* until they finally also appear in the circle dance of the philosophy of history's constellations, indeed of the entire world-process.

It is not hard to push ahead into this other way of listening. Of course externally nothing is given at first but desire, except perhaps presentiment. Even the latter remains for the most part appreciative, passive, leisurely, and thus still completely lost in the void. It already contains all depth, but on this level, as the *initial* mere indulgence in sound, is as yet unusable, is false, random, arbitrary. For only what is shaped can appear, which after all we have said is not to demand that the shutters be kept closed in order just to trace only the faint, circumscribed light shining through the cracks. Nonetheless, what operates behind it, full daylight, also contains "form" or has form within itself at least as a lower objective determination, and by this determination there reappear the concepts of the individual composers, of the composers as concepts. Here the creator and his "what" act as the respective form: not randomly, as it just happens to be; rather, it is only there within a historical-periodic system of the objects and spheres of musical individuality. Here the sound acts above all as a *means* for expressing oneself, as a medium that must be broken but nonetheless conveys us buoyantly. Here harmony additionally acts as *formula*, and above all—already making its way completely into the personally meaningful—the particular rhythmicization, the graceful, consistent, dramatic counterpoint, acts as the *form of technique*, the *type*, the *sigillary character* of great composers. Rhythm and the three aforementioned types of counterpoint are already *lower* objective determinations in themselves, and thus determine precisely that historical-periodic system of the ascending objects and spheres of musical individuality appearing in the great composers up to now. But these forms are of course only *lower* objective determinations, and the musical object which must truly be brought out has not yet been accomplished. Just as the most intricate fabric does not yet write poetry, which after all it is not supposed to do; just as dramatic-symphonic movement only posits a space of a very general readiness into which the poetically executed musical drama can then be "arbitrarily" inserted: in the same way, between the most transcendable species and the final sigillary character of great composers, or even the final object, the ideogram of utopian music generally, there yawns an empty, dangerous abyss to hinder the crossing. It is not possible—even in the theoretically most illuminated, philosophically defined rhythm, counterpoint—to arrive directly at what is present to the weeping, shaken, inwardly torn, praying listener as a presentiment; to put it differently, without this finding-out-something-particular-about-oneself, this feeling-oneself-expressed, this human overtaking of theory—as we can only discuss it at the end of this investigation, as the interpolation of a new subject of course most profoundly akin to the composer, and this subject's new, historico-philosophically metaphysical speech-vision—every transcendent typological correlation to the *apeiron* stands idle. Hence on this *longer musical-historical stage* of presentiment, sound once again appears as the one experience that was meant, as the explosive "Aha!" when the fog clears; the sound, the heard, used, perceived, clearly heard sound, the sound sung by human beings, the sound that carries them; no longer as a means, certainly no longer as astral shrine, but certainly as the highest aura of receptivity, as the ultimate material of the soul, of the kernel, of latency, of the self-symbol, to which music as such is applied; as the *highest phenomenal* of musical expression and ideogram, of the musical spirit realm. Hence where poetry disturbs the musical circles, it can genuinely expand interpretation, can anamnestically draw it in on the archetypal map, far beyond mere commentary.[29] "Our very deeds, and not our sufferings only / Restrict the progress of our lives,"[30] certainly, but there is still another lifeblood operating here—a propulsive concept of the artistic character, the "final" artist as the metaphysician of art, in other words as the final guardian of the artistic object, as the creator of a *Gesamtkunstwerk* of a *contentual* nature—in the homogeneous medium of the speculative concept. There is consequently an automatically creative aesthetics, a not only annotative but spontaneous, speculative aesthetics, and only here, in its interpretation, will "absolute" music be established, only here will music's utopianly expanding castle be revealed.

MEANS, FORMULAE, FORMS, AND PHENOMENALS OF
TRANSCENDENT MUSIC THEORY

The Note As a Means

So nothing here may sound by itself, then.

Only in us can it blossom and awaken. The sound is intensified by us, qualitatively colored and at once dispersed. We alone are the ones who raise it up, even more: who make it define and animate itself with our life. Of course it is no accident that just this tender, transparent body is chosen. As surely as intoxication is not in the wine but in the soul, just as perceptibly is there something in the natural sound that floats and speaks toward the other side, and this makes it alone suitable as musical material. But, to mention only the perfect fifth: all of this is only beautiful because it was chosen, because it occasions further, synthetic relationships, and only in the breach with these direct inclinations can a human being sing.

Harmonic Theory As Formula

So what counts is to sense oneself all the way through.

Whoever just listens, and he might be very moved at the time, does not even notice anything about how the notes are combined, and it would mean nothing to him to know. Certainly the artist requires dexterity, except on holidays. It is more than mere dexterity, and much that appears inadvertent derives from extremely cool deliberation working with proven methods. That is why it tends to show off so energetically, and why composers by tradition usually divide into teachers and students, with all the critical assurance that formulaic language and technical expertise bestow by rights. Already for this reason one cannot speak theoretically without acknowledging the theory developed by the composers themselves. Could one not here hope that the mind where this technical and logical information comes together might already just objectively, through the mutual attraction of the two domains, discover something incredible? In fact in philosophical circles there seems to be a certain, unavoidable kind of raising of the eyebrows, even a sort of aspiration to continue thinking linearly (perhaps still deriving from the old faith in mathematical precision) as soon as concepts such as the third or the Neapolitan 6th or the cross-relation, in fact the entire, already in itself intellectually so abstract-seeming figure of harmonic theory, enters the field of view. And not only Franz Grillparzer's poor minstrel; Hoffmann's Kapellmeister Kreisler also has moments just like the young Wagner's, when the numerical relationships within music, to say nothing of the mystically intensified rules of counterpoint, nature's Sanskrit, in themselves provoke a shudder. And yet as soon as Kreisler, the Kreisler who everywhere burrows into infinitude, stands before the total, resounding musical reality, he is displaced from the formal margin to the real center: the scaffolding has long collapsed, he coincides again with the deeply moved layperson, the *reality* of modulation is the miracle itself, which lives in the inner spirit. Even so, we possess a large number of excellent books on theory, and if in the pages to follow we refer to Schönberg's book to settle the practical issue, that is not—however agreeable we may find this—because a creative composer wrote it, who only aspired to a descriptive and not a natural system, but rather for the more profound reason that it is typical that here precisely the most accomplished methodologist is concerned that form not become such an end in itself that it excludes its object.

~

Whoever can, may compose as he pleases. Here everything breaks up powerfully for someone who inwardly must. For him, however, if he knows technically what he is doing and personally what he can leave aside, absolutely nothing can still be ugly, impermissible or dissonant. He may compose in free, floating divisions of time; indeed, he may write any sonority, even if it seems to have absolutely no harmonic derivation and can be justified only through the voice leading. Thus one can no longer even speak of nonharmonic notes. Every sonority is possible, and may for that reason alone, as purely a sonority, be posited as harmony.

A discord exists somehow independently as little as does a *key*. It seems impossible to exclude it from the score, to say nothing at all of the fact that the entire dominant effect has been shaped and comprehended only on the basis of a maintained tonality. Nonetheless Schönberg, for example, indicated no key signature for the last movement of his F# minor Quartet, although according to its main theme it belongs to f# major, even if the most expressive constructions in it, the altered quartal chords, are liberated from every mode, from every *tonality*. The note from which it all emanates can hover quietly in the air, after all. Instead of concluding the piece on the same note, there is still the possibility, as Schönberg writes, of indicating the relationship more conspicuously one time and blurring it the next. What thus results is a kind of infinite harmony that no longer needs to announce the departure and destination points every time, and even less may fear journeys of discovery in the broad fields of the tonal vacuum. Anyway, it has been the case for a long time now that it is no longer the cadences that govern the harmonic developments of a piece. So it is also unnecessary to set up other keys in order to come to the aid of a wavering tonality, in other words to erect new, subordinate, here and there certainly surprisingly useful means such as perhaps the exotic whole-tone scale, into a system. There is nothing for which the chromatic scale would not suffice, as soon as one simply gives up sanctioning every possible deviation from the old scale and then at the end nonetheless upholding the cliché of the sovereignty of tonality. If this rule is to be achieved, then all leading tones must stay out if they cannot be tied, and above all certain proportions must be observed within the modulations, as Classical composers actually did. But one simply cannot act free, and exploit every possibility of such a condition, while not wanting to face the actual dangers and obligations of being free. In Schönberg's neat turn of phrase, it really appears as a disturbing asymmetry when the relationship to a root is maintained after the harmonic possibilities of the augmented triad and above all of vagrant chords are applied not just occasionally but continuously, under the pressure of the imperative of continuous expression, which ought to stand above the axioms of tonality. The song then concludes with "new," "infinite," or "unfulfilled"; it travels without arriving, the meaning is in the wayfaring, and the formerly operative center, the root, or the stationary voice, the sustained pedal or even just its ideationally perceived requirement, which only becomes real again in the reprise, has disappeared with the fluctuation or suspension of tonality. Instead there are many groups of tonics; indeed every chord can achieve harmonic definition through its own tonic; there are intermittent tonal relationships or just shifting centers; and the sense of a totality that permits a work to be concluded, in order to necessarily lead it back from the condition of ideal infinity to real finitude, need be no harmonically necessary termination, even if living form, like artistic form, previously did not permit the inner limit of the work, as the proper shape of its form, to be dictated to it except from out of itself, out of its own disposition, growth and *a priori*. Thus the limiting element here must be derived from something other than the tonic of the whole, and there is no doubt that this something can absolutely not be a premature interruption, since it pushes toward no finitely attainable target, but rather attains its high point and potential full stop in the strongest, most genuine expression of an inner power, boundlessness, infinitude, in other words in a tonic now explicable only in rhythmic and certainly not in harmonic terms. Anyway, when Schönberg requires a deeper substantiation, the harmonic almost always becomes the contrapuntal. What may arise almost by itself, unsought as a chord, although constantly dispersed as such into the parts, can simply not be harmonically justified or grounded. If for example one has two voices in C major move in contrary over a stationary harmony of c-e-g, an abundance of the most splendid and interesting dissonances will occur, without these sudden and fantastic chordal riches having any source but the counterpoint of the simplest finger exercises. Even there, however, anything can stand for anything else, and so, however self-evident a precondition contrapuntal diligence may remain at least technically, only the whole human being, only the artist's moral sense may finally really decide if some harmonic-contrapuntally baffling spot indicates that a "mistake" was made, or if this is some pointless rumination, or if one just has to accept some unknown rule, that is, a unique one, necessary only here, a likeness of a particular inner animation, fullness and sonorous density, in itself empty and nontransferable. It would be equally beside the point to want to find a particularly intelligible cause of the empty combinatorial wealth, of the harmony's basically endless chordal permutations, within the contrapuntality, the wayfaring of the counterpoint.

Our definitive emphasis on the inner necessity that explodes, besides dissonance and tonality, all of *harmony's independent expressive correlations*, thus proves itself in the most favorable way. The simpler a song's mood, of course, the more clearly its sad or happy feature can be displayed. Thus it always is with Zelter, but never when Schubert sets his bitter "Heiden-röslein" in a major key. For what kinds of feelings are these that can so readily be identified as displeasure in the darker minor mode and as plea-sure in the brighter major, or, as Schubert asks: can there even be "happy" music? And what terrible superficiality does this monochrome technique make of pain and pleasure and of the still deeper thing that is neither the one nor the other, but is just what Shakespeare praises so very ambiva-lently in music, "moody food of us that trade in love"? Even before now the simple duality of major and minor, registering emotionally as softness or brilliance, and with its basis in the lesser or greater blending of the har-monics, perhaps also in the minor triad's characteristic of developing downward, as the drop from a higher root note into the depth—already before now, in other words, this classification by mood had lost its mean-ing in numerous works. Perhaps no one would even guess that the Ger-man "Moll" and "Dur" meant sorrow and joy respectively if their ono-matopoeic names did not derive from the rounded or angular shapes of their customary symbols (the German "b" and "h") as the *B-molle* and *B-durum* of medieval musical notation. Thus Bach is already very often completely indifferent to the mood supposedly expressed by a mode; in-deed in his music one now and then finds minor used for determination, and major, particularly when the third predominates, for kindness or melancholy. What is more, just as the seven former Church modes have dissolved, so will the two remaining scales, major and minor, someday perhaps find their dissolution in the chromatic scale's affinity for leading tones. Already the augmented triad beginning on the third degree of the minor scale cannot still be perpetuated as emotionally a minor chord. Not only may it arbitrarily be carried through in either major or minor, but also possesses, like those chords Schönberg called "vagrant"—that is, para-tonal, roaming at the borders of the key—a not at all unequivocal alloca-tion to an emotional character incarnated in major or minor. One does find the augmented triad in Hugo Wolf, as well as in Puccini, as the chord of brooding, but Wagner's completely contrasting applications of this chord in the *Schlaf* motif and then as an arpeggio in the cry of the Val-kyries or chordally in the Nothung motif make one take notice. It appears that an extensive arbitrariness attaches to the character-structure of just this important and for a more modern, expressive harmony so very typi-cal chord, and with respect to major and minor a certain hermaphroditism. It is therefore entirely correct when Schönberg, there where a chord sounds very expressive, also wants to see the cause of this expressivity only in the novelty. That is why for example the brilliant and harsh diminished seventh chord, which was once new, provided the effect of novelty, and so in the Classical period could stand for agony, anger, excitement, and every other strong feeling, has, now that its radicality has vanished, sunk irretrievably into mere light music as the sentimental expression of sentimental matters. Therefore the new chord is only then written when what matters to the composer is to express something new and incredible, which moves him. This can be a new chord, too, but Schönberg as well believes that the unaccustomed chord is only assigned to a hazardous post in order to accomplish the extraordinary, in order to say, in a new way, what is new, namely a new human being, in other words in order that the new sonority can help a new emotional world achieve symbolic expression. It is just as impossible to comprehend the novelty in the effect, in a chord's receptive allocation, but in the fact that it is unusual, and for that reason already, or rather only, qualified to express even the most excited and powerful feeling, as it is unthinkable to deduce, as functionally ulterior or constitutive, the necessity of the choice, the formal-causal allocation, that is, the harmonic-expressive equivalence of such a chord, outside of this usage, its merely symbolic usage. What could it be, then, this strange identity between the inner and the tonal totality of pulsions, this coincidence of expressive truth and structural truth, this "natural" system of chordal physics moderated or permitted by psychology, if not the unwavering continuation of a "tonal" instinct, that is, an instinct borrowed from us, a borrowed sonic vitality that can simply be no further conventionally marked out by a harmonic *logic of expression*?

The selection is certainly trained by the discipline and order of traditional procedures. But all that remains afterward as the source of order are the expressive imperatives of genius, its strength, its flowering and truthfulness, in both the compositional and the object-theoretical sense. Then every harmonic system becomes ultimately irrelevant; what seemed at first like nothing but proscriptions and laws becomes merely an obstacle to the untalented and a training for the talented, who soon enough will have to decide for themselves how far they may go and what the nature of the subjectively irrational element shall be that may set itself above and beyond bar lines, dissonance, harmony and tonality. That someone is something, might truly need this or that form, have this unmistakable primordial color and personal aura about him; that in terms of the philosophy of history someone might be overdue as that person who he is: basically this remains the only essential reason we can give for distinguishing Kaulbach from Michelangelo or Bungert from Wagner, for even distinguishing the copy from the original, and not the minor differences of some mere regulatory system of the conciliatory, pedagogical sort, which would actually make it impossible to dismiss Kaulbach through concepts such as "decorative tableaux" or "historical painting" without also seeming to apply to and condemn Michelangelo as well. The mere, currently most suitable formula is not even necessarily personally meaningful; it is certainly no suprapersonal cipher, and even if it were, it would be valid only in an epochally restricted way, and not in the way that what has been up to now the most expressively suitable—in other words historical tradition, irrespective of its former expressive-symbolic connectedness and necessity—could become theory, a harmonic object-correlation that disregards the imperative of choice.

Rhythmic Relationships As Form

In contrast, the beat seems not entirely free of reflection.

It is not only that we find our way within it as we breathe. This interior emptiness could be valid at most for the soothing, fastidious, elevated emotional value of the verse. Rather, there is palpably a deeper kind of life operating in musical time. Not only that it progresses differently than the external time in which it takes place, but that it also readily seems mobile, expansive, historical.

So in a particular part of the bar, perhaps, a sharply struck drumbeat comes due. That it does not arrive, or arrives at some other point, can destroy the character of the whole. A little goes a long way here: one can slow the simplest popular ditty to the pace of a hymn, or, conversely, transform Wagner's Pilgrim's Chorus into an unspeakably vulgar waltz merely by accelerating the tempo, indeed even suggest its affinity to some old collegiate drinking song. Or one attempts to disregard what is written above the staff and perhaps move the 21st measure of Beethoven's D minor Sonata to the beginning, thus striking out the "now" and "finally" of this measure, the entire superbly situated triumph that the tonic, D minor, achieves there. Then it will be clear how, particularly in Beethoven, everything depends on suspense, on the occurrence of things at the proper time.

It can certainly more often confuse than clarify, this power to make pulses throb audibly. From this vantage one can understand Wagner's hatred for rhythm, which of course refers to something other than the simple Italian sort of rhythm: rhythm, to reconcile us with the dream, seems to extend a helping hand to us as mere visual beings; composers, by dividing and phrasing, rhythmically ordering the notes, come into contact with the visible, plastic world. Into the simple brightening, darkening, and shifting, into the magical flow of the tonal structures cut the bar lines, and a resemblance to the way in which the movements of visible bodies intelligible reveal themselves to our observation. The outward gesture that was defined through expressively alternating, regular movements in dance consequently seems to be for music what bodies are for light, which would not be visible without diffraction just as music would not be perceptible without rhythm, without the coincidence of plasticity with harmony. In other words, according to Wagner, it is the most exterior aspect of sound which here faces the world, which in the consistent development of this, its exteriority, requires opera's lavish spectacle, while its interior opens up as the immediate dream-image of essence at rest, freed from its rhythmicality's phenomenality and correlativity. That would also mean that temporality can indeed play a pedagogical role by clarifying individual scenes, but that just as the *Ring* leads us into the coarse, the broad, the low, and the visible, while Palestrina and the chorale style indicate a change of meter almost only by a slight change in the harmonic ground color, so also would truly ontological music as a whole be compelled, like the early Christians, to banish rhythm from its realm. We cannot entirely agree, however much these objections apply to much vacuous structuring, to a certain common, of course not only temporal, corporeal vanity about quartets, as well as to much of the distraction and interference by Dionysian dance rhythms in Wagner himself. We need no longer necessarily curse temporality if we consecrate it, moreover, and not only because Beethoven and the syncope already have occurred, and the music for *Tristan* in particular, this surging, this utter inconceivability, possesses extreme temporal structuring and rhythmic cultivation. Rather we are moving toward a working method, philosophically as well, to which time signifies something other than absolute mundanity, than the mere course of this world, than merely penultimate, still dramatic action, precisely insofar as the essence wandering with us, through us, no longer "rests," and fixity is no longer the sole theological state. Thus in this new momentum, in an intuitive rubato schooled ever more deeply in Beethoven and Wagner, in a mysteriously animated and syncopated adagio as the organically abstract rhythm, the soul, precisely, can count itself more deeply, without any concession to plasticity or heathen biologism. There are already cases now where—as in the jerky movement peculiar to the Priest's adagio in the *Magic Flute*, Tristan's awakening, Parsifal's homecoming and the mystical midday, but foremost the entire prelude to the second part of Mahler's Eighth Symphony—where some correspondence to an occult tempo, to the oddly dotted rhythms of an occult advance or ascent seems to appear. There usually the second music sounds, that different way of sounding, the mysterious breath, music's mysterious atmosphere, spontaneously vibrating and filled with the other side like the air in Tintoretto's *Last Supper*. But not only here, rather where the whole progress of a movement is concerned—its deep-seated, as yet barely discovered *relationship to the rhythmic tonic as such*—there above all the temporal shaping becomes substantial: no formula, but a form, no crutch on a naturalistic basis and no mere trivial corporeal beauty, but the cipher of a spiritual action that happens essentially inside, in the object-domain of music itself.

The rhythmic tonic is superior to any harmony precisely in Beethoven; it relieves it of its duties, and with the progressive demolition of tonality it is ever more destined for victory: how else should one even now be able to understand Beethoven without this music within music? He moves about restlessly, he relinquishes in order to gather energy, he compresses quietly and imperceptibly in order to ignite more terribly later. He leads, pulls, sends back and forth; he treats the little melodic structures like lifeless entities; he sees masses of music before and below him, this colossal strategist of time, from which he selects the ones most suited to his intentions. Whole groups of notes follow one another like a single lean, economical, increasingly tense succession of generations: and then, in the "now," in one single, rhythmic-dominantly overblessed measure of genius, the flash of extravagance happens, and the gigantic masses spill out. By doing this, by composing not themes but rather an entire movement, an entire sonata, Beethoven lets the variations in our energy play along, impels time into the previously tranquil counterpoint, and by means of this dramatic form creates the image of a story where not only the inmost stages of our life reappear in succession, but the previously so ghostly reality of time itself automatically raises its head as well. If temporality still happens intermittently, as in a novel—highly important, but to become visible only through the hero, through his age, his disillusionment, maturation, whatever—then the sonata packs time together as though it were something discrete, and lets the enigmatic work order itself be heard. There is a glowing and pounding within; there is an anonymous calling, waiting, knocking, entering, arriving, hesitating, an exuberant simultaneity here that otherwise appears onstage only during the most concise of all dramas; the arrival in particular, however, is the primordial secret of Beethoven's music, and it is essentially a rhythmic secret. The light and the heavy count, the phrasing's groupings, half-subjects and periods are a discrete fluid substance here: each thing in a Beethoven sonata has its time, a verifiable inalterability appropriate to its placement in the moment, its gravity and dignity, its birth and appearance in the metaphysical timetable, and the apparently subjective schema of this time is not only simple coherence or mere, cunning, formulaic dramaturgy, but rather, since every effect originally has a metaphysical background, and at the same time sigillary allegory, the most objective rhythm and the inmost, realest effective schema of our Luciferan character. Here is flame, and the most mysterious stroke of the clock: the first movement pushes dramatically beyond, the second rests within itself, in the lyrical fullness of its immediate reconciliation, the third movement, above all the coda, opens the inner door, the march as secret chorale, and makes its late, somber, ecstatic confession—a finalmost syllogism of the discovery of the soul.

∽

So the beat is actually and fortuitously full of objective-metapsychic reflections and correlations.

We are the wanderers; it is our coming and going that occurs within things. Or rather, the trip has already begun materially, and we live within this time, physically and organically, and either we just barely keep up or as creative beings we overtake time, leading, plunging into what has not yet really occurred. There is therefore a single tendency, everywhere most profoundly related if not identical, that structurally connects precisely the symphonically framed course of events and the remaining historical-productive course of events. For in both cases the process moves out into the distance, and the conclusion can only come from within, can come in absolutely no other way than out of the process, and as its goal. In both, time is completely the persistence of "then" within "now," in other words conservation, persistence, development, inheritance, preparation and collection, until something can be fulfilled, and thus musical-historical time—purified, noticed, charged with purpose, musical-historical, motivated by Reason and Providence—or rhythm, as the music within music and as the logical element in the cosmos, achieves its effect. So occurrence, with its own power of shaping and of overview, also enters into a new spatiality, in order thus to remake an accidental succession into the comprehended juxtaposition of a "developed" inventory—*musically* in the chordal-contrapuntal spatial substrate of a fugue or an entire symphony; *philosophically* in the luminous, qualitatively discontinuous historical space of a self-contained epoch, or of the entirety of world history—just as soon as its totality, notwithstanding the decrescendo of contemporaneity unfurling again at its respective finale, can resonate with enough integrity and utopian commitment. Ultimately, in the one as in the other, active time presses toward an unknown goal, and it is more than likely that in more particular areas of music the same problem of the goal arises objectively that animates the total process of the symphony of history, or more deeply: of that philosophy of history that concerns the ethics of inwardness. The great composers' migration into a spiritual dwelling—into the region of individuality that was born to them, into the moment of integral self-being—the moment imbued, arrested, and broken open to become itself, resounding and deferred to the most private sanctum [*Stube*], as the thing-in-itself of music as well—is itself nothing but the passage of music's time into its space, and as such a conversion of its specific temporal form into its specific spatial form; accordingly, in the following, the final spirit of fugal and sonata rhythm still lying above the actual tempo, as the spirit of hierarchies—to have subject—can then be correlated to transcendent counterpoint.

Bach's and Beethoven's Counterpointing As Form and Incipient Ideogram

For if we do not go along, absolutely no note moves.

Of course it can take a few short steps on its own. But these are soon concluded, the descending fifth at once brings everything back to consonant repose. Only the scale leads on, and it is already a purely human construct.

Now of course nothing is easier than to have a melodic idea within a scale. Nearly every strong beat, even a train's pounding wheels and noises already induce one. It is becoming much rarer to come upon a *propulsive*, melismatic idea, and just as the first few lessons make one sing worse, the expansion of this idea in several voices—which by no means need be "already" fugal, but may also content itself with chamber-musical subtlety—at first damps every melismatic splendor, in order to destroy the false and thereby set the genuine kind properly on fire.

Now does this beginning—originating with us, powerfully weaving itself together with us—have depth? Here something other than the notes playing so freely, linearly, and songfully emerges. The *melos* rises up, the theme governs: the development, the creative Beethovenian eruption above the theme, where the latter becomes a mere opportunity and no longer the sole driving force. Thus—insofar as it is not a means, a formula, but a form—the manifold types of *counterpoint* are entrusted with music's final transcendent correlation. It is the counterpoint, harmonically kindled, from whose shaping powers everything springs; counterpoint occurs, and the great event ensues; one can bend the branches and twigs aside, and then one sees from where, out of which undergrowth, the wondrous tree's flowers have assembled themselves into a crown. But if it is not even the case that sulfur, phosphorus and friction explain the flame, how could there ever be a Newton of this grass blade, this highest-order organicity? Even here, the human being who makes music, the essence of Bach or Beethoven that makes use, is still the direct measure of everything and even of the counterpoint, at least the indirectly transcending kind.

Naturally we have still hardly understood the brilliant flow and warmth that resulted. One readily assumes that students will not often be in a position to write a fugue, but one nonetheless concludes their training with it. In other words, the metallic and instrument-rich nineteenth century did not fail to leave some mark on theory. Since its great chordal achievement is right on the surface, we gleaned from it a theory of harmony, which stands above the fugue chronologically and in a certain sense in terms of developmental technique, but which nonetheless, as only the lopsidedly emphasized, specific characteristic of an apparently not very contrapuntal century of music, must yield precedence to the old counterpoint in terms of sphere. What the sonata thus yielded, namely a developmental technique specific to it, nonetheless remains without a theory. It will not suffice to explain things merely harmonically here, for Beethoven will simply not be sworn to his modulatory tactics and skills. And what would it be about the *Apassionata,* indeed even about the fugal overture to *The Consecration of the House*, that could be grasped with a new theory of harmony alongside the old counterpoint? Everything lags precisely in a harmonic sense far behind Bach, who tilled a restricted field infinitely richly, and if Beethoven harmonizes more rhythmically, then the deductive locus of this rhythm lies in a different counterpoint than Bach's. The liberation of the voices as of the dissonances, the new chordal-contrapuntal system of tensions that transports toward great climaxes, the sonata's succession and thematic duality operate, as always, outside of the old *Gradus ad Parnassum*, however much improved. We certainly acknowledge that the sonata has the same rank as the fugue, but while the fugue has since old Fux's time been progressively cheated of its contrapuntal dignity and lawfulness, the theory of the sonata is caught in the anecdotal tone of a mere, extramural theory of form, and the reconstruction of its form, its own, undiscovered counterpoint beginning in the rhythmic harmony, is subject in sonata theory to arbitrariness or, what is almost worse, the tyranny of the program, an almost completely nonmusical logic. Thus the dynamic theory of the sonata lags far behind the rich but static theory of the fugue and the higher *mathesis* of the musical as such that has up until now only been abstracted from it. It is important that one's work be flourishing, filled-in, filigrane; at times it is equally very necessary that one return now and then not just to chamber music but also to the old bilinear style, in order to supply new life to a harmony easily depleted and increasingly problematic in its expressive means. But song, enthusiasm, the spirit of love, the modern storm, the gigantically crashing ocean of Beethoven's music-spirit are more important yet, and if the sonata's voice leading has developed holes, if it fails to cultivate the particular within the exhilaration of the whole, then logically these errors cannot be cured with the old but absolutely only with the sonata's *own, specific* counterpoint.

This counterpoint does not simply set one thing next to another, but articulates the sound and develops it. Development indeed already takes place in the fugue, as the actual elaboration of the parts, whereby the theme simply wanders, however. A part begins, presents its thoughts briefly; a second part commences, imitating the heard theme in the upper fifth or the lower fourth, though with certain considerations for the preservation of the key, most important among them the reciprocal responses of tonic and dominant. During the statement of the reply, the first part continues with a counterpointing usually exploited again later; if the fugue has three voices, the third follows with the first theme again in its initial form, the *dux*, and the fourth then takes up the reply again, the *comes*, such that at the moment when all the parts have introduced themselves with *dux* and *comes*, and the movement has reached its full complement of parts, the first development is also over. There may follow, depending on the theme's copiousness, another four or five developments, all determined by exact rules, which allow the parts new counterpoints every time, richly unfolding intricacies, which according to Riemann is nevertheless only good insofar as at least characteristic motifs recur thereby, until finally the last development appears, the *stretto*, the masterstroke of *Engführung*, that is, the compression of *dux* and *comes* into one another in canon. Of course this simplification is adequate only *ad hoc*, and fails to account even for Bach's simplest expositional scheme, the interpenetration—illustrated in Kurth's excellent analysis of Bach's bilinearity, for example—of linear movements. But nevertheless, here in the fugue there is only entry and no event, only patience but no admixture of impatience; any surprise is as foreign, indeed disadvantageous to the theme, which is intended only to be repeated often, as it is to the uninterrupted progress of the fugue itself. For insofar as the fugue is obligated to take every part into consideration, it maintains a certain mediality or neutrality, which thus gives preference, harmonically and rhythmically, to a certain persistency, lack of caesura, gravity within the motion and the flow. The fugue, however flighty and lavish it might be internally, is as a whole composure, structure, stratification, is, *cum grano salis*: the medieval idea of society, in music: it is also not the breathless discovery of a truth, but like meticulous exposition of dogma. Only in the sonata, then, does the chaotic, lavish and Baroque burst forth externally as well, as an external, an overt Gothic; freedom, personhood, Lucifer reign there, not Jesus with his definitively closed theocracy. Beethoven sounds completely different, then; the willed-through, the thought-through element, the grasp and the attack as such, and his development, rising over a bithematic tension, transports one into the unknown, to the strangely familiar return on another level. Here appears—as we have already so often portrayed it—the powerful first theme, which then encounters a gentler, more songful second theme, as a rule in another, probably related key, both still empty and incomplete. Most often the first entry is repeated, whereupon after the double bar the more airy and incorporeal, tonally more agitated, destructive and then again antithetically generative development section appears (ideas live easily side by side[31]), colorful, with rich modulations, combining fragments of both themes and through their conflict contriving more or less thrilling intensifications, out of which, with the return to the deliberately avoided principal key, the two themes finally reemerge, with the second theme's antagonism to the first eased, however, by the acceptance of or greatest possible approximation to its key. Insofar as precisely Beethoven is the greatest master of this art, and the first movement of the *Eroica* its everlasting model, the question of the sonata's blueprint can be concentrated foremost on the problem of the new, the unsuspected, the productive, of the shattering, self-intersecting, self-elevating succession in the *development section*, which must thus stand for the entire contrapuntal art, which we want to define, of the sonata as such.

In the development everything grows urgent and heated, spirals upwards; the draft becomes violent. The brass rings and crashes, wild units intersect, a fiery exhalation makes them glow. What has been discarded above all here is mere exposition, the purely expository modification of themes assigned at the outset. Only one principle usually persists, that no actually new material need be procured for the construction of the development apart from what had already appeared in the exposition. On the other hand, complete freedom governs the selection itself; the composer has no binding obligation either toward a single theme as an entire, mechanically indivisible construct, nor, certainly, toward all the initial themes. He can restrict himself to mere motivic fragments of the theme; indeed, the guiding thread of tonality may even be abandoned if only the discarded key absolutely reestablishes itself after all the vagaries, the secret and in the end triumphantly issuing functional cause of the entire not only propulsively but dramatically generative harmonization. The theme is predetermined, then, only as that doubly thematic sprouting and germinating that propagates itself and wants to become kinetic. One simply cannot represent things as if this theme, if not already a fixed construct, were at least just stationary tension, containing energy stored up within itself for later. Then of course it would be simple to break away and move out, even if only with the objective that the tensed material should shrink back down to mere melody without any new accruals from precisely the conflict of the themes; nonetheless it certainly often appears that way with Mozart's still inauthentic sonatas, which have not yet come into their own. But neither Beethoven, nor Bruckner, nor even Wagner, who does not even put the theme at the beginning, can be given as evidence for this mere "clock spring" or "tensed bow" theory of thematics, and anyway the theme almost always exists in the finale as the product and not the actual *prius* of the development. Everything depends on what one does with the theme; as little as Jean Paul's cheerful Schoolmaster Wuz, who has no money to buy books, and so, in order to acquire a library, must invent his own from the titles in catalogs—as little as this absolute phenomenologist of thematics thereby gains any experience of the status of contemporary literature, so little is the mere, crude theme—be it ever so well conceived, distinctly outlined and propulsively composed—a nucleus out of which, automatically or in association with other nuclei, the symphony's forest grows. If the purpose is to push forward and inward, then the already deployed *chordal energy* gives better service. And indeed not only in the sense that certain inessential tributaries spring from the inner voices, to issue into a progress that would still happen without them. Rather, there is here a particular formative energy that retunes, reshapes the series of notes, indeed renders it unrecognizable to the lay listener; that leads beneath entirely different skies, and as such, foremost in the development section, most powerfully underlines the wandering, faraway, estranged quality of the action, complete with the longing for the tonal homecoming. Beforehand, precisely, the rhythm in Beethoven had already seized control of the harmony, contributed a powerfully propulsive dynamism, and imposed the latter's *rhythmic cultivation of the tonic.* The respiration of the rhythm no longer permits the voices to distribute themselves only chordally-vertically, let alone homophonically relax, and even less, furthermore, does it allow a unified sensibility—in the sense of the frictionless, fugal self-differentiation of a single thought—to present itself in every voice. Rather, the force that rhythmizes builds downward, draws a polyphonic process to itself, so that it will bring together the vertical segments, so that, notwithstanding its inclination toward filigrane polyphonic activity, it will favor the climaxes that resolve into a single stratum, the passages where the notes join together as the sonorous, supporting columns of the achieved splendor, and precisely by so doing are able to place the adventurous, self-intensifying, self-deciding, dynamic-rhythmic harmony into the service of a new form, a *counterpoint of succession.* Whereby it is precisely *as a whole* that this succession first represents a *horizontalism* again, one that finds itself more fundamentally dependent on the harmony's turning points, transitions, and corners—above all, however, on the rhythmically emphasized stopping points—than on the irresolute voice leading of an architectonic counterpointing. Rhythmic, too, remains the focus on the chord, on its almost continuous, secret collaboration with the rhythmic dominant which it underlines, not just something accidental, contrapuntally secondary; rather, it honestly becomes the *prius* of the compositional process, the chamber-musically rich melodizing ends up in the middle, and so the resplendent white heat of the orchestra, the *prius* of the triumphant, rhythmically expanding harmony, the harmonically underscored rhythm finally even becomes a *prius* not only of the standpoint, but of the cause as well, the cause of the dramatically motivated sonata from Beethoven to Bruckner. Certainly it is *ultimately* not the generative chordal and rhythmic energy that lets the sonata expand. For this might characterize the new element, perhaps even extensively support it, but even the richest possibilities for dominant tension and a rhythmically fueled chordal energy would not be able to deduce out of themselves the breakthroughs of the new element under discussion here, something neither posited nor intuited in the theme. What probably *contributes the decisive moment is the contrast in the disposition of the two themes*; in other words, one can penetrate into the full interior of Luciferan music only by the help of the *bithematic theory* of the sonata, and of that unity wrested from the opposition, which as the "abstract" of the triumph coincides only accidentally, so to speak, with the mere pathmark of the first theme.

Here the notes spiral completely upwards, catch fire, but the violent flight also has a purchase. By pushing forward, escalating, something else emerges, the struggle, or the soul of the correlation being born out of itself. Hence in Beethoven the particular is nothing and life in a context everything: energy, straightforwardness, a contentious departure and a resolution which is no possession but exclusively an attainment. And so in his developments—his truly conflicted developments—Beethoven acknowledges no opportunity for the theme's subtle, calm, solitary self-enrichment, but only the emotionalism of its application as courage, the sweep of the story given in its own harmonic-rhythmic substance. With Beethoven one enters a room and breathes the correlation in, one feels most insistently how everything compresses by turns, and acquires by the variations in barometric pressure, so to speak, a knowledge of the terrain's heights and depths, and even more, one attains a true nautical intuition, even an innate intuition for the atmosphere and its laws. How here, from a quickly forgotten inflection or at an apparent endpoint, a tiny structure begins to grow, as yet almost invisible and insignificant, how it gains strength, enlists allies, takes up a conflict with the old and soon overgrows the entire situation with its powerful limbs, a sovereign fulfillment. It is impetus, fatigue and misfortune, argument and triumph in this music, given in rapid succession or in great strokes, so much so that all the springs and levers that the rhythmic harmony alone seems to have applied become superfluous before this furiously antagonized interior, Beethoven's interior, and the *bithematic fruitfulness* that objectively unfolds by the counterpressure of another. He hangs buds over the lamp so that they will bloom sooner, just as even the familiar adagio-flowers, in this very unvegetal composer, look quite natural between two precipices. Hence Beethoven also does not speak uninhibitedly in the adagio or the *cantabile* of the variations, in his slow, peculiarly laborious, agitatedly languishing movement, but rather far more typically, and alone definably, at the beginning and in the finale, where what matters are the powerful emotions and the tremendous accumulations of that strategy of his that goes right into a human being. The slightness of his themes—almost all positioned as merely the taciturn witnesses of a dynamic state—already forces him to create something new in progress, something other than the mere elaboration, unraveling, or merely architectonically counterpointed variation of the very similar theme. In Bruckner, too, though he exceeds Beethoven in the love, the thoroughness, and inventiveness of the chromatically melismatic element in and above the theme, the intensifying element is neither stored in the theme, nor, as we have seen, in the harmony and rhythm set up after the theme in order to round it: rather, something else, something primordially proper to the symphony, has risen up, that as yet has no name, though it could approximately be designated an evocative succession or a no longer architectonic but rather dramatic counterpoint. It is a mighty, cyclical broadening cultivated over several movements, that stretches the earlier dominant tensions of a few bars into an entire movement, in other words creates an enormous verticalism visible perpendicularly, as much as it transforms the themes driven close behind one another into a succession, and into a juxtaposition, an only retrospectively apprehensible superimposition within the context of an entire destiny in music: into a new, purely conceptual horizontality of the equalization of forces, a *horizontalism first visible in the whole of the dynamic-dramatic unity*, a horizontalism of flashes, vast conflagrations, magical, gigantic words, the magic of the march and inexhaustibly wide triumphal terrains. The symphony is sonority that is only just taking shape; its form is impatience, destruction, escalation, a constant sighting as yet without lingering, absolute vision; its counterpoint does not set *linea contra lineam*, but *complexum contra complexum*, and in this re-membered "historical" horizontalism first provides the simultaneity, the totality, the shape borne upwards.

For this purpose, then, the voices had at first to become lighter, also pause often, in order to acquire and retain momentum. Since then, how-ever, the sound has filled out again, become more songful and filigrane. A difficult new simultaneity: the organically interwoven string playing and the violent symphonic fire with its lethargies, climaxes and the spirit of the future. What Schubert nevertheless initiated, Bruckner and Wag-ner's polyphony have taken further, and Beethoven's now and then thin, unsonorous symphonic writing, dedicated only to the functioning of the whole, melismatically only punctuated, has become identifiable as pre-cisely its least essential and most easily dispensable element. Afterward everything could again become right hand in piano music, or an individ-ual, richly blossoming solo passage within orchestral ensemble playing. It has turned out, to a certain extent, that there is an evidence, a chamber-musical subtlety, a contrapuntal minimum still underlying the fugue that represents only *one* of its potential forms.[32] This subtlety is always just a means, always just a cipherless, meaningless, reflexive formula, just as the entire theory of harmony was, but its different, specific superstructures are objectively determining forms, depending on the rhythm. If one nonetheless makes the fugal application unconditional, if one suppresses everything else that the sonata has brought in terms of succession, of the meaningful competition between the harmonic and the contrapuntal, es-pecially of counterpoint within the dramatic harmony, then the fugue's counterpoint will also become reflexive: as something applicable to every-thing and thus to nothing, not even to itself, as a kind of ingenuity pat-terned on a single one of its concretions and hence become drab, which has lost precisely its transcending, differential valence in the properly as-sembled *system* of counterpoints. If therefore the mobile and yet regular, transparent participation of the voices has returned, if above all Bruckner allows varied melismatic play, and all remaining signs indicate that mu-sic is moving toward an ever higher degree of filigrane, carving, and in-ner power, this does not immediately suggest a copyist's return to the canon, as though Haydn had made a mere housecoat out of Handel's brocade, as though Mozart had backslid from Bach's Baroque into a light Rococo and Beethoven into the stark Empire style, as if, finally, Bruckner's and Wagner's polyphonic symphonic style had broken off the old architectonic counterpoint in favor of a minor handicraft all around their illegitimate dramatizing. Even the other demand, that the *ultimate music* should correlate to the fugue's melismatic-contrapuntal balance as an actualization, in the same way that reality correlates to the corrective, signifies no disregard for the dynamic sonata, no "Onward to the fugue!" Rather: the historical Beethoven is closer to the "real" Bach than the historical Bach is; the gradual convergence to the old music of space is an *acte accessoire*, a fundamental Beethovenian accomplishment, a purely substantial act of grace crowning the perfected system, and so the *total dramatic counterpoint* remains as the place of preparation laid before the ultimate music, before the ontology of music as such.

Then again, here too the ear hears more than the concept can explain. Or to put it differently, one senses everything and knows exactly where one is, but the light that burns in one's heart goes out when it is brought into the intellect. For that reason, then, in order to correctly understand what is contrapuntally intended, a new self must be set *above* the counterpoints as mere indicative form, the self experienced during listening, the individuality of the great composers themselves who apply the different types of counterpoint, as the properly expressive-descriptive seal, indeed, even as the incipiently undistanced ideogram. It is not possible here to explain something purely intellectually and then immediately to correlate it beyond. The game has to follow rules, certainly, but what the needy human being seeks within it, beyond it, does not. Thus for example it is said that Beethoven connects the complementary themes with greater discernment than Mozart. This obviously does not suffice to explain the heard, the most colorful activity: it is not only better when Beethoven errs than when a theorist is right, but also this aspect, wherein Beethoven is strict and wise, ultimately cannot be reflected as strictness and wisdom in terms of counterpoint as form, nor of the second, kaleidoscopic counterpoint of succession. To the same extent, what is formally given—which here also means, always, what is given according to the *form*—should no less fail when the point is to deduce not only the "where from," which could if necessary still be "explained" by means of the contrary friction and purification of the themes, but the "where to," the storm in which this music flies past, the What For and Whereupon of the storm and the nameless struggle, the deeper Why and What of the rewards of victory and all the remaining spiritual forces of this game, so meager and so aimless in terms of the formal cipher. Certainly everything is well ordered, then; there is just as much "mathematics" in here as there is order, and certainly to that extent the types of counterpoint—like the relational, structural and morphological systems of the banquet, the festival, the dance; like strategy, functional theory and systematization generally—can be developed within a taxonomy: the essence of music is thereby as little if not less depleted than logic and categorial theory can give an account of metaphysics. For what one infers from the scaffolding, that is just the provincial stage where Garrick played Hamlet, or, to be exact: Bach and Beethoven, the *great subjects themselves, appear above the form they utilize,* the indicative cipher, the merely lower objective determination; appear as the calling, creating, expressive-descriptive seal, indeed precisely—since here the needle sinks as when near the pole—as incipiently undistanced ideograms, as indicators of the musical metaphysics of inwardness. So little does the mere compositional layout encompass what the deeply moved listener immediately knows and comprehends: music's hall of the mirrors and its guests, this theater of magic and illusion; and without the new, autogenous, metaphysical commitment of a subject who will carry on the essence of Bach or Beethoven, even the more profound forms of counterpoint remain mere, higher orders of mechanization, which can in no way continuously guide us across to the fugue or the sonata *in their ideal state.* It is Bach and Beethoven alone, then, who exist ultimately as transcending counterpoint: Bach and Beethoven alone, and something within our receptivity which can answer Bach and Beethoven as the generative and underivative force, as the living force by virtue of which all this happens, as the sole essential tenet of discontinuous music theory, as the great encounter of a particular subjectivity compelling one into its sphere, and as the individual named Bach or Beethoven that is *prima facie*—in terms of the philosophy of history—so general and canonical that, like Plotinus' angels, it can stand as the operative category of this sole possible transcending counterpoint.

There are four great ways of having counterpoint, then, and all of them *prima facie* possess an objective relationship to ethical facts. Now of course it was precisely music to which we assigned a markedly eccentric role in history. But then music is historically nonconformal for just the reason that its hitherto short, late-beginning history recapitulates the history of our kernel; because, in other words, the history of modern music, as "belated" music as such, is too large for modernity's space, and correspondingly, as was already evident from our presentation of rhythm, this art form's marked historical eccentricity is grounded in the totality of its categorial recapitulation of the philosophy of history and the ethics of inwardness. There are in other words four great hierarchies of having counterpoint, and these possess a constitutive correlation to the metaphysical-ethical spheres of the self, albeit one to be complemented by listening, creating, and not simply demonstrable directly, without a leap. Accordingly Mozart is Greek, offers the small, secular self, gentle, is Attic counterpoint, pagan joy, the soul conscious of itself, the soul of feeling, the stage of the self that takes the form of play. Bach is medieval, offers the small spiritual self, powerfully built, sacrally complete, a ruby glass of music, architectonic counterpoint, filled with love and hope, with the remembering or actual self-soul, with Adam's atoned soul, in other words the self in the shape of faith. Beethoven, Wagner in contrast have broken out; they summon, lead into the *great secular, Luciferan self*, they are seekers, rebels, putting no hope in the given, full of militant presentiments of a higher life, underway on a nameless expedition of discovery, as yet without apparent spoils; they are the masters of dramatic counterpoint and of the assault on the inner, final heaven. But what is still pending, the great spiritual self, the upper stages of being-human, a music completely arrived, will become the art of the future Kingdom; this unimaginable music's actual arrival, crowned by eloquence and victory, would have to condense the counterpoint of succession into the simultaneity of a statement, of the meaning of a sentence understood and then possessed in the same movement, of a *musically* superlegible, prophetic language *a se*, a truly speaking meaning, which is music.

The Note Once Again: Not As a Means, but As a Phenomenal

If we do not go along, then, nothing can continue singing.

That a note has consequences to which one must give in is certainly not based in the note itself. That one has to sound out which way the phrase wants to turn, how long it has a need to descend, and where the point is at which it pulls itself together in order to ascend: all that would not even be possible without an empathetic, powerfully applied effort of will, which remembers, travels alongside, and anticipates just those consequences which are not even present yet in sound.

Certainly the note in itself also leads itself forward and builds itself up by means of related frequencies. In the overtone-rich pealing of bells it excites even distant chords, and in every other struck note at least the three partials of the major triad. In this way the note pushes forward by itself, and a movement inherent in it reaches toward other notes by cadential compulsion. It rejuvenates itself, builds bridges, forms relationships of a fifth, and insofar as it treads the path of octave, fifth, third, in other words the path of the first melody, defines for itself certain points in the harmony to which it is drawn quite independently of our wishes, purely numerically.

But now of course that is a meager sort of singing, which soon fades again. It is the singing of the basses over a sustained fundamental, a rise and fall essentially only of pure fifths; the riches of dissonance are absent. Once the note has arrived back at the tonic, it stays there; the descent of a fifth is too short, the tonic is a pit and its consonance more the tomb than the womb of music. Things would absolutely not even really continue if only the natural chord progression predominated, if there were no new leading tones, scales, suspensions, anticipations, fragments of other directions that were intermittently heard and then immediately, deliberately pursued. The only crucial thing here is to think in terms of the scale, which dissolves the compulsion of the circle of fifths and as such posits the deliberately chordal as well as the freely contrapuntal system. Certainly, then, what is given must be used; one can also concede that the singing teakettle and the gale blowing past the chimney already in themselves let us hear something like a wondrous spectral language. And it likewise remains remarkable that the charm of the simple, triadic, primordial facts have often been used by Marschner, Beethoven and Strauß with great melodic success, but really only as raw material, in itself completely meaningless, extramusical, and in contrast to which the explosive melody of the scale, which has thirteen notes in Siam and seven in Europe, already represents a purely human, unphysiological and certainly unphysical construct.

This is as much as can be accomplished, then, without our hands' fruitful violation of the note and its related frequencies. The note, if it is to become musical, depends absolutely on the blood of the one who takes it up and performs it, like the shades that had to give an account to Odysseus: not of themselves, but of the interrogator. The full extent of all potential partials or of exploded tonality, into which the more modern music again dares to go, is good, and will supply new impulses to the depleted Romantic and even Bachian systems; but every so-called aesthetic acoustics remains barren if it does not serve a new metapsychology of sound. Hence the life in the sound, precisely while it is being played, and its particular determinacy, its intermediary, unbroken material idea, is ultimately never the essential intention. Such a thing has never occurred to even remotely the same extent, at least till now, in visual and plastic art. Precisely because sight, and the optical element as such, does not constitute their body, less of the material element needs to be sacrificed here. Therefore it also reappears more faithfully, as a more remote accompaniment, only diffracted into wood or as a filigree of light through the trees, or adapted in some other quietly natural way. In contrast, precisely because music reaches more closely, deeply, it also adapts the sound more deeply, the totally broken sound, as the stuff of musical essence as such: and must therefore, precisely on the grounds of its deeper correlation to the inspirited sound, to the sound of spirituality, the physical sound, all the more decisively give up everything within the means which still acts only for itself. Thus while Erwin of Steinbach only gives up the stone of the Strasbourg cathedral because he actually thinks in terms of wood (certainly not only for that reason, for *why* does Gothic man still think in terms of wood after building in stone? but precisely by falling back on the at any rate still physical wood, and remaining faithful to it, he avoids the clarity of a decision)—in the Beethoven of the B♭ major Sonata or the *Diabelli Variations*, the prestabilized harmony between experience, material, and the concrete thing-materiality perhaps generated and encountered only within the material is seriously disrupted. The asceticism of Beethoven's piano compositions has often been remarked, and it is characteristic that Hans von Bülow, who so often seeks to mitigate Beethoven's "acoustic atrocities," would describe precisely the later work, the *Variations*, as "the most sublime developments of musical thought and sonorous fantasy." Bekker is not entirely wrong when he remarks that the B♭ major Sonata and the *Diabelli Variations* are in the end unplayable, as though written for an instrument that never existed and never will; that both these works work not with real sound but with incorporeal, purely cerebral tonal abstractions, in order to employ pianistic language only as an approximate, fundamentally preliminary alphabet. As meager as sound may therefore be in terms of worldly fullness, in the power to assimilate the forms of the broad and polymorphous external world, this largely artificial product also remains limited in its deeper ability to step before the throne of the inner, purely inwardly illuminating musical God with the works of its *autonomous* determinacy. One arrives, one carries oneself over, one twists the sound into a mirror and the floor into a ceiling, but only such that everything will live in us and only be stimulated by the sound; that we are in other words far too generous when we kiss the mirror, which really only surprises us with our own image—and surely not such that one had perceived one's own meaningful state of animation by means of the sound [*"empfühlt" am Ton*], through it: as something that might only have awakened through our listening, but now that it has awakened and been condensed by us and enveloped in quality, might exist independently as the *praeludium* of an extrahuman physics or metaphysics of sound.

One cannot expect that, already because the external means have increasingly begun to seal themselves off and die. Certainly, and now we can finally discuss this, it is no accident that it is precisely sound—note: sound utilized by human beings, radically broken up, that has the musical impact—that just this delicate, translucent body should be chosen as the vehicle of musical states. For someone who is deeply moved must close his eyes. He longs for the darkness, for evening; there is a twilight about everything more profound within us. It flees the day; its manifestation as something wafting, mysterious, humming is more favorably disposed toward conditions of poor visibility. Just as ghostly cries and apparitions generally await the dark of night, where our strange, inner dreamwork may go and strike undisturbed.[33] But music's unique magic resolves these depotentiations of sight into a benefit, something more immediate, into a more luminous sense, into the idea of a spirit world, so uncanny in itself. So Shakespeare has a character in the South say: "How sweet the moonlight sleeps upon this bank! / Here will we sit and let the sounds of music / Creep in our ears: soft stillness and the night / Become the touches of sweet harmony."[34] *Yet it remains black magic, music does, and still profoundly near to the Ossianic character, to rain, autumn, and the profound delight of early nightfall, to the gloomy sky and the heavy clouds, to fog and to heroes riding across the lonely heath, to whom ghosts appear in the shape of clouds, no differently than they appeared to Bach and Wagner—facing the compass point where this world goes out and goes under.* Wagner's and Schopenhauer's theories of spirit vision provide the key: just as beyond every dream there still dwells a kind of inmost prophecy [*Wahrtraum*], which begins by veiling our sight, thus making possible the appearance of ghostly figures in the furthest background of the inner dream world. We are only able, goes the theory, to convey what we see there to the awakening process, and to awakened consciousness, by means of a second dream mediating the true content of the first only through an allegorical form, because already here, with the brain's expected and finally full outward awakening, forms for the cognition of the outside world in terms of space and time need to be applied, from which then, obviously, an image completely commensurate with our common life experiences results. Nonetheless the great poets, Shakespeare first and foremost, already set up their brightly lit stage exactly where the more muffled sonic world passes into the more apparent but also inferior optical world; and more importantly, it is the same dream that here engenders Shakespearean apparitions, as they are made to resound by the total awakening of the inner musical faculty, and there Beethovenian symphonies, which must likewise unfailingly stimulate the listener's unveiled, less somnambulistically enfolded vision to a clear awareness of those shapes, great poetry's dense, unforgettable, superreal spirit-shapes. But one must here *differentiate* dream from dream: one *sinks*, and leaves only a derivative, moonlit landscape of the day's contents, a mere recollection of what has already been; and the other *crosses over*, is a twilight occurring first of all through the sonorous subject, the ultimately ontological verbal substrate, a *not yet conscious knowledge* of what will occur over there one day, in an "over there" that has not yet happened; of course such that here also a recollection, a finding-a-way-back-home is operative, but precisely to a home where one has never been, which is nevertheless home. But the body of this last dream in the middle of the night is always of gold, is sound, golden sound; for just like the significant human being who makes more mistakes than others because he can never gauge just how insignificant to him, how inhomogeneous with him the world is: the final God, the fluttering of the final God, can no longer find a place in any framework of mere opticality or pictoriality, of material valences. If color still clings strongly to the thing, and can therefore also be vacated by the thing's spirit: when brass sounds, the clashing and ringing froth over to remain not a feature of the brass, but stand out above it as a new, human attribute, such that the means of hearing and perceiving oneself are finally closer to the spirit than are color, or stone, or this now uncategorial material's questionable homesickness for God. One could say that since time immemorial music has glorified the other truth, the pious fraud, the constitutive imagination, the new philosophy among the arts.[35] Only sound, this sensory riddle, is not so laden by the world, is sufficiently phenomenal for the end, that—like the *metaphysical* word—it can return as a final material moment in the fulfillment of mystical self-perception, laid immaculately on the gold ground of receptive human latency.[36] That can and hence absolutely shall not mean that natural sound in itself is already a metaphysical part or even just a spiritual enclave within nature, but the correlation remains undeniable insofar as hearing sound, hearing and perceiving oneself within it, in other words sound's potential application to extrinsic, incorporeal spiritual categories, certainly do permit one to assert a similarity between this material and the "material" of what is meant by "God." If one nonetheless were to go further, and read something heteronomous and by nature astral off what sound inherently is and provides, this would be an impermissible relegation of music back into a mathematical kind of natural science, where it tends to appear just as infrequently as mathematical moments appear within the phenomenology of musical effects. Which is why there is no way to get from even a purified sound—in the sense of being subdued by degree, measure, and quantum, as would still be appropriate for a physical, indeed even a psychological object—to a *willed and musical* sound, to the complete untenability, in purely acoustic terms, of tempered tuning, of enharmonic modulation, of infinite chaos avoided: to the conflict in its melody, the dissonant variegation of its harmony, the deliberate succinctness of its thematics; to the manifold, human, filigrane, time-spatial succession, superimposition of the counterpoint as the most artificial construct in the world: to the *denaturalized* sound as an almost already purely metaphysical object and first phenomenal of all mystery.

Nevertheless one has not shrunk from letting sound land only completely outside us. It was not so long ago that one equated *do, re, mi, fa* to the four elements and the seven notes of the octave to the planets. Not only the Vedas wail their mysterious monsoon ragas, not only the intervals of the Chinese stringed instruments are tuned to the intervals between the planets, but even Dietrich Buxtehude took it upon himself "to charmingly depict the nature and character of the planets" in his seven keyboard suites. And regrettably, Shakespeare continues, to Jessica: "Look how the floor of heaven / Is thick inlaid with patines of bright gold: / There's not the smallest orb which thou behold'st / But in his motion like an angel sings, / Still quiring to the young-eyed cherubins." Here the true, the inner night has been forsaken; a false, *purely astronomical theory of music* dominates, as Kepler above all finally conceptualized it. Here even the particular registers are supposed to correspond to particular planets, the minor key coincides with the perihelion, the major with the aphelion, in fact the entire tonal system with all its harmonies is described as the pale reflection of the solar system, or in Pythagorean terms, as the sevenfold refraction of the primordial solar note, as the *lyra Apollinis*, and is only legitimate within this system.

One gains little by renaming these correlations more spiritually, for even then the sound will not land within human inwardness. Thus Father Singer's speculations, for example, seriously attempted to deduce the minor key's sadness from the fact that it rests on the diminution of the second note of the triad, and hence refers to Golgotha, the descent of the second person of the trinity. This might sound irrelevant and absurd, and Christianity's language of Jesus as the light of the world also misleads us about the unfathomability of astral magic, but the only thing recapitulating itself here as well as in the modern theosophy of music is that unproductively mystical way of plucking out form *par tout*, which, as Abert has shown, was able to command the submission of the entire medieval view of music to astronomy, numerology, instrumental symbolism and astral mysticism. Even in Schopenhauer the ponderous bass still mirrors stones, the tenor plants, the alto animals, and the soprano who carries the melody the human realm, and thus the orchestra becomes a cross-section of the world[37]; even in this most Christian of philosophers, then, music's transcending objective correlation is still directed toward the cosmos: for here again man is not the *point* of nature, but rather just the strongest, most diurnal, clearest objectivation of Will, and as such appointed precisely to destroy the illusion of individuation in the face of universal Nature. For Schelling the musical gold nevertheless lies entirely embedded in the number 7, and Kepler's Pythagoreanism triumphs in such an aesthetics where it applies to music, so totally that in Schelling not even Schopenhauer's at least still seething and twitching Hindu automatisms, but Pythagoras, in fact Egypt itself, becomes music's most direct deductive locus. From Schelling comes the proper conceptualization of the principle that music is nothing but a suggestion of architecture, and the latter frozen music; thereafter it becomes an easy matter for this philosopher to destroy music with forced structural and megaspatial systems of obsolete astral correlations. He loves only Greek music, which he assesses as quintessentially melodic, and thus correlates to the ordered, planetary world; he loathes modern music, which he calls confused, arrhythmic harmony, and as such reduces to the centrifugal comet world; by such means all of "unarchitectonic" music, all music since ancient Greece, is deprived of a home in the planetary system and so of the possibility of a substantive, logically objective debate. Sound can lead into such extraneousness, such senselessness and complete inobjectivity, when Schelling begins and continues to trace it from natural premises, however Christian his guise. For it is as though the Christian soul itself, this quintessentially musical soul, had not even awakened, as if the fires, the torches of our yearning and our labor had not yet burned through the crystalline astral vaults, and the most profound thing in the world could still only be conceived as most objective thing of the *completely cosmic type.* All the stronger, then, is the absolute admonition to keep only to human receptivity in any decipherment of the tonal factor, because it knows nothing of any astral mysticism in music, and to the singular miracle of genius, which likewise posits no transcendence but the spiritual transcendence homogeneous with it.

It is therefore better to believe that sound need only melt our hearts, need only soothe and wound us, in order to bring about the pilgrimage into the self. It is better to believe only in the reciprocal correlation between the note's movements and the soul's: in proper agreement with the Church fathers, above all with Augustine and his doctrine of music's power to illuminate the heart, of its magical journey and still secret landing in the *purely ethical-mystical Castel Merveil* of music. What is here being held aloft by the fervent arms of the wish to return home is not the contrived lie of a however pleasant world of appearances [*Schein*], which as appearances must be lower than truth. It is nevertheless equally little— whereby appearance would admittedly be revalued as a certain consoling and misleading reflection [*Widerschein*]—the promise of some depopulated alternate universe, of some sensory reflex of the universal conceived since time immemorial as depopulated, be it fixed as *nous,* as *pneuma* or as the Will-to-Life, as the nirvana initiated in reflection. For Schopenhauer too is still quite far from understanding music's true correlation to the *apeiron,* to the extent that he anchors it only passively, cosmically, and not in the individual, heroic, Christian element: in other words, to the extent that he indeed concedes to music the power to supplement appearance with the thing-in-itself, but nonetheless defines this thing-in-itself only as something metaphysical, of an indeterminate, deindividuated, aprocessual, indeed of the already empirically most real kind. The self-encounter, We-encounter (and there is in every true artist a profound passion to correlate epistemologically), which as the basic concept of the philosophy of values corresponds ultimately to the Apocalypse, to the ultimate revelation of the We-problem, the basic concept of the entire system of philosophy, may allow truth to persist neither as a simply inductive logic of facts, nor as the Greeks' definitive totality-logic of the greatest universality and therefore greatest reality. Rather, and here it is precisely the responsible artist who stands closer to the philosopher than does the unsubjective empiricist, there is another truth than the truth of what exists now, a truth that pertains only to us, to the compass of the world that we experience in our coloration of it, comprehend as we accelerate it, and consummate in religion, to an absolutely "subjective" and yet highly substantial world—beyond the merely empirical-comparative inventory of the present situation and its easily achieved logic of Being—directed not at the elucidation of things, nor of humans, but at a first adequation of longing to itself, at the interiority and the unknown self-perception beyond this world. And that is certainly why humans cultivate strong objective correlations in music—in large part still of the artistically specific type, and, after the appropriate conceptual expansion, of the immanent type as well—before and beyond the laws of the transcendental synthesis of artistic-imaginative apperception and its phenomenal, of its material-phenomenal fulfillment-moment. It is the suddenly indirect correlation to the unseen Man, to the approaching figure perceived in the sound-image, of the Master, of the Servants, the eschatological ground of the soul, the restoration of Cosmic Man, of *the secret, absolute figure of humanity, from the labyrinth of the world.*[38]

On the Thing-in-Itself in Music

Only a few even get far enough to be able to hear themselves purely.

They end up beneath themselves, plunge into sleep, dream falsely and arbitrarily along the sound, drowsily and vaguely recoloring what had been buried as well as what has not yet come.

The better kind wake up, perhaps, not simply bringing themselves along just as they are, but then they also go dry. As connoisseurs, they brace themselves on the framework and believe that through it, through the means they have seen through, the forms they have comprehended, they are being musically objective. Thus these rational types are also on the wrong track, and one would almost like to set the sensual sleepers right, who, however dully and erratically, at least move spiritually within the spiritual element. For however much it is only form which shapes, discovers, helps what is dawning to emerge, the musical miracle can hardly be comprehended through form alone if the most expressive personhood does not lead upward through it. Its question lies in the expression of what can be sung.

~

Unfortunately what fell precisely to the sleepers reveling beneath themselves was something that had already been heard many times before. For after all, the falsely associative listener rediscovers himself particularly easily in Wagner's peculiarly blurring character, too. Certainly not because here, even more than in Beethoven, small, long familiar, once respectfully incorporated forms have been shattered. Instead, an expressively even more deeply grounded form took their place, showing how extraordinarily much more musically Wagner was defined than he himself, who transposed musical into dramatic logic, wanted to acknowledge. It more than suffices here to point to the subtleties, to the floridly weaving *melos*, to the extraordinary handiwork of the *Meistersinger*, to the harmonic innovations, adaptations, and gigantic tensions, but above all to *Tristan*'s syncopic and polyrhythmic wealth, and more to Wagner's highly specific counterpoint, which Bruckner then exalted; anyway, there is simply no way to exclude Wagner's genius from the development of music, especially not purely technically. If—albeit with questionable justification—one could call Beethoven's symphonies operas in disguise, then one would conversely, much more certainly, have to grasp and appreciate considerable stretches of Wagner's musical dramas completely musically—without knowledge of the text and its purportedly sole substantiating coherence—as legitimate intensifications and developments, as elaborations of a purely musical logic. That has to be said against a mistaken and then again tremendously growing criticism; nevertheless, and of course, Wagner in many ways gave a great boost to the languishing sleepers, insofar as he lets listeners, in spite and even beyond all his technique, falsely arrive at themselves. He gave the dreamers who merely revel beneath themselves the all too somnambulistic opportunity to encounter the heat, the ambit, the dream-stratum of a merely animal memory. It becomes clear precisely thereby just how little good *work* by itself can determine or salvage here. For Wagner's peculiarly sultry, sensuous character lies beyond melody, harmony, and rhythm, and proves to be caused by his peculiar *theory of the object of music.* This is finally what forced the suppression of the sound, its objective restriction to what is numb, drowning, sinking, subconsciously unconscious, animalistic; the human conscience that struck back did not so much let the sound, its inborn spiritual language have its say, but held it down, blocked, inadequate, and overcompensated the murk through textual intelligibility alone. As such the "motifs" were indeed Romantically transferred to the orchestra, but the actual release and expressivity above them were not entrusted to the music, but rather, in an exceedingly Gluckian kind of Classicism, to the visual element, the text, the drama as music's ultimate tonic—but then of course only the expressivity of "verworrener Vorstellung," the *petites perceptions* of dreaming monads, the *confusa conceptio* of pained, unfree affects guided by inadequate ideas all over again. In this way, then, Wagner's music—blocked, not allowed to finish speaking, robbed of the hour of its self-discourse, of its *humanly absolute poetry a se,* robbed "poetically," to be precise—pushed ever further outward into realms of unfreedom. Certainly not without often cresting, without flaring powerfully up into the spiritual, not without luminous presentiments of the other, supraconscious side, but still on the whole tending toward the animalistic and the pagan, landing in the automatism of delusion, in the frightened or ecstatic cries of the inhumanly driven creature, in the raptures of satisfied lust, or, finally, in spite of the grail, in the deserted shadowland of the dead Pan.

~

So we drift along here, and craving is almost all that wants to sound. Even the renunciation offered here operates with a worldly luster. Its heaven seldom lies very high above the strand where Tannhäuser dreams in the arms of passionate love.

As we know, Wagner only occupied himself with Schopenhauer late, long after the bagpipes had begun to lure him. But however completely the composer of the underground developed out of himself, his art seems nevertheless like an immense test of the *Schopenhauerian* philosophy of music. In reality, the prototype for almost all of Wagner's objective correlation can be found in Schopenhauer; but the latter neither teaches nor expresses anything about Beethoven's or Bach's objective correlations or even about the unimaginably expressive future of arrived music—even in

the world as Representation, it is the world as Will which quintessentially
remains the object of music.

For here we really remain below, and this way of no longer being, but
only seeing, finds only craving, and hardly anything to satisfy it. Indeed
our eyes close readily, but the interior that consequently appears in
Schopenhauer resounds only impulsively, frenziedly, full of fears or fleeting pleasures; nothing more can be found here. The arts adapted to the
light and to the principle of sufficient reason here mirror the same substance from the outside, but in the shadow of its correlations; their models are at best the forms of the objectivations of Will, these strange intermediate constructs between multiplicity and unity, between illusion and
reality. Nevertheless, precisely, the way that Schopenhauer's Will is immediately proclaimed in the cry, and the way that time's reflexive phenomenal form only still envelops, like a flowing veil, nature's kernel living
in the human heart: according to Schopenhauer, this is how *music* speaks,
no longer of phenomena and their endless interrelations, and no longer of
their objectivations or Platonic Ideas, but rather of the all-one essence itself, of nothing but weal and woe, of universal Will and nothing else, as
the absolutely most serious, most real thing.

Here one desires to rise no higher, then; one enjoys the music and is at
the goal; the sound expresses life completely. Although it may not actually paint and imitate appearance, the Will's gradations certainly project
into music: such that here the entire world is mirrored from its deepest
registers up to the human voice above, all the way to the leading melody,
which most purely and at the same time most mindfully expresses the
mutably restless essence of Will. But Schopenhauer ultimately places no
decisive emphasis on the particular correspondence between music and
the mundane gradation of Ideas; what remains important is rather just
this: Everything that happens relates to music as just an arbitrary example; to any clothing of flesh and bone, to any operatic or mundane scenario, music has always just a mediate relationship; music expresses the
essence of Will *in abstracto*, so to speak, without any accessories, and
therefore without motives; music is the extracted quintessence of the feelings, the passions; in short, music is the melody to which the world *as a
whole* is ultimately the text, so that one can as well call the world "embodied music" as "embodied Will."[39] Indeed, Schopenhauer ultimately
isolates music so completely from every and any parallelism to the objectivations of Will that he even asserts: All the other arts objectivate the

Will only mediately, in shadow form, from the outside, by means of the Ideas, and since our world is nothing but the manifestation of the Ideas within plurality, then music, since it ignores the Ideas, is entirely independent also of the phenomenal world, ignores it altogether, could to a certain extent exist if there were no world at all; in short, music does not phenomenally posit the manifestation of its Platonic Idea, like the other arts, nor the cognition endlessly shunted from the one to the other as in the sciences, but rather it posits everywhere and at the same the One, the All-Pertinent, the timelessly, spacelessly Identical, precisely the Will itself as the thing-in-itself—on which, precisely, is supposed to rest music's inexpressible intimacy, its power to offer a somnambulistic revelation of the *world's inmost essence*. Although the stratification of the world that projects into music is therefore ultimately not essential to it, music is nevertheless still built unshakably into the inmost essence of the world, and only of the world: so cyclical, in other words, is the reassurance that music here grants us. The highest aesthetic elevation above the world only plunges man further back into the center of this world where music is supposed to eternally work its subhuman spell. The shaft of the soul, of reversal, of presentiment, is here completely sealed, and one cannot see what might force it open again. Nothing is darker here than precisely "the ineffable intimacy of music," nothing remains more incomprehensible than "the language of music, so rich in content and meaning, the like of which would be unbearable composed in a language of words," and which Schopenhauer nevertheless is supposed to have completely deciphered. Vainly Schopenhauer affirms—vainly according to precisely the deepest conclusions of his philosophy—that every music is at its destination, since its object really remains always just the Will. Equally futile remains the claim that music could exist to a certain extent even if the world did not, for the world could really only exist insofar as music here lets the world reappear with heightened significance, as in other words music represents an objectivation of the total Will just as immediate as the world itself, so that consequently—far from being a panacea for all our suffering—it more confirms and affirms than averts the universal Will whose cries it lets ring. Nowhere does Schopenhauer's philosophy in itself lead into the shaft of the soul, into an oceanic tranquillity of temperament, into the void where he teaches that the universe is to be found, and which he nonetheless makes completely transcendent, although the mysticism of an "absolutely Christian philosophy" should really just begin here. Precisely inwardness, in spite of every ultimate negation of Will, finds itself completely disavowed: "As soon as we turn inward, and, having directed our perception inward, want to reflect on ourselves fully, we lose ourselves in a bottomless void, find ourselves like the hollow, glass sphere out of whose interior a voice speaks whose cause is nowhere to be found there, and, when we thus want to grasp ourselves, we catch, with a shudder, nothing but an insubstantial phantom."[40] In short, spirit in Schopenhauer may be a lyre, but the plectrum is always *objects*, and these, the world and its substance, finally confer the same contents that it is the lyre's task to sound. Whereas: *even in the world as representation, ultimately only the world as Will, and never representation's secession from the world, remains the real object of music.*

However much they are part of the illusion, human beings are consequently even less able than such parts to act independently. Rather, they are merely the scenes of the action, cheated, ironized puppets in the hand of the all-one false idol and in his play. They believe they seek their ownmost, and yet just carry out the business of the species, such that absolutely no original "motivation" acts in them, but only the same fatalism, occasionalism, the same transposition of "efficient cause" into primordial principle occurs here as in Romanticism's other reactionary systems; even if the concepts of "motivation" or "efficient cause" are unsuitable for someone who despised the principle of cause. Individuals and their particular, their not only compulsive will are nothing before the Will of the One, the alone real wave of the universal Will or perhaps universal Spirit. Thus Wagner also found his philosophy here; much of *Wagner's music* as urge, delusion, the metaphor of the firefly, ocean swells, clouds of steam and the deep sleep of the unconscious expounds the same raging and forever static automatism, the same unsubjective nature legend. Certainly Schopenhauer occasionally breaks through his unseemly immanence, and the heavy world rolls aside, but if much of this life already sounds to him like an orchestra preparing to strike up a great and beautiful symphony, then for him music truly averts no misery; then to this aspect of Wagner's music, as of Schopenhauer's philosophy, the world, as the object of music as well, remains always just the devouring and regenerating river of birth and death, as which Krishna revealed himself in his true divine form to Arjuna. As we wanted to say, a strangely unsubjective animal lyricism ensues, foremost in the *Ring*; these people are no *dramatis personae* advancing into the space of an encounter with each other and with their own profound destiny, but rather blossoms on a tree, indeed even just bobbing ships unresistingly obeying their subhuman ocean's sufferings, labors, love, and yearning for redemption; over whom, in every decisive moment, the universal wave of Schopenhauer's Will thus sweeps: of that craving for the thing-in-itself, in other words, and its tyranny, which is not only foreign to the moral will of Beethoven's music, but which also diverts, envelops the specifically Wagnerian initiation of a fervent-spiritual *espressivo*.

~

Yet the task awaits of soon harkening toward oneself purely and deeply. The essential thing is to finally direct the aimless kind of hearing toward oneself, to take hold of the soul. Better technical training for the lay listener would certainly help, so that he could have at least an initial purchase against the fugitive depths.

Meanwhile the listener ultimately receives precisely only himself back, strengthened, interpreted, after being thus shaped and outfitted. The deeply moved, profoundly inexpert listener must remain carefully preserved, comprehended, in order to reappear as the one for whose sake everything happens beyond the tonal framework and its rules, that is, at the location that intends and expects him. The artist as well, who after all is progressively giving up such meaningless expedients as tonality in order to more extensively work out such transcendent forms as rhythm and counterpoint on behalf of his own cause—the great artist is also, in the end, only his own listener. He is the first to accomplish, on behalf of all, the intention of meaning toward what is inward, in order thus to first— recognizing, just as he is recognized within the collective space—hearken toward the brightening amazement, the approaching utopian ground of the soul. This means that precisely the listener, instead of the expert, instead of mere formal analysis, must be objectively clarified, and *the interior of everything that harkens toward itself, shaped sound as the mere aura of the listener encountering himself again, must be placed at the end of music.* Not before the work, absolutely not, but rather beyond, above, even beyond its false, pagan domain is where music's spirit realm stretches; emphatically removed from every mere "psychology," fundamentally superior to Schopenhauer's paganism as the object of music, a pure-understanding-oneself-in-existence with the We-problem and its metaphysics as object and substance. A new self, the self precisely touched by presentiment and by the convocation, must therefore also be newly committed, beyond any concept of musical form, must be newly installed as a function of meta-physical aesthetics if deeply moving experience is to be salvaged and rein-forced, if the What For and the spiritual end of music—one long, re-sounding heresy—are to be adequately conceptualized. For it flowered; music as sight, as clairvoyance, the visible world, and also God's traces in the visible world disintegrated; music, for a deeper reason than had ever before appeared, is the newest art, the heiress of visibility, appertains to in-teriority's form-eccentric philosophy of history, its ethics, its metaphysics. We must finally draw the right conclusion from this evening lateness and this overtaking of every form or type: now the calling and the listening themselves step forward, the power of time and gigantic strategy, crying, pounding, knocking, namelessly dawning clairaudience and the birth of the kernel, of the sonorous, not yet existent, undesignated kernel of every thing, the difficult birth by the hearth of music—and insofar as here every epoch's clairvoyance has been transformed by seriousness, soulless intellect will end in disaster in art as in philosophy, and the existence like the con-cept of music will be achieved only conjointly with the new object theory, with the *metaphysics of presentiment and utopia*.

To the latter, too, certainly, even when it stands as near as possible to us, we come near only in dreams. But it is no longer a dream recollecting the past or burrowing into the various baser passions. Rather only that yearning which brings with it what was unfulfilled, what could have ab-solutely no earthly fulfillment, the waking desire for what alone is right for us, which glimmers in the well-correlated sound. It is so deeply fa-miliar to us, it renders good and clear, leads into the heart, and the only thing that was ever meant there gazes mysteriously in its own direction: "Where is Paul the thief?" asks Matthias Claudius; "gone into the woods; and I after him, looking frantically through the bushes and trees, intend-ing to beat him wherever I found him, and my blood boiled—when there in the distance the gracious lord's huntsmen began to blow their horns. I had never felt this way; I listened, stood still and looked about. I was right by the stream; horses, cattle and sheep stood on the banks and drank; and the huntsman blew. 'Money or no, I won't hurt Paul.' I for-gave him in my heart, there by the stream, and went home again."[41] Even higher into that feeling of "becoming better," becoming oneself, ventures E. T. A. Hoffmann, and that stranger "who told him of distant, unknown lands . . . whose language spontaneously faded into a marvelous ringing," and the most familiar faraway place opens up, the certainty it gives that somewhere and sometime "a higher wish, one exceeding the sphere of earthly pleasure, will be fulfilled, which the spirit, like a chastened, fearful child, will not even dare to express."[42] And completely in this direction, music's most genuine direction, leads Jean Paul's question: "Why, when music redoubles our sad or happy emotions, even creates them, do we forget how more supremely and forcibly than any other art it tosses us abruptly back and forth between happiness and sadness, in the blink of an eye—I ask, why do we forget her outstanding characteristic: her power to make us homesick? Not for the old, abandoned land, but for the virgin land; not for a past but for a future?"[43] So completely is music simultaneously the pledge of the beyond, a song of consolation, black magic, yearning and our own arrival, the nighttime flower of faith that strengthens us in the final darkness, and the most powerfully transcendent certainty between heaven and earth: *not Leander's fervor, then, which Schopenhauer had alone intended, but rather Hero's torch burns absolutely, much more surely, in the interior of great music*, as the spontaneously flashing dream sky of the human soul. Wagner turned back the pages, Schopenhauer plunged into an ever more hopeless world; disregarding Kant's warning, he sought the name of *the thing-in-itself within Being as it exists, within Nature*; and even if the universal God he intended here turned quite honorably into the devil, Schopenhauer nevertheless pointed music toward the mere hearing of this Being, this state of the world, and not to the presentiment of seclusion, not to the discovery of a treasure, of our inheritance beyond this world, beyond this world's next bend in the road. He did not point to Beethoven, to the gigantic rhythmic shape of his "upward," his Luciferan-mystical kingdom; not to Bach, the song of the spiritual soul, shining into itself, to the great, towering organ fugue with its staircases and stories, a single self-illuminating, gigantic crystalline glory; not to the promises of a messianic homeland beyond every expedition, beyond every Luciferan assault on heaven. There is only one thing we can still want, however; only to what is unsayable, after our gestures and words have grown rigid, is sound appointed. Ghosts and masquerades emerge, the play of true vision, the funhouse mirror for comic and the magical mirror for tragic opera: "music, moody food of us that trade in love," and that music that must ring out as soon as the supernatural enters the plot, until—in accordance with Busoni's genuine insight—what is impossible in music connects with what is impossible, visionary in the plot, and so both become possible. But finally, as soon as everything grows silent on this earth, within earthly action—completely dispensing with the text and even the Shakespearean world of dreams, the world of dance, masque, intoxication and magic—then music assembles the features of the other word, the Word from another larynx and logos, the key to the inmost dream within the objects' Head [*Haupt*], their own newly meaningful expression, the multiply singular, final expression of the Absolute. Now still a fervent stammering, music, with an increasingly expressive determinacy, will one day possess its own language: it aims at the word which alone can save us, which in every lived moment trembles obscurely as the *omnia ubique*: music and philosophy in their final instance intend purely toward the articulation of this fundamental mystery, of this first and last question in every thing. For the *thing-in-itself*, still only "appearing" within spiritual yearning, and thus also having precedence over music, is what moves and dreams in the immediate proximity, in the blue around objects; *it is this, which is not yet; what is lost, presensed; our self-encounter concealed in the latency of every lived moment; our We-encounter, our utopia calling out to itself through goodness, music, metaphysics, but unrealizable in mundane terms.* The farther, the more undivertedly the sound thus enters itself, the more perceptibly does the primordial mute also emerge, telling himself the most ancient legend: but he is what he tells himself. If the lived moment, arrested within itself, broken open, deferred to the most secret sanctum, thus finally begins to sound: then the times have changed; then music, the miracle-working, transparent art that accompanies us beyond the grave and the end of this world, will have successfully drawn the first stroke of the exact likeness, the completely different naming of a divine name, one as much lost as never found.

The Mystery

We want to know where clairvoyance has disappeared to. A river trickles out on dry ground. Suddenly, far away, another river emerges, which had never before been seen on this spot, and which can have no source in this arid region. Can one connect clairvoyance to music with the same certainty with which one associates these two rivers? One never saw them together in the same place, but as one retreated, the other grew slowly and, so it seems, increased by the same energies. Of course it is not known whether they consume the same amount of energy or are in structural sympathy. If we thus ask what it was before, that is now music, in order thereby to discern more exactly what music is, then even the acknowledged affinity in itself will not yet suffice for a closer definition.

For we are gradually becoming blind to the outside. To what lies above us we became blind already long ago; the light of Christian illumination is also gone. Our sensory eyes may have opened later than the extrasensory ones, and only appeared as the latter were closing; or rather, through the sensory, rebellious, intrusive opening of our eyes, the extrasensory world increasingly receded and finally disappeared completely. Earlier, in the days of which we preserve legends, external things were veiled or entirely invisible, but behind them, in utmost brightness, moved their group-souls, the naiads, dryads, guardian angels, Sirius and the hunter Orion, the night sky's colorful clouds and all the nearness of the other world. Nevertheless one recalls that Roman admiral who dared what had been inconceivable, to have the sacred foul who would not eat, thus giving an unfavorable prognosis for the naval battle, thrown in the water: if they will not eat, let them drink! And that, moreover, in the age of the sybilline books. And so our sensory organs soon developed more acutely, the visible world grew densely, oppressively, conclusively real, and the now invisible extrasensory world declined into a belief, into a mere concept, into the Platonic-Plotinian Jacob's ladder or pyramid of ideas. Even the oracles became ambiguous, indeed incomprehensible, and so worldliness, the sensibility initially developed only for reckoning only with strategy, jurisprudence, calculability and the real causal nexus, was reinforced ever more rationally until finally, by the time of Augustus, every sensory or even intellectual contact with transcendence had disappeared. Then Jesus was born, the metempsychosis of God himself, and humans, by the grace of this light shining even into the darknesses, in other words this incarnation, earthly sojourn, the making public of the mystery of the *logos*, perceptible to even the most sensory organs, could once again be assured of the supernatural. But for the last 400 years, since Luther and the Renaissance, despite a reemergent secularity, despite even the renewed force with which something free, virile, operative, Luciferan, rational is stirring, and plunges into this world and the world above, we have seen a dual principle at work. For it is gradually becoming gloomy all around us, having already drawn shut above us long ago. The night advances further and not only unilaterally as in Roman times; instead even the sensory foregrounds begin to recede, as surely as the higher,

Christian light occurring there long ago receded. Nevertheless: the self's light burns brightly within, always brightly now, and unequivocal powers could awaken expansively there. Our soul weeps inside us and yearns beyond, posits God and the dream; but what the darkness of night chases before itself like Orpheus chased the shades is born purely of the soul and has nothing but this inmost Eurydice as its goal. The subjects are the only things that cannot be extinguished in any external or upper darkness, and that the Savior lives and *wants* to come again: this is then as now irrefutably vouchsafed to us; but He, and God Himself, like everything objective, have forfeited their own power of being able to come, and act visibly; the age of the completely pure subject-magic first implanted in us by Jesus, of the most complete Luciferan-Paracletan unfolding, has arrived. Hence there is only one salvation here, and that is the defiant connection seeking itself above everything alien to us, between the moral self that can only still shine a light in the night of what is external and higher—between this self and the silent, absconding God who hesitates before his transformation into the Holy Spirit, as the cries, prayers and deep nominative power of heroic-mystical "atheism" itself.

And so, while we are gloomy and pregnant and yet nevertheless radiate beautifully back to ourselves, a different kind of clairvoyance has returned. It was already there before, and now operates so to speak on the ricochet, but everything about it has changed, become solitary, less supportive, more productive, no longer mirroring what is alien to us but instead radiating into the emptiness before us, already in its very function. Visual accuracy has changed; the Persians, Chaldaeans and Egyptians, the Greeks and the Scholastics, *none of them with any music worth remarking,* these masters of the complete and unified, of stable figures and definitions, reflections instead of creations, have their reward there, the reward of pictorial clairvoyance and the guaranteed heaven full of nothing but visibilities and objectivities; but the new man has been granted, instead of the old realm of images, instead of the old, homeless exuberance, the consolation of music. This is why the great composers became significant in such measure as the rootedness as well as the other secure, spiritual ties of myth loosened; indeed, not even folk song and church song are the final sources of nourishment, nor do they convey, obviously, now that they have disappeared, music's ultimate substance; and music has grown and become constitutive in the same measure as philosophy has actually been forced, been graced, to aim at practical action, at substance as process, at truth as the sublation of the world. There is hence a different kind of light in this clairvoyance of the ear, of music and of creation; and its planet, in complete contrast to the ancient mysticism that dealt with complete, in themselves very clear realities, has not yet rotated so far that its other side, facing away from us as much as from itself, can yet be seen. If we were thus to ask what it was in those clairvoyant but musicless eras, which now, within modernity, begins to appear as music, in order to discern where to and to what end there be music, then the recognized affinity between clairvoyance then and music now only suffices to define the common level, but not to define the change in function nor even to summarize the contents of the thing that has progressed. It would be the worst divergence if here, because of the similarity of both these royal roads, we also wanted to retain the old goal, if in other words the day born entirely of sound, the day born of sound meant only for spirit ears, the enormous, inner, heavenly image of music, the primordially intuited sonorousness of *devachan*[44] in contrast to the prismatic aura of the merely astral world—if in other words the broadly, integrally, sonorously gleaming dark of the lived moment should now nevertheless be populated with the figures of astral myth or even the still partly astral myth of the Trinity. Rather something different, unnamable, our secret splendor itself rises up; "but let's be gone, the dark is come, / the air turned cool, the mist descends, / for evening shows a home's true worth"[45]; and not without the most profound reason did the chaos, the Luciferan and also satanic overthrow of everything higher, the paradoxically darkened Advent nights of modernity first become the birthplace of music. But thereby also the birthplace of our ownmost, historically inner path: as deliverance not only from the body, but from every mere duty and every bare, merely interpersonal definability; as the release from every technical system, from every transcendence *in which man does not appear*; as the release toward an ethics and a metaphysics of inwardness, of fraternal inwardness, of the secrecy disclosed within itself that will be the total sundering of the world and the dawn of truth over the graves as they dissipate.

Here we need not fear being disappointed, even betrayed. It is no longer permissible to say that just as dreams dissipate when one wakes, so too must that which lives only in the self and is otherwise unconfirmed be absolutely inessential. This may apply to our minor excitations; here it may of course be that only the body's blanket tightly wound about us can convey to us life's joys and sorrows. And just as in our sleep we believe we are suffocating under avalanches when the blanket flaps over our lips, so will this clay, this body certainly pass lights and sounds and cold into the 70-year-long sleep of the immortal soul, and out of this the soul constructs the expanded history of its sorrows and joys: and when it wakes, very little of it will have been true; indeed, one can add to this statement Jean Paul's, that no part of it was true, all of it is reflexive and shares nothing with the spirit moved by yearning, which keeps at a remove from not only the body but every interpersonal definability: nothing, not even an antagonism.[46] If however what the *sound* says comes from us, insofar as we place ourselves into it, and speak with this great macanthropic larynx, then that is no dream, but a solid ring of the soul, to which nothing corresponds only because nothing outside can, and because music as the inwardly utopian art lies completely beyond anything empirically demonstrable. But we need not be concerned that this higher and better thing than us might not again shrink down into us: just as little as we should be indignant that in music—though it is certainly still mostly true in the visual arts—a sort of barrier has been set up, and man must constantly look in from outside and wait. Here one need not console oneself, disengenuously console oneself, that we more easily overcome our own tears than we could overcome the angels' nameless jubilation, and one need not now, with desperate jealousy, try to break into the symbol granted us by music as into the visual likenesses and symbols of ancient eras. The servant's entrance of mere reflection has been forced open, and a different symbol appears than the allegorical kind that was alien to us, at least half extrahuman, that would have crushed us, burnt us up if it had become fully visible, like the uncovered Zeus, and whose still unresolved, transcendent ungraspability within the visible world, what is inclined toward us, had constituted its character as symbol. As its only erroneous, allegorical symbolic character existing only for us, behind which still lives, as in Egypt, perhaps our own darkness, but also the fatal clarity of error, of alien light, of astral myth. But sound accompanies us, and does not in the end withdraw allegorically back into a homeland foreign or perhaps even forbidden to us. If sound remains only indicative, unreal, then this unreality has surely not been put into symbols, its puzzle language does not want to conceal from us something already resolved supernaturally; music's function is rather the most complete overtness, and the mystery, what is comprehensible-incomprehensible, symbolic in music is the proper object of humanity *objectively* veiled from itself. Sound accompanies us and is We, not only in the way that the visual arts, which had seemed to point so far beyond us into the rigorous, objective, and cosmic, accompany us merely to the grave, but rather in the way that good works accompany us even beyond the grave, and precisely for the reason that the sublimity of music, the new, no longer pedagogical but *real symbol* in music seems so very low, so much just a mere fiery eruption in our atmosphere, while it is really a light around the farthest, certainly innermost firmament, indeed the very problem of Self and Us. Shaped sound thus does not remain something across from us; instead, there is something within it that lays our hand over our heart, that invokes us with us, transposes us and hence answers our needy, eternally questioning receptivity with itself, at least with its undiverted, purified question of the homeland, reverberating as itself. So the sound creates as much a superreal as an unallegorical circle of meaning, symbolic only with respect to the still incomplete state of its ornamentation of the self, a circle of everything human beings can intuit about themselves, of the undistanced gnosis of the We-problem as such, superior to any type.

In other words: clairvoyance is long extinguished. Should not however a clairaudience, a new kind of seeing from within, be imminent, which, now that the visible world has become too weak to hold the spirit, will call forth the audible world, the refuge of the light, the primacy of flaring up instead of the former primacy of seeing, whenever the hour of speech within music will have come? For this place is still empty, it only echoes obscurely back in metaphysical contexts. But there will come a time when the sound speaks, expresses, when the true chandeliers can finally be installed in the higher self, *where what still sounds to Brangäne like horns blowing, Isolde in the silence of night will hear as a fountain,* where the new composers will precede the new prophets; and so we want to allot to music primacy in what is otherwise unsayable, this kernel and seed, this reflection of the colorful night of dying and of eternal life, this seed-corn of the inner, mystical ocean of the Servants, this Jericho and first dwelling of the Holy Land. If we could name ourselves, our Master [*Haupt*] would come, and music is the only subjective theurgy. It brings us into the interior's warm, deep Gothic sanctum which alone still shines in the uncertain darkness, indeed out of which alone the light [*Schein*] can still come that must wreck and burst apart the chaos, the unfruitful power of the merely existent, the crude, fanatical groping of demiurgic blindness, perhaps even the coffin of God-forsaken Being, for the Kingdom was preached not to the dead but to the living, and therefore just this, our hardly known, warm, deep Gothic sanctum, will on the Morning of Judgment be just the same as the revealed Kingdom of Heaven.

The Shape of the Inconstruable Question

L'acqua che io prendo
giammai non si corse
—Dante

I am by my self.

Here one finally has to begin.

But where do I suffer from being not enough? Where am I askew, where have I been corrupted? Where am I secure and genuine? But of course we are neither one nor the other, but rather muddy, tepid and to see us is to want to vomit.

That is little enough, and almost everything immediately follows from it. Even what is good, because man immediately languishes in weariness, and nothing achieves any color. Only this is finally clear: that we mean little to each other, can pass unsuspectingly by one another. Or when we do know—when the possibility of helping, of becoming another draws near us, while we work, even with ideas—then the nasty way we have of warming our hearts with vanity appears, and the prospect still remains empty. Moreover most people around us, particularly since they have been entangled in a money economy, are so lethargically filthy that none of them, once they are scalded and marked, comes near any more difficult inner stirrings. And the emancipated, intellectual ones decay with all their soul, however elegantly they may have put talk, sentimental experience, a moral sensibility in the place of action when the other acts, when the other needs help. They are far from feeling: I am at fault, not the others, and if they are dark, then I have not shone enough for them. Instead they split moral life off from itself, contemplate it lifelessly and easily like everything else, and so the collectively inner character of its essence is misrecognized, squandered. It has fallen to the criminals to feel fear, remorse, guilt, the stirring of the germ of the spirit in us, and our hearts stay lethargic.

OF WHAT IS GENUINE IN US

I myself am, however, in order to work.

Then our listlessness finds itself even more deeply startled.

For who am I, that I can work? Am I worth so much, or am I so well loved? It cannot be felt everywhere; our inner chill is dropping off the scale. Where else could what I can do come from, since we find nothing in us that could live up to it? That nevertheless makes every blossom a springtime, that lets every idea spread, great, solemn, and practical. Yes, this ability even reflects back to show a direction, and who I "otherwise" am now glows much more strongly in what I know and can do. The weak ones may be as hollow and false as the words accessible to them; it only makes the artist even more solid, responsible, more overwhelmed by a love he can never deserve, at whatever remove he stands to himself, to his knowledge, to his works that are not so hollow and false. He can take to heart James' words: "Therefore to him that knoweth to do good, and doeth it not, to him it is sin."[1] Haydn may have felt something similar as he fell to his knees upon first hearing the "chord of light" in the *Creation* and thanked God that he had created this work. That is not necessarily humility and certainly not pride, or need not be. It is the moral, initially apparent experience of grief for the artist who breaks down when measured by these standards, and would like to surrender his overwhelming skill to God.

Now of course this still presupposes that I myself believe in the work. But if an individual is not very strong, certain in his color, then this age all around us will certainly not make it easy for him. It is not only easier for this age to believe in the visible than the invisible, amazingly, but even within the visible, what is discrete, subdivided seems even more real than the whole. The trend now, long supported by technology, is to locate the more easily movable, easily variable elements in order to move the whole from there; in other words in order to effect a cure at the lowest possible point. That has an effect; it leads to that total dismantling of anything original, that recognizes only the mundane, the calculable, and even then only the simplest impulses, contents as variable, and thus acknowledges these alone as real. As practically beneficial as this approach in terms of subcomponents, this technique of minute variations has proven, it is decisively and perhaps incompatibly opposed to the power and conscience of "Behold, I make all things new."[2] Unbelief weakens the soul, which no longer finds any clues to the blossoming, the phototropism and the fullness elemental in itself.

In this way human beings collapse into themselves, without a path or a goal beyond the quotidian. They lose their properly human wakefulness, substantiveness, existence; they forfeit their polarity, their comprehensive teleological awareness; and finally everything grand, powerfully massive, atomizes under the "knowing" gaze into false, disenchanted details; every blossoming becomes a whitewash, or ultimately mendacious superstructure. Certainly those who are actually satisfied with this state do not even come into consideration here; they do not think and they shall not be thought of. Higher stands the one who is at least desperate, just for being desperate; but the artists above all, out of the deepest awareness of their constructive powers, battle against the all too technical or even resentful dismantling. Nevertheless: not even the artist can always be present everywhere, can always easily believe in that which lets his thought light the way in him, above him. This ultimately still exposed doubt, desperation, this shortage of the deadly seriousness of the unconditional Yes to the vision, is a second experience of grief, the worry of the productive human being that even as such, he is not completely true and genuine.[3]

OF FOG, ALEXANDER'S CAMPAIGN, AND THE
MAGNITUDE OF THE YES

We are not even free to be so true.

But perhaps it is only so difficult because secretly we could already be this genuine.

Now of course we are still inadequate to what we create, and it often seems as if it were just the house which is unhoused. Not only analytical nihilism destroys; rather, more deeply, in the very center: we are presently wavering in the greatest blackout, one of the interior as well as, above all, of the exterior and the superior, that has ever occurred in history. It absolutely still remains to be felt how, to all of us, everything solid has gradually become not a matter of experience, but just a base habit. Perhaps Nietzsche believed sufficiently in what he said, perhaps Schopenhauer, who experienced so powerfully, perhaps Spinoza, *more geometrico*, but all of them lack the deepest sense of also being dragged along into it, and there is no substitute for the road to Damascus. Kierkegaard as well only believed in being able to believe, and Dostoevsky by no means overcame the Grand Inquisitor's poison, and just as Luther had to confess in only twice having believed in God, Pascal's *Apology* includes the sincere thesis that it is still more advantageous to place one's hope in God's existence and judgment—a logic of the wager that could never have turned to reason so persuasively, appraisingly, assuredly, so utterly differently than the medieval proofs of God's existence, if unconditional fervor had not also died out in Pascal. Matter in this our modern age is burdensome, and souls have become increasingly unpitying and ungenuine, so that Christmas, Easter, and Pentecost seem like one long Good Friday, like merely the insubstantial knowledge that the Redeemer has died, but as if he had been murdered in the crib, and the presentiment of glory floats emptily overhead. So unconnected with life, and then again so irritatingly concurrent with the void, as if coarseness and baptism, the most secular Renaissance and the most ecstatic Baroque, the lowliness of the most wretched Philistinism and the waking dream of music and speculation found themselves next to one another, or even alternated repeatedly, in this astonishing modern age. But it is just this, on the other hand again, which lets us feel that in our strangely weary and obscure life something important were not right. At least despair remains: that we do not believe, that the inward human being stands half still, motivated and attracted only cognitively, but what remains or is even reinforced is the presentiment of our hidden power, our latent ascent, our genuine possession, finally unhusked, finally drawn perfectly near.

~

So we at least long to voyage into color. The settled life is over, and what juice is still in it has become increasingly sluggish. But deep within us something else wants to ferment, and we seek the grain that would not grow here.

And so we go East; resisting it has already repeatedly been shown to be pointless. The Greeks warred against the Persians, and triumphed at Marathon and Salamis, but Alexander married Roxane, dismissed his Macedonian bodyguard and died in Babylon. Scipio destroyed Carthage, but the Semite Peter destroyed Rome, and the Emperor Theodosius' confession to the Bishop of Milan was the late and definitive revenge for the Battle of Zama. The Franks again warred against the Arabs, winning at Tours and Poitiers, but the Pope proclaimed the Crusades, and with the champions of the Holy Sepulchre, the chivalry and the *minnesang* of the Song of Songs, the Gothic as well as the scholastic arts, wander from the Orient back over to Europe. So the way—at the beginning and certainly at the end, with the collapse of the evil, hard, narrow, frigidly faithless life of the European world—to find help has always gone East. How many times already, how very plausibly even, has Europe in the face of the Orient, of the arable chaos of every great religion—become a circumscribed peninsula whose destiny remains to seek contacts in order not to grow cold in its smallness and purely intellectual attitude, its religious anemia. Nevertheless, to the Greek-European arrogance of complacently normal eras, the world, the history of the Orient—which certainly once formed a whole, and which in Isfahan possessed a center as it were, a medieval Olympia to which Tangiers, Tunis, Cairo, Istanbul, Baghdad, Delhi, indeed even Peking sent representatives—has tended not to become known even in outline. But at twenty Alexander, the youthful man, the boy of the fairy tale, purposely turned to Persia, following his dreams, only not so vain and insubstantially young as Alcibiades before him, and after him, in a much purer way, Otto III, but with visions and aspirations of guiding Greece over to Asia and bringing great logos into history, and powerfully enough to compel the indifferent coincidence of a nominal world empire into its own logos. He certainly did not set out to curse and then, against his will, to bless, in spite of the order given in advance to the Lacedaemonians and Athenians, to exact from the archenemy; he went to Troy a second time, but not to destroy it, for at home there was no longer a Tiryns or a Maecenae; rather, Alexander, the chosen commander of the Hellenic alliance, left Greece in order to descend to his "preliminary stage," tired of all the artificial occidentalism, no differently than Heraclitus, Pythagoras abandoned the all too human statues, the *euphrosyne* without depth, and the world's perfect *sphaira*, in order to unharness longing, neo-Platonic transcendence, the construction of domes within this world. As even the ground echoed the tread of the barbarians: it had become dark, pagan splendor long gone and only still shining like a distantly receding sunset, but in the Church a light still burned, another light and not only below, but the stars burned anew from the beyond over to us, as the fiery glow of a faith that no longer believed in this world and was no longer of it—now the magical mythos truly drew across Europe again, high above all the aftereffects of antiquity, an angular, Gothic, transcendently overarching reality, defeating even the onset of the Renaissance, outlasting it. What Alexander, the truest Greek, gave up, Michelangelo, Schelling and Schopenhauer gave up no less, in order by means of Europe to bring something mysterious to the deed and the incisiveness of the concept.

But we also, we most of all, late Western men and women, search further; like a dream the East rises again. Our souls also, sick and empty, move according to an *ex oriente lux*. Since the turn of the century, since a certain decline of the smugly cultured Philistine, it has twice come close. In Russian warmth and expectancy: the rivers, the steppes, an India covered in fog, is how the whole of measureless Russia seems to us. And above all, once again, pertinent, thinking mysticism and metaphysics themselves, the spirit of the North, is probably joined to a supplicant Asia through a related inner turbulence, through a properly theurgic piety: for Zion's sake refusing to be silent and for Jerusalem's sake refusing to stop. From just this point onward, consequently, transformative but empty Western man can finally advance into the greater depth beyond. Indeed, just that expanding anamnesis that imagines the world, which came over Europe after Augustine, would not have existed in the world without the highest Orient, that of the Bible, nor would the reinterpretation of the properties of God as archetypes for human beings exist in the world above. Foremost, however, there would be no final prospect radically related to an Absolute [*Überhaupt*]of life and striving; apocalyptic awareness must be ascribed completely to tiny, also primordially possible Attica. Ascribed to the Bible, with its altar, standing in the East itself even after a final East and Orient. And: "Next year in Jerusalem!"—even this post-biblical prayer, in this case pertaining to the Europe of the diaspora, likewise stood symbolically within the profundity of a truer Christ-shapedness than Europe had had, or, on its own, without the voice from Patmos, could ever have had. Whereas: an anamnesis arose from the not only maternal Orient, which is more human than even the Greek Adam, and which showed a however Attic mundane fullness, whereof the world is absolutely still not full, quite the contrary.

So we are not only unhoused, but within it something else truly advances ahead of our dismal lives. Otherwise we could not even recall, in such seeming digressiveness, perhaps not even historically, how it was and how it wants to come back to us. So in this elective affinity, this productive understanding and perhaps even "misunderstanding," we nevertheless feel like that Persian king in the Book of Esther who in sleepless nights would have someone read to him from his kingdom's chronicles, and so learned of the Jew Mordecai. More than one forgotten, unpaid debt burns within *Geistesgeschichte*, more than one deed that went unrewarded, more than one bold dream still awaiting fulfillment. Through our century it can come to be, the awareness of the Unconditional and the concept of the Absolute can find a new, an unsuspected strength. All the more does that fog descend, and that acute loss of certainty, which sets a limit on our conversion and would again like to confuse the energies, obscure the goal. All around us also rules the devil of the cold again, who desires precisely that one not believe in him, nor see his cloven hoof, and who can best rule undisturbed as pure nothingness, as complete demystification, barring the mystery from us. But out of this simultaneously arises the paradoxical courage to prophesy the light precisely out of the fog, or in other words: *the No could not be so strong if there were not among us, at the same time, a dangerous and battle-worthy Yes*; if at the same time, below this veiled life, below the nihilism of this modern age, a power unknown in morality or fantasy were not therefore at the same time stirring, whose path is just for this reason blocked by terrors and obstacles without number. Nearly everything has thus fled to us, from inhospitable life, to us as the gardeners of the most mysterious tree, which must grow. In us alone burns the light, in the middle of the collapse of earth and heaven, and the creative, the philosophical hour *kat exochen* is here; what helps to fulfill it is the constant concentration of our waking dream on a purer, higher life, on a release from malice, emptiness, death and enigma, on communion with the saints, on all things turning into paradise. Only this thinking wishful dream brings about something real, harkening deeply into itself until the gaze succeeds: into the soul, into the third kingdom after the stars and the heaven of the gods—waiting for *the word*, turned toward the enlightenment of a great maturity. The urge to correspond with oneself draws soul into this dreadful world, into its unknowing, its error and its guilty conscience of its finality; everything that is has a utopian star in its blood, and philosophy would be nothing if it did not form the ideational solution for this crystalline heaven of renewed reality. Life goes on around us and knows not where it goes; we alone are still the lever and the motor; external and certainly revealed meaning falter: but the new idea finally burst forth into the complete quest, into the open, uncompleted, dreaming world, into the landslides and eclipses of Satan, of the very principle that bars us. In order that, girded with despair, with our defiant presentiment, with the enormous power of our human voice, we may also designate God, and not rest until the innermost shadows have been chased out, until the world is bathed in that fire that is beyond the world or shall be lit there.

~

And yet first: shall be lit, for we do not yet burn freely, and, precisely, nothing is already fully authentic even in itself. What has remained, then, even beyond the fog, is the desperation of not really believing in anything, of first needing a presentiment and then already seeing the end, and closing the path. In the end, however, it is not totally as if the tender shoot of authenticity and genuineness had already been completely discovered in us and only concealed again by the simultaneous excess of consummate sinfulness and immanence as negative transcendence: as if therefore music, and the anamnesis of the modern age, ever more closely circling the Unconditional, had already rescued forth what is most authentic, most genuine of all from the world's unknowing and error. Rather, in spite of all our significant trust in the existence of continuous, particular Orients in the modern age, as testimony to the unstifled process of salvation in the soul: what is *most inward* in us itself simply lies in deep shadow even past the insubstantial fog, incognito to itself, *in a moral-metaphysical incognito*, as it not only socially causes every attention or inattention to be expressed only as ultimately revocable, under consideration, reflexively, but especially, in the ethically productive elucidation of the I and the We, never lets the deepest authenticity totally succeed: the union of our intensity with itself, their reencounter and congruence beyond the vision. In this way, in other words, even if the situation did not immediately become apparent without a nameless, mysterious ascent, a kind of forbearance reenters: that all we can do for the moment is prepare, provide words and concepts, until an identification takes them up and grants equivalence. What speaks here, cognition's prayer: May it truly be thus! May this be truly the right gaze, the gaze pertaining completely to us, into the overpowering enigma of existence!—what in this way again retreats from every brilliance of already accomplished vision, is again the flaw of only partial concern, of the playful, the often only intellectually artistic element in so much production, still drifting on an intermediate level, uneaten in its all too objective evidence and all too abstract even in its obscure optimism and the latter's transcendent jubilation. Which certainly holds, indeed especially holds for every traditional, certifiably objective

ecclesiastical splendor and—with *aliter sed eadem*—for every perfectly detached panlogism. There is consequently not only the shadow that the enemy hurls against our strength and against the light that shall be lit beyond the world. But precisely also: human strength even *in hoc statu
nascendi* still has its particular spiritual shadow, its unknowing of the
deepest depth as such, and the *center in itself* is still night, incognito, ferment, around which everyone, everything, and every work is still built.
Nevertheless the world at hand can not overpower the potential light from
the end of the Bible: with *l'ordre du coeur*, finally, with the new Jerusalem
instead of the old Rome.

KANT AND HEGEL, OR, INWARDNESS OVERTAKING
THE ENCYCLOPEDIA

I.

Who is nothing, however, will no longer encounter anything outside,
either.

Without ourselves, we can certainly never see what shall be.

At least this much was anticipated by Kierkegaard, and especially by
Kant: he gives "subjective" spontaneity, our only salvation and declaration of color, now that nothing else can still provide color or substance,
its due.

Certainly, in the way Kant lives and speaks, he is not immediately rich.
His themes, all of them, are played out within a very fortuitous frame.
We see English skepticism, a Prussian sense of duty, a desire to believe
but an inability to, crippled presentiments, and a miserable life into the
bargain, apparent in the majority of his examples and in certain un-
speakable definitions, as for example of marriage.

This is what Kant has to work with, and where his thought begins is
restricted enough. He asks how the formula for gravity could be possible,
in order to circumscribe the rational faculty with this possibility. One can
justifiably doubt whether these boundaries and these theories of the
spirit's transcendental composition, faithfully oriented to Newton and
nothing else, really have any more significance within the greater phenomenological expanse of consciousness. For one can clearly just as well
ask about the conditions of possibility for Javanese dance, Hindu mysteries, Chinese ancestor worship, or, if one wants to be Western European, and insofar as one can substitute scholasticism for Newton, scientific as well, how Christ's sacrificial death, the Apocalypse and certain

other similar synthetic judgments are possible, in particular if one does not want to survey just a single nook—eighteenth-century Europe—but rather the entire spirit apportioned to us human beings. That is why Kant's mockery of the world of the shades, of the aerial architects of speculation, signifies so little. What difference should it make to the other that a procedure is posited as a model and is in fact valid for every gray duck, when for the other, which because of its rarity or height cannot be posited as a model, it is therefore not valid, for it is a swan and obeys other rules. From such a starting point nothing can critically be proven, and so, as in a certain form Max Scheler already saw, and quite differently before him Eduard von Hartmann, the transcendental dialectic with all its prohibitions—to the extent that one perceives other contexts than the ones available to the phenomenology of Kant's time—is nothing more than prejudice and tautology. So from this point, and of course only from this point, it remains insignificant if the procedures that make possible pure mathematics and Newtonian science as the only accepted cognition cannot be applied to God, freedom, immortality, hence to the objects of morality and religion, and thus denying these epistemological complexes the character of empirical reality.

But there is another Kant, and this one is inexhaustible. It is deeply moving to watch how this power in him, alien and indifferent, conflicts with the frailty of his constitution no less than with the limits of his individual cross-section of experience. He may defend himself against his own genius, but it testifies to the power of this genius, which could bring anyone to his knees, that it once again destroys any explanation or evaluation on the basis of the contingencies, presuppositions, relativisms of the phenomenology of his time. That is why the question, how may something universally be valid, remains great only in Kant. Otherwise the question remains incidental, academic, a history of the sciences that becomes a theory of the sciences, structurally eternalizing everything limited and accidental in the state of those works selected as canonical. The same holds for the universally valid judgments of an *a priori* moral and aesthetic nature, where a Kant is needed so that above the restricted contentual material a supercontentuality of the formal production, pertinent to the most extensive content as well, can nonetheless emerge. How something might *a priori* be possible—this simply cannot be limited to the function of judgment, to the "logic" of nature, morality, beauty; however much a progressive transcendental-realistic correlation to the therein operative, persistently operative things, acts of will and ideas might deepen the purely *formal* exclusivity of the *a priori* in favor of a *real* determinative character of all "experience," better yet: in favor of an *a priori* as the metaphysical deductive cause of what should be, what is "logical," canonical in the world. But Kant, as we noted, possesses the momentous ability to make his own meager contents translucent, and to subordinate them transcendentally along with—insofar as that certain motion in the depths allows it, that is, the philosophy of history that is about the metaphysical—the Hindu mysteries as well as the Apocalypse, to the one who needs them. Hence English astronomy is merely his opportunity to find all the additional and scientifically pregnant connections within empirical logic, and the ban on applying these categories to Prussian moralism or to Kant's enfeebled metaphysical intuitions, in other words through the "unhappy" infatuation in what has been understood as metaphysics until now, opens the way to postulative logic on the one hand, and to the honest, great, subjective-ethical metaphysics of the age of a remote God on the other.

For precisely, we are simply no longer so fortunate that just anything can be received through the senses, or simply instinctively. Instead, Kant seeks to prove that the process which necessitates synthetic judgments from experience takes place independently, beyond perception. Neither the particulars nor the whole of this most esteemed part of Kant's investigations, insofar as it relates to the coherence of the natural world, is tenable. Apart from the remarkable fact that something "is," the naturally given phenomena: dampness, or the sound of shears cutting through silk, or even just the gait of a German shepherd dog, or whatever else, which are themselves experienced completely beyond mere perception, can not be reconstructed with Kantian categories, absolutely not by anthropomorphizing them, synthetically, nor theoretically, in terms of their inner relations. Especially the self that here wants to free and prescribe to itself and instead only "produces" the objects of nature, the epistemological self, is therefore, according less to function than to level, completely different from the ethical self. It can be illuminated by reflected light from the ethical self, the first properly productive self, but it can not itself take over the portfolio of production, of artistic responsibility, of prescriptive supervision, for the experiential world of the critique of pure *theoretical* reason, of the not only value-free but value-hostile world of physics. The laws and numerical constants of the natural world are not, as Kant thought, likewise situated within a system of "reason"; they are absolutely just "found," unevidently given, but not "assigned" to us in the more deeply home-ward—intellectually revealing—sense of this concept. Meanwhile, of course, the real issue in Kant is ultimately not even Kepler or Newton and the objectively valid connections between the phenomena of external na-ture, but rather that unconditional totality of determinations, those basic limit concepts that can only be willed or thought, but not recognized, in-sofar as they can perhaps be "experienced" in an immediately practical way, but can not be "intuited," insofar as their object is no empirical real-ity, in other words, and which are finally unfolded in a metaphysics of *as-signments*, as the Unconditional's regulative ideas of reason.

Here we first, finally become free, and the outer encirclement breaks; the genuine self steps forward. No matter how the things that still exist respond: hope makes one partial to precisely the well-fabricated [*er-dichten*] but otherwise unverifiable idea. For we are able to escape our-selves, and our quasiphenomenal form of existence, insofar as we form intelligible characters. Here the world's labyrinth and the heart's paradise become visible discretely; the world in the *focus imaginarius*, in the more hidden, intelligible part of our subjectivity, begins to appear as hope for the future. Precisely because theoretical knowledge finds itself restricted, as the knowledge of mere phenomena, belief, practical knowledge, the practical expansion of pure reason becomes free, and the postulates ap-pear, theoretically not provable, but in practice valid *a priori* uncondi-tionally. Here, by leading the same function that at first restricted us me-chanically *back onto itself*, onto precisely *the ethical self*, we are moving toward another rationalism than the thinking, theoretical Cartesian sub-ject's, destroyed by the natural world. We are moving, precisely through this rationalism of the heart and its postulate, so from away the produc-ing and the being-produced of a merely reflexive mechanics that respect for the law can be defined as the effect on us of the moral thing-in-itself, and our citizenship in a realm of higher and also contentually more pro-ductive intelligences secured. Meanwhile this effect on us obviously rep-resents no application of the category of causality, which is after all for-bidden here, but rather—as something rationally incomprehensible and paradoxical, the purely axiological inclusion of ideas of an Uncondi-tional as well, indeed the productive emergence, shared involvement, the adequation to this very effect—as the morally archetypal function and its inventory.

Here we are left alone with ourselves, then: indeed, no longer protected by anything outside or above, in fact. We must be good, although we know nothing of the real or, seen more exactly, even of the contentually ideal legitimation of value. We are lonesome, and stand in the dark of an infinite, merely asymptotic convergence toward the goal; even the remote star shines only a very uncertain light, illuminating nothing else in the sky; it can hardly be grasped as constitutive, and yet everything that does not completely go under in the general forms of a critique of pure theoretical reason—the particular, the specification of nature, as well as the decision by individuals for culture—must be subordinated to and organized within the moral law's primacy. But what appears as faith here is precisely only able to express freedom, immortality and the universal moral order in God as particular, plausible *postulates* of a second truth, relating only to a sphere of validity, to a not yet manifest, supersensory element of citizenship in intelligible worlds, and so does no damage to the obvious heroic "atheism" of this theory. In other words, there is no need for the customary complaint that in this way Kant tacitly maintains validity in the form of content. What is more important is that although Kant will certainly not further commit himself to any earthly particulars, his incredibly honest and grand sensibility is reaching firmly for the objects of its hope. Every hypothetical or relativistic quality has been eliminated from them, and if the most certain values and ideas nevertheless receive a regulative accentuation, this relates predominantly only to whether the idea *exists* and not to whether the *idea* exists. Here moral nominalism has pushed its point of unity extraordinarily far above any earthly reinforcement, without absolutely losing this point of unity, defined moral-mystically. Certainly, amid the clearest recollection and disclosure of the final given, the great Christian pathos of danger dominates, taking the field against the methodologically closed systems of physics or jurisprudence as well as against every assurance that God is already in his heaven, that is, against every duplication of the Platonic panlogism impermissible in modernity, but the constant problem of the *real* determinant of even the most unhypothetical imperative has not gone away, and the moral As If really appears here essentially as a theological Not Yet. Perhaps Kant even offers too much rather than not enough of a good thing here, as Hegel rightly sensed, insofar as within the Good one catches sight of that contentual and real indeterminacy of the postulate which, out of the fear of "sensual," empirical, hypothetical dependency, determines our behavior only regulatively and with such cautious diffuseness, as if our determination extended infinitely far above experience, in other words above this life. As important as it is, however, that the will be relieved of every particular purpose and turned toward the Absolute, this equally urgent obligation still finally arises within this inner norm, this Absolute of the moral will: to let a sun rise, a goal applicable at least as an objective moment of purpose, and thus to vault a heaven over ourselves that is no longer endlessly elusive but rather, as in Eckhart, again fundamentally attainable, utopianly real. The complaint should far more be the reverse—against the objectives of a continuous, unpenetrating methodization—that Kant here makes validation infinite, that he is precisely too little, too tacitly contentual, insofar as he defers validation into an *infinite process* with a *result posited* only from *the prospect of the spirit*, as only a *formal-a priori idea*; and Hegel's aversion to this sort of criticism, against this perseverance in method as such, be it undertaken with modesty, sobriety, or enthusiasm, as the case may be, had justified grounds, even beyond his utterly reprehensible Hegelian "realism." Hegel's theory that everything rational is already real concludes a premature and total truce with the world, but Kant's only approximative infinity of reason, practical reason in particular, makes of the world an ocean without a shore: what comfort is there for the shipwrecked, indeed for travelers, if no arrival is possible? Against "Kant's deduction of practical reason, and the latter's absolute blindness," Baader thus observes, with indisputable religious justification, and certainly not out of infatuation with either this world or some already arrived afterworld: that here Kant had not gone deep enough; the analysis of the phenomenon of "practical reason could more immediately and easily have resulted in spontaneity, its artistic unfolding; that in our conscience we become aware, with immediate certainty, of being perceived in our inmost life activity, as engendering the will; our reality, as abundant life and as divine reality, announcing itself to us as it unfolds outward within us." Indeed one can discern the deliverance of Kant's utopian spirit from method and from its bad infinity into the religious sphere itself, when Baader continues: it is completely contradictory and somewhat ironic to presume that one should give up a real life one knows without having the least hope in the *reality* of the other life whose affirmation is demanded; "only religion bases its demand for the negation of a contrary, false life completely on affirming and fortifying a different and better life, whose evolution keeps pace with the involution of the worse life."[4] In other words: nothing is valid without a being,

however threatened; rather the Ought or the Valid relate only to the abstract distance, to the mere, still unrealized essence of a law or value perhaps striven for but not yet implanted, however dark even for its part the
reality-degree of this logical surplus may appear. Indeed there exists, considered logically, from the standpoint of a utopian-absolute subject sur-
passing time, absolutely no discrete sphere of validity, but rather only an
supramundane sphere still to be evangelized, still valid over the distance,
a utopian reality. One which, insofar as it brings fulfillment, is certainly
not guaranteed, but which does not therefore involve a mere infinite striving after it, but rather involves Kant's postulates themselves—even as postulates of actualization.

II.

Now there is certainly no better gravedigger than the completely contentual concept. The essence of *Hegel* is to have brought all inwardness
outside, and to have closed off everything that remains open in Kant, in
favor of a certainly accessible but also regrettable achievement of an ex-
plicitly concluded system.

Someone who has it good finds it easy to be good. Hegel does the same
thing, but at the wrong place; rather than being good, he finds everything good, in order not to have to be good himself.

Thus one ceases to suffer and to will here, to be human. This shows itself in Hegel's annoyance with every demand. He wants to balance himself out, without there remaining the least sting in anything that seems to
him essential about the world, anything that the cold, lucid, dispassion-
ate concept might discover on the side of the objectively existent. Thinking oneself too good for the world, says Hegel in a characteristic phrase,
only means understanding the world better than others.

But Hegel is too rich as well as too poor to still be able to demand anything. His true inner attitude varies from one case to the next, and as a
whole, too, can be determined only with difficulty. In any case it remains
obscure who is speaking here so continuously and conservatively, but also
so absolutistically, whether it is the unfeeling Privy Councilor in him, or
else the passionate friend of Hölderlin and exuberant, Gothic phenomenologist of Spirit, who no longer thinks an earthly present alongside the
perfect Now.

At first, of course, we lose ourselves completely here; nothing about us is answered or resolved. Whether we suffer, whether we can be blessed, whether we are immortal as individual, existing human beings—the concept does not care. For the philosopher is on the way toward no longer being human; he leaves the worst to us and proudly departs an existence that so little affects the interests of abstraction. But the trouble with existing, as Kierkegaard says, is just that those who exist find existence endlessly interesting. It is easy to discern thereby whether a man tested by life is speaking, or a Münchhausen. Who only tells a story—say, "We left Peking and got to Canton; on the fourteenth we were in Canton"—is simply changing locations, not himself, and so the continuous form of narrative is in order. But here in the spiritual element, changing location means changing oneself, and thus every direct assurance that one has been here or there is only an experiment à la Münchhausen. Against it Kierkegaard posits the task for *subjective*, un-Hegelian thought: to apprehend oneself as existent and to understand oneself in existence. We and always we alone are addressed by Christian parables, and individually illuminated, strangely. It is Man, the first, last and freest being, or, seen even more nakedly, the We that grants itself the Messiah and then labors in the anticipation of him. But Hegel, the detached, objective philosopher, supposedly gives in to the temptation to take this all into consciousness as a mere occasion, in order to remain otherwise untouched, indeed even by taking the easy way of embellishing it, talking and speculating about it on better days, to hasten toward honor and fame, the more urgently the cause of finding oneself and of interiority demands a confession of faith. Thus it is far preferable, as Kierkegaard says, to be angry with Jesus, yet constantly in relationship to him, than to be a speculator who has understood Him, who makes theoretical material out of the sufferings of the glorious ones, and who finds Christianity true "to a certain extent." It became obvious how little we possessed after we allowed our effort of comprehension to be diverted in a way which was not even demanded, but which burdens man, as question, with the world as answer, and lets every other problem deteriorate into one determined *ad hoc* by the potential for its solution by the *Encyclopedia*. The detached, objective philosopher, in contrast, should be able to deal with even Christianity's most terrible demands at a remove, by his rootless cleverness, and to make every leap or obscurity into merely a momentary paradox at which the movement of speculation does not pause. To this unconcerned and worthless academic plenitude, then, the abstract thinker

Hegel, with objectivism's clear conscience, doubtless contributed his share, with an enchantment of construction all too remote from the self and all too freed of subjective participation [*Dabei*].

On the other hand, Hegel is also ultimately complete, and precisely therefore accustomed to comprehending from above. For philosophy then appears within time only as long as it has not grasped its own pure concept. It is, as Hegel expressly says, not just the higher level but the highest where the spirit resumes its education, impelled by the sublimity of the end. For Hegel, therefore, the movement from the uncultivated standpoint, past all its enfolded memories, to absolute knowledge, is only propaedeutically of importance. Everything has already been authorized by Providence; secular history is already transformed into sacred history; thus the philosopher who is required to notate the orders of the world spirit transforms and translates reason into nothing but mandates from on high, with a certain trump. The way it works in Hegel, in other words, according to his unadmitted principle, is that heavenly cards are shuffled into the earthly deck as though they belonged there and had always been part of it, that—putting it differently—the last remaining, the latest human being reassembles already solid formations out of the already completed process, whereas the whole, even what is empirically useful and certainly what is spiritual in these prehistories, is selected from the end of the *a priori*, or inserted from the object of thought into the object. Whereby in other words every kind of wishing or should-have-been, every laying-bare of the heart's convolutions, every insistence on subjective ideals and their antihistorical rationale, is traced downward from the highest level, and all this out of the same *panlogical pathos of perfection* with its eternally completed final word pushed back undifferentiatedly into the empirical. Characteristically, formal logic only appears at the end of Hegel's formal-metaphysical logic, and likewise the truth of this formal-metaphysical logic as a whole is only revealed in the sequence of religions and philosophemes at the end of the system. As the thought which knows what it is, then, it exists in Hegel no earlier and nowhere else than after the completion of the work. It is entirely a correlation to itself, historically and certainly metaphysically complete, and as a true infinity or as absolutely present depth of all factors, a circle looped into itself, indeed a closed circle of circles. The soul disappears, but the concept now itself become substance, like the activity of comprehension, the secretary of the world-spirit, triumphs in an unsubjective, panlogical objectivity.

Thus everything becomes so necessary and so clear that one should only have to mature enough to understand it. How else could Hegel dispute virtue, that it refuses the earthly course of things, which knows nothing of virtue? Hegel does not sneak up on the facts, as one used to say; rather he improves them, as if everything rational were real, and life itself wore the seven-league boots of that human feeling of being better. Meanwhile he improves things only intellectually, but nevertheless presents these merely intellectual clarifications as real, as so real that to the dissatisfied claim against so much freedom, so much Lutheran abdication of conscience to the state, to existence, there remains not even an intelligible, not even a consolatory beyond. In Kant the Ought was still defined as a something that occurs nowhere in nature, for which the guiding idea of history resides not in the fact, but absolutely and *a priori* only in the *problem* of an empire of moral ends. Now Friedrich Brunstäd has observed, with the utmost acuteness, that the *Phenomenology of Spirit* tried retroactively to do the same for practical reason that Newtonian natural philosophy, as something already at hand, had done for theoretical reason: in other words, that Hegel's philosophy of history would like to provide the fulfillment system for the primacy of practical reason. Only in Hegel one precisely does not notice where the empirical ends and the logical begins: he wants to find everything which is, proper; he still senses an idealism in the blue Hussars, a necessary estate in the feudal lords, a profound meaning in original sin, but then the so to speak messianic subject which after all establishes this utopian peace is not named, nor, above all, is the mixture (particularly active in Hegel's history) of the semifinished logical products of sound experiential knowledge with the closure and axiological deduction of the system ever raised to an object of investigation, in the sense of the epistemological problem of reality. Thus a peculiar situation appears in Hegel, where one time too little world is acknowledged, that is, too little movement, resistance and individual difference, and another time too much world, that is, too much that simply accumulated and is now presented as real, the falsest satisfaction and fulfillment of the Ought, too much of the already manifest truth of the matter, too much of the logically already perfected state of the world, and where all genuine experiential knowledge, all Hegelian empiricism, can therefore be understood as such only on the approximative scale of a Scholastic "realism" (this initial secular-ecclesiastical overthrow within philosophy), as empiricism. Out of which, finally, developed the further dubious element, a *final* ef-

fect of the premature, all too ratiocinative final word: that Hegel destroyed the soul and the freedom of his God outside, inside and above, in
favor of a merely intellectual process, overly mediated, bringing nothing
new, having purely a restorative, calculable outcome. What is the assurance supposed to mean here, then, that in human consciousness, which is
recapitulated history, God comes to himself? Of course this sounds ma-
jestic, like the mightiest subject-magical audacity of the old German mys-
tics, but if one looks more closely, and above all observes this weak, intel-
lectualistic God, then clearly the self who thinks, as well as the God who
is thought, proves to be dethroned and banished to the perimeter of an all
too mundane and encyclopedic consciousness. Here one needs to recall
Baader's profound words: that only the devil needs material, psychological and mundane mediations in order to exist completely. For as the fallen
souls sank inexorably downward, God arrested the earth in its plunge into
Hell, created matter out of pity, and rescued errant human beings from
hopeless destruction when he, by means of his Creation of all of inorganic, organic and psychological nature, made a perceptible material of
duty, and on the other hand, through Mt. Etna's eruption of all matter
and nature onto the devil, let the devil approach us only through them,
thus keeping Tartarus from harming us directly.[5] It makes no difference
here how correct these volcanic metaphors are; all that is important is that
God's highest state cannot be connected to this merely academically successful, only mundanely mediated consciousness, that if the truth is to be
seen there must be another kind of inwardness and "subjectivity" than
merely the intellectual world historian and absolutist's, and that only dis-
satisfaction, moral dedication against the *Encyclopedia*'s seemingly exhaustive realism about God, can be called to the Absolute and its reality,
a reality not pantheistically mediated.

Certainly suffering does not already need to be invoked everywhere, or
from below. Many simple things already show themselves to be complete
and, so to speak, capable of analysis, without it concerning them. The situation is quite different, however, when suffering, as the danger of frustration even in every higher real context, is denied. In Hegel the deed is
lacking, the sorrow or despair that even within the totality of history and
culture calls a person to action. That is why, where the concept overesti-
mates its reality, suffering adds savor, and the squalor, the adversity of life
becomes a harmless ceremony. Hence Hegel, considered exactly, acknowledges real historical progress only insofar as nations let Spirit enter

their consciousness, though it is quite complete without them, too, and their sequence then represents a particular way to comprehend, in time, the idea's timeless, in itself completely immobile, perhaps emptier and less fugal, but nonetheless already concluded mobility. Nowhere is the concept of development defined any differently: it is already based on an inner determination, an assumption existing in itself, which then simply brings about its representation. Just as a teacher at the blackboard "develops" essentially already completed mathematical theorems or philosophical schemata, so in Hegel is only the concept, the didactic disassembly and reassembly of completed cubes into a completed pyramid, and not the substance, allowed any "development" or metamorphosis. One can recognize here how the unceasing struggle of individuals against that alien, dark, wavering, merciless current that signifies life and world reduces merely to a difficulty within human and at best God's own receptivity. One can thus imagine no more innocuous reduction of every danger and every kind of fruitfulness than the manner in which Hegel on one side lets realization consist entirely of intellectual material, indeed lets it come out as merely the dialectical reversal of abstract thought, yet on the other hand transforms it into a function completely in the service of the concrete idea. And if the universal's particularization of itself is already defeated by inferior reality, by the inferior, purely existential bounds of the logical, and only possessed a certain methodological significance during the constructive phase, one can appreciate how much more violently the self-disclosure of the abstract, and its only apparently negative concretization into the concretely and really total, had to fail before cases of higher reality, in other words before the upper, *existential-moral* limit of the abstractly logical. Here the immoral belief in an already completed framework of the world and an omega, already completely disclosed in the alpha, of the absolute Idea, the regression principle of Hegel's dialectical method as such, takes us no further. One searches in vain in Hegel for that sensibility which alone directs us upward and is aware of the danger, which manifests itself in Kant, in Fichte's words: that there must be, beyond the mere repetition of what is or was, a knowledge grounding the deed, or a vision of that world that is not but which shall be, which drives us to act; that in other words one is not supposed to endure the world by the will of God, but make it different by the will of God, which, defined existentially-morally, in complete opposition to the dialectical kind of anamnesis, is certainly not the will to restitute some already past and precisely known cultural alpha.[6] In Kant, in other words, philosophy was a solitary light meant to burn up the night of this world. In Hegel philosophy becomes a headmaster, or indiscriminate lawyer for the Being that hired him, and the night of the world retreats into the merely ignorant subject. Here spreads the beautiful warmth of the classroom, so that everything painful, unendurable and unjust about life, the constant necessity of its refutation, the self-immolation of nature and the entire Herculean passion of the idea, can be developed as something safe, always occurring, never occurring, whose proper exposition is either just written on the blackboard, or else, in accordance with the eternally resolved, eternally completed logological silence of actual reality, is a mere ceremony: whose process, in other words, proves grounded only in transcendental-pedagogical and not transcendental-productive deduction. That is truly a restoration directed against Kant, but Hegel has no more refuted the Kantian Ought than the lying Schnaps of Goethe's *Citizen General* is a Jacobin, than content at any price could preserve the true form-character of Kantian philosophy, of philosophy as such. As a practical-transcendental, transcendental-real method on behalf of a *logos* that has not appeared, realized in the world at best by means of more or less preliminary, more or less indirect signs and symbols. So if here the tension between what was attained and what ought to have been has vanished by their being variously combined or imperceptibly played off against each other, then—notwithstanding how often, more or less without acknowledgment, the real is posited as the utopian, the utopian as the real—the Ought and the Valid have paid the greater price for the Spirit's regrettable worldliness, its world-reality. Hence it was certainly not only the murmurings of a benign spirit that induced this feverish desire merely to comprehend, this dialectic of the conclusive posited as real, this coastal navigation of mere systematization, all the way around the known continents, in order finally—so completely contrary to the true, deliberately constitutive method of Kant's philosophy that reaches far into the darkness—to let the inner God appear extrinsic, and his utopian *a priori* as an already real rationality.

~

Nevertheless, in the end: two types conflict here between which one may not simply choose. For the reason alone that here, far from any agreed alternatives, Kant cannot be done if Hegel is left out. Kant remains inward and infinite; his demand just fades away in eternity, contentually weak; certainly in contrast Hegel seems the more brilliant, magnificent, powerful manifestation, reminiscent of Handel and Wagner, as a philosopher of expanse and of a whole that would like already to be the true, with the objects, subjugated and thought through, following in the system's train.

But not everything inward need be slight and weak. For one thing, one cannot tell from a merely external circumspection if any of this is still moving or even wants to move. On the other hand, of course, one can see further in Hegel further than in Kant, in the Hegel we mean here, because Hegel has built well and thus can stand on the battlements; because he understands intensification, and above all, instead of unarticulated, unmediated feeling, understands the mediated thought that secures against every kind of avoidance or Don Quixote, against a false, disengaged, unreal radicalism. Meanwhile, and here Kant nevertheless triumphs in the end, the concepts, the forms, the spheric orders—even if, unlike in Hegel, they are correlated to an accelerated, motorically-mystically restructured world—are nothing final; rather, what is inward, its understanding-itself-within-existence, what is intensive finally appears above them, these mere directives and certificates, as the only equivalence [*Deckung*]. The spheric order is perhaps constitutive, but at the same time it has its limit within this constitutive function, as is already shown by the "crossview" Hegel maintains of all the spheric orders of law, tradition, art, religion, say those of Greece, or of the Gothic, a crossview by means of concepts that correspond interspherically almost everywhere, and break through the spheric perimeter. And the *final thing*, selfhood and its countenance [*Gesicht*], that immediate evidence, inaugurated by Kant's rationalism of the *postulate*, of properly understanding oneself, of the deepest utopian part of the conscience, can certainly be outlined only metacategorially and metaspherically, in the Kantian spirit of being affected by the thing-in-itself alone. "It does not seem to me," says Kant in the "Dreams of a Spirit Seer" that ironically betray his deepest principle three times over—"It does not seem to me that some kind of affection or unexamined inclination has deprived me of deference to any grounds for or against, save one. The scales of the understanding are not entirely impartial, after all, and the arm that bears the inscription *Hope for the Future* has a mechanical advantage causing even slight reasons falling into the corresponding pan to far outweigh speculations that in themselves have greater weight."[7] This is however the only "inaccuracy" that even

Kant "most likely cannot correct, indeed would never want to correct"; and the time has come to install, purely and exhaustively, such pious deception, such primacy and pragmatism of practical reason with regard to the actual, to the moral-mystical evidence of truth, such a metaphysics of thought conscience and thought hope. Certainly, who speaks in tongues, improves himself, but who prophecies, improves the congregation: yet more important is that the self that improves itself not be lost in the world. So it seems necessary at this point to let Kant burn through Hegel: the self must remain in everything; though it may at first exteriorize itself everywhere, move reverberantly through everything in order to break the world open, in order above all to pass through a thousand doorways, but precisely the self that desires and demands, the not yet implanted postulative world of its *a priori* is the system's finest fruit and sole purpose, and therefore Kant ultimately stands above Hegel as surely as *psyche* above *pneuma*, Self above Pan, ethics above the *Encyclopedia*, and the moral nominalism of the End above the still half cosmological realism of Hegel's world-idea. The goal would then have been attained if what had never entirely come together—glossolalia and prophecy, the spiritual and the cosmically total—were successfully unified, so that the soul could overtake and outshine the expansive world, but then did not remain narrow, and merely a subjective or humane idealism. Rather, after the end of glossolalia, of the Self- and We-encounter, the movement out into the world, into the world-encyclopedia, must really begin, for whose sake alone the Self-Encounter takes place; but precisely not in order to be lost in the world, but to destroy the false, dark expanse in it, to make it into the *world* of the soul, with the *omnia ubique* of the We-Problem at the beginning as at the end.

On the Metaphysics of Our Darkness, of the No-Longer-Conscious, the Not-Yet-Conscious, and the Inconstruable We-Problem

THE DARKNESS

But then I cannot even experience and occupy myself. Not even just this: that I am smoking, writing, and do not want precisely this, as too near, standing before me.

Only immediately afterward can I easily hold it, turn it before me, so to speak. So only my immediate past is present to me, agrees with what we experience as apparently existent. So this is what it means to live? This is how it looks from inside when one has become what one saw before one as a child or a youth? This is how it looks as myself; this is the love, the life that I read about; this is how it is subjectively, how it feels to me when one turns twenty, thirty, forty, fifty, as old as my mother was then, my parents' guests, all the adults, objectively observed? Never to be there: so this is the "real" life of this woman, this man; they were still twenty and that was their entire fulfillment? When does one really live, when is one consciously present oneself in the vicinity of one's moments? As urgently as this can be felt, however, it always slips away again, the fluidity, darkness of the respective moment, just like this other thing that it means.

THE NO-LONGER-CONSCIOUS

Only then, in other words, can I see what I just wanted and experienced: when it has already gone by in something else. But the wanting, observing gaze incessantly changes, too; the contents it observes sink from view, and soon I no longer possess as experience even what just passed.

Nevertheless, past desire, past experience does not cease to exist or to influence, even when it is not immediately conscious. In dreams above all returns the desire that had subsided during waking hours, and takes control, excited yet no longer exciting anything, of the hallucinated contents of memory. As Freud showed, they stand for forgotten or unresolved wishes, or wishes that our moral vigilance, moral adulthood cannot consciously permit. The unconscious, breaking through, becoming accessible to consciousness in dreams and in certain psychoses, has for its mainspring and motive force sexual desire, or the will to power, or whichever continuity one orders the different kinds of motor behavior into—in themselves already inherited, remembered, still creaturely. As such it is well known that mostly infantile wishes fill the abyss of what we dream. This shows that nothing lives in this space, volitionally or intuitively, that was not once present to consciousness, during childhood or prehistory, and then sank, was repressed and buried. Such deep-seated kinds of drive or experience can persist here that not only can the sexual impulse carry on its radically debilitating work, not only does the will to death of Freud's radical derivation persist within the organism and its unconscious, a tendency to reestablish inorganicity, but an environment, indeed an entire, defunct magical world can again be dreamt or atavistically divined that longer exists, whose forces and contents no longer determine our lives. Only now and then do features of the so to speak higher, human volition appear within this kind of remembering; only now and then does the darkness of the dream achieve an enfolding affinity to the mystery of the presentiment that speaks out of it, protected from the all too insolent light; certainly transmutations of what was appear now and then in memory, pointing to something expansive, utopian, essential, dispersed in the past, and so rescuing it. Otherwise, however, all that can be gained by immersing oneself in the chthonic, the defunct, in one's own sleep or any other unconscious blossoming, in the torpid condition of nature, is only recuperation, relaxation, or some initial protection, but no power right for us, for the soul has its own inception far from any creatureliness, where there is after all not only the flame that blossoms and burns upward, but the stone that drops, and precisely the flame of the *sursum corda* glows in the originary heat of the intention upward more purely than in the impure nature of the autochthonous, of prehistory, of heathenism as well as of the protective chthonic husk. The sleeping dream itself, then, usually derives in every sense from the past, decomposes what was just present into a past, holding on to the past in its lifeless fragments, its stereotypy, in mere "nature's" tendency to repetition. Indeed, finally: even a natural science that only wants to grasp what is, without us, and how it was, which observes only what was, only matter, and breaks down every phototropism without remainder into a creaturely "before," loses every vitally utopian current and finally encloses itself within an empty mechanics: even such a slack science, a science directed toward what has slackened, is finally trapped in the no-longer-conscious, in a past so stabilized that only stones still tumble there.

So the drives that appear again here, and what they impose, remain far behind us, are no longer right for us. In no way can the grasping of color, the upsurge of joy be derived from it, and certainly not what is better, higher, purer, the drive upwards, the individual conscience. Rather the reverse: the sexual drive, the instinct for self-preservation, the will to power, form mere enclaves, mere dismal, covert, involuntary, automatic prologues of our "genuine," "right," "human," "spiritual" will and instinct. Certainly the animal drives, however ravenous, contaminated by egocentrism, enclosed in craving, already contain the will to return home, the completely alert drive, just as in the ordinary wishful dream an aprioristic wishful dream, a waking dream, can take effect. A legend of happiness or of the will to be happy is just as trivial a matter as it is potentially the

most sublime; it is the same thing that the tailor of Seldwyla and the
knight Zendelwald sought in Keller's *Seven Legends*, what moved Martin
Salander's daughter the second time again, and then more deeply in the
legend about the pot of gold at the end of the rainbow—and it cannot be
gutted even somewhat by means of some reduction to or rabulistics of
sexual imagery.[8] Similarly an artist can certainly give himself over quite
completely to the free influx of ideas, repressions, and associations, the
happily obscure ancestry, the wondrous sons of chaos, the chthonic "half-
nonsense" out of which Goethe, just like someone who had just awakened, wrote down his *Harzreise*, though, precisely, instructively, a fan-
tasizing still obstructed by animality, drowsing fitfully, will really only
follow streets that are shorter than any halfway exorbitant reality's, let
alone the truly productive waking dream's.[9] As a whole, then, in spite of
various prologues and various enclaves dispersed within animality: everything that fulfills these creaturely drives, all the contents of their world,
their unreal, bygone world, as well as the ancient parallel world that can
perhaps still become recent to our atavistic clairvoyance—all this is at
best a cipher for the true, authentic volition and for the contents of its
truly intended fulfillment-world. The scientific given itself, however: discovered by the slackened I in itself, rotated under us and revolving under
us in its God-forsaken automatism, independent of the experiencing,
comprehending, present subject—is not even a cipher, but rather just the
schematism into which the dead bury what is dead, prescribing to it its
structures and laws.

A related fact is that even these structures and laws, that even this secularized myth of destiny, that is, the entire factual logic of the scientifically given world is beginning to lose all functional regularity, and not
just substance; that thought independent of the experiencing and comprehending subject, as the natural sciences require, increasingly loses even
a recognizable, a cognitively functional objective correlate. For scientific
thought might want to grasp what exists without us, and how it was, but
it goes no more deeply into it, and holds on to just the beginnings, the
fragments. Scientific reason has always been imagination that had learned
from its mistakes: with an approximation, an ideal type at the beginning
that was practical when the real world demanded some reduction, correction, damage to and dismantling of the spirit. Meanwhile the damage
has increased so greatly that scientific reason must wither into a bare
schematism, a reflexivity that lays out its now fully alogical *vis-à-vis* only

through computational approaches, through more or less economic models, without the energy or the ambition to find the reality within this alogical horror, within the totality of this consummate desolation. If science could mirror its world, the whole of the obstruction, the immobility, the lack of flow, the "regular" stereotypy, the mechanical freedom from value: it would reflect—apart from a few ciphers, which of course on the other hand science could not register, since the apperception of them presupposes a presently living subject and a utopian elective affinity—it would reflect the realm of the buried "past and gone," a suffocating immanence, a mechanically absolute "in vain."

NOT-YET-CONSCIOUS KNOWLEDGE AND THE
DEEPEST AMAZEMENT

And then we ourselves simply do not occur merely as something remembered. Precisely: we live [*leben*] ourselves, but we do not "experience" [*erleben*] ourselves; what meanwhile never became conscious can also not become unconscious. Insofar as we have never and nowhere become present through *ourselves*, neither within the just lived moment nor immediately afterward, we cannot appear as "such" in any area of any memory. Matters stand differently, nevertheless, with the *hoping* that turns what was experienced forward, above all with the hope that lives in us as the "quietest," "deepest" longing, that accompanies us as the "waking dream" of some demystification, some nameless, uniquely right fulfillment.

Already as children we are constantly impatient, waiting, finally making sure of ourselves in it. It stays with a person, so fervent and enigmatic, making us jump on Sunday evenings every time the doorbell rings; will the right thing finally be delivered? Thus that *open* questioning, effervescing, covert uncovering opens up everywhere new life begins, as the expectancy of emergence as such. Precisely because the words here merely intimate us, distantly and yet quite closely, hardly still played about by images and yet at the same time as though we had also been taken so far away, so near, a kind of remembering is at work that has almost nothing in common anymore with the creaturely drives from which it is apparently supposed to derive, or with its defunct world. What could the art of revealing beginnings still mean here? Does not in truth an *originary* point lie here, which begins to glow by itself within human love, artistic genius? What life promised us, we want to keep it here above, for life: and never can this "unconscious" of an entirely different kind, this living, hoping, intuiting directed forward, this striving out of the darkness into the light, this in truth not yet conscious essence, as the "unconscious" of the completely other side, high above, be reduced to the moonlit landscape of what was. Of the normal or chthonic dream and its contents, forming a dead circle of creatureliness, past, myths of destiny or mechanism around us. Rather, the demonism of genius commences with itself; love is already no organic but rather a theological state, located on a different level than our creaturely drives, and especially everything else intensively spiritual in us has its own energy source. Very far from the mere dreams of the animal spirit or the earth spirit, very far from the chthonic incubations of what was, what was buried: and belonging to whom else but the elevated, reborn, revolutionary serpent; whom else but the true prophetic god Apollo; whom else but the originary spirit of the Messiah in our ownmost depths, who precisely first enables every *eros* to be divested (not "masked") in colors, wayfaring, festivity, homesickness, homecoming, mysticism? Above all in days of expectancy, when the imminent itself intrudes into the Now, in the power of happiness, most strongly in music, which from beginning to end has our spiritual existence as its goal, and wants to deliver to it the word (that word whispered into our ear every night; it always seems to be the same, and yet we can never understand it), above all within artistic labor itself, is that imposing boundary *with the not-yet-conscious* clearly overstepped. A dawning, an inner brightening, trouble, darkness, creaking ice, an awakening, a hearing nearing itself, a condition and concept, ready, against the darkness of the lived moment, the nameless *a priori* brewing in us, near us, before us, in all of being-in-existence in itself, finally to kindle the sharp, identical light, to open the gate of looking in one's own direction. As Leibniz showed the spiritual *roots*, and thus demonstrated to the *Sturm und Drang*, to nature's dark sides as well, the *fundus animalis* of the *petites perceptions*, so does the utopian philosophy of a way of thinking that shines further upward, of the soul shrouded in incompletion, mystical careers and an expanding glow from the future, begin to explore the higher-order unconscious, the *fundus intimus, the latency of the primordial secret in itself moving within the Now*, in short the creative unconscious of our spiritual *coronation*.[10]

~

Hence there is still a stirring in us that lately reaches inward and upward. It is evening, there a genuine dreaming might most easily find itself, and yet there we are the most deeply brightened and touched. Of course this hoping and, making it clearer, this *amazement* often ignite completely arbitrarily, even inappropriately; indeed, there is perhaps not even a rule here by which the same causes of it within the same person could be found.

It is questioning in itself, an inmost, deepest amazement, which often moves toward nothing, and yet quiets the flux of what was just lived; lets one reflect oneself into oneself such that what is most deeply meant for us appears there, regards itself strangely. A drop falls and there it is; a hut, the child cries, an old woman in the hut, outside wind, heath, an evening in autumn, and there it is again, exactly, the same; or we read how the dreaming Dmitri Karamazov is astonished that the peasant always says "a wee one,"[11] and we suspect that it could be found here; "Little rat, rustle as long as you like; / Oh, if there were only a crumb!" and upon hearing this small, harsh, strange line from Goethe's *Wedding Song* we sense that in this direction lies the unsayable, what the boy left lying there as he came out of the mountain, "Don't forget the best thing of all!" the old man had told him, but no one could ever have come across something so inconspicuous, deeply hidden, uncanny within the concept.[12] No horror, image or feeling fully includes or concludes here; one can see that it is not only the great discoveries, the sails of great ships still below the horizon to the average eye, that the genius of the not-yet-conscious foresees, that populate his utopian space. More deeply, rather, it is the *values of amazement* that are carried by the state of presentiment, and ultimately reflected: something small, the kernel within so much impressive empty emballage, a Messiah who appears not in a flash but warm and nearby, as our guest, the discarded cornerstone within a metaphysical perspective, the wafting, comprehensible-incomprehensible symbol-intentions of the *tua res agitur* as a whole. The simplest word is already much too much for it, the most sublime word much too little again, and yet perhaps what is true of these small, penetrating, and yet, followed through to the end, always the most authentic of all emblems, was true till now only of the greatest things: of the Delphic Sybil, of the miracle of the "Holy Night" in the *Missa Solemnis*, of the reverberations of ourselves in all great music, of the primordial experiences of great, dark poetry, of Faust and his always rationally incommensurable production, as Goethe writes, of all these constructs just before dawn, which one namelessly understands from somewhere, which, in their question-as-answer, their answer-as-question, already fulfilling themselves almost completely. What is felt,

meant here is the same every time: our life, our future, the just lived moment and the lighting of its darkness, its all-containing latency, in the
most immediate amazement of all. Our moral-mystical concern and our
self-ascertainment in itself is meant; some surplus based on nothing extrinsic, the surplus of the *moral-mystical existence-meaning in itself,* is
proper to every such experience and especially to every artistic concentration of symbol-intentional profundity. That gives them their tremendous promiscuity with respect to time, space, and terminus; that marvels
on through these constructs in a philosophical lyricism of the final border standing above every discipline, spiritually *kat exochen,* arch-imma-
nent and thus metareligiously superior, exterior, even to the formations
of faith, to the other world.

If one nonetheless would like to designate here somewhat, one should
consider that what has just been said must be crossed out each time, so
that nothing can solidify. Nevertheless, precisely, the darkness lightens toward evening and its own morning, in the amazement of all these vague-
precise symbol-intentions. To them applies what William Butler Yeats
wrote of Shelley and his symbolism, and how inevitably the boat, the vision of the boat that drifts down a broad stream between high mountains
with caves and peaks, toward the light of a star, ceaselessly accompanied
him: "I think too . . . that voices would have told him how there is for
every man some one scene, some one adventure, some one picture that is
the image of his secret life, for wisdom first speaks in images, and that this
one image, if he would but brood over it his life long, would lead his soul,
disentangled from unmeaning circumstance and the ebb and flow of the
world, into that far household where the undying gods await all whose
souls have become as simple as flame, whose bodies have become quiet as
an agate lamp."[13] Of course not just differently for everyone and thus os-
cillating only psychologically, so to speak; rather, symbols also flow functionally; one must remember the rule that they more or less circle only
the one primordial word, which in turn more closely surrounds the still
unarticulated primordial secret: in other words, symbols do not at all
solidly attach or assemble themselves into a plastically self-completing inventory of moral-mystical symbol-intentions and their concepts, their
types. Rather, again and again, diagonally through every meaning, there
appears the one, the unnamed, unnamable, *spiritualistically* confounding
the order, just as the true Gnostic Basilides said about precisely the "concept" and the "order" of the primordial word itself, quite destructively:

"What is called inexpressible, is not inexpressible, but is only called so; but that of which we speak is not even inexpressible"[14]; which denies, then, already in principle, that the ontic symbol-contents ultimately are shaped like a representation, a world, or that they are fit for hierarchy. Above all, however, instead of the still mundane fixation on mere images of the outside (leading outside, even if perhaps into a higher outside), that consciousness of *mystical soul-intensity in itself* must dominate that addresses us, means us only through symbols, and itself would like to brighten our lived incognito; there appears, in other words, that powerful, primordially symbolic intention, so close and yet deep inside, the *visio vespertina* and at the same time the brightest chapel of the heart, which Eckhart means in his sermon on the eternal birth and the one hidden word that came in the middle of the night, where all things were silent in the deepest stillness: "See, just because it is hidden one must and should always pursue it. It shone forth and yet was hidden: we are meant to yearn and sigh for it. St. Paul exhorts us to pursue this until we espy it, and not to stop until we grasp it. After he had been caught up into the third heaven where God was made known to him and he beheld all things, when he returned he had forgotten nothing, but it was so deep down in his ground that his intellect could not reach it; it was veiled from him. He therefore had to pursue it and search for it in himself and not outside. . . . There is a fine saying of one pagan master to another about this. He said: 'I am aware of something in me which shines in my understanding; I can clearly perceive that it is something, but what it may be I cannot grasp. Yet I think if I could only grasp it I should know all truth.' To which the other master replied: 'Follow it boldly! For if you could seize it you would possess the sum total of all good and would have eternal life.' St. Augustine spoke in the same sense: 'I am aware of something within me that gleams and flashes before my soul; were this perfected and fully established in me, that would surely be eternal life.'"[15] Of course on the other hand in Eckhart, as forcefully as he immediately asks, "Where is he that was born King of the Jews?" the light-substance is still very high, very remote in space, shifted away from the subject and the We to the supradivine God, into the highest depths, into vertiginous depths of angelic light, which truly can least of all contain, resolve, the only secret, the secret of our nearness.[16] Rather it must be the moment just lived; it alone, its darkness, is the only darkness, its light is the only light, its word is the primordial concept that resolves everything. Nothing sublime lives whose sublimity is not such that it conveys a presentiment of our future freedom, an initial interference by the "Kingdom"; indeed Messiah himself (in Collossians 3:4), the bringer of absolute adequation, is nothing but the finally uncovered face of our unceasingly nearest depth.[17]

More on the Adequation of Amazement, and the Pure Question

As sublimely as the condition of amazement, presentiment may point outward, then, underway it still finds every kind of deceptive solution—and not only in its "unconscious" intention, which can be dragged down to the merely no-longer-conscious, but rather precisely in its adequation as well, on its objective side—that stops, that repeatedly develops static forms dissipating and equalizing the utopian surplus in this our existence.[18]

But one should finally refuse to let oneself, what one meant, be so quickly put off. Hunger must not be cheated; it only knows that this cannot satisfy it, nor can that, but of what will finally allay it can have only a presentiment, as it is not yet here. Certainly the question how one imagines bliss is so far from forbidden that it is basically the only one permitted. Meanwhile even this question, trying to brighten the twilight, already aims frivolously at something named, accustomed, already commits us to a weak, restrictive word.

This is not what one wanted, or even asked for; one could drown trying to understand all this, which ultimately remains alien. We stand there no wiser than before, perhaps less, for our longing did not enter with us, and yet the wrong kind of abundance came. Everything was so totally different before; there were sighs, restlessness, moonlight, wind, the clock's ticking, the old man's stories around us as around Heinrich von Ofterdingen; but whatever is given to us: we remain always still outside before what we create, the painter does not enter the painting, the poet is not in the book, in the utopian land beyond the lettering, and even the girl, the blue flower, as clearly different as she is from any other treasure, finally falls into the adept's arms from outside, remaining outside. The question that we are lies so near, whose one word resonates secretively within every moment, brighter than bright in this dark chamber, in the self-mountains of amazement rising steeply by us: but if one just seeks to ask it in outline, then on the way it also becomes curved, folded, bent over, *construed into shape*, disassembled into the manifold pseudo-enigmas of the outside, until like a buyer who had wanted something entirely different one is finally loaded down with what was most easily available; the uncertain wish itself is forgotten. One sought the essence of the world, and as one had it, it turned to water or later something lofty and unmusically ceremonious that could not be too remote to provide a clear conscience and the highest concept. Indeed, the higher the category lay, the more joyfully the Now was given up, the more perfectly the sign of distance seemed to rise over the tepid old nearness: all things that do not concern us, all self-presentative ideals, and God in particular a thing, the "highest" thing, the nature "of the highest object [*Objekt*]," as in the Byzantine state. The needy human being wants to have only one thing, flowing, dark, sorrowful, primordially luminous, resolved quietly inside him; and then ensued those countless distracting "problems" and answers defined only by mundane objects, pure cosmology, the potential for solution: action and reaction, spontaneous generation, the origin of the species, the Catiline conspiracy, the filiality of Jesus, such that man, in other words, if he finds himself just once on the stages of this extrasubjectively illuminated, extrasubjectively ascending science or pyramid of ideas, forgets the question originally motivated by self-amazement, indeed unthinkingly allows the *Encyclopedia*, the plaintiff having disappeared, to present itself as the day of absolute maturity and the comprehensive answer. Just so does that senseless game also persist of "the universal enigma" and especially its "answer," which honest philosophers are only supposed to suggest, but which every philosopher till now, reducing the primordial question to a more convenient scholastic problem, the *ad hoc* problem of a system's beginning, affects to have located in some monumental term. But one should understand here and remember: by its very nature, the solution, at least, will never be expressed in a book, and as little in a mundane church as in any academic philosophy, once one finally constitutes the correctly understood question differently as the absolute *crisis*, which, once come to pass, *means nothing less than the unavoidable end of this world, along with all its books, churches, and systems.* No secular reader could still rise from the study of this metaphysics, this metaphysics reserved solely to the Messiah; he would at once discover himself in the world beyond existence, in the Jerusalem of shattered time, transformed suddenly in a moment and *as this moment*: as the revealed Kingdom of heaven that had been his dark, deep Gothic *sanctum*, existentiality and latency. For this reason only one thing is ultimately left for precise, ontic discussion: to grasp the question about us, purely as question and not as the construed indication of an available solution, *the stated but unconstrued question existing in itself*, in order to grasp its pure statement in itself as the first answer to oneself, as the most faithful, undiverted fixation of the We-problem.

One man above all here left behind the merely external, thinks his way into what concerns us. *Kierkegaard* alone left what is ultimately alien behind, is the Hume born to us, who awakens far differently, more significantly, from dogmatic slumber. We are: that alone is the concern where what is truly fundamental is involved; one looks out the window onto the street, but in the silvered glass, in the mirror alone does one see oneself. Only in the cloudy, shimmering aspect of being-there [*da-Sein*], which feels and wants to become aware [*innewerden*] of itself, is one together with the truly infinite, the immediate, out of which alone the truth looks toward us: it is moral, is character, "but the sea," says Kierkegaard, "has no character and the sand has none and abstract intelligence has none either, for character is precisely interiority."[19] And: one should not make something objective even of God; rather just this would be pagan, and a pure diversion toward a will o' the wisp and a false expanse; everything depends on the discarded cornerstone and on Eckhart's insight, slight in the most utterly Christian way: "What the heaven of heavens could not contain, that now lies in the Virgin's womb."[20] Only that cognition, Kierkegaard teaches, which relates essentially to our existence, is essential cognition, existential pathos, in contrast to which all alienated, dispassionately systematic procedure represents nothing but a cheap, mendacious way to process oneself out of the immediacy from which the truth regards us utterly; or as Kant similarly formulates this purely existential pathos: "God and the other world are the single goal of our philosophical investigations, and *if the concepts of God and the other world did not relate to morality, they would be useless.*"[21] Kierkegaard, like Kant, means the force in the direction of the kernel, which of course need not lie firm and round under the husks, with a sweet taste, but is itself at first full of confused utopia interwoven with the darkness of the lived moment itself. And this force should finally prove itself in this respect, that it also intensifies the grasp of the inconstruable question as subject-magic by the subject on itself, on the phenomenal of its freedom: with a new, inner conception of evidence, that takes absolute care to want to be edifying, that possesses the finally awakened will to the human-spirit instead of to the world and its world-spirit, that confirms the primacy of practical-mystical reason even, and particularly, on the highest heights of metaphysics.

Again the Darkness (of the Lived Moment) and Its
Mutual Application to Amazement

We have seen, we have nothing at first, whether outside or inside, that would let one hold on to oneself. That is why it remains so shadowy, never immediately to experience anything lived, while the Now by which we alone "are" still always thumps and haunts.

It is not easy, say, to attentively observe a point from which one must intentionally look away. Similar, but far more difficult, is retrieving the always momentary out of the melancholy shadowiness of its being-there, and possessing it in the present, without veils. There is certainly not just one simple weakness: certainly, completely unmetaphysically, there are enough people who simply cannot live, only watch the others or avail themselves of the pictures, the reports of experiences which they themselves could never have, and so they must have substitutes. But here the issue is *the darkness of experiencing in itself,* and of precisely the intense and completely potent kind of experiencing that can only be grasped with such difficulty, whose curtain with its thousand folds breaks over consciousness and enfolds it. The operative complaint here is being able to experience nothing but what is already past or only just appearing, whereby what approaches at least stands closer to the dark self, while "life" itself, grasped as the sum of its moments, dissolves into the unreality of these moments.

We do not even really know what absolutely just "is" or even who we "are"; if anything is ghostly, it is someone who wants to present to himself the one who presents. Here everything converges at first, and combines in precisely the Now that is being experienced. We have seen that only just after it passes can what was experienced be held up in front of oneself, and it is organized spatially, in the intuited form of its simultaneity, which diverges from the flow, so to speak: half still just experientially real, and half already a juxtaposition of inactive contents. When the past is regarded as such on a larger scale, as a world of the no-longer-conscious, as a world independent of the experiencing, apprehending subject, this world, as has already become clear, becomes the object of science. Within partly organized experiential reality, space as merely the intuitive form of *simultaneity* was still an enclave of time, surrounded front and back by the latter as the intuitive form of *vitality*: history still maintains this somewhat, it understands a succession of effective units, albeit merely lining them up; in physics, on the other hand, the model of scientific conceptualization, objects are organized into such a typically ahistorical field that here time itself figures only as a sort of spatial dimension. Only the philosophy of history, also reviving what was, utopically overhauling it, places time, the intuitive form, the operative sphere of active life, at the center; and as for the concept of hope, of the philosophy of value, when it recognizes a stiller kind of simultaneity, a "spatiality" of ensembles, shapes, categories, spheres, these are all finally centered around the *true simultaneity*, around the far-near "inner space" of absolute life and existential disclosure, where the Now first brightens. Because however the Is, the Now, or—the actualization is already so difficult to see experientially or inspect scientifically: that is why a prophet is without honor in his own land, that is why every age appears corrupt to itself, mere civilization, that is also why the historian is so painfully subject to the course of history's becoming the present again, the decrescendo into "currency" within the system of history, without his political judgment necessarily learning anything from his historical judgment. What thus lies midway between memory and prophecy—we ourselves, the midpoint moving, floating through the ages, at which we find ourselves in every lived moment—is a shadow, the hidden seed, the flowing, partial correlation of consciousness to itself as experiential reality, a sheer, blind, self-absorbed, indirect being-affected, a dark island where nonetheless not only the entire impetus of the movement of the world, but, after movement stops, arrests itself, in other words after its conciliation, the true condition of being, the true reality and logicity of the world seems to be hidden. The self's intuition of itself, however, is only a problem at all because until the hour of the process, the "world-process," the rotational and objectivational process *kat exochen*, no placing-oneself-before-oneself, no revolving-oneself-beyond oneself, encountering-oneself, no more total reflecting of any lived moment had succeeded: no concentration of mere partial consciousness into being-identical-to-oneself, achieved being as such.

So it goes without saying that even this: that we humans are, represents only an untrue form, to be considered only provisionally. We have no organ for the I or the We; rather, we are located in our own blind spot, in the darkness of the lived moment, whose darkness is ultimately *our own darkness*, being-unfamiliar-to-ourselves, being-enfolded, being-missing. Just as all the indistinctness there derives from the subject's present condition as the still dispersed, unassembled, decentralizing although never disconnected function of consciousness as such. However, this function operates only indirectly, either punctually, as actual momentariness, or, when it wants to get nearer to participation, then spatially or spherically, so that the dispersed subject's consciousness arrives at basically only the past and its laws, without ever being able to advance into the flowing future, let alone the great presentness, to be realized as well as to meet up with one realizing himself. Yet—*and this is of decisive importance*—the *future*, the *topos of the unknown within the future*, where alone we occur, where alone, novel and profound, the function of hope also flashes, without the bleak reprise of some anamnesis—is itself nothing but *our expanded darkness, than our darkness in the issue of its own womb, in the expansion of its latency.* Just as in all the objects of this world, in the "nothing" around which they are made, that twilight, that latency, that essential amazement predominates where merge the reserve and yet the strange "presence" of seeds of gold blended into, hidden in leaves, animals, pieces of basalt; *whereby precisely the very thing-in-itself everywhere is this, which is not yet, which actually stirs in the darkness, the blueness, at the heart of objects.* And God within must not just become visible to us in order to be, so that the entire world-process is eleatically reduced to the coordination between two "separate" realities; rather even God—as the problem of the radically new, absolutely redemptive, as the phenomenal of our freedom, of our true meaning—possesses himself within us only as a shadowy occurrence, something objectively not yet occurred, only as the coincidence of the darkness of the lived moment with the unconcluded self-symbol of the absolute question. That means: the final, true, unknown, superdivine God, the disclosure of us all, already "lives" now, too, although he has not been "crowned" or "objectivated"; he "weeps," as certain rabbis said of the Messiah, at the question, what is he doing, since he cannot "appear" and redeem us; he "acts" in the deepest part of all of us as the "I am that I shall be," as "darkness: of the lived God," as darkness before his self-possession, before his face that will finally be uncovered, before the departure from the exile of true essence itself.[22]

So it seems, indeed it becomes certain, that this precisely is hope, where the darkness brightens. Hope is in the darkness itself, partakes of its imperceptibility, just as darkness and mystery are always related; it threatens to disappear if it looms up too nearly, too abruptly in this darkness. We tremble in hope, in amazement; something comes over us, and people like to say that at such a moment someone is passing over where we will be buried; but in reality, insofar as we thereby experience the genuine question, a word is approaching the inmost focus of our and thus all being-there, is passing over our final self. The darkness of the nearness thus perhaps still intensifies the darkness of the secret, which of course would precisely not seem so dark if it were not in the deepest way the darkness of the nearness itself; thus the "dreaming" Epimetheus in Goethe's *Pandora* sees little more, does not recognize hope, Elpore, the unconditional Yes, when she comes too near, and only at some remove does she who cannot be grasped become audible as the flashing of the *in aeternam non confundar*.[23] But the secret quite precisely never stands in the dark, but rather is called to dissolve it; *thus does the darkness of the lived moment awaken in the resonance of the amazement that comes over us,* and thus does its latency arrive at an initial "visibility," the enjoyment and the superabundance of being affected by the We. Much therefore indicates the reciprocal connection between the darkness and the amazement of the question: at first negatively, insofar as neither can ever be seen as such, thus remaining ultimately unobjective, and then more positively, insofar as both not only formally represent the *novum* in itself in the world, but also materially intend the same We, maintain the same objective correlation to the subjectivity which is to be excavated, and to our moral-mystical incognito. So closely do the darkness of the lived moment and the essence of the inconstruable question touch, that exactly the symbol-intentions of the central kind remain partly invisible, sharing in the abruptness of the current angle of vision, as well as able to mark out the path for those who yearn, who are amazed at the very nearest latency in us, the direction toward, the direction of the centrally applicable "existence-word," the password to the We-disclosure as a whole. Here a crossing into the final answering is making ready, into the eating-ourselves, the being-resurrected-into-ourselves, the reciting-to-oneself of the only theme: a crossing into a completely experienced anamnesis adequated to its kernel, into an intensively and thus operatively objectivated presence of personhood and the incipiently brightened question.[24]

Here, then, is where thoughtful hope resolutely holds on, lifts itself precisely out of the Now and its darkness, into itself. Thus does the heart's thought first cast its light forward into the land where lightning flashes, that land that we all are, in which we all move, which we finally enter decisively, harkening toward our arrival, our absolution [*Lösewort*]. Here is not merely a new path into the old, certain reality; rather reality itself proves to be broken open toward where the *fundus intimus* finally appears in all its centrality, and just as in legends and the ancient epopoeia, man, infinitely stronger than himself, travels again into the unknown world, into the adventures of a soul-space extending to an unknown limit. However, the philosophical insight that is especially intended here is the lamp that transmutes into gems, the arrival of the minister in the prisons of the demiurgic Don Pizarro.[25] Is the activity of the great work, of the water of life, of absolution; magical idealism on the basis of the prophetic dream waiting in the head of every thing, of the inconstruable question, of its thing-in-itself: that this is, in other words, which is not yet, which the final future, finally genuine present is, the self-problem finding itself in existence, still unknown, incomplete utopia. Then again philosophical thought also proves to be turned toward myth, a different one than before, toward the final myth before the great turn, toward that myth of utopia that has immemorially motivated the Jews like the philosophers by their nature; which to them both, these anxious worshippers of an unseen God, the ultimative absoluteness, makes every theology of a definitive, pictorial factuality seem suspicious. Whoever wants to pursue the truth must enter this monarchy: but not as if the secret compartment in every object contained still more grandiose scrolls and documents, as in earlier eras, when a gigantic emballage came with every profundity—gods, heavens, dominions, glories, thrones—and were considered essential to it. Rather Odysseus returned to Ithaca soundlessly, sleeping, that Odysseus who is called No-One, and to that Ithaca that can be just the way this pipe lies there as it does, or the way this otherwise so inconspicuous thing suddenly acts so that one's heart skips, and what was always meant seems finally to regard itself. So secure, so very immediately evident, that a leap into the not-yet-conscious, into the more deeply identical, into the truth and the absolution of things has been made that can not go back; that with the suddenly final intention of meaning by the object toward the observer, the countenance of something still nameless, the element of the final state, embedded everywhere, emerges at the same time within the world, and will never leave it.

THE POSSIBLE SITES OF ABSOLUTION

But exactly here, totally inside, nothing can happen just by itself. The impulse, as it collects and appears on a higher level, must be unselfish and communal. It must transfer into commonality, moving outward from here to understand what is urgent, brightening. The egoistic I remains imprisoned within itself, but for the spark in us, once we bring ourselves to it, the purer, higher life will certainly become urgent and bright.

There is so much outside that would never occur to someone; it has to be given through the senses. If we want to comprehend what kindness is, or love, or any other archetypal figure of the *human* landscape, our determination of everything that just happens to be there becomes suddenly independent, nourished in itself, by itself, clear, comprehensible, a determination within a concept of value. Goethe similarly says that knowing how to hold court is not innate, nor how to behave in parliament or at an imperial coronation, and in order not to offend against the truth of such matters the poet must learn them from experience or tradition; the region of love, however, of hatred, of hope, of despair, and what the conditions and passions of the soul are called, is in the most precise sense innate in the poet; he possesses their contents through his power of anticipation, beyond any observation of the natural world. In every single powerful experience of a spiritual kind there is thus an ontic surplus value intended toward the symbol, and no less so in the *ontos-on* concept; Christ's statement: "Why callest thou me good? there is none good but one, that is, God"[26]—thus uses the quintessence of goodness in a singularly ontic way: as a judgment, all the worse for the facts that do not agree with it, far from needing any inductive proof, valid without world, all the more valid without world, valid in its own self-presence. As soon as one articulates and defines just the *concept* of humility or kindness or love or soulfulness or spirit, the result is immediately valid in all its unavoidably moving profundity calling for realization. Every object of moral-metaphysical expression is thus simultaneously the reality that has not yet been fully achieved, that nonetheless already compelling, essential, utopian, ultimately sole "real" reality. Here—related to *the conclusive significance of the ornament*, of the *philosophy of music*—here the conceptual needle drops that had otherwise always pointed the concept into the distance, toward something else; for the pole itself is close by. Here in these deeply moving symbol-intentions the facial features of absolution take shape, as the upward flash of the We-problem, the ground-problem most closely concealed in the darkness of the respective lived moment.

This chart of the incipient evidences thus—deciphering the palimpsest of hope and the deepest amazement somewhat in respect of its ground—has its site in an ethics and a metaphysics of inward community; there can be no *Enzyklopädie* of the truths of love and of spirit *outside* of great metaphysics. But certainly one can already now point to these signs, which have once again become intelligible in themselves. They are finally like the same moon over two distant lands, at whose sight betrothed lovers think of one another. The insights that bind us all, turned toward Jesus and the already rising presentiment, can be provisionally registered even if the final concepts are still totally pending. Nevertheless the office of transcribing such elucidations must be taken up anew, and drafting a new *Dictionnaire* of properly understanding oneself has become a metaphysical duty. No longer with the obsession of elucidating the contents by the light of one's own time instead of the final, utopically intended light; and this tireless anamnesis hardly devotes itself to the eidetics of each and every established fact, but rather just to implanting what is given as us: to those simply evident things, in other words, where thinking-oneself becomes equivalent to becoming-oneself, attaining-oneself, being-oneself. Just as far, however, be that method, in the wake of Bergson or Nietzsche, of indiscriminately denying the *spirit*, where precisely such evidence becomes most thoroughly apparent, and putting in the place of mystically pure spirituality either a loose emotionality or an intoxication to provide an enthusiastic immediacy against the concept and against reason. Certainly any shallow, unmysterious understanding is evil when it is nothing, has nothing, encounters nothing; certainly, too, every deeper knowing, if it is to know only what is worthy of knowing, indeed what is alone knowable, must begin emotionally. But the labor that follows is certainly of a new "rationalism": in its diagrams and typologies, in its rethinking of the world in respect of soul, in its expulsion of unknowing as the ground of the manifestation of this world, in its generation of concepts in the direction of knowledge; it is a rationalism of the heart and precisely not just of the heart, but rather grounded ultimately in the postulates of a *brightened emotionality*, of the spirit which brightens. Similarly, Kant still did not entirely eradicate the self of reason after Cartesian rationalism's destruction by the *empirical* world, but rather narrowed reason's domain "theoretically," in order "practically," that is, with respect to the *moral-mystical* world, to let it more adequately be rebuilt to give primacy to practical reason. Not Dionysos, then, but the spark, the thought of the soul, the spirit of the soul, the *illuminated* ground of the soul, is the highest mystical concretion, is equally the very last seal, like the very deepest inwardness and content of the very last adequation; *wisdom alone keeps watch over the constitutive stretch of the homecoming.* But finally also within the spirit: as far as the latter stands from Dionysian-creaturely rapture, just as far does the integrally and paradoxically eruptive absolution of the We-encounter stand from the reverse constructions of the kabbalistic alphabet, which is disparate, falls back on just the formative principle in this world of formal development, on the regency of creature and world, in other words only follows the emanationist path *backward* to the universal principles, instead of teaching the battle-cry of *secessio plebis in montem sacrum* itself, the logical lineament of the *postulate* and the *paradox.* The quintessence of the highest, evident objects also does not obey any of the world-spirit's pyramids of ideas, but is purely part of the inventory of the exodus-spirit, and only from such explosively understood, antimundane knowledge, directed toward the outcome and not the origin of the world, will the *verbum mirificum* sound, will the features of the identical substance of every moral-mystical symbol-intention take shape.

Here, in other words, in the wake of the comprehension of amazement, that new, primordial, inmost evidence-concept finally reappears, which simply does not take care not to edify, which confirms the primacy of practical-mystical reason even and precisely on the highest heights of metaphysics. The soul's thinking simply will not learn from its mistakes, but strikes out past every external and upper void. The existing world is the world of the past, and the despiritualized object of science, but human longing in both forms—as impatience and as waking dream—is the mainsail into the other world. This intending toward a star, a joy, a truth to set against the empirical, beyond its satanic night and especially beyond its night of *incognito*, is the only way still to find truth; the question about us is the only problem, the resultant of every world-problem, *and to formulate this Self- and We-Problem in everything, the opening, reverberating through the world, of the gates of homecoming, is the ultimate basic principle of utopian philosophy.*[27] Only then should the intention toward the secret, still not existent joy above our Head, the disclosure of the all-redeeming existence-word fail, when that within us which has not yet shone will also have shone; in this way, however, philosophy finally begins not only to be conscientious, but to suspect what for, and to have a conscience; its *anamnesis*, its synthetically expanding messianism *a priori* finally creates the Kingdom of the second, the alone truthful truth: to find, to accelerate, to consummate, in the world, against the world and its mere, factual truth, the traces, the concentric promiscuities of utopia.

A slight systematization of that stirring within us, evenings, reaching inward and upward, has already been attempted. First *spiritually*, by the impression rising as over a void, already by the mere droplet, falling, by the image of the hut, the wind, the heath, the night in autumn. Here already, however, in the hut and the evening, a *direction* to the hoping and wondering was shown; mostly, however, it is the falling of the shadows outside, the lighted window, the warm, deep Gothic sanctum, the direction in which the world runs out, and Christ enters. Finally the self-evident *concepts* of a moral-mystical type—kindness, hope, the heliotropism of the wondrous—came into view, and there is no doubt that precisely here, above even the most extraordinary metaphors, our deepest concern with ourselves takes place. All these contents, however, wherever they turn up, are more than just arbitrary causes for amazement, more than just the arbitrary dissolution of the darkness of the lived moment by such amazement; they also cannot be conceived as their opposite, say as something that appears different to everybody, appearing to the ship as the coast and to the coast as the ship, but they bear absolutely the stamp of unambiguity and necessity. At the same time, however, it was also emphasized that utopian conscience must dominate here, that we can not already set up an inventory of securely connected symbol-intentions and their types, a regular *Summa Ontologiae contra immanentes*; rather, every moral-mystical symbol, in other words every ontic symbol, only circles the one primordial word, the highest symbol-type of our developing absolution, in a wide network, which in turn more closely surrounds the still unarticulated primordial secret, the kernel of lived intensity, of mystical soul-intensity in itself. A corresponding, parallel sequence is of course unmistakable, precisely the one that moves through this entire work up till now—from the first slight in-itself, through ornament and music, and ultimately toward the discarded cornerstone, the mystery of the Kingdom—by means of ever more deeply excavating, ever more closely sounding self-expressions, We-definitions, adequated only by the illuminated ground of the soul, by the unveiling of the inner image at Sais. Language here becomes increasingly pictorial by itself; indeed, it does not hesitate at finally preserving symbol-intentions within concepts. This may appear strange to the kind of thought that is all too easily "factually" fulfilled, or remains totally abstract and disengaged, though just the converse, that we humans now see only the backs of things instead of the faces of the gods, remains the real anomaly. However tightly our inner eyes may be closed, the soul nevertheless keeps its strangeness to this world and its draw toward that world; accordingly it should become an easy matter by means of certain indications to sense precisely that which is too available as something strange, remote, and that other being-concerned-by-evidence, in contrast, as a conversation, in the loneliness of a foreign land, about friends back home. By such means, by simple as well as dense symbol-intentions, the thinking of the soul sees into its ownmost, wondrously illuminated depth; consequently, then, it is just the existential idea—far from being thereby diverted from itself—which in the end necessarily encounters the religious archetypes as part of its uppermost region. With the dawning of the evidence, the evidences of the dawning, which can reach from the love between man and woman up to the great difficulty of the image at Sais.

THUS WOMAN, AND THE GROUND IN LOVE

We do not want to be lonely there where we finally live. Even the weak are not allowed to be restrained; only in love do they flower. It begins with the vivid women, in eagerly mixed dreams that demand of the body at the very least something which can humanly not yet be given otherwise. We ripen to love at variable tempos, and the air between girl and boy is charged with the sudden, connecting flash well before the soul can comprehend such a confusing charge: meanwhile feelings are aroused, raptures and chivalry. Moreover, since one never completely forgets a first love, since one's memories of her are framed as enduring images, and indestructible places within them, this apprenticeship in love has for the better man a constantly flowing, wistfully fruitful beauty which nothing can replace, let alone dismiss. The true path of love, once followed in earnest, can absolutely no longer be concluded anecdotally. Unless it is through that adventure of fidelity still to be undergone, which is called marriage.

There, too, the desperately lifeless man could save himself, by being more than just complemented. And not only because his base depletion, exhaustion, and the question as to what should happen with these two people after the sexual act are most elegantly resolved by marriage, or could be, by its festive routine, full sexual partnership: by the aristocratic aging of the erotic relationship within marriage, love's only possible late style. Rather precisely because here the average, socially all too divided man can or could also fundamentally partake in the warmth of a woman and of the evening hearth, in the fragrance, the abundance, the melody of her being, and thus recover from the *bürgerlich* death of his nature. At any rate in the home, part shelter, part corrective to an otherwise so bloodless general altruism. Indeed, even the busily fulfilled, productive man, after marriage has risen around him, and the beloved: the bright, lovely soul, quickly and powerfully impassioned, with a quiet, devout, perfectly inward vitality in her steel-blue gaze—only then finds a way from his adventures to a deeper, erotic complex that needs expanse and time in order to develop; and only past this expanse, past his disconnected land adventures, do the high seas swell, does an enormous steamer carry him to the more total journey into the undiscovered, broadly rounding cosmos of his life.

Now this remains quite remarkable: that woman and man should not have to combine in order for the child to be born. Even bees are familiar with the virgin birth, and in the unfertilized ovum of an echinoderm, which otherwise reacts only to fertilization, chemical stimulation has brought about division and segmentation; in short, neither organically, nor, especially, psychologically, does a mingling of the sexes, the sometimes nonetheless available spiritual surplus, really seem necessary so that new life will originate. If one nevertheless wants to insist on the necessity of fertilization, which certainly represents no rejuvenation or renewal of the genetic material, but still perhaps an arrangement enabling the combination of two different hereditary tendencies, then it still remains difficult to understand exactly why flies, toads, turtles, whales and similar species, interchangeable among themselves and in no respect variable, still need to combine the father's stature and the mother's vivacity. It is completely conceivable that an organic-psychological parthenogenesis could continue along this entire stretch, so that finally even humans, all of one gender, would be propagated purely as cuttings from the same stem, and perhaps only every 500 years would lovers, loving couples be "born," the ardor of a completely erotic rut, the true recomposition, from which the resulting generations would then have to live for half a millennium. That is conceivable, but it is conceivable precisely just among animals, and here alone could a birth occur without the sexual act that in fact seems to drag us down into animal drives again. In *human beings*, on the other hand (and in every higher organism, as a prelude), fertilization, the counterpart to every parthenogenesis, begins with the highest possible necessity: originary, and leaving behind the methods of mere zoology. That means: a child and a pair of lovers shall be born among us that have become *one* body, *one* soul, a prototype of the mystical circle of the love of all; here operates an originary beginning, which is love, as we have already grasped, not an organic but a theological state. Precisely as the beginning of a function really only attained in the human being: correlated to the birth of a human child, but foremost *to the accomplishment of the bisexual archetype of the lovers themselves*. Purely for our sake is there love; purely for our sake, for purely superanimal causes do the two vials pour out; purely through us does the copula as the necessary act of love begin, does sexuality first blossom completely into the *erotic* as its complete fruit, sought, intended in itself alone: far removed from being merely an artificial breeding, a superfluous detour, an inessential superstructure, or an ultimately extraspiritual gloss over simple animality. We mingle, then, and begin to glow through one another, so that the child will already be doubly animated, so that the beloved will be complete receptive in the embrace, augmented to herself by the man, if a soul is even to be born. And furthermore: Julia, Isolde, do not even need this child, this cry of unborn generations, in order to be completed in, beyond the man's cry, with gaze averted, turned toward their own superabundance, giving birth to themselves as women, granting the lover, in the fire of a higher fertilization, the deepest dream. Love thus radiates high above all friendship and the always just penultimate mysticism of male societies, a mysticism of the state and not of the Kingdom; indeed, the Faustian, which as something purely masculine one has always tried to set above eros, is after all as surely allocated and subordinated to the erotic as the experimental method is to the result that it first records and adequates. In Faust, consequently, the process pending between the sexes has its locus and its outcome: that woman needs man like a dream its interpretation, and man takes hold of woman like an interpretation the meaning—both on love's path toward androgyne unity, in the interiority, the human form, of love.

For ultimately it is only I who am to be conceived, and not woman alone, but a significant man also conceives, and brings forth in great sorrow.[28] He, being more childlike, is here already closer to woman than to the average creature of work; he grows old and then young ten times over; he is as fertile as the young soil, and woman far more thoroughly comes toward him at the end of his work in a constant vision. The work holds her dear hand out to us, she beckons everywhere. "My hair was wet with his tears," sings the girl in a Lithuanian folk song. But perhaps this is still too weakly felt, not so virile, rather with a small child's smile, and merely creeping immaturely back into the old incubatory warmth. So this may lead deeper: "God has abandoned me," lamented the lover, but the girl said: "I will not leave you," thus already disclosing to this isolated, magically destitute man the sources of the more unbroken existence that in our dreams is superior to world and gods. So exactly this, this great, perfect, redemptive, profundity for which woman longs when she is awakened rightly, is for the artist the most colorful embodiment of his categorical imperative of production: that he, that his work be worthy of her; that he carry her colors and do battle for her as the measure of all soul and of the absolute *a priori* given to the work. Nothing can be completely false or lead off the path where a woman has gone along, looked in, nothing which she garlanded, which she clearly foresaw, which aroused her deeper fantasy, nothing wherein she found herself adequately echoed; and if that French ambassador undersigned the Treaty of Utrecht "on the radiant loins of my mistress," a complete parallel to this frivolous allegory nonetheless recurs in every higher situation, of the protective, sigillary, and symbolic power of feminine sensuality, of the devotional evidence counterposed to every decision generally. There are three things, says Mohammed, which constantly fill me with reverence: sweet fragrances, women, and my eyes' solace in prayer—whereby he embraces, in such a completely different, mystically near region what Kant ceded to the starry heavens and the moral law. But this is not only so because woman, once inseminated, is the sooner consummated. Gretchen vanishes and is freed from all motion, in order nevertheless to appear in heaven earlier than Faust. But she rises at the behest of the *madonna gloriosa*, for in woman operates the purest amazement, presentient and fulfilling, most deeply flowing, at once virgin and mother. Thus she utopically holds the garland: at once muse, sibyl, mystery, and inscrutable guardian of its depths. In this way she is the dreaming womb, and in the vault of the inconstruable question echoing so consolingly through the land of the loved she is at the same time the hanging lamp, the symbol of the hearth as it will be on arrival. What man is, he sees drawing ahead of him; but when it reenters him, returns, and with him who was answered, achieved, productively attained, ultimately becomes adequate again, then it is of a feminine nature. He has not only conceived the ideal in feminine form, in Goethe's mysterious words, but the final thing that absolutely awaits man *is woman in form and essence.*

⁓

May it also happen thus by our method of dissolving into and keeping watch within the other. Certainly this does not mean that ultimately one could truly arrive in us when we have not arrived in the other, but the self neither vanishes along this path, nor is it merely the other self where it then appears. Love indeed transforms a human being into what he loves, but because the lover does not seek within the other only the natural, fellow human being, something Jesuan now appears, unerotically, within the so much rarer charity: helping from below in order to do for the humblest of our brothers, and for precisely the most obscure principle, what one would do for Jesus; in this way, in charity toward oneself and toward the other, enduring the labor of the transformative, collective self-encounter. Christian eros is *caritas*; it looks downward and moves it higher; it will not let a particular I fade heathenishly into some All-One, not even within the *tat twam asi* of a nameless universal flux; rather, precisely, the I like the Thou are preserved in a third term, in the future omnipresence of everyone in everyone, in the mystical figure of the Servants, whose being and whose leading light is Christ.[29] Here operate, ultimately above all, the three great regional categories of hope, love, and the faith that one day will transport even the mountains, nature into God, with a *fraternitas* even without a father. So the basic metaphysical phenomenon of true Christian charity remains this: that it lets one who loves live completely within his fellow, without sublating his soul or the soul of him whom he loves but into the We, into the salvation of all these souls, the preserved And and About Us no longer marked by anything alien to us.

CHRIST, OR, THE UNVEILED FACE

Here the lamb must perhaps first bleed. Certainly, the door posts were already painted with it once before.

Even now the Jews commemorate the children saved by this substitution. And the other, different element occurs everywhere, seemingly related: breaking someone on the wheel; nailing him to the cross, which is the wheel with the rim left off, as a legal but also a solar symbol; the mourning for Baldur; and all the sacrificial features of the very profound Hercules legend. All this seems convergent, at any rate, and one might think that since Siegfried, the founder of the ancient Germanic initiation, could be wounded only in the place that Kriemhild's cross-stitch indicated, and in fact Jesus later bore his cross on the same place, the same redemption, the same magic of the solar disc is being sought everywhere here, a Christianity that is also druidic-Germanic, so to speak, albeit by astral paths. But if one continues to look, then very little still comes together, and precisely the sun itself, which would seem to connect it all, which would seem to connect even Christianity with mere *astral myth*, wavers. So for Fiji Islanders the sun and moon were once man and wife; they separated, and now the sun wants to devour the moon, but the stars give her red furs where she can at least rest nights. On the other hand there are Native American solar legends about two brothers who with their arrows shoot a ladder up to heaven, in order to climb up and kill the sun, which their father, the resin, has stuck fast to the tree for him, and then the older brother ascends to the throne of the sun, the younger brother becomes the moon, and the original sun finally no longer even exists. Solar mythos of a higher type, such as Mani's late system, diverges completely again: the sun and moon are two water buckets, and indeed such that the moon receives the departed souls and the light of their good works into his barque, in other words becomes "full," in order to hand over these materials for the construction of the kingdom of Ormuzd to the sun, who then delivers them to the supreme god by "columns of praise," until finally all the light imprisoned in the world reaches the top through the two intermediary vessels. Thus we can see, across quite a geographical expanse, how nothing actually agrees here, how everything in these astral myths has to waver back and forth, as an area where the mystery of the Son of Man has not yet occurred, and which therefore will hardly allow a reduction of Christianity to astral myth: the myths themselves diverge too greatly. Only in one respect do the old views go hand in hand: there, namely, where it is a matter of the holy one landing on the sun, instead of the sun landing in the being of the Savior, as in Christianity. Even when Osiris rises from the dead, the great sparrow hawk of the morning, his eternally seasonal divinity always returns just to the springtime, when the sun waxes and grows brighter, returns to the history of the natural year; indeed in the cult of Mithras the sun appears less as the companion than as the god himself, and even if from a distance such great figures as mother, Typhon, and son come close, they are still only earth, night and sun, so that the human realm stands for the astral, conversely, in the ponderously mysterious tendency of all these nature deities and their concept enclosed in false sanctity. If the sun itself still accompanies even the life of Jesus, beginning with his birth on the winter solstice, if it far more encompasses his ascent to heaven as a reborn vegetal and annual god: closer inspection nevertheless reveals what is redemptive, what is most important, that all that is only the legacy of heathenism and of Near Eastern miscegenation, sharply distinct and distinguishable from the prophets, from the Gospels, which proclaim not the sun but the Son of Man, not the world but the *exodus* from the world.

Certainly, then, it is manifestly the lamb above all who bleeds here. And likewise, who in the peril of the exodus paints his door posts with lamb's blood, his firstborn will death pass by. Doubtlessly the other Passover could easily be connected to it, but is not this passage already contaminated by heathenism? Even in the story of Esther and Mordecai, an astral saga intrudes, and as for this latter Passover: there are still suggestions of lamb's blood, the slaughtered kid or Joseph in the pit, the one sold off to Egypt, the white steer or the boy Horus of later memory. If one wants to invoke the Scriptures elsewhere, above all Deutero-Isaiah, then the passage on the sacrifice of a lamb in Isaiah 53,[30] where salvation is moreover derived from the way the lamb dies than objectively from the act of killing, is contradicted by the later passage from Deutero-Isaiah or Trito-Isaiah, and in any case by other passages from the same prophetic complex: "He that killeth an ox is as if he slew a man; he that sacrificeth a lamb, as if he cut off a dog's neck; he that offereth an oblation, as if he offered swine's blood; he that burneth incense, as if he blessed an idol."[31] What contradicts it above all is that its God, not sleeping, but in the times of Moloch and a flourishing polytheistic stellar worship even among the Jews, has already refused the sacrifice of Isaac, on Mt. Moriah, on the mountain where "The LORD Will See," as the text expressly says, and on the memorial to the three shofar tones blown on the Day of Atonement.[32] The unhesitating submission, the moral conscience, if necessary sealed by death as well, suffering as a means to destroy the old Adam, this true principle of suffering: all this comes from the life of Jesus, can absolutely not be eliminated from the revolutionary morality he directed absolutely against every creatureliness, but: the dogma of the vicarious, once and for all accomplished sacrificial death, *as an chthonic-cosmic magic*, was clearly added by St. Paul from Near Eastern cults of seasonal gods.[33] Hence there is more than enough of an astral-mythical,

"Babylonian" element in the Old Testament as in the New, but at best as a shell, usually as a contrast.

Everything thus confused with the passage of the year is a thing of the past, and a Dance of Death. The other element can no longer be delineated by it, nor does more guidance stare out at us from what is inanimate than from what is our own, which has gradually revealed itself. One might expect a bonus after traversing the entire silence of the stars, in contrast to which the Thou of the human encounter might contain depths, but not the deepest. Then precisely the most perfected self would again have to rebound back toward the stars, and the Makarie of *Wilhelm Meister's Apprenticeship* would stand high above Myshkin in the spheric series of mystical intuition, as a Prince Myshkin of the most impenetrable outer soul, of the massif of physical and solar nature, silent like God. Then the turn would be inevitable that man, and the Son of Man as well, should form only a key, only a method into the most difficult lock, the one hidden treasure and mystery, the not only heuristic but contentual Bethlehem of physics, and the key itself need have no substance. Nonetheless, in spite of all that: the outside can no longer close the circle of this problem astral-mythically; only the end can still close it, soteriologically, and this conclusion is based without any doubt purely on the homogeneous problems of the subject and the philosophy of history, on the *parousiai* of music and ethics. The Son of Man's torch has also burned through the crystalline vault along with its calendarial enclosure, and this had occupied a place where it did not belong. In accordance with apocalypticist's words about the new Jerusalem: "And the city had no need of the sun, neither of the moon, to shine in it: for the glory of God did lighten it, and the Lamb is the light thereof."[34] That is why, then, however necessary it might also be *to retrieve all the correspondence of a deeper sort from nature*, which the Christian mysteries inadvertently also seem to celebrate—that is why, then, that Mithras, and the entire myth of the solar god's *decline* and his *ascent* that also rescues us, that is guaranteed to us, are to be kept away from Jesus, on purely metaphysical grounds as well. If the death of Jesus is supposed to presage anything for us, it is simply that two members of the story of Jesus, namely humans and God, were deaf, failed, and gave the prophet who could have been the Messiah over to his death through Satan, and indeed in such a way that the latter was hardly defeated, the innocent blood was hardly spilled into the world's hatred, that human beings were hardly ransomed from Satan by this payment, in other words absolutely not as pleasantly as a Scholastic thought: "And what did our Redeemer do to him who held us captive? For our ransom he held out His Cross as a trap; he placed in It as a bait His Blood"; hardly as contentedly panlogical as Gregory of Nyssa's explanation: that Satan, since he saw in the God-man only the man, swallowed the barb of divinity along with the lure of humanity.[35] Rather, nothing in this world was ever more futile and, *qua* heathenish analogy to the dying and reborn annual god, at the same time more apologetic for the practices of this kind of world-order than a vicarious restitution by means of crucificial or sacrificial magic.

More important and more fruitful, therefore, is what the life, the words of Jesus himself convey. And indeed not only morally, but precisely also, without Paul, as the promise of the deepest logological contents. Thus the partly astral text about the sacrificial death, which instead of the gospel of Christ posited a second gospel, a gospel above Christ, can logologically be disregarded in a pure, not yet elevated Christianity of not only morality but cognition. Obviously it is always doubtful whether that can ever succeed without "accessories," but there is here too something like an non-construing ontology.[36] That is: the eternal, utterly incomparable rank of the human soul; the power of goodness and of prayer, the most deeply grounded morally good as the seed corn, as the vital principle of the spirit; the tidings of the salvation possible through service toward one another, through submission, becoming the other, filling oneself with love as the spirit of the convocation and of the most universal self-encounter; above all the tidings of the new eon of a godhead unknown until now. As the heretic Marcion with his gospel of the stranger God, and especially the heretic Joachim of Fiore later understood better than the hierarchical Church with its God the Father, its Lord God who is just like Ammon, or Marduk, or Jupiter, too. Only thus will this day, our wounded, hot day conclude; it collects itself to accept every longing for God-likeness and fulfill it in the omega, as the alpha finally made good—without domination, with congregation, without this world, with the Kingdom.

But it must happen in us; only here will people become free, can they encounter themselves. " . . . and it doth not yet appear what we shall be: but we know that, when he shall appear, we shall be like him; for we shall see him as he is," writes John in his first Epistle.[37] Only in us do the fruitful, historical hours advance; in the deepest soul itself the primrose must bloom. "Behold, I shew you a mystery; We shall not all sleep, but we shall all be changed. . . . For ye are dead, and your life is hid with Christ in God. When Christ, who is our life, shall appear, then shall ye also appear with him in glory,"[38] preached a different Paul, who in the Epistles to the Corinthians and the Colosssians baptized not into sacrifice but into prayer. But there is not just the obscure Adam in us whose longing for the knowledge of good and evil was in any case allayed by Jesus the Savior and by Asklepios, the returned, white, whitened serpent of paradise. Rather the obscure Lucifer stands higher, and his longing for *being-like-God*, his true divine sonship, patrimony, also still remains without a return and a clarifying justification in Jesus himself, a triumph, clarifying God himself, of his own truth. Only in this truth that remained secret in Jesus, was kept secret for later, for last, when exactly this face might be uncovered, but who has become restless since he was forsaken a second time, since his cry on the cross faded away hopelessly, since the head of the paradise-serpent hanging on the cross was crushed underfoot for the second time—only in this concealed aspect of Jesus as the *antidemiurgic* principle as such can one understood the truly theurgic aspect of him who rebels as the Son of Man. So in the "Our Father" itself, in its *kiddush hashem*, as the hardly praiseful but rather assertive consecration of the Name: so awaken, so may Thy name be hallowed, so may Thy kingdom finally come, "and forgive us our sins, *as we forgive those who sin against us*. And lead us not into temptation, but deliver us from evil"—all pleas to God, summons, that he finally abandon the dark ground of Moloch within him. He could once speak "light"; now a different word begins to glow, He himself, His name, the name of all "Truth," of the goal toward which everything is born and draws, for here the Son and the Father, indeed even the Holy Spirit are only the sign and the direction in which moves this great keyword redeeming the primordial beginning, *kiddush hashem*, the transformation, consecration of the name of God, the supremely concealed *verbum mirificum* of absolute knowledge. The Greeks had understood in tragedy that man is better than his gods; Christian mysticism not seldom had its own *kiddush hashem*, according to which the Christian God too might be like a bushel over the light of Jesus and Lucifer. He shatters here and breaks open, God does; his book is devoured and the creative space of the convocation opens—that, then, is the quintessentially eschatological and not theological meaning of the "uncovered face." In a reversal of movement not only out of love, but out of transcendence downward, toward human beings, such that in the most extreme *novum* of this New Testament it is just his heavenly Jerusalem that "comes down," and "adorned like a bride," not like a sacrificial altar or even a throne of grace.[39]

That someone stumbles: that passes. But it means very much more when instead one must bleed.

It has certainly been said that here there is absolutely nothing that happens temporally. Only the dramatic spectator should need preparation, a preparing of his soul for the leap of the great reversal, of the hero in thick air. Even his death, his seemingly heroic end, is only there for our human-psychological examination. Tragic humans, so Lukács, are already long dead before they die, and the tragic awakening itself, the self-disclosure and the becoming-essential, is only a moment, without any experiential duration.

Now doubtless all of this, guilt like death like destiny, can be elaborated just as seen from here, just formally-ethically, as it were. Then the hero is the way he is; he goes his way and becomes guilty. That means he perceives everything into himself, nothing comes to him from outside, he experiences his deed as something that had to happen to him. He says "yes" to everything that has happened to him, and because he perceives it as his deed and his guilt, he conquers it; he knows what his destiny is and delineates everything within himself connected to his activity and his individuality. *Next*, the hero must die; he lies broken at the outcome of his struggle and his exertions, and suffers death. But then everything was really already directed toward this end, not as a misfortune or a punishment (for Gunther, says Lukács, can stay alive in—Paul Ernst, whereas Brunhild and Siegfried must fall) and still less as something terrifyingly senseless, something suddenly cutting off the flow of life. Rather, dying tragically is supposed to be the privilege of the great, insofar as it is the same as the form of the tragic miracle, and, insofar as it makes a life complete, the form of the most secular life or miracle. One's death thus represents the revelation of one's character, the form's doorway into the hall of the judge, of self-judgment on the Platonic idea of humanity. So tragic death, on this view, can be defined only as something that happens absolutely from here, a recursive, immanent, completely unmystical compulsion to form, to *horos*, to shape and the definitive terminus of the self, the way the psychology of tragedy is from the outset only the study of dying moments, and the ethics of tragedy has as its categorical imperative to drive anything, once begun, toward death. *Third*, argues Lukács, the hero does not step aside, his outline does not waver, he attains his destiny. Everything externally oppressive and unclear he also takes on, silently and reverently, as which has been granted to him, wherein he shall have justice, wherein he will be fulfilled, most visibly in the clearly heterogeneous action of the "historical" drama. One can see: what becomes essential here is that ultimately only human beings really determine their fate, as strangely and heterononomously it may seem to approach them; it is not, as is still the case in Shakespeare's *Macbeth*, prophesying witches and predictable marvels, nor, as in the ancient Indian, late Greek or Spanish legend or salvation dramas, God himself who is involved and so guides the characters as well as the destinies. Rather, naked souls here conduct a solitary dialog with naked destiny; or: only when we have become completely godless will we again have tragedy. Tragedy is a becoming-God, a disclosure of the God only still living, sleeping in man, God's monologue within the creature, a disclosure of God before himself, but the immanent God thereby awakens the transcendent one to life. And because, as Lukács also recognizes, the souls of human beings have never trodden their deserted paths as forlornly as today, because nature and destiny have never been as terrifyingly soulless as today, that is why we can expect another birth of tragedy. In other words, God must exit the stage (for, we would add, he does not exist, but may only be valid; there shall be nothing but God), but a spectator he must still remain: as this is the only kind of piety still possible, it is also the historical, the utopian possibility for tragic ages, epochs without a heaven.

We intentionally and respectfully offer this thorough presentation of fundamentals with which we ultimately accord, but then only ultimately. One sees how forcefully Lukács here, in his "Metaphysics of Tragedy," excuses himself from every question of guilt and justice, every Aristotelian concept that has deteriorated into a scholastic issue, unfortunately every transcendently metaphysical form of thought, at least in connection with classical tragedy, which extends so to speak from Paul Ernst up to Hebbel, then through Alfieri, Corneille and Racine, and finally to Sophocles as its aprioristic climax. It is certainly striking that all the dark colors are missing from this depiction of decline. They have already been conceded to life: there everything is disordered, never does anything flower into true life, but drama allows the attainment of fullness, it shapes finally "real" human beings, and so the anarchy of chiaroscuro comes to an end. The twilight is divided, not by the exclusion of chance, which would produce only the shallowest and most listless kind of life; rather, tragedy no longer requires chance, it is nowhere or everywhere present in tragedy, and tragedy has incorporated it into its world forever, the world of free-floating homogeneity, of the necessity of encountering oneself in the other, of the destiny unfolding necessarily out of and toward the characters.

But, one must ask, where do murder, death, and tragic darkness remain here? And here is the point where Lukács, or the immanent path, diverges irreconcilably from the transcendent inquiry.

No one could still remain visible to us after fully encountering himself. Man can not yet live through to the end in this world if elsewhere the stage provides the moment of crisis. He can not inwardly consummate himself, can not elevate external conditions, even just as something which the hero does with them, to the peripheral scaffolding of his form, let alone reshape misery into self-mediation, into destiny, into an expression of his life or the demonstration of his life's potential, merely in order to respect the secular nature of the stage and reserve for art the definition of purified life, life without disappointment, in completely immanent form. Certainly my hour strikes when I go tragically under, I can include it in me; a profound person has this kind of death that sets limits, sets a seal, as his hour of judgment. Accordingly, the self should coincide with destiny: character [*Gemüt*] and destiny [*Schicksal*], says Novalis, are names for the same concept; if one has a character, then one also has an occurrence that always recurs, are Nietzsche's profound words; and for Hegel the tragic individual always reaps only the fruits of his own deeds. But if one now thinks all of this in a *real* way, outside of this subtle, profound inclusion, outside of drama's peculiar immanence as well, thinks it with a *historical* and at the same time *religious* focus, which is where Lukács is leading when he transcends at least morally, when we can finally gauge the problems of our self-consummation and our external distance from God from his use of tragic form as a cipher: then the broader context for any possibility of a meaningful death, for death as a sublime inner ceremony of conclusion, for immanent self-perfectibility generally, becomes conceivable only as a sort of karmic theory, strangely, in accordance with which, then, every life could certainly be made immanently meaningful and homogeneous, insofar as here precisely the entire indifferent, meaningless causal nexus of destiny can be meaningfully deepened and correlated toward our pre-existential kernel. This was certainly never the intention, but one thing remains indisputable: that the tragic human being can stand firm, without slipping into the world that surrounds him, only when this world that (according to Lukács's definition of the tragic as a formal-ethical immanence) drives him back into his exposed, strict, statuary unity and selfhood—can basically do nothing to him, insofar as it is blind and indifferent, insofar as its sun may shine on the righteous as on the unrighteous, and no less on the unrighteous. To be freed for self-judgment is already such a tremendous thing that it already—precisely through the external or the higher world's lack of the power: to diverge from tragic destiny—in itself presupposes this world to carry a tacit, positive divine charge, that in other words—and this is unavoidable—historically and religiously reconceiving the Lukácsian immanence of tragedy in precisely this seemingly self-consummative form leads to a transcendental philosophy, entirely inadequate to tragedy, of the kindness and God-fullness of existence. If anyone had ever visibly, actively, self-achievingly, morally consummated just himself, as the person who he is—in other words, not only as though formed at a distance, as in the visual arts or in music: still *before* the leap, symbolically—then not only he but the entire world would be at its destination, and the problem that ought to have been of such concern to Schopenhauer, the relation between the redemption of all and a single, successful, morally real self-redemption, would become actual. For the game of tragedy, of action, is open on all sides; it is no hermetic retort where life's essences can gently organize themselves into a metaphysics in installments, nor an unpenetrating enclave, amid the world-process, of the most immaculate metaphysics. Rather one finds in tragedy the seemingly most oxygenated, compressed, impermeable location within the process, one that lets the true, outward-inward life, the effectuating morality, the apocalyptic kernel itself glow more brightly, and not just its virtual, tonal image. Which is precisely why tragedy, in complete contrast to any other art, can represent not so much the self-encounter as the *encounter with the obstacle*, the encounter with Satan, on the grounds of the impending *real, absolute* self-encounter, the understanding of the goal.

Therefore: the hero must die in reality before he can truly come to himself. Therefore also: it is still more than a bitter *game*, the tragic, and death in tragedy must continue as something terrible and dark.

Things are stirring dangerously around us, we who want to explode our darkness. But now something else moves closer, becomes quieter, less obtrusive, and is nonetheless exactly this thing which one has always known by the names Evil and God. An inflection, a dialogue, a stopped grandfather clock lets us hear the thunder of the Last Judgment. Or: life tires us out, and the rattling window, the oven that always smokes, the otherwise very nice desk which still, every morning, requires a slice of cork under one leg so it will stand straight, the terrible, hostile, vampiric figure of the cook from Strindberg's *Ghost Sonata*: all these small, peripheral and thus always incurable poisons, totally inhomogeneous to us, are able to divert to themselves the quintessential necessity of bleeding, the murder of all light in this prison, madhouse, mortuary that is the earth. In return, of course, the sublime, the Christ enthroned above the clouds, draws together more tightly, and the words by which our eyes are closed: "Sleep without dreams, and when you wake, may a sun that does not scorch, a family without shame, love without flaw greet you"[40]—Strindberg's unassuming funeral song brings home to our souls the same heavenly increase that is otherwise only revealed in the most splendidly broad and least implanted background abstraction, in accordance with the new, deeper, now conclusively morally engaged transcendence of the end. But the hero nonetheless, indeed precisely because of this more quiet nearness of murder and of light, still stands in a charged space; there is a something beyond, and it decides in a flash. The purely comic hero can perhaps come to life in single strokes and within the novel, because the comic is a condition: but the tragic is a moment, and thus requires purely the drama, through which its hero advances toward a final act as toward a niche or an apsis where the singular flash of the unsettled god of sleep, god of destiny waits. The tragic hero, striking his blow at the moment of crisis, moves toward a background just for this reason drawing together by dramatic compression, measured against which the comic as reflexive, the tragic as constitutive, absolutely first become transcendentally possibly. Therefore one can certainly concede that authentically great tragedy could develop in this age of a distant God and in the heroic atheism operative there, only this does not at the same time mean, as it does for Lukács, that the frenzy of external life has no power, that in other words the inhuman, or at least the slimy, gelatinous, unpredictable, arbitrarily stalling, falsely complex, moody, maliciously fortuitous and intermittent element within the external causal nexus could simply be overlooked as something sim-

ply and indiscriminately alogical. In fact the nothingness of this godless
world could very well become the actually coactive background, such that
all this desperate crashing into the sand shifting all around us, all the
vague reluctance in the transformation, in the principles of the human
encounter, in the crust of the interior-superinterior light, would be clarified as that tragic battle and dispute over authority, which since the soul's
beginning has been pending between man and the first principle that has
still not subsided, between Lucifer and the demiurge.

Of course sometimes we step forward from it all as though we were
well and truly free. For alone of all creatures we can laugh; we are
strangely liberated by laughter, the simplest sensibility, as well as the most
sublime, when it sufficiently overcomes what it includes. At the bottom is
the joke, superficial and meaning nothing, which cleverly, but not out of
profundity, brings unrelated elements playfully together. Then come the
humorous novel and the still inauthentic comedy, meaning, things are
not so bad, but here our hearts are not eased, not because something there
just skips over this wicked life, the laws and the authorities, but simply
because our boss is just not a king, although it says so, indeed he is not
even a good boss; it is the comedy of miniaturization, merely quantitative
alleviation, the reduction of the senseless or even of the overt eruption of
tragedy to a bagatelle. Essentially different, already because of certain hu-
morless features (since one may certainly not just confuse the humorous
with the comic), are the authentic comedy, the comic drama and above all
the great comic novel. Here the hero is obliged to have nothing but himself before him; he lives completely within a false, powerless, and—for his
abilities at least and *prima facie*—unreal, unconstitutive illusion, whereby
of course, by means of this possibly noble, indeed sublime, but never constitutive monomania, he himself experiences failure after failure, misfortune after misfortune—but unsonorously, avoidably, unresonantly—disgrace after disgrace in the world as in the higher world. This is reversed as
soon as the hero becomes canonical, in other words in the fatal necessity
of true tragedy, which still gives every one of its shattered heroes a shimmer of the Prometheus who will someday triumph against Zeus, or a rem-
iniscence of the Moses of kabbalistic legend, who must die against his
will, but then, after he was able to drive back even the angel of death by
means of the great name of God, and Yahweh himself has thus had to appear, slaps even Him in the face, uncomprehending, not wanting to comprehend, and then returns first to the realm of shadows instead of to the

promised land. Here the depiction of a life would be at its end if a highly significant trail did not still curl upward from below, which slowly escaped from true comedy as *humor,* and has absolutely no place in a tragedy. That it is possible, humor, does not mean laughing through tears, in the sense that one could always still lead a happy and dignified life after being imprisoned in dreams again, while the ground of the world is unchanged, and actually sad. Rather this easing, this uplift means precisely—and here a subtle, enigmatic beam of light, an insight nourished only from within, inexplicable, unsupported, mystical, flashes into this life—that something there is not right, that the tears should not be taken entirely seriously in the face of something invincible in us, however dreadfully real they might appear together with the ground of the world from which they derive; that Goethe's statement: "gentle rhymes, like rainbows, are best drawn on a dark ground,"[41] might hold for the deepest, but not for the most essential utterances; that in other words the significant, perhaps acknowledged but in no way guaranteed buoyancy, the incomprehensibility of joy in itself—stands closer to truth and reality, which really need not be the ground of the world, than does everything oppressive, verifiable, indisputable about factual conditions with all brutality of their sensory reality. And so this incomprehensible buoyancy can become presentiment; the comic hero too can be loved and comprehended. Then a smile stirs again, but the nameless smile of a new way to be moved to tears. It can even quietly touch on the comic; the humorous can radiate at this point into a new kind of comedy, but in an entirely different sense, namely insofar as the mistreated, misrecognized individual lets things and persons imperturbably pass through him, and in this way it is finally no longer the *individual who ends up in comic conflict with the world,* as in comedy, but the *world ends up in conflict with the individual,* in this comedy of the inessentiality that got in the way. Then the "comic" hero, so understood, with a new, soon reversed comic aspect, stands closer to the depth itself than the tragic, the dying hero suffering from having taken world and destiny and demiurgic world-spirit all too seriously, this hero with his disengaged subjectivity that triumphs, despite being metaphysically adapted, merely by means of a sporadically comforting *reservatio mentalis.* Just as it signifies a great Scholastic profundity that Dante's work, because it does not begin well and ends badly, but leads from hell to a certainly still guaranteed heaven given "uncomically," without any existential irony, was in all simplicity called a comedy, a reborn comedy like every epic or drama of grace, whereby precisely humor, as a creative and reality-positing pragmatism of the spiritual, can finally be elevated objectively, indeed perhaps one day above every destiny.

What has been written [*gedichtet*], is real; we are the poetic human beings to be seen at an externalized remove in formalization. They move not only across the boards or within the idea or in the artistic hoax of an immanent formal perfection that no longer recognizes any dissonance but a sounding, aesthetically fruitful one. Rather poetry's great figures advance in a peculiar, object-theoretical procession of individuality through history, over history, on the solidly [*ge-dichtet*] shaped, utopically real level of what we see as essential as such. This adjoins poetry's reality to the substantiated legendary phenomenon's, though distinguished by characteristic utopian objective and spheric degrees, and so the ultimate correlation of the tragic problem to the life of Christ becomes unavoidable, who likewise perilously defeated destiny without having escaped it, after all, since it was able to strike back. The hero thus does not die because he has become essential; rather, because he has become essential, he dies; only this turns a serious having-become-oneself into heroism, into a category of tremendous destiny and of tragedy, which raises the man up whom it crushes, by crushing him, and only this suprasubjective correlation places the tragic into unconsummated-consummated contexts, into the self-consummation, self-invention destroyed midway, into the pitiless old conflict of Prometheus, of Christ, with the upholder of this world and the guilty conscience of its end.

THE IMAGE AT SAIS

So only we drive everything forward from below.

We do not rest from moving it again and again, from letting everything move, beginning below. We lash out around us, call, create, accelerate, remember the unknown "where to" and kernel, until it remembers itself. Nothing is important but to loosen the crust and throw off the mask of unknowing around us.

~

But grasping upward impurely can never succeed.

We humans alone have become free, therefore of course selfish as well and easy to mislead. Thus we pushed upward too early, unready to enjoy the apple, the apple itself unripe as well.

What one thus achieves depends on what sort of person one is. Going

upward, most are overcome by a strange fear. They feel themselves floating, the ground disappears; in the more intelligent, of course, this is combined with a kind of flying, yet still just as strangely torn back and forth
between repulsion and attraction. Just this could also be felt in the artist's
twofold experience of sorrow: being found not good enough and not devout enough in respect of what had proven necessary. With an uniniti-
ated, guilty hand, with the overhaste of mere curiosity, the veil can never
be lifted from the image at Sais. The youth there surely did not see the *final* truth; this was not what took away his good cheer, it was not this sorrow which dragged him to an early grave, this was not the truth to which
he came through guilt, and which did not seem pleasant to him. Rather
he saw himself, perhaps, as Novalis profoundly called this miracle of miracles, but himself only in the twofold form of the experience of sorrow
before the transcendental entrance. To the novice at Sais came the guardians of the threshold, this initial view of the higher self itself; these came
before his unpurified eye, and here the mere neophyte broke down. He
saw his self as it still lies in creaturely bonds, and its remove from the
light; he saw his self as it might radiate in full, redeemed, future glory,
and in turn its remove from the existing darkness, from active unbelief,
from not-being-identical-to-oneself. By the first guardian of the threshold his God appears railing, furious, a *mysterium tremendum*; by the second however his God appears as fervor and love, as the miraculous abyss
of our own heavenly glory, a *mysterium fascinosum*. The youth before the
image at Sais thus experiences completely the moment of final conflict
that is here, precisely here, before, and so that, a door can finally open.
The image at Sais thus stands as a construct also having a share in us, indeed as symbol of the inconstruable question of being and its very ornament, strictly before day.

At the same time, however, what so horrified the youth as he raised the
veil also becomes overt. In fact he saw even more than himself stepping
forward doubled by sorrow. Past the guardians of the threshold was at the
same time a far more terrible abyss, from which Gorgo peers out. The
youth stood across from the *absolute* guardian of the threshold, the de-
monic power of the great In Vain, of eternal death without peace, of absolute frustration. The keyless neophyte saw himself seemingly dead in an
eternal grave, turned to stone, with full awareness, burning with an aimless longing *in perfect nothingness*, past which Isis looms, past which the
still unbarred alternative of eternal death extends, of a quintessential cos-

mic meaninglessness all around. The youth of Sais, then, precisely because he cried out: "What do I have, if I do not have everything?" instead saw, with his unwavering phototropism—into a completely negative outcome and reconstruction, into an apocalypse—though only as the blow of the axe, and as hell—of all In Vain. In the form of Christ, the adept would absolutely not have desired to "behold" the truth as something complete; instead its preparatory element is warmth, human sound and anamnesis, and its Kingdom, the deepest of any amazement, is not of this world as it is.

⁓

We alone, in other words, drive ourselves, upward as well, only by going through.

What we are, we do not know; we are still restless, and empty, and like ourselves, but kept hidden.

In this way, too, only we, the manifold, and not, say, the world or God, are given from the outset. But only in respect of what is coming will we be able to recognize what we sought or "were" before we entered the movements of time, this act through which we entered, and posited time, world and God as our leader, as something "objective." Quite on the contrary, we were none of that yet, for the beginning will only have happened completely at the end, and it is not questionable to say that it is enigmatic; for since it is we whose beginning remains enigmatic, since the darkness of the lived moment, so near to us, therefore still contains the enigma of the beginning, the enigma of the existence of the world at maximum strength, then after all just this explains the entire world-process—searching, trying to solve the enigma—of the elucidation of the We and of the darkness, of the primordial problem reclaiming itself as answer. That is why the old question, to what extent may the manifold be derived from the One, is also posed wrongly, in this respect: according to the question not we ourselves, the Many, but God was initially proposed as the quintessentially One, as *causa sui*, and so something immobile, in itself fundamentally unenigmatic, the universal shelter of logic, has to include the greatest enigma. We and we alone, then, carry the spark of the end through the course. Only within time, after a thousand disruptions and obstructions, does what was meant from the beginning, always, what is present without being disclosed, force its way out. The time of history in which we labor pervades the mundane space where our life itself appeared, into which we install our works, the geography of the human lands, of their architectures and their spiritual sites; here is the permission and the possibility to presense, to find, to realize values, *a priori* possible constructs, and finally to let the last thing as such, even if it be posited extratemporally, extramundanely, nevertheless emerge through time, through the world, against it. It is uncertain how long the time and space with which we work and yet so paradoxically shatter can continue as the scene or, certainly, as useful ciphers for shaping rhythmic time, aesthetic, even religious space. More deeply, however, it is unknown to what extent we human beings, our mystery finally solved, will be resurrected, toward what end the last, the only absolute one of our self-elucidations, self-realizations will lead: toward the Last Day, the Day of the Servants, the seventh day of creation, beyond all the vanishing, nebular realities of this unreal, untrue world subject to the Apocalypse.

But whoever truly goes also takes along the space where dawn finally breaks. With us things awaken completely beyond their currently applicable laws, and move within feasible potentiality. *We however carry this spark of the end through the course, and the spark is still open, full of unarbitrary, objective fantasy.* That is why in everything which we shape, eternally shape—finally with experience, Baroque, music, Expression, self-encounter, the age of the Kingdom all in philosophy—a storm prevails that comes from what is inordinate in human nature and pushes toward the Word's tongue of fire, toward the pronounced *individuum ineffabile*, toward the tearing of the curtains and not only in every ancient temple— a spirit of unconcealed utopia, as the spirit of the hidden human being, finally, shines in.[42]

There is still nothing that could encompass this, certainly, here where we drift unfamiliar to ourselves, immersed in darkness. But the thought of it is at hand, for only we proceed slowly forward, darkly, atomistically, individually, subjectively, within everything moving or amassing, as the unresolved utopian tension constantly undermining everything shaped. This: that we will no longer be suppressed, our Christian-messianic being-thought within this drifting existence, in the dark, in the primordial problem of the lived, all-concealing moment, a rethinking of the world in respect of the macanthropos inside it, is at the door: that we may finally seriously recognize ourselves as the principle guiding every transformation in this world, and without which there would be no process and also no hope, no *problem*, God or heavenly kingdom. The purpose of finally pronouncing the moment is to win ourselves back from the world, with a pure hand to touch the evil spell of unknowing, of the resistant unknowing that alone turned us to stone, disguised us as plants, animals, partial natures, mundane structures in the most diverse false shapes, and keeps the soul in the sleep of death, in exile from itself, isolated from the expectant truth of the finally uncovered face. If the world is a sphinx who throws herself into the abyss when her riddle is solved: this lies not within its having become (for this world is an error, and void; in the face of absolute truth it has only the right to be destroyed); rather, the enigma lies within the true image at Sais, and this image alone is the figure of the Self-encounter, the darkness of its lived moment and the shudder of the absolute question. The unknowing around us is the final ground for the manifestation of this world, and for precisely this reason does knowing, the lightning flash of a future knowledge striking unerringly into our darkness and the inconstruable question, constitute at the same time the inevitably sufficient ground for the manifestation, for the arrival in the other world.

Karl Marx, Death, and the Apocalypse

Or, the Ways in This World by Which the
Inward Can Become Outward and the
Outward Like the Inward

The Lower Life

So am I. So are we still.

But is not all this already far too much? For who would help must absolutely go back, yet be there anew.

I repeat: that is enough. Now we have to begin. Into our hands life has been given. To itself it became empty already long ago. It pitches senselessly back and forth, but we stand firm, and so we want to become its initiative and its ends. New and expansive, what lies beneath us opens up for the first time.

We are also inside it, however. This is how one moves, and we too fall asleep. We too were embryonic, became plants and animals, for we do not know who we are. Not, certainly, as though we had only evolved out of plants and animals, but had not been there before, within. Rather the converse: every organism first became on the way toward human form, which had always been *meant* by us alone. So little did man appear last and as though fortuitously, that everything that took shape before him is pure larve, indeed deformations and errors, which the proper kind of presentiment had first to remove and eliminate.[1] Individual creatures, perhaps, once become, accommodate to the flora or move exactly to the rhythm that their structure, and the environment to which their structure is attuned, dictates. But of course not even hares could arise through mere adaptation to the environment, to say nothing of lions, if it were merely impressions of the milieu that assembled, and not potential victors over them. Rather there is a free, open, human-seeking quality in the progression from algae to fern to conifer to deciduous tree, in the migration from the water into the air, or certainly in the strange delarvation of worm as reptile as bird as mammal, in the struggle for skeleton and brain. Tentatively, and led by a strange presentiment, not yet implanted, burning like a flame over every separate living creature, there takes place here a testing, retaining, rejecting, reusing, erring, reverting, succeeding, a delegating to reflex, a leap toward a new formation quite familiar to us. There is an impulse toward the brightness, but still beneath larves and within the persistent constraints of the genus itself, to which animals are in thrall; only in man himself can the movement toward the light, proper to all creatures, become so conscious, or be carried out. The life of the animals beside, below us, remains constrained here, above all larval; their shapes and their heads themselves are masks, and their slowly changing, in themselves almost ahistorical species and genus keep them under a spell, as an almost complete fate. Which is exactly why the temptations of all these forms had to be experienced all the way through, until at least the characteristically uncompleted being: Man, was established. Man alone, in other words, is here the latest and yet the firstborn creature; only he broke through, exceeded the genus fixed for so long among the animals. Under pain of destruction, he became the toolmaking, detour-making animal; thus he could also not get by with inborn reflexes, the earlier signals. With time he becomes only more dependent on deliberate planning, in the building of nests and related activities: absolutely artificial, and yet right on the front.

Our lower relatives pass expectantly by us now. The topsoil, the plants, the worms, the tame as well as the wild creatures: all of them, too, variations of something that is not like that, that is encircled, that has not yet come out. The pulse of life beats, however, after the leap toward the only creature that changes has succeeded through work above all: beats only within human beings. In what they, organically quite defenseless, initiate with their new standpoint and viewpoint, by starting to make history. A history of hedgehogs, even of cows in fifteen volumes, would really not be very interesting. To their own species humans are certainly dangerous, like no other animal. But they are equally capable of giving light to this species and to the place it occupies, like no outer fire can do.

The Socialist Idea

So we need ourselves first, above all. For that, however, the outer path must be cleared.

But will not everything inward in particular already be far too much then? Does not a great inwardness, which traversed the self-encounter in ever rising loops, ever higher levels of integration, reduce precisely the simple power to turn back *socially*, to do right in politics, and to think? Thus we also step back here somewhat at first. But it is no less already essential that we kindle a light before our feet. Precisely the one who was a thousand steps ahead can help more easily and closely than someone who blindly gasps along or adds his voice to the currently feasible.

So we repeat: What just was will probably soon be forgotten. Only an empty, horrible memory hangs in the air. Who was defended? Foul, wretched, profiteers were defended. What was young had to fall, forced to die for ends so alien and hostile to the spirit, but the despicable ones were saved, and sit in their warm drawing rooms. Not one of them was lost, but those who waved other flags, so much flowering, so much dream, so much spiritual hope, are dead. The artists defended the middlemen and kept the home front warm for the instigators; the clerics in the churches and in literature however betrayed their Lord for the sake of a uniform, an enlisted one, more cheaply than Esau, more cheaply than Judas. There has never been a more dismal military objective than imperial Germany's: plunder and brutality, the enslavement of all and the arsenal of the reaction; a stifling coercion, imposed by mediocrities, tolerated by mediocrities; the triumph of stupidity, guarded by the gendarme, acclaimed by the intellectuals who did not have enough brains to supply slogans.

We repeat again: And of course, as though one had not been burned badly enough, this is how it remains even today. The War ended, the Revolution began and with it, seemingly, the open doors. But correct, these soon closed again. The black-marketeer moved, sat back down, and everything obsolete drifted back into place. The profiteering farmer, the mighty *grand bourgeois* truly put out the fire in places, and the panicked *petit bourgeois* helps to enfeeble and encrust, as always. Nonproletarian youth itself is more coarse and stupid, has its head thrown further back than any youth before; the universities have become true burial mounds of the spirit, hotbeds of "Germany, awaken!" and filled with the stink of rigidity, corruption and gloom. So those who have apparently been restored completely reenact what the reaction of a century ago auditioned, as Hegel's friend Niethammer already lamented: "Just as worms, frogs, and other vermin often follow the rain, so do Kajetan von Weiller and his crowd follow the dark day spreading across the entire civilized world."[2] They reenact that Restoration's recuperation, when the cloddish slogans, the corporative state were recalled; when the traditionalism of *Vaterland* was rampant against the truly Christian, indeed even quite properly medieval idea of humanity; when that insensible Romanticism appeared that forgot Münzer yet revered the junk of heraldry, that ignored the true German popular tradition, the Peasant's War, and saw only knights' castles rising into enchanted, moonlit nights. Once again, predictably, the writer helps apply the brakes; indeed, Expressionism's former priests—incinerating what they had just recently exalted—rush to help incompetent literary homesteaders patch together misrepresentations from the tasteful ruins of the past, in order to bar the way for the vitally formative sensation of the future, of the city, of the collective; in order to insert the reaction's black market deception into a better ideology; in order to make their lamentable hygiene, their doubly imitative Romanticism absolute. Instead of this petty generation being ashamed of itself for mostly failing before a principle of which it had nevertheless had a presentiment, the postulate of the very dawning of creative Expression, it now in addition to all that slanders even the presentiment, the historical-philosophically overdue principle itself, because to its misfortune it found only this petty generation. Meanwhile the West with its millions of proletarians has not yet spoken; meanwhile there stands, unbowed, a Marxist republic in Russia; and the eternal questions of our longing, of our religious conscience still burn, undiminished, unbent, unredeemed in their absolute claims. What is more: we Socialists have at least learned from the same outlook on reality that came a century ago; Marx thoroughly purified Socialist planning of every simple, false, disengaged and abstract enthusiasm, of mere Jacobinism, and we have especially not forgotten the spirit of Kant and Baader above. Whereas the Romanticism of the latest reaction has inherited absolutely nothing proper, is simply coarse and backward, is neither factual nor enthusiastic nor universalist, but simply numb, obstinate, withdrawn, soulless and un-Christian; so with its pathos of the autochthonous it can elicit only the decline of the West, in completely animalistic stupidity, irreligious extinction: faded blossom and for today only civilizational atrophy, a navy, and the pessimism of historiographical registration as the only goal, but for Europe only prompt, eternal death.

Consequently the inner glow won for us elsewhere may certainly not glimmer only on high here, but must move back far into the medial life all around. From this place of the self-encounter, so that it may become one for everyone, there consequently also springs, inevitably, the arena of political-social leadership: toward real personal freedom, toward real religious affiliation. Here, then, a *second* point has been attained, where the "soul," the "intuition of the We," the content of its "Magna Carta," streams responsibly into the world. To be practical in this way, to help in this way on everyday life's structural horizon and put things into place, precisely to be political-social in this way, is powerfully near to conscience, and is a revolutionary mission absolutely inscribed in utopia.

Certainly its light fears becoming somewhat feebler thereby. However, even if its luminosity darkens at first, one has to persist: this light must be moved from the inner sanctum onto a broader domain. To some, certainly, even this restriction is not yet enough of a renunciation, and they become indignant whenever some concept cannot immediately be resold or exchanged, in other words whenever the nevertheless inextinguishable ultraviolet of the genuine, great thought does not absolutely immediately describe party appeals and statutes. But for this reason the seemingly more remote revolutionary *concept* is not "rootless" after all, or "impossible" or "abstract" in the capitalist age; rather, since the thinking subject is located not only in its time, and the collective from which it speaks is not only socially collective, it can be achieved absolutely eccentrically to time as the inventory of Oughts (that is, of our tasks even beyond the historically given) and thus in a suprahistorically concrete way, as an absolutely constitutive presentiment of the goal, knowledge of the goal. As a whole, in any case, we have here reached the place to strive—instead of for the mere self-way, the pure soul-expanse of the self-encounter, even the most direct shape of the moment and the question—for another, practical-exemplary level of concretion. To shape a path from the lonely waking dream of the inner self-encounter to the dream that goes out to shape the external world at least to alleviate it, at least as *locus minoris resistentiae* or even as the instrumentation for the goal. And just this, the explication of "glossolalia" as "prophecy," of the metapsychological as the socially, ultimately cosmically metaphysical system, distinguishes the passage to the "world" of the soul, which is neither of this world nor of that, but is nonetheless not simply acosmic and closed to the cosmos, but turned toward the new, all-pervading power of the subject-object space. Accordingly this passage, precisely as such, turns back, gains height precisely by flattening out, gains the resonant energy of utopia precisely by sinking in level, gains the cosmic element reverberating throughout its hitherto only vertical salvific intention precisely by also confronting the state of society; for how could there be an inwardness, and how would it notice that it was one, whether as sorrow or as truly paradoxical joy, if it stopped being rebellious and desperate against everything given? If here too, then, in glossolalia's transition into a still unelaborated, provisionally social part of a "world system," we are working in a different metal than has been customary in the domain of self-invention: only when the goal-invention is added, after all, does the ore of the social world begin a ferment and a process that will open a passage for glossolalia itself from Kant to Hegel, and on the other hand, for the natural "Hegelianism" of the state of the world, the passage to "Kant," to the absolute Ought, to the problem of a Kingdom of moral beings.

So one should remain sober here at first. Only after what is false has fallen away can what is genuine live. And not many are aware of how much coercion remains to be unlearned.

It is not possible to imagine precisely the state unceremoniously enough. It is nothing if it does not let us manage things in a beneficial way, then obsolesce correspondingly. Everything else in which the state oppresses or lulls us should finally fall away, and it must hand back everything but the organization of dreary matters. If fear and lies depart, it will become difficult for the state to exist, let alone arouse greater respect.

Perhaps through this thing that restrains its coercion? This, says Anatole France, is equality before the law: that it forbids rich and poor alike to steal firewood or to sleep under bridges. That so little hinders actual inequality that it actually protects it. Or shall the state prove itself as a Solomonic father through what it facilitates, the public administration of justice? The weak are defenseless, but the cunning ones are protected; people do not trust the courts. There is no feeling for people or for cases; academicism, pedantry dominate, and the entirety of legal protection is circumscribed by the horizon of property, in terms of the method as well as of the object. For since the lawyers are trained in no other way than formally, precisely the abilities of the exploiter class in calculation, mistrust, and underhanded accounting find a cognate basis in this formalism, still apart from the fact that the contents of any possible economic system can be inserted without contradiction into the abstract amoralism of jurisprudence. Not only the fact that most attorneys will take anyone who comes to them, like taxis, to name only one example; not only the fact that the judge in a civil trial could be compared to a bad clock that only moves when pushed by one of the parties—without his own aspiration to demonstrate the truth: all of law, far and away the preponderance of criminal law, too, is merely the ruling class's means of maintaining a rule of law *protecting its interests.* There too, where not only cunning persists in its accustomed deals and triumphs legally, where the state itself takes the prosecution and investigation of crimes into its own hands, punishment, far from establishing justice antithetically, becomes in its punitive aspect an immoral barbarism and in its deterrent aspect the most skewed prevention and most failed pedagogy that could absolutely be conceived *post festum.* If there is property, then there is no law, no cause for its spiteful, vacuous categories; the rest is medicine, or, as "justice," pastoral care.

But now this wicked coercion wants to be useful, too, distribute gifts. It recognizes *Bürger* who are apparently worth something to it, citizens, and above all it promotes its servants. Thus comes the salaried presumption, the bestowal of honors, the civic clergy, the claim to be God on earth. But what else could bureaucracy mean than that the right man should find the right position within a purely technical system of administration, whereas the War and all the white terror generally showed what kind of God inhabits the interior of a despotism. Or is the murderous coercion of universal conscription for the stock exchange, for the dynasty, perhaps supposed to demonstrate the moral substance of the *poleis,* insofar as here we have passed through one of the most ignominious hours of history, and the state happily be used again as a springboard to the fury, the logic of natural catastrophe? Things went so far that the state finally even deviated from corporate interests in the capitalist countries where it had become the board of directors. In accordance with its feudal-alogical character, the state as coercive formation culminates in the military state, which proved to have such an abstract monopoly on power that in comparison even corporate interests, the previous causal base, appeared as in a sort of ideology—so completely, against all bourgeois rationalization, all socialist misunderstanding, did the state reveal itself as a discrete, heathenish, satanic coercion-materiality in itself. May it have a Bolshevistic function for a time as a transitionally necessary evil, but the truth of the state is really still beneath any socialist perspective: it withers away, it transforms itself into an international regulation of consumption and production, into a great instrumental organization for the control of the *inessential,* which no longer contains or can attract any meaning, and whose purely administrative Esperanto is beneath the different national cultures that should be the next valid category of social cohesion. The comprehended state hence simply signifies nothing but a relatively static excerpt of economic, occasionally military, basically administrative history; on none of these levels does it contain anything independent, spiritual, that would not be ideology; rather on all these levels, and particularly on the last, the only justification it can have is the simplifying, frictionless functioning of its organizational method, placed in the middle of illogical life, its only, entirely instrumental logic, the logic of a state of emergency.

May the right conduct consequently burrow from below as soberly as possible into such things, in order to move them. That is why Marx taught, so that we should never again have to find, test what is possible right now: all that matters is always just the next step. This corresponds within the revolutionary act to the known fact that here the oppressed wage-laborer, with justified self-interest for his part, saw himself as above all useful and called to an important office. Marx finally calls self-interest, as for the most part the strongest driving force, by name, and: the proletariat has nothing to lose but its chains; its interest, indeed, its simple and how much more its comprehended existence, is already the dissolution of capitalist society. Here there is no longer a natural poverty, no longer a class of serfs oppressed seemingly just mechanically, as under feudalism, through the weight of society, but, precisely, still oppressed intrasocially; rather, an entirely new class steps forward, social nothingness, emancipation as such. And precisely to this class, to its *a priori* economically revolutionary class struggle, Marx, in a magnificently paradoxical conjunction, gives over the legacy of all freedom, the beginning of world history after prehistory, the very first true total revolution, the end of every class struggle, liberation from the materialism of class interests as such. The alliance between the poor and the philosophers, between the egotism most strongly ignited by the *vis à vis de rien* and the moral purity of communism has allegedly already been concluded; or as Marx formulated similarly: philosophy cannot be realized without the proletariat's abolition; the proletariat cannot abolish itself without philosophy's realization. In particular, this alliance is possible for Marx because the proletarian in himself already represents the dissolution of society as such, because with capitalism the last of the social forms that are dialectically even possible, that could even be abolished, was attained, and socialism hence posits no apparent class conflict, no transformative moment of contradiction at all. In general, however, this alliance between interest and *such an idea* was absolutely not doubted by Marx, or even seen as a problem; that it even seems possible at all is obviously based on this: that the human Will to happiness has not been completely corrupted, that the Will as revolutionary class interest is morally already more easily defined, or at least becomes definable, through the simple fact *of the commonality* of willing; that finally, however, interest also needs the idea, the testimony of its suffering, willing, in order to be effective, as much as the idea itself needs the course of the world as the instrument it will finally refute, outwit. The highest concerns can certainly not be pursued through such an indiscriminate application of reason, such a theory of the cunning of reason taken over from Hegel: on the contrary there exists in Christian morality, in Kant, in Schopenhauer, a completely comparable recognition of the contradiction between creaturely interest and the paradox of the Good, the idea of the Good: whereas the first level of a world that lies so deep in wickedness can obviously only be explored through a creaturely compromise, consistent with Marx's despair at the political evidence of the Good. At any rate the proportions which Marx allotted to interest as the voluntaristic moment and the Idea as the seemingly providential, panlogistic moment are hardly clearly defined. He wants to act volitionally and change the world; thus Marx awaits not only the appearance of conditions, but rather teaches us to create them, posits class struggle, analyzes the economy in terms of the variable elements useful for active intervention. On the other hand, however, the occasionalism restored by the Romantics but above all by Hegel—in a splendid reversal of subjective into *objective* irony—the theory of an all-utilizing world reason, henceforth utilizing precisely the subjects, also influences Marx; and the same man who drove the fetish character out of production, who believed he had analyzed, exorcised every irrationality from history as merely unexamined, uncomprehended and therefore operatively fateful obscurities of the class situation, who had banished every dream, every operative utopia, every *telos* circulating in religion from history, plays with his "forces of production," with the calculus of the "process of production" the same all too constitutive game, the same pantheism, mythicism, upholds for it the same ultimately utilizing, guiding power which Hegel upheld for the "Idea," indeed which Schopenhauer upheld for his alogical "Will." Precisely this manifestation of the problem of the relationship between "sub-jective" Will and "objective" Idea proves the necessity of a fundamental metaphysical rethinking neglected by Marx; history is a hard, varied jour-ney; only potentially does continuous *activity* become time, time's very objectivity, charging time, refashioning it into a *locus minoris resistentiae*, indeed even into a related autonomous dynamic of this objectivity. Where we obviously enter the same problem-level where the discussion at the Council of Trent took place on the relation, the relative proportion, of freedom and "grace" and their potential synergism.

Until now everything has usually been brought down to dollars and cents, while on the other side the soul could always only shine in from above. The businessman laughs during his *earthly* business, and the levers are in his hands; a misunderstood Jesus offers encouragement in the *ideal* domain, seeks in vain to shame us by not resisting evil himself. Marx on the other hand finally sensitized us against the external method, which by itself so readily makes us inflexible, and then, separately, against the good man who thinks freedom already comes with him, in order finally to unite both; his conduct is guided so to speak by the Jesus of the scourge and the Jesus of fraternal love simultaneously. Sometimes the conquest of evil may succeed more quietly, as the rider on Lake Constance succeeded through heedlessness, and, more deeply, the saint in special situations succeeds through the kiss of righteousness, through a creative disregard; but as a rule the soul must assume guilt in order to destroy the existing evil, in order not to assume even more guilt by an idyllic retreat, a hypo-critical connivance in injustice.[3] Dominance and power in themselves are evil, but it is necessary to confront power in terms of power, as a categor-ical imperative with revolver in hand, wherever and as long as power can-not otherwise be destroyed, wherever and as long as everything diabolical still balks so violently at the (undiscovered) amulet of purity, and there-after finally discharge authority, the "power" even of the good, the lie of vengeance and its right, as methodically as possible. Hence Marx pro-vides, as this *third* term, a sufficiently complicated sensibility and a vari-ation of the identical revolutionary concept: in order to be able to think purely economically alongside capital, against its injustices, just as the de-tective is homogeneous with the criminal—where nothing but the eco-nomic aspect has to be considered; and only afterward to imagine a higher life, as soon as the space and the liberation of the idea have been won, and the measureless lies, as well as the unwitting embellishments, excuses, superstructures, variables of purely economic functions, can be destroyed in favor of the always and finally genuine idea of society. Here a separate procedure is operative that wants to define economic relations not with spiritual means, with a "league of the just," but rather places the economy outside of spirituality, and deduces the spiritual from the economic; or, as Marx himself similarly defined the proper maxim of the scientific socialism gained through him: it is not our consciousness that determines our being, but on the contrary our economic being that determines our consciousness, the breeding ground of ideas.

Ultimately, of course, this alone can not make the sober view fruitful; man does not live by bread alone. As extensively important as the external may be, and must be attended to, it still only suggests, it does not create, for human beings, not things, not their powerful process, outside of us and wrongly turned over onto us, invent history. What must still come economically, the necessary economic-institutional change, is defined by Marx, but the new man, the leap, the power of love and of light, morality itself, has not yet been allotted the desirable degree of autonomy in the definitive social order. Put differently: if primitive accumulation, the feudal and then the capitalistic modes of production successively determined particular moral and cultural systems, at least in terms of sphere, then the obsolescence of every discrete economic element, in other words the finally triumphant socialist mode of production, must bring in its train certain moral and cultural consequences, an equally "correct," aprioristic kind of sensibility and of culture, which can not just be defined as free thinking or a banal atheism, in accordance with the Philistine cultural ideals socialism has taken over from the bourgeoisie. Certainly socialism could not have been grounded if Marx had been submissively devout, if he had insisted on an Arcadian state of the world where rational distribution gives everyone what he needs, if in other words Marx had organized only consumption and not above all production: with his practical eye toward an inexorable industrialization, with his unromantic coldness and his materialism as a powerfully demystifying rigor. But precisely when this narrowness persists too long, man is simply saddled again, precisely in economic terms; oppression is only curtailed and not lifted. In just this way production is finally taken out of the hands of the subjects again, and a phantasmal process of the general, of economic developments in themselves, goes its own way: like an idol, occasionalistic, detached and even in the future indestructible. This is consistent with the fact that Marx, by really aiming his thrust, even where he did not weaken it into a "revolutionary development," only against capitalism—a relatively recent, derivative kind of decadence—and not also against the ceaseless, primordial locus of all enslavement, brutality and exploitation: against militarism, feudalism, a world from the top down as such; here the ancient socialist movement had already been reduced, misdirected and trivialized just by its opponent. Similarly there can be no doubt (from a religious viewpoint, closely related to the foregoing) that the indiscriminate ideology-critical distrust of every idea, without the need to exalt an idea oneself, does not encourage anything brighter; that even when Engels took up a dialectical-synthetic recon-struction of the condition of liberty, equality, and fraternity predominat-ing in the ancient communistic *gentes*, the social-constructive labor he expended was not confronted by a particularly clear and impressive ideal-constructive emphasis. Heart, conscience, spirituality, the communion of all the living, fraternity, *philadelphia* and the end of all isolation, found in the French Revolution, this truly not just "bourgeois" breakthrough of heretical history, its *closer* earthly reflection. And in this age, where God's desperate red sunset is already sufficiently in all things and neither Atlas nor Christ holds up his heaven, it finally appears that Marxism is no spe-cial philosophical accomplishment if it remains aesthetically fixed in the status quo in order to posit nothing but a more or less eudaemonistically instituted "heaven" on earth—without the music that ought to resound out of this effortlessly functioning mechanism of the economy and of so-cial existence. One can thus say that precisely the acute emphasis on all (economically) determining moments, and on the latency of all tran-scendent moments, existing but remaining in mystery, *moves Marxism close to a critique of pure reason, for which a corresponding critique of prac-tical reason has not yet been written.* Here the economy has been sublated, but soul, faith, for which room must be made, are lacking; the actively intelligent gaze has destroyed everything, certainly often justly, all the private idylls and uncritical reveries of socialism's hermits and secession-ists, who wanted to distill just for themselves a beautiful parallel earth from what is best on this earth, and dismissed the rest of the globe's phlegmatism; certainly the all too Arcadian, the abstract-utopian kind of socialism—appearing since the Renaissance as the secular mode of the thousand-year Kingdom [*Reich*], and often merely as insubstantial drap-ing, as the ideology of extremely sober class objectives and economic revolution—has been disavowed on good grounds. But then the utopian tendency in all these things is neither comprehended, nor is the substance of their miraculous images located or redirected, nor is even the primordially religious wish rescinded which in every movement or objective of a reconstruction of the world absolutely wanted to make room for life, in order divinely to essentialize itself, finally chiliastically to install itself into goodness, freedom, the light of the *telos*.

Only then will the deceivers truly tremble; what is right will appear. Magicians will no longer invoke the spirit, which will no longer lead beyond the light. But more than just a partial enlightenment is necessary, more than the kind that neglects the old heretical dreams of a better life rather than investigating and inheriting them. Only in this way, and not by means of the wretchedness of a vulgar atheism, can the ideological oxygen be cut off from the businessmen as the heroes, the negotiators and leaders, and their storehouse of beautifications be barred. Only someone who speaks not just for the earth but also for the wrongly surrendered heaven will truly be able to demystify the fabrications of bourgeois-feudal state ideology, namely unseductively, and the "enthusiasm for an equal share in enjoyment"[4] will no longer be what it seemed to the Prussian state theologian Stahl, the sole stimulating aspect of communist social theories. Certainly we will no longer work out of necessity, indeed we will work much better and more productively, our boredom and wretchedness is a sufficient guarantee of that, and there—as is already true for the teacher, official, politician, artist and scientist—pleasure in one's ability will replace the profit motive as a sufficient motivation, at least for practical occupations. Especially for the social valuation of this motive, in accordance with the tremendous, intensifying potential—fully capable of replacing the monetary stimulus—of contempt or esteem, of honor and of glory. Only very extrinsically do dangerous alliances appear in this hardly *Manchesterian* "state of the future": as Hegelian correlations to Prussia, especially to the universal state, to the very principle of organization—the more readily, more urgently does the duty thus arise of placing Marx into the higher space, into the new, most real adventure of disclosed life, into the What For of its society. That is: of bringing the usually all too truncated construal of society back into Weitling's, Baader's, Tolstoy's utopianly superior world of love, into the new force of the human encounter in Dostoevsky, into the Adventism of heretical history. Hence utopia's distant totality offers the image of a structure in no way still economically profitable: everyone producing according to his abilities, everybody consuming according to his needs, everyone openly "comprehended" according to the degree of his assistance, his moral-spiritual lay ministry and humanity's homeward journey through the world's darkness. Only thus can the new life, now radical as well as orthodox, be understood; only thus may the most exact economic logic and austerity be linked to political mysticism, and legitimate itself thereby. This logic removes every hateful sort of impediment in order, under the sublation of the economic private sphere, to hand it over to a communitarian society, but in return it lets the true privacy, and the entire, socially unsublatable problematic of the soul, step forward stronger than ever, in order—at the height of a structure that will only become reliable and orderly under socialism—to affiliate it to the Church, one necessarily and *a priori* posited after to socialism, oriented toward the new content of revelation. Only in this way will the community, freely electing itself, have space *above* a society that merely disburdens and a communistically restructured social economy, in a structure without violence because without classes. But a transfigured Church is the bearer of the furthest discernible purposes; in life she stands beyond labor, is the conceivable space of a continuously flowing tradition and of a connection to the end, and no social order, however successful, can do without this final link in the correlative series between the We and the final problem of the What For. Then human beings will finally be free for those concerns and questions which alone are practical, which otherwise only await them at their hour of death after their entire restless life up to then had done nothing but seal them off from everything essential. It is as the Baal Shem says: the Messiah can only come when all the guests have sat down at the table; this table is first of all the table of labor, beyond labor, but then at the same the time the table of the Lord—in the philadelphian Kingdom the organization of the earth finds its ultimately coordinative metaphysics.

The True Ideology of the Kingdom

I want to be nevertheless. But what is still left for us, especially now?

Will not everything inward go too high for us, especially now? For we must *die*, after a short delay, and perhaps corpses need no such broad drapery just to go the way of all flesh. The fraternally inner wealth no less becomes a brief phantom, disintegrates into tree bark like the gnome

Rübezahl's false treasure: if no energy arises in it to withstand even death, conquer it, in other words not only to go all the way through from below but also to become a powerfully upper part in itself, and the essential element of eternal life.[5] We repeat for the last time, then, to further fulfill an "objective," which here is of course opposed to more than just the slogans about the Battle of Cannae and the exclusion of the *creator spiritus* thereafter: This is how bad things could, had to get with us.[6] Certainly I would sing for my supper. But this dance around the golden calf, better, the calfskin with nothing underneath: this still came as a surprise. It means we have no true idea of socialism. Rather we have become the poorest of vertebrates; whoever among us does not worship his belly, worships the state; everything else has sunk to the level of a joke, of entertainment. Still we stand here expectantly, have longing and brief knowledge, but little deed, and—which explains this lack—no breadth, no horizon, no ends, no inner threshold, presentiently crossed, no kernel, and at the center no gathering conscience of the Absolute [*Überhaupt*]. But then here in this book a beginning was precisely posited, the unlost heritage was taken hold of again; the way that the Inmost, the Other Side shines again here, it can be no craven As If that denies the Absolute along with the Not Yet, and no insubstantial superstructure; rather, above all the masks and all the defunct civilizations rose the one thing, eternally sought, the one presentiment, the one conscience, the one salvation; came forth from our nonetheless unriven hearts, from the deepest part, the realest part of our waking dreams: as the last thing left for us, at the same time the only thing worthy to remain. This book—which will never make peace with the world—led the reader all the way through, first to our still unused nature, to our secret Head, our figure and awakening convocation, to the center of our artistic principle; precisely this already rang out by our interpretation of a simple pitcher, interpreted as the *a priori* latent theme of all the "visual" arts, and then as central to all the magic of music, illustrated finally by the ultimate possible self-encounter, by the comprehended darkness of the lived moment, which leaps up and hears itself in the essence of the inconstruable, the absolute question, in the very problem of the We. This deeply, it had to be said, only the *internal* path can lead, also called the self-encounter, the preparation of the inner word, without which every gaze outward remains empty and no magnet, no force to attract the inner word outwardly as well, to help it break through the error of this world. Of course in the end—*after* this merely *internally* concretized vertical—may a broader current spread out, the expanse, the *world* of the soul, the shattering, reverberating diapason—of the We-problem, the *external, cosmic* function of utopia sustained against misery, death, and the husk-realm of physical nature. In us alone does this fire still burn, this final dream, which Augustine meant: "Deum et animam scire cupio. Nihilne plus? Nihil omnino"[7]; in us alone does the absolute light still burn, a *sigillum falsi et sui, mortis et vitae aeternae*, and the fantastic movement toward it begins, toward the *external* divination of the waking dream, to the *cosmic* implementation of the principal concept of utopia. To find it, to find the right thing for whose sake it is worthy to live, to be organized, to have time: that is why we go, why we cut new, metaphysically constitutive paths, summon what is not there, build into the blue all around the edge of the world, and build ourselves into the blue, and there seek the true, the real, where the merely factual disappears—*incipit vita nova.*

~

Yet still we live our lives away quite briefly. We shrink as we mature. Very soon after we yellow, lie rotting deep below.

Certainly we try to imagine, to practice for what will happen after us. But no gaze can go upward without brushing against the *death* that fades everything. Nothing seems to us, the way we exist and experience, to take us over the caesura, to let us reverberate across.

One stands constantly outside; this strange circumstance can simply not be illuminated from here. Some who came back in the end depict what had appeared to the bystanders as convulsions and dreadful spasms as a vivid if not cheerful dream. But an old Jewish saying describes death in its gentlest form as if a hair had been brushed from our lip, and in its more common, more terrible form as if a lump had been torn from our throat.

So at first not much winds across from the other side that could lead us and help us. When it comes time to die, a kind wish will not become father even to an idea, far less to things that exist. On the other hand, those comforting images can also not prevail that we find all around us and yet never need approach us any more than proverbially. There is not much difference in itself whether we say: it's lonely at the top, where certainly the consistent connection between a mountain peak and Goethe creates no further obligations, or whether pupa and butterfly, winter and spring, "A new day lures us to new shores"[8]—whether these metaphors already seem to present us with an afterlife from the outside. But even if dying unto death is unknowably abrupt, it looks as if the prospects of permanence, in other words what remains identical on this side and the other side of the caesura, could be more convincingly established *through ourselves.*

For we move about within ourselves in a clearly palpable way. We are aware of it; the steps can be heard even when the one moving about remains shadowy. The impression remains undeniable that in us a hand governs the glove, and perhaps could remove it, too.

Hence that everything simply ends with death is a minor impression, and it still says very little. One might simply not be interested in what comes next, as though it might perhaps be worthwhile to collect news about life as constant change, against which death would represent a fixed state about which a single report rather than all the news would then suffice. But this kind of skepticism is really far removed from precisely the ascertainment of fact, or if it should actually present itself as an assertion, or even just as the asserted probability of the destruction of personhood, then this is surely not a careful demarcation, the closing of a chapter for lack of additional material, but rather in itself already a theory about the unknown, to which theories of the indestructibility of personhood, with a completely equal hypothetical weight, could immediately be opposed.

And indeed not only in this way: that we will all soon experience it, one way or another, but that we must nonetheless remain equally ignorant about the beyond. For having experienced nothing is absolutely no proof, whether of the No or of the Yes, while even the least thing that could be experienced would *eo ipso* have to be put on the account of the Yes. Consequently every religion's numerous albeit inauthenticated reports of such experiences, and foremost their fully unanimous teaching that there is an afterlife of the person, represent a certain however just regulative plus. Or as Chesterton says: "Somehow or other an extraordinary idea has arisen that the disbelievers in miracles consider them coldly and fairly, while believers in miracles accept them only in connection with some dogma. The fact is quite the other way. The believers in miracles accept them (rightly or wrongly) because they have evidence for them. The disbelievers in miracles deny them (rightly or wrongly) because they have a doctrine against them. . . . The plain, popular course is to trust the peasant's word about the ghost exactly as far as you trust the peasant's word about the landlord. Being a peasant he will probably have a great deal of healthy agnosticism about both. Still you could fill the British Museum with evidence uttered by the peasant, and given in favour of the ghost. . . . If you reject it . . . you either deny the main principle of democracy, or you affirm the main principle of materialism—the abstract impossibility of miracle. You have a perfect right to do so; but in that case you are the dogmatist. If I say 'a peasant saw a ghost,' I am told, 'But peasants are so credulous.' If I ask, 'Why credulous?' the only answer is—that they see ghosts. . . . The fact that ghosts prefer darkness no more disproves the existence of ghosts than the fact that lovers prefer darkness disproves the existence of love. If you choose to say, 'I will believe that Miss Brown called her fiancé a periwinkle, or any other endearing term, if she will repeat the word before seventeen psychologists,' then I shall reply, 'Very well, if those are your conditions, you will never get the truth, for she certainly will not say it.' It is just as unscientific as it is unphilosophical to be surprised that in an unsympathetic atmosphere certain extraordinary sympathies do not arise."[9] But even if Miss Brown were to say it, we would still, *joco intermisso*, certainly reject all efforts of a scientific kind, in other words the efforts of a potential *experimental* research into inherently suprasensory materializations. It may be that something could be ascertained thereby, though in any case less now than before, when clairvoyance could be practiced more thoroughly. Those who still have it—the Seeress of Prevorst was once at the forefront—and those really not so intelligent or perceptive, but rather listless, often dormant souls who think they see, are too poorly prepared—for just the reason that clairvoyance can no longer exhaustively account for all the connections—to be able always to distinguish the merely neuropathic from the actual visions here, or the merely still unanalyzed stellar clusters from the actual nebulae, so to speak.[10] To say nothing of the constant possibility of also being deceived in the actual occult sphere, insofar as the "lower elementals," the "cobolds" and "poltergeists" of old German domestic legends pretend to be the souls of the departed, as these all too atavistic types themselves say. And even if such illusions need not be feared, perhaps because the experimenters know how to keep at least the elementals at a remove by being agnostic about them, it is a sorry sight when what should be profound is made creepy, or such musty old notions are compiled, or that higher realm of rational beings that Kant acknowledged in the conclusion to his *Fundamental Principles of the Metaphysics of Morals*, and methodologically had to acknowledge, is devalued into a sphere of transcendental physiology. One may have as much presentiment as one likes, dreams may come true however often and however extraordinarily: it is certainly not our true, hidden essence that predicts lottery numbers. Indeed, one can even have a consistent dream city where one recognizes everything in the most precise way, fountains, bay windows, plazas, and which is called—Denver: all this is really quite unimportant within a transcendent application, because here the point is not to duplicate the lower realm, and because we should still expect something better from the beyond than a mere Baedeker for higher-order tourists. This also applies to such an estimable, unjustly forgotten man as Carl du Prel, who likewise saw, or thought he saw, the As If, duty and morality, the meaningfully difficult reality-degree of this object-series, confirmed by means of a coarse kind of magic, a so-called experimental metaphysics—a transcendent seed cannot germinate in laboratory dust.[11]

For precisely, we already feel ourselves to be just inhabiting our bodies anyway. Thus a foot, an arm could fall off, without our self losing anything thereby. One can thus possess what is most distant more experientially, and already to have affirmed it phenomenologically somewhere. In just this way a dying man was once able to say of himself, strangely enough, that this life had of course been nothing, but how he would have to laugh if there were no other. And a French nobleman said of himself, with just as unguarded and absurd a profundity: "I can take care of myself, but I will be able to manage without myself, too," whereby he wanted to say that he regarded death with equanimity. How very easily the Chinese die: they stab themselves to death in an enemy's house in order to create legal inconveniences for the latter; the poor are ready to be executed in another's place in return for compensation; criminals die as coolly as we lay ourselves to sleep every evening, prepared to awaken as the same person. The Hindus too do not fear death, but rather quite properly only life, and death only insofar as it is an element of death, of the transience, the mutability of life; accordingly a surfeit of life leads immediately to a longing to have escaped life along with "death," a longing for eternal peace. Conversely again, precisely the will to life can point to death, toward a different death of course, toward death as release, certain of its power to overcome death, and beyond it to attain permanence in itself, repose; hence du Prel already reported of somnambulists: "The more deeply they were immersed in transcendental existence, the greater was their reluctance to return to sensory awareness and be reunited with their bodies, which they see lying before themselves as objects. Only on the lower levels of somnambulism is there a fear of death (apparent as a fear of the 'danger' of the deepest sleep state; in deepest sleep itself, however, whose symptoms approach those of death, somnambulists often resist the will of the mesmerist who wants to wake them." Now of course this resistance could also derive from other, more neurological sources than from a conquest of the fear of death; meanwhile, who has not known the curiosity, the craving for knowledge, the paradoxical pleasure of the great wayfaring, the longing for death out of a *transcendent vital exuberance* itself, the absolutely transgressive and exploratory pleasure in the "quintessence of the lovely, slumberous fluids," in the new day, in the fiery chariot of a desertion one nonetheless refuses?[12] Certainly this un-Christian assurance concedes too much to death as such; the power of evil within death, the paradox of its absolutely only potential connection to the pillars of heaven, the most profoundly dialectical function of such a *copula spiritualis*, is not comprehended; and meanwhile of course no one can be overcome by fear who is certain of his immortal part, in whom a love from beyond has even taken part, in whom the *non omnis confundar* above every corporeal and every debasing, mundane empiricism, which he was given and which will again be received, has already united. There the soul's inmost element energizes itself, an essence full of mysterious power, full of deep, undeveloped meaning: "Do you know," cries Alabanda in Hölderlin's *Hyperion*, in the same sense, out of this same profound self-awareness, "why I have never heeded death? I feel a life within me that no God has created and no mortal begotten. I believe that we exist through ourselves, and are so intimately connected to the cosmos only by free choice"—but the natural contract may also freely be canceled when it fails. In short it may be doubtful that we could already find death within us if we had not already seen death all around us, and accordingly inserted ourselves into it empirically. But it is completely certain that every single correlative act within the correlation, "I feel, I desire, I think" not only accompanies, but is ultimately sustained, so that the self, the synthetic viewpoint, shines almost constantly, as individuality certain of itself, into the corruptible, forgetful mechanism, regulating it. Here rests a seed which is indestructible, precisely the enfolded self, the *darkness, the question, the meaning, the ground, the center of the self-encounter of us all*, shadowy no less as still an act of consciousness than as an object of consciousness wanting to objectivate itself, and yet the very realest support of our personality. For this permanence is completely given to us, and so, precisely, at any moment phenomenologically discoverable for purposes of making oneself evidently present. That we must nonetheless die is only empirically discoverable, and that there must even be in every case a psycho-physical parallelism, that in other words the death of the body also means the destruction of the soul itself, that there can be no psychological life without corresponding physiological activity, is merely the working hypothesis—already punctured by science as well, since Bergson —of physiological psychology, and is already regionally inferior to the phenomenological evidence of being-in-oneself, of the spiritual substance. Even if external experience did not lead far enough, unambiguously enough beyond, in other words, at least—*pour être heureux ou malheureux il suffit de se croire tel*—the dissimilarity, the corporeal superiority, incomparability, ultimate invulnerability of our soul, meaning precisely: what remains identical about the kernel, on this side and beyond the caesura, can still be adequately discovered phenomenologically. Here, in accordance with Schelling's prophecy, on the strength of the already hazarded illumination from *Hyperion*: "For of course the souls of those who are entirely preoccupied by earthly matters will simply shrivel up, and approach a condition of annihilation; those however who were already preoccupied in this life by what is enduring, eternal and divine, will be eternal with the greater part of their being."[13] By no means, then, does personhood simply emerge from the body's machinery like apostles out of a clock tower, destined to perish along with its empirically knowable mechanism; rather, the soul is defined by its eidetically real nature as indestructible, and the body as well as its death seem like simply an empty spectacle next to the resonant, the personant, the personal, like almost everything else in the ineptitude of the available empirical reality.

～

So strangely, in other words, do we often already watch the change in us. But during this change we nevertheless take at least one significant standard with us. It would not be possible for us thus to suffer from our insufficiency if something in us did not also press on, ring out more deeply, and want to push far past everything corporeal. It would not be granted to us (though we constantly do it, and in precisely this does the power of not-yet-conscious knowledge, of presentiment and amazement, prove itself through us) to anticipate, directed toward something before us for which we are destined, if we did not feel like children, but then

one day the perpetually locked chest opens where the secret of our ori-
gins is hidden. Thus a powerful and unconcluded volitional and apper-
ceptual mass within the tendency, a true soul-spirit of utopia, proves to
be at work here. This is also partly the reason why pain is felt so strongly
and pleasure so very much more weakly, and is already so much more
difficult to grasp, to shape. But it is also partly why the joyful and valuable elements in our life, the elements that have become our gains, can
be retained all the more exactly and substantially, at least in memory, this
strongly postmortal, highly metaphysical gift. Of course the great standard reveals no less truly terrible absurdities, insufficiencies and finally,
above all, our own restricted blood supply, in the final understanding:
the subject's inability to withstand, to carry, to guarantee all too extensive, all too far-sighted continuity of purpose. About this last thing, in
other words—however one might feel with the utmost certainty at the
sight of one's lover: this soul cannot perish; or at the revelation of the inner meaning that a person in his inmost aspect cannot die—about the
definition and nature of the immortal soul, how to endure the passage
toward this soul, even the most evident phenomenology can tell nothing. But now, precisely here, where this has become clearly visible, appears the point we promised, where the self-encounter begins to radiate
extensively over the question of death, thus inciting the problems of our
historical-mystical survival in the face of death, disruptions and the final
destruction of the world.

Here above all we are broken up; the self certain of itself now withdraws entirely. But while it previously seemed that such expanse could
only be achieved through a diminution, only so to speak through an—organically or socially—adaptive downgrading of the waking dream, of the
knowledge of the goal, nonetheless a leap: *exitus*-exodus is posited within
the We itself, on its own level. In the organic or the social domain, the self
effected, reinforced, guided what it had merely befriended, objectivated
itself by stretching like a violin string across every thing, every social situation it encountered, on the basis of their negligibility and vacuity,
whereby it naturally also gained a greater plenitude, expanse, depth in itself. But now the daughter of Zion confronts only herself, in herself, in
her own imperilment, in the most critical *de te res agitur*, whereby it is
precisely death which provokes the metapsychic-metaphysical *probation*
of the soul in the world and in the terrors of the world above. Here, then,
the innermost and the "outermost" locations are attained, and at the same

time the most direct passage from the one into the other, the soul's most direct entry into the "world," into what is free, great, scenic, into the theater of decision and what is finally most real about metaphysics, such that death, the *provocation* of metaphysics through death, at the same time brings about the *full spheric expanse of the metapsychological.* The inner light here becomes fully extensive, no longer a light on the field as in sociology, but a shaft of light from the canopy; to put it differently: death, insofar as through it, against it, above it, the inner principle can step fully into the open, insofar as its hostile sting, the blow of destruction, involves the very most central application and rebirth of inwardness—death's accomplishment is thus to furnish a journeyman's test of our self. It tests the height reached by us, the value of our inner metapsychology; it examines its strength, its uses, its durability, its suitability for mobilization and against the most terrible reality; it introduces a subjectively alien factor and thus solicits us directly from the subjectively ideal sphere, from the free-floating realm of ideal self-definition, into the "cosmic" element of danger, of dispersion, and yet finally the soul's proof as it gathers itself again from the mechanism of this fatal world—in short, death brings about the *birth of metempsychosis out of the strength of metapsychology.* Consequently the task and problem here is to make our acknowledged permanence triumph over empirical adversity, over our own insufficiency, that is: to overcome, through the power of transmigrational dispersal, and finally through the Apocalypse, as the absolute work of the Son of Man, the history that cannot be experienced in its entirety.

THE VULNERABLE BODY

What is lying all about us will long remain.

Only we move away, stay warm, and yet one day will go pale and blind by what covers us.

Thus do we breathe, and die in parts in which we do not even exist. However healthy one may feel, we carry a body that is often only as similar, or ultimately perhaps not even as similar to us, as flowers or pretty stones could be. Animals exist in their bodies, and never come out, but a human being cannot return to his body's center of gravity, never meets up with his body where he wants to play toward his own center, not in the leap, nor in the dance; here especially he fails to meet up with the body that he far more leaves behind and breaks up. Of course just the one who appears as he is has permeated his own flesh, so to speak purified it with and as its eye. But it is precisely the animated body that does not accompany the one who animated it for long: that is, astoundingly briefly.

CONSTRICTED INDIVIDUALITY, TERMINATION

Nevertheless we stir within; we can do it uprightly.

Still, where to go with this sensation of oneself, with the indestructible particularity of the respective self given to us? Really, very few find it pleasant to be born with this wicked heart and these fixed levels of talent, whereby to someone who hates himself, moreover, envy of another's apparently unreasonable favor tends to be more a poison than a balm. And does this not lead us to the real enigma: our defiance against the very constellation that let us be born into this "state," these prospects, this time. Most children's epitaphs can already be written even before they get here, so precisely and inescapably are they normally detained by the houses in which they emerge apparently randomly, for a reason unaffected by any social fluctuations. Here defiance snatches at the void: neither the parents nor any representatives of the capitalist social order, living or dead, can in any particular case before us be designated as personally to blame for such an apparently arbitrary dispersion into the social stratum. If there were finally a social leveling here, there would remain the variously well-dispensed natures and talents.

But a hateful doubt also lies in wait for the socially, the intellectually more fortunate, and the health and vitality which lets one ignore death is for most of us really just the secularized remnant of an older kind of piety, our debt of transcendent certainty to a bygone religious culture, long overdue for cancellation. It is horrible to have to live and work this way, and afterward they throw us in a grave; at best only our image carries on after our death. Even this work, however, shines beyond the grave only within others, who likewise must die; it is no independently animate, free-floating mode of existence, and even if it were, the soul can still not possess an existence of its own through such an effect. For a short time there was light, an enigmatically promising upbeat containing strong telic correlations it could not complete by itself, and then, to the larve bled dry, life becomes like a measureless nothing, as if previously there had also been nothing: as though, even if one added up a thousand upbeats, there had been absolutely no personal history before the void that is death, as though no memory of the work could persist. Precisely the generations pass away; in endless sedimentations they lie above one another everywhere, shrunken together, and even if one leaves aside the sentimental interest in the loneliness and the dreadful sepsis of our demise—nevertheless achieving some consolation through posterity's remembrance, the so to speak continuously upgraded courier system, the relay stations of memory extending into infinity—even then, indeed especially then, the functional problem persists: who or what lives life as a whole life, *as the broad, historical life granted to "humanity" as a whole?* Do the relay stations of historical-cultural memory exist by themselves? Will not in fact the Amati and Stradivarii remain preserved someday, but no one will be able to play them, and the scores for the Ninth Symphony will appear as lifeless and illegible to another culture as the Incas' knotted script? Do successive cultures, irrespective of their perhaps immanent connections, separate themselves from one another, *as no longer capable of coexistence,* without anything identical about their problems, anything enduringly comprehensible in their solutions? Is it even worthwhile, considering the pathetic brevity of our existence, for us to accept a task not only for children and family and the already now transindividually existent state structure, but for everything more expansive that can never be grasped *as a whole* by any single soul, and that exists as just a conceptual reality, as history or humanity or whatever objectivity? And what could human history, human culture even mean in and of itself, after not only the individual, the nations repeatedly submerge in them, become unpresent, but their historical summation is also threatened by the possibility of an ultimately disengaged isolation? By the danger that merely clever animals in some remote corner of the galaxy will rub their eyes, decorate each other with peculiar honors, and mistake the twinkling in their brains for knowledge; by the possibility, in other words—and then death would be anything but a *musagète*—that even our most convincing works, even our humanly most evident self-elucidations, will only drift like debris down some nameless river, or surround us senselessly, with only the reflexive, *ad hoc* meanings that our minor provinciality of a culture has imagined for them in the midst of a consequently wholly unfeeling universe.

THE POWER OF TRANSMIGRATIONAL DISPERSION

And yet it still means a great deal to be able to die. There is something generous about it that at least allows us to travel away. And indeed either permanently, or just like fog or the clouds that rise and yet circulate. One can thus assume either that we become completely separated and can never return, or that a new life, a life from the beginning, is again and again granted, disclosed, and poured out for us. The former, harsher conception, already positing everything as final, forms the content of the simple doctrine of the immortal soul.

That the soul migrates, on the other hand: among both Jews and Christians this is spoken of only covertly, in fact almost not at all. For among Jews, what happens on the other side is absolutely seldom the subject of discussion; Sheol, the shadow realm, covers up every mystery. But there are certainly intimations between, or, better, within the lines that now and then point to the latter conception of death, in other words to a transmigrational line of thought. Thus in Job 1:21: "Naked came I out of my mother's womb, and naked shall I return thither." Further in Genesis 3:19: "In the sweat of thy face shalt thou eat bread, till thou return unto the ground; for out of it wast thou taken: for dust thou art, and unto dust shalt thou *return*"; in Deuteronomy 33:6 (according to the Aramaic translation by Onkelos): "Let Reuben live, and not die [a second death]; and let not his men be few"; in Ecclesiastes 1:4 and 1:9: "One generation passeth away, and another generation cometh: but the earth abideth for ever. . . . The thing that hath been, it is that which shall be; and that which is done is that which *shall be done*: and there is no new thing under the sun." It also seems that the sentence in Exodus 20:5: " . . . for I the LORD thy God am a jealous God, visiting the iniquity of the fathers upon the children unto the third and fourth *generation* of them that hate me"—could best be interpreted as applying to the identity of the self, particularly when one recalls the Yahweh who did not want to destroy Sodom because of ten just men, after all, and when these could not be found, had Lot, his wife and his two daughters led out of the city by angels. Of course, these are only a few passages, which become no more conclusive if one differently emphasizes a "hither" or an "again," or the same soul in different "generations," not to mention that only a later, kabbalistic interpretation had this emphasis. Since Jesus also leaves these questions completely unanswered, and only spoke of a final resurrection on the Last Day—in spite of many suggestions, as in Matthew 11:14, where John is supposed to be the reborn Elias, and although the Church later had to accommodate itself to a longer timespan—the doctrine of immortality, even after the New Testament, this *abbreviated* form of the doctrine of the transmigration of souls, where Jesus reckons with the most immediate nearness of Judgment, remained the essential dogma of the Christian

Church. All the more strongly, however, did post-Christian rabbis re-member transmigration as the divine spark's already intracosmic power over death. A statement by Rabbi Meir ben Gabbai discloses in brief form the entire intensive-ethical foundation of this doctrine, of this already mundanely implanted and operative postulate of a white magic we pos-sess against death's black magic: "You should know that this work [the re-peated translocation of souls] be God's mercy on Israel, so that the souls of light may be worthy of the highest light and, as our rabbis, hallowed be their memory, have said, all of Israel may attain a part in eternal life." Everywhere, then, where mere initiates speak of the wayfaring and not of the "Messiah" who of course will abolish all occurrence in time—indeed in all the world's occult doctrines, not only in Buddhism, but equally in the central Sudan, in druidic Ireland, among the Sufis, in the Kabbalah, among the Cathars, throughout the old Christian Rosicrucianism, this second, more just, more loving doctrine—transmigration, this more ap-portioned, complicated form of immortality, forms as much the final les-son for the neophyte as the recurrent, comparatively verifiable *arcanum* of the mysteries. Under the aspect of multiple lives, then, as Lessing also em-phasized (in his *Education of the Human Race*, significantly), there can never be too much death and end for one person alone.

Moreover, death may already be sufficiently comprehended within our afterlife. However, to say nothing of any other issue for the moment, where shall we consign birth, this *descent* of a soul created at the begin-ning of time, as the doctrine of immortality after all explains it? Why should this incarnation, if we concede even a single occurrence, be re-stricted to it, and are we forced for the sake of this singularity to main-tain the conclusion that the same number of souls keeps rolling stub-bornly on? But if there is nothing that limits these souls but the Last Day, then of course one may conclude: the world will end when God wills it, or rather, that it will end was already conceived by God in advance such that it will truly end at the proper hour, and the entire spiritual substance will have been used up and incarnated as soon as it is no longer needed. But it could also be argued, conversely, and perhaps with more justice, in view of the arbitrariness of everything created: if the Last Judgment is supposed to limit the souls, then the number of souls also restricts the Last Judgment, meaning, the latter would by definition be given when the meaningless, bad finitude of the number of souls were finally de-pleted by their unique births, so that then—which would be intolera-

ble—the purely mathematical concept of a fulfilled quantum would take
the place of natural philosophy's concept of the catastrophe, or the metaphysical concept of a leap within the divine *mysterium*. But according to
the intramundanely transcendent idea, value-idea: metempsychosis, the
mere *number* of souls is already well complete: what is pending, and so
poses deeper problems than those of the quantum, is the *maturity* of the
souls, and this first determines the end, then.

In other words, if it is permitted to us to leave this earth differently
than do things that remain, than animals who must die with no self, with
no memories, with no works, dilettantishly: then it represents a more
profound right to be able to come back to this earth. Then we take ourselves along as we have become to ourselves and assumed ourselves, as
someone inward, depending, or someone still incomplete, without knowing ourselves. Often, however, one can already arc so far away from here
that even if an actual foredeath would hardly be endurable, one can nevertheless think about inner luggage for the terrible journey, for the pitch-
black ocean by an uncertain sail. "The frantic chase of life comes to an
end . . . Come! We shall see if a fire burns in the hearth," C. F. Meyer has
the weary Ulrich von Hutten say, and this inner thing we carry across, its
resonances, its relucences, fill the beyond.[14] "In the dream it was better,"
a saint cried here below already, but what Jean Paul reported of the last
hour of this life at least remains, at least applies: "When everything in our
broken spirit fades and dies off: poetry, philosophy, struggle, joy, then the
night-flower of faith finally springs forth, and in the final night fortifies
us with its perfume."[15] And still more deeply shines a smile that never
passes away and permits no ruination, looks at us with its eyes, from
which we can take a light within death; the sound transcends abundantly
that had already come over us as we lived, that compels the dying to take
courage and to hearken upward: "They heard it all around them, and
knew not what they heard. / But the seraph took up the numinous weaving / of his lyre, and still in the sweet torments of joy / strayed, with un-
steady hand, down its radiant strings," sings Klopstock in the 12th canto
of his *Messias* on the death of Maria, the sister of Lazarus, and she died
because she could not bear the rapture which the heavenly voice poured
into her breaking heart. Indeed, truly: death here lays bare the deeper
sense of hearing by which it must then be grasped, by which our life must
triumphantly be entwined with death, morally traversed like a single moment by the disembodied spirits, in the declared shadow state of the be-

yond. If people only know who they were, then it would be an especially easy thing for those who have been *reincarnated* to remember their previous existence; but certainly, too, we do not know ourselves within existence, do not know the sleeper in the dark chamber of the lived moment, and so we have no standard by which to recognize our soul within what is different, earlier, to ascertain its selfsameness just as Heinrich von Ofterdingen saw the metamorphosis of his own form through all the ages portrayed in the hermit's cave. But *final* images were always and everywhere still dark and incomprehensible, even if particular dream figures might surprise the soul with an intimate delight: and, in just the same way, people everywhere lack support for a *decisive anagnorisis* in such claims to remember oneself "at a later time"; My name is No One, said Odysseus to Polyphemus, and of course, in a truth most dismal, this is still always the human name wherever finality stands for identity. Meanwhile, finally, although it seems to be denied to us to see more deeply inward or even recognize ourselves as the same, as the wanderers, there is still the all-overpowering vision of which so many testimonials of insight and anamnesis relate, and that Delphic votive gift still appears at whose sight Pythagoras called out, half unconsciously: "My shield!" and which was Achilles' shield, suspended in every great event. Memory itself is already a very strange gift, where the intimacy of the lived moment is preserved for another time, and the concept of the transmigration of souls, as the unity of Epimetheus and Prometheus, is absolutely able without contradiction to add hope to this gift, a higher metaphysical enigma. This is why, then, our lives flash before our eyes when we are in mortal danger; this is why Pericles commended himself in his hour of death, saying that no citizen had suffered an injustice through him; this is why, according to a profound kabbalistic tradition, the same angel who began as a little flame on the head of the embryo, and escorted the soul through higher realms during the mother's pregnancy, stands by one's deathbed when the final hour draws near, as the angel of death, and now a human being recognizes his double protector, and recognizes by him, by this terrible gauge and index of the beginning and the end, how much closer he has come and how great is the sin that either left his life open in respect of his ideal or wiped it out. My deed is my property, says the Buddha, my deed is my inheritance, my deed is the womb that bore me; my deed is a family to which I alone am kin, my deed is my refuge. Every ancient initiation was meant for passing over, for ranging through: "I strode through the portals of death [the illusory coffin, the coffin of Lazarus], crossed the threshold of Proserpine [here the soul stolen from the underworld, from Pluto, from the past, from matter, recognizes itself as the same], and after I had traveled through all the elements, I saw in the middle of the night the sun in its brightest manifestation [poverty, suffering, the threat that the light will be snuffed out, the total December night of the world, the birth of Horus, Mithras, Christ, the Messiah]"[16]—what Apuleius here relates of the Eleusinian mysteries expresses the entire content of comparative esotericism, that of Christianity as well, within a mysticism of death.

But departed souls should become young and incarnate again; they seek us here below, and breasts, comely bodies are their way of attracting us, clothing themselves. An embrace between lovers is the bridge across which the dead stride back into life; they were the guests and they are also the hosts; the will of the unborn souls mingles perceptibly, although not completely, with the man's strength, the woman's charms. The souls, however bright they have become, still do not thereafter leave the intramundane cycle; precisely they do not want to leave it; the saint also returns, and returns precisely in bodily form, ripens into the destinies of the living; the saint, says the Buddha again, sacrifices by eating: he practices a great renunciation by still being here, by being a teacher, by still lingering on the plane of unknowing; indeed even great geniuses, having become as it were unaccidental, unsubjective, enter the historical schedule as the heirs of their own, utterly discontinuous maturity, of a kind that could not even be gained over a single lifetime. Stories of divinities who sojourn here offer a mythically very similar lesson, and precisely the birth of Christ would have been the incarnation, the journey through the grave, the all-pervading journey across this earth by a divinity oriented toward humanity, by the Son of Man within God himself, if Man like God had not failed in this highest reincarnation as the contact between all of heaven and all of earth. In this way the souls live, right up to the end, our collective circulation between the Here and the There that is not truly a Beyond if the Here does not finally appear fully within it, and they function right up to the end as the organs of that great soul-migration, that *cosmic process of self-recognition*, which the lost, riven, unknown Soul-God or Holy Spirit describes in accordance with the true gnosis of the doctrine of the transmigration of souls. In the world as its passage, and in human beings as the heads [*Häupter*] of the world, as the final place of preparation, resurrection, the burning problem-cycle of the *still undiscovered world-idea.*

PROSPECTS AND CONSEQUENCES OF OUR BEING-THERE

Now the point, however, was that we are trapped all too cruelly within ourselves. What motivated us was our so very darkly fortuitous birth into a particular circumstance: the brevity of life and then the indiscernible something else into which it leads. The problem which arose foremost was: who lives this life in its totality, and is it possible to raise over the existence thus fashioned something that always concerns us, and also something in common, something ultimately visible *to all*? The doctrine of the transmigration of souls, this penetrating application of the certainty of the We to the improvident course of this world, should have proved itself as the strongest antidote to the contradiction between our brief time and the historical time we cannot live.

First, of course, is it even desirable to reinforce such a twisted path? Is the outer life so orderly that it can be trusted to carry out rewards and punishments, let alone flawlessly? And above all: is the upper realm so moral, are we so well governed, do we even want to be governed so wisely and patriarchally, that our karma is dictated to us like a syllabus, whose negative entries, under penalty of a regression or a disaster in a subsequent life, we must pedantically and academically balance out? Is it not more devout to hold to this disorderly life rather than to the merciless schooling that this unbreakable causality of suffering, purgation, and bliss represents? Finally, if we already have a used soul, and the individual takes up the threads of his work precisely there where he laid them down in a previous existence, should not a cowering desperation be the necessary consequence for those living in the cellar, who after all began no later, and the coldest kind of Pharisaism of their "status" for those better-rounded natures to whom everything—luck, talent, favor—then has to appear as their true "inheritance"? So that in other words only mediocrities whose life flows away tepidly and vaguely, combined of simultaneous night and day, could discern in the doctrine of karma something like better times to come, and a song of consolation? Much in all these objections is correct, but here the solution must be found with the help of the idea that this migration is after all hardly set for us heteronomously, by external circumstances, and by a God along with them.

Not only that we can all include death in us as we age. From our first hour onward we respire the fatal air in which we actually first mature, historically. That articulates our lives for us, provides stages and colors, brings out an attitude and a countenance, rescues us from the immobile child or youth. And in fact the inclusion goes even further: the pulsing kernel in us has freely left the death-blow behind, along with all the rest, and over the longer course as well. What remains behind is filthy enough, but there is nothing that could appertain to us less than the vacated corpse, which can thus be painlessly washed away after the tremendous excretion of death. Here we have not only escaped such that the slamming door no longer snags our coat, which anyway belongs to us no differently than a husk or a vein of ore might; for it was already too late for annihilation, and the leap of the soul, even toward the individual, historical soul, had already happened; rather, we were even able to enlist death, organically underivative like conception, into the service of our light in a way that drew out more than half again as much energy as misery. Not only *within* this life is the "Die and become!"[17] already operative, did we force many of the grim energies of death to become the devil who must build St. Martin his church, who could usefully become the motor of self-renewal, the mortification of selfishness, the night of love and the liberation of our bodies; of precisely the death of *world* through us. Rather we drew from death, from its power, in itself the most malign, most horrible power, from its thunderbolt against everything human, significantly human, at least in itself operatively tragic, satanically intended—we drew from it, even *on the other side of* this one life, the idea of a recurrent beginning, the witch's potion, a wide, departing and recurring, in other words strongly intermittent *dispersal of our self across all of history, an intermittence to the soul's various historical existences,* with the dream of a final, undefeated, fully matured self-presence at the end of the world.[18] Hence everything here is determinable only from the standpoint of the self and not from outside; hence the migrations and the karma and that we ourselves can be the cause of our future life (note: of its purely characteristic habitus), an instrumental outwitting of everything outside or above, of the world's still uncorrelative automaton, and not at all, as it might initially have seemed, the senselessly flagrant system continuous all the way down to Desdemona's handkerchief, of a panlogism of the concrete machinery of coincidence, fortune, and success. Certainly a karma of the soul is hardly causally determinative for the course of the world itself when karma is the moral-panlogical basis or even the equivalent of destiny, of *tyche* and of automatism, of the pure mechanism of events; rather, from its migrations the soul gains only the power to bend external destiny to itself, to use it, to shape it to be ironically conformal with itself, to use it, like death, as the equipment for very unworldly goals, to achieve this destiny intelligibly, in the midst of the empirical world, by going through this world. To return to our point, then: we do not devise our natural body, perhaps, but certainly the expressive one. So it still very much remains for us to change our seemingly invulnerable character historically, within time as within eternity. So no social or any other destiny, no false or failed encounter that befell or hindered us here could be already singular and decisive for the soul's destiny; rather, our born radius of action should extend past any particular social differentiation, at least subjectively, and would hence be equipped not to heed it as the final element within our one single participation. Then this would apply: nothing in this life is unique, nothing accidental is irrevocable, the five foolish virgins could find oil *after* midnight as well,[19] the *status viae* lies far beyond death, which hardly represents an inflexibly formative *status termini*; and if in accordance with the ephemerality of every local actualization, pessimism remains finally organically and socially ineradicable, our ability to shape our true Son of Man as an enclave of meaning ultimately extractable from "destiny," precisely as it affects us individually, has still not been buried from the perspective of a *return of our own not-same, same*.

But for us who live over and over the final thing that we did not fear to see thereby also begins to be very near. We have to set the course; on us lies the agony of choosing a direction, but we immediately go along as ourselves and not as mere memories; we follow the good, living way, the way of the goal, to its end, since we ourselves are this way.[20] Wieland's Herkules, who chose, and chose the deed, hardly felt himself to be "a fool who died so that when he lived no longer, he could snatch an unfelt existence from the lips of other fools"[21]; rather, the stone may fall downward, but consciousness, once attained, burns steeply upward, bearing ever more gold. If there was until very recently still a question, what permanent element is it which lives this life in its entirety: then we are completely the ones, who also live our afterlife, as ourselves, wherever we remain faithful to ourselves and hold ourselves fast by our kernel; we live life, not at every moment, but intermittently, and above all at its end, as the entirety of life, as the broad, historical life allotted to "humanity" as a whole. Or to put it differently: insofar as we reappear, our existence can spread far over history; indeed it should be possible for us to figure as the same human beings in different centuries, it should be possible to experience our own—even, since we can never experience our own deepest subject, if accompanied by no memory of our identity—history, and to that extent—this is what the resurrection of all the dead in the simple dogma of immortality indicates, after all—through history's final event, never far from the chorales of life, to be subjectively existent. *Everything could pass away, but the house of humanity must remain preserved and stand illuminated at full strength, so that one day, when destruction rages outside, what we have gained can live there, and help us— which leads us directly from the transmigration of souls to the meaning of the true social, historical and cultural ideology.* Understanding past epochs would not even be conceivable, let alone deducing the historical-rhythmic return of living epochs, in other words individualistic and "abstract," that is, theological epochs, if there were not an alternating entry, an alternating current so to speak, of two different spiritual natures, such that we can now understand Greece and the Renaissance, say, as the work of strangers, and Egypt, the Gothic and above all the merely incompetently interrupted Baroque as the work of our brothers, indeed of our own self. Thus history is already properly divided into two spaces through transmigration—one lower and mundane, the other higher and invisible—between which this rotation between groups and epochs takes place, insofar as in the higher space, as the space of the departed, as the intermediate realm between here and there, history, or the typology of the next time-space, receives its particular *essential* causal stamp. And most of all, precisely, above the history we are able to repeat again and again, replay more meaningfully, transmigration causes every subject to be present simultaneously at the *end* of history, authenticatedly present, guarantees the concept of "humanity" in its one day most concretely inclusive, absolute entity. What human beings are pursuing is the world's prime of life [*Mannesalter*], and their time, the time of the circulation of the soul, historical time with its extensive continuity of purpose, well and deeply substantiated, at least in the subject, is the true, constitutive scene of the mysteries: the water flows, the earth's lava has cooled, even the organic world's great mutations are long since spent, but human beings have remained at work, and now they are the ones to conclude a broad, historical, subjective metaphysics, the life of this all-surpassing time that thunders against heaven and of its impatient testing of the Name of God.

FORMS OF THE UNIVERSAL SELF-ENCOUNTER, OR,
ESCHATOLOGY (1918)

Too much still persists all around us, and ultimately we still *are* not.

Only inwardly can nothing affect us enduringly; here we have set out on another path, and built our own house.

But most work without knowing what they do, and base it only on trite, inferior goals. So our fierce collective striving is guided by nothing but the profit motive, a flimsy, barbaric content, which soon enough expires from its own sterility. It helps us little, in contrast, when other, more idealistic endeavors also appear, for as long as they are not granted enough power to decisively transform, decisively to be put to use, then the cooperative factor, the spiritual factor, remains as arbitrary as the economic factor of meaningless record-breaking. The one merely an abdominal question, the other a lie roundabout the social question, or, after hunger has been stilled and luxury liberated, a game, a buffoonery, an amusement and an entertainment, a science in itself, the exploration of the soul of the gnat, or as Dostoevsky mocked, a treatise on Hanau's significance for the Hanseatic League, and on the particular and equivocal reasons why Hanau did not even attain such significance in its time—in other words the spirit becomes a baseless and basically odious cliché. Of course, one single reversal, and the night of our fragmented activity would become measurable and bright; even in infatuation the human face is turned in one single direction, and human beings still labor under sealed orders to institute freedom.

For then came the tireless expansion, the automatic operation, and our relentless attendance by mechanical power. There will still come the inevitable emancipation of humanity by technology, and its now irresistible consecration of life, namely the potential abolition of poverty and the emancipation, compelled by the revolutionary proletariat, from all questions of economics. There will also come a progressive and not strictly imperialistic inclusion of other cultures and phenomenologies into one common viewpoint, in accordance with the ancient missionary program. There will come a federative gathering of the nations themselves that can no longer be thwarted, the parallax of a distant star, the *multiversum* of a universal republic, so that the waste of isolated cultures will cease, and our fellow human being, who is meant by the word "morality," can also be born. There will finally come the rebirth of a church with no *poleis* and infused with the paraclete, summoning anew something fraternal within a human lifetime, preserving anew the fire signals and unity signals of human fellow-travellership, spiritual confederation. We are not becoming free for ourselves, as should already have been evident, just to fall asleep more easily, or to universalize the agreeable idleness of a particular upper class; we are not struggling to regain Dickens at best, or Victorian England's cozy fireplace; rather, this is the goal, the eminently practical goal, the basic motif of socialist ideology: to bestow on every human being time outside of work, his own need, boredom, wretchedness, privation and gloom, his own submerged light calling, a life in the Dostoevskyan sense, so that he will have set things right with himself, with his moral party membership, when the walls of the body fall, the world-body that protected us from the demons: when in other words the fortifications of the mundanely ordered kingdom are demolished.

And now a distant fluttering also goes before us, the soul grows bright, the truly creative idea awakens. What proves to be called to active intervention here, that will certainly come at the right time, on time [*zurecht*] within the philosophy of history, by right [*zu Recht*], even if not those people living now but only something preceding all time should be its receptive witness. Just as something in this book struggles to understand what is to be done, and to disclose the world of the self, finally and seriously to abolish that immoral game of the "world-enigma" and its seeming, its merely hypothetical solutions, to commit ethics and a philosophy open to the extraordinary [*das Ungeheure*] to the most constitutive thing of all, the seventh day of Creation: even these initial sketches of a system were not written for the public living now, but rather—helping, leading, conscientious in another way—as dictated by the philosophy of history, for the human spirit in us, for the Spirit of God within the present age, as the indicator on its gauge; and every book, in its meant-to-be, in its *a priori*, the power of this book of utopia, would finally like to be like two hands clutching a saucer, carrying this prize to its destination, filled with the drink of the self-encounters and of music, explosives against this world and the tropic essences of the goal, held aloft to God.[22] Only in this way can what is useless, anarchic and all too objectivist, literary about creative artifacts as such even be framed, set off: by means of a historical-theological background which lets us assign a flow, a current, a direction, a redemptive value and a metaphysical site to everything that humans create above themselves in the way of works. The site of another attempt, a restless mobilization, the site of true socialist ideology, the site of the plan for a great campaign by civilization and by culture directed against human baseness, against the world's stupidity and value-estrangement that smashes everything together—guided by the conscience of the Kingdom.

Nothing can consistently come to us here outside of the ordinary way of dying. But of course precisely for that reason our always busy arch-friend looks for ways to find, deceive, and torment even the souls that have escaped by means of transmigration. Just for the reason that inwardly, in the shadow of the towers we have built, nothing still defeats us, our bad conscience about the end has sought, in all our four hundred years of itinerancy and emancipation, at least to delay the process. Thus evil no longer initially approaches us as pride, but as sleep, fatigue, the veiling of the self and the distortion of the beyond, in a much more terrible way: for that one no longer believes in the devil, that one no longer has an eye for an already amassed transcendence, this constitutes the enemy's truest triumph, and assists his vengeful undertaking. Hence there are two points above all, and indeed focused precisely against those two criteria for philosophical ascertainment as such where the malignancy of the hateful, vengeful moment we have overtaken, the Satan within God, develops. First it can harden our hearts, and cause us to shut ourselves off from our neighbors. Thereupon it can interfere even more fundamentally, and mark off our wanting-to-be so abruptly, satisfy it so prematurely, that every more definitive fire within dwindles. And it seems that the cold, poisonous fog, so damaging to our respiration, not only so hardens our hearts that envy, obduracy, resentment, a murderous rejection of the likeness and the brightness can lodge there, whereby we commit the one true original sin, the not-wanting-to-be-like-God. Our bad conscience of the end also knows how to weaken, to harden our spirit so much that here the other part of this original sin insinuates itself, namely delusion, contentment with the world, the state as its own purpose, the omnipotence of the world brought about by our worship of the diabolical, and so embeds in us a tolerance for our remove from God, a not-wanting-to-be-like-God, as the true and deliberate formula of Antichristendom. But none of this is yet the anti-God's *truest* trump: the spiritual element has not yet deteriorated enough, and is too well combined with counterforces; in the final hour, a too explosive bitterness has broken out against every kind of domination, against the profusion of systems, against all the maliciously pointed or inward-curving works; in other words, our absolute conscience is too much provoked by coldness and also by any kind of dazzling impregnability; looting breaks into the false temple of the image, of the work, and into everything in cultural mortmain. But precisely in the fact that here our radical higher light begins to burn more brightly, begins to burn through world and illusion, we now see—as the final, most terrible, absolute counterattack—which *other*, long unheeded powers we have still to unharness, what a power of disruption and frustration can still operate within the stupidity of a simply impartial, God-forsaken causal nexus, how powerfully the demiurgic principle, so incited to vengeance by its other, is still able to retreat to its truest, powerful-invalid makeshift, which is still our space, and what a terribly final, absolute kind of dying and what fatal means are still available in *the physical world*: as the pitiless scene of our Kingdom.

We have certainly begun to emerge from it, alone of all those who remain sealed off downward. But while we do, the lower world keeps moving, the pulleys keep turning, and the blind, empty jostling of chance becomes the rule of this life. It can affect us randomly, bringing frustration, death and misfortune; so the lower world appears quite strange to us, but often already vengeful, too, as in the lost letter, the mediocre doctor who just happens to live nearby, that extra glass of wine the locomotive driver drank before the crash, although on the other hand steam drives the machine, accident and benefit all jumbled together—so foolishly, so maliciously random is this world's causal nexus. We ourselves are in the middle, disrupted a thousand times over, entangled in and subject to chance affinities, of which one still says a great deal when one calls them chance; when one still calls the monstrous stone that is nature, which slipped from our hands and now takes the value-free path downward into the abyss, blindness. Flaubert is the poet of this agony, our life's agony, of its inane, nerve-racking stupidity; the world is a tower where a prisoner sits, and the tower cannot also be humanized; the world is a wheel of Ixion onto which humanity is nailed, and hardly, as heathenishly infatuated astral myth would have it, a Christianized zodiac onto which zodiacal man, macrocosmic man can be applied while preserving all his depth. External nature indeed vaguely and broadly suggests certain inner mysteries, makes of the charnel-house a spiritual scenario, just as if behind the external sun there were actually concealed a Christ: but these are at best distorted correspondences, nature's summer is without ceremony, only at Christmas does the spirit-sun first shine its brightest light, Christianity is the paradox against all creatureliness and all nature, in the Apocalypse heaven will depart like a rolled-up cloth, and the Kabbalah teaches, not without reason, how it was out of precisely the debris of nature that the hostile demons emerged who wanted to destroy the human realm.[23] The mere physical world is still an impediment in itself; it is the collapsed house in which no one lived, is a rubbish heap of cheated, deceased, degraded, misled and ruined life, is the kingdom of Edom as it was, as it still is outside of Israel, outside of the human family, the spirit realm, and always the place where Ahriman's counterattack, a premature end of the world, a forestalled Apocalypse, is in danger of breaking through.

Quietly, now, the ground here begins to tremble that seemed no longer to reach us. We have nonetheless absolutely not completely escaped them, these mysterious processes operating by all appearances in the region lying below us, bearing us. What happens from helium up to lead, this decline in weight and this explosion slipping downward toward the simpler deposits of electrical energy: this is an exact uncoiling, a disintegration of what had been compacted together, and as a whole the first intelligible chemical indication of an entropy already long operative within the physical world, that is preparing to clear away and level the ancient, powerfully vaulted physical edifice. Here a warning signal of the end can already be heard, a quiet, distant trembling; a small, unusual cloud, never before seen, announces the approaching storm, and so, somewhere behind us, in the subterranean processes of radioactivity and not only just entropy, the second law of thermodynamics, the physical world collapses. One sees all this advance calmly and uncorrelatedly enough, of course: but should there not be, in this process moving so strongly toward the end, a place for the leap? Certainly entropic cooling alone could not contribute to the end of the physical world, as here the counterweight is dropping only very gradually; it is an extremely slow decrease in potential, still entirely within the dimensions of finite, physical time, and as a mere relaxation of the universe also far removed from any kind of explosive abruptness. Nevertheless, disregarding entirely the fact that radioactive decay is only appearing now, is in other words historically concurrent, is perhaps even functionally connected to the historical place of present human labor: is it not precisely then that these tremors should occur with so little correlation to our disparate age, such a *discontinuity* making everything groundless, letting these two moments, the disappearance of matter and the religious day of maturity, break apart in the most danger-

ous way? That hence simultaneously makes nature, this barely still sustained nature, this memorial slab, this arduous, fatally clear rubble heap
of worlds that God smashed, according to the Kabbalah, because no human being could be found there—that makes this monstrous, mindless
backdrop, this hard, slaggy, godless husk, accessible to every malign
metaphysical intervention without any potential resistance by heaven?
One knows, one can definitionally know, that the world as a process begins as well as ends in time; the unknowing that maintains it is, in its
seething relationality, not a permanent state, and must find its metacos-
mic limit point in either an absolute In Vain or an absolute Absolute.
Thin and slight thus becomes everything that does not help us past the
burning vapor; the terror of the millennium is not given to us, and none
of the prophets of the end of the world who have appeared in the meantime, always to be disappointed, can compromise the end's jet of flame,
Jesus' words concerning the Day of Judgment. The decisive blow is still
pending, and the countermovement toward the goal, no longer divisible
into rations, makes it obvious what a terrible breach is left open by the
potential death of matter, in matter's sickness, in a depopulated, uncanny
nature that has not yet been summoned to itself, not yet blossomed into
itself, open to every contamination and every explosion, to the true, inferior act of explosion, the Apocalypse as an *act of nature* fundamentally
disconformal with the day of maturity.

   For when we die, even when, as always, we die as someone who still
needed much life in order to be "complete," the earth still remains, and
the weapons can be passed on. But if one strangles us and we suffocate,[24]
the mountains and the islands move out of their places, and heaven departs like a rolled-up scroll[25]; if air and soil are taken away from us, the
sun turns black as sackcloth of hair, and the moon becomes as red as
blood[26]; if for us who are incomplete and unsheltered all the world's time,
the world's entire countenance thus dies out in the raging thunderstorms,
led by the devil himself, of the world's midnight hour, in the immeasurable collapse of every foundation and every firmament: then we stand
naked before the end, half, tepid, unclear and yet "consummated," consummated as by a tragic situation, although defeated by entirely different
wishes, connections and tempi than those of our work and its time, so laboriously wrested from Satan; rather, *Satan's* apocalyptic moment dominates now, and nothing carries any weight at this premature, satanically
arbitrary, but irrevocable conclusion to the work but the fullness of our

achieved purity and preparedness, our emotional wealth and spiritual anamnesis, our *having-absolutely-become* as the summoning knowledge *of our name, of the finally discovered name of God,* so that it will not all be in vain, so that the way will not be cheated of its goal and all its benefactions—life, soul, works, worlds of love—be ruined without leaving so much as a seed in the dust of our cosmic dissipation. Only the good, anamnestic person holding a key can draw forth the morning from this night of annihilation: if those who stayed impure do not weaken him, and if his call to the Messiah is illuminated enough to rouse the saving hands, to secure the grace of arrival for himself, to awaken the inspiriting, gracious powers of the Sabbath kingdom, consequently to engulf and immediately to vanquish the brutal, satanically dispiriting flashpoint of the Apocalypse.

Here the issue is absolutely not whether we will be admitted or not. Who could admit us or not, who could judge us, *nil inultum remanebit,* in order that he be not judged?[27] That we and a God are frustrated is the only judgment over us and Him, and it is terrible enough. That is why, however despairingly he turns his gaze toward the revelation, the tribunal in the Apocalypse of St. John commands reciprocity: in order to be just.[28] We too would rather hold on to our unavenged sufferings and our fervent, unappeasable anger, like Ivan Karamazov, than have to watch how everyone, completely innocent children along with them, has to suffer as the price of eternal harmony. Why are they, who really can have no share in the entire adult complex of sin, retribution, forgiveness, made to "furnish material to enrich the soil for the harmony of the future?" asks Ivan. "And if it is really true that they must share responsibility for all their fathers' crimes, such a truth is not of this world and is beyond my comprehension. . . . Oh, Alyosha, I am not blaspheming! I understand, of course, what an upheaval of the universe it will be when everything in heaven and earth blends in one hymn of praise and everything that lives and has lived cries aloud: 'Thou art just, O Lord, for Thy ways are revealed.' When the mother embraces the fiend who threw her child to the dogs, and all three cry aloud with tears, 'Thou art just, O Lord!' then, of course, the crown of knowledge will be reached and all will be made clear."[29] But Dostoevsky will not cry aloud; the children's tears remain unrequited; they cannot even be requited, whether through revenge or forgiveness; the being does not even exist who would have the right to condone such things in this world, his world; and if children must suffer to help pay the full price, the surcharge for the purchase of the truth, then this price is too high, and Ivan Karamazov, as a man of honor, refuses the ticket to the ultimate harmony. This means, one could have to see everything, and be there as it happens, that expense of the world's finale in the moment of eternal harmony, that suffices for every heart, to still our anger, to atone for all the atrocities committed by human beings, to absolve all the blood spilled by them, for the possibility not only of forgiveness but of justification for everything that has happened to us—and yet there lives in Ivan Karamazov and in us a force that will not accept that, that in Dostoevsky's inconceivably profound statement believes in God but refuses his world and no less the end result, the panlogistic day of judgment and atonement.

For this reason, too, we do not want to believe in him who is, the disintegrated one, but in the one who is valid. One cannot want or venerate the world, the Lord of the World, and then at the same time want what will heal or be healed by the world. It would ill become the distorted system that somehow guides the transformations of things as they exist in nature to tolerate every earthquake, shipwreck, war, and then be distressed only by the sinful perplexity of the human heart. At first there existed absolutely just one tendency, with man vaguely in view, but through Adam, through Jesus, the twofold essentiality of the direction awakened: the God of this world, ever more clearly becoming Satan, the archfiend and the interruption, and the God who continues on with Jesus, with Lucifer, the God of a future Ascension, the essentiality of the inner brilliance, of the *shekhinah* or true divine glory. What holds us in its inept and then vengeful hand: blocking, tormenting, deluding us, the spider, the kill or be killed, the poisonous scorpion, the angel of death, the demon of chance, of disaster, of death, the homelessness of everything meaningful, the dense, banal, almost impassable mountain range separating us from all Providence, the wizard of a "pious" panlogism—all that *can not* be the same principle that will one day pronounce judgment, and then claim always to have been watching over us by inscrutable, suprarational means, and, in spite of the "Fall" caused by our overweening pride, to have kept us close to its heart. There is in God, as our depth, this double self, at first confused, unclear, unseparated, but then awakened with complete clarity, and set apart, and indeed in such measure as humans have started on the path of wanting-to-know-better, as the serpent who returned within Christ and made the true Revelation more nearly audible against the wrath of the demiurge—as in other words our Luciferan nature rebelled in real terms through the tower of Babel, and in ideal terms through our Fall, as well as the angels', against the principle of an errant, depopulated, physical beginning to the world, and as even the prophets, Christ himself, proclaimed a wanting-to-create, a wanting-to-know or wanting-to-be-like-God, formerly called "original sin," as the highest postulate. This comes completely, however, from the heroic principle in us, from Lucifer, from the rebellious and finally homeward-turning principle, from the subject's wanting-to-know-more, from the rebel toward a goal, from the kernel of intensity and the commander of a hidden subjectivism finally recognized as no longer *mediator* but *conqueror*, as the seed of the paraclete, from the banner of Michael and the halo of Jesus; as in him, at the same time, the weak, far-removed final God, the utopian Idea, the Idea of the Good, proves itself, which, unlike the black sun, the demiurge's true and alone fallen nocturnal shape, no longer battles Lucifer or depicts him instead of itself as Satan. But the goal of this battle is surely that the removal of the physical world will be met with purified souls, with the souls' finally discovered *Absolute* [*Überhaupt*], with the unriven Paracletan guardian spirit of what is inmost, of the Servants, with the word from the essence, with the keyword of that Holy Spirit who for his part could let nature, this rubbish heap of error, disappear so completely that for the evil ones, as for Satan, one would not even need a gravestone, let alone a hell. Certainly spiritual life radiates beyond the body, there is a spiritual germ plasma, and transphysiological immortality is unaffected by the loss of the body. Nevertheless for spiritual life to reverberate beyond the annihilation of the world: for that it must first have become "complete" in the deepest sense, and thrown its towropes over the post at the landing on the other side, if the spiritual germ plasma is not also to be dragged down into the abyss of eternal death and the goal be missed on which the organization of life on this earth above all depends: our Master [*Haupt*], eternal life, accessibly grounded Servantry, an immortality that is also transcosmological, the one reality which is the Kingdom of spirit, the *pleroma* of the Holy Spirit, the foundation *in integrum* out of the labyrinth of the world.[30]

The Countenance of the Will

We live without knowing what for. We die without knowing where to.
Easy to say what one wants, now or later. But no one can say what he

absolutely [*überhaupt*] wants in this after all so very purposive world. "I'm surprised how happy I am!" says an old inscription.

And yet what is left for us here, we who suffer and are dark, is to hope far ahead. If it remains strong enough, becomes pure, possesses itself undivertedly enough, it will not go to ruin—hope will not let us go to ruin. For the human soul embraces everything, including the other side which is not yet. Hope alone is what we want, and thought serves hope, hope is its only space, its semantic content and its object scattered into every part of the world, hidden in the darkness of the lived moment, promised in the shape of the absolute question. And because what is—it can no longer be thought, but only still rethought—can be brought into line with the soul, because a kind wish can be father to an idea as well as to those things which alone are true, because of this finally antifactual, antimundane, world-sharing homogeneity between idea and *not*-being, *not-yet-being*, it is now only the empirically factual and its logic, and no longer the utopically factual, the imaginatively constitutive, which appears inaccessible or transcendent to the *creative concept*, indeed appears as the "metaphysics" forbidden by Kant. That should not be understood to mean that the other side could be shown to be merely "possible," for that a river could freeze over is possible, conditionally possible, or that plants have sensations is possible under hypothetical conditions, on the presupposition of still unknown premises, or that desert spirits can exist is possible under problematic conditions, on the presupposition of still unknown premises, perhaps entirely outside of the present radius of experienceability as such; but *that we will be blessed, that there can be a Heavenly Kingdom, that when seen evidently, the dream-content of the human soul also posits itself, that it is correlated to a sphere of reality, however defined*: this is not only conceivable, meaning formally possible, but *simply necessary*, far removed from any formal or real examples, proofs, concessions, premises of its existence, postulated *a priori* in the nature of the thing, and therefore also having the *utopian*, intensive inclination of a precisely given, *essential* reality. Within the concept of the bright, sacred soul, the timeless one, which it was our sole undertaking to divine and teach with the methods of philosophy, through the objects of faith: "He that overcometh, the same shall be clothed in white raiment; and I will not blot out his name out of the book of life, but I will confess his name before my Father, and before his angels."[31] Benevolence here has no limits, and the true thought summons the one single magic spell we seek, at whose sound every creature throws off its veil, and by whose flaring the God-bearing soul discloses its dream to itself, the dream of the presentiment, the dream which in the end will be the truth of the whole world. Hence in conclusion: we ourselves advance, by thinking, suffering and longing, into our inner mirror. We disappear through the small, painted door of this marvelous palace and can no longer be seen, in this world or in the other; the all-propelling, all-concealing moment has arrived and broken open; time stands still in the inner space of absolute unveiling, absolute present. Precisely that too was messianically meant by the Second Coming, and in an explosion it flies at the outside, the put-in-the-way, Satan the Demon of Death, the encrusted *ritardando* of the world, everything that is not of us or even obstructs us, of the plural Singular who hopes for himself, of our heavenly glory; while inside, in the Gothic sanctum of the Self-Encounter, this entire, spacious and apparently so very real world will itself one day just hang on the wall like the image of some innocuous memory.

But when nothing but Soul is willed, willing itself is immediately revealed therein. In its depths this impulse is at the same time the content, the only Arrival, the Equivalence [*Deckung*] of the movement. As its philosophy once again reverberates through the world, opens the gates of Christ everywhere—that is, the adequation of human longing to itself—reveals the secret Human Being, something always meant, always utopianly present, this identical substance corresponding at the same time to every moral-mystical symbol-intention. Thus we are the travelers and the compass at the same time: the finally self-equivalent [*gedeckt*] intensities are and themselves remain the enigma *before* the category as well as, *after* the category, the only solution that was meant, appearing above even the highest ideal transcendence till now. If, therefore, the thing-in-itself has appeared as this which is not yet, which in other words stirs and dreams within the lived darkness, in the deepening blue that now surrounds objects, at the same time also beyond all thought as the content of the deepest hope and awe, then the thing-in-itself now—in accordance with the final unity of intensity and light as *their* self-revelation—defines itself more precisely as *the Will to our true countenance* and ultimately as *the true countenance of our Will.*

Toward it we now reverberate, force what is inmost outward. None of our constructs may still be independent of us; man may no longer let himself be absorbed by the means and the false objectifications of himself.

Just as the machine and the state must be kept down in a merely disburdening role, cultural works may only still be erected as methods for the
accumulation or logical invention of Soul, with the requirement that they
be potentially convertible back into or across to the latter. Everything
alienated from man is worthless, every cultural objectivation is relevant
only as a subvention or a token, insofar as in the Name of God, to whom
we owe our purity as he owes us redemption, metaphysics and ethics
alone will be the gold standard. "Know this," says an old manuscript of
the Zohar in a related sense, "know that there is a twofold view of any
world. One shows its external aspect, namely the general laws of this
world in its external form. The other shows the inner essence of this
world, namely the quintessence of the souls of men. Accordingly there are
also two degrees of action, namely works and ascetic disciplines; works
are for perfecting worlds with respect to their externality, but prayers are
for causing one world to be contained in the other, and raising it up."
Within such a functional correlation of disburdening and spirit, Marxism
and religion, united in the will to the Kingdom, flows the ultimate master system of all the tributaries: the Soul, the Messiah, and the Apocalypse, which represents the act of awakening in totality, provide the final
impulses to do and to know, form the *a priori* of all politics and culture.
That is where this is going: to color, accelerate, decide everything with
ourselves; nothing is complete, nothing has already been closed off, nothing is solid all the way to its center—the only thing now is to gather the
lower parts that were split off, to let our Head [*Haupt*] continue growing
out of history, to force the state to accompany our fraternal congregation,
and finally to bring the grain of the self-encounter to the terrible harvest
celebration—"But we all, with open face beholding as in a glass the glory
of the Lord, are changed into the same image from glory to glory, even as
by the Spirit of the Lord."[32] For we are mighty; only the unjust exist
through their God, but the just—God exists through them, and into
their hands is given the consecration of the Name, the very appointment
of God, who moves and stirs in us, the presensed gateway, darkest question, exuberant interior that is no *factum* but a problem, given as a prayer
into the hands of our God-summoning philosophy and of truth.

The present volume, written between 1915 and 1916, first appeared in 1918, then again with some revisions in 1923. The latter edition is the basis of the reprint, the third volume of the *Werkausgabe*. It exhibits a number of deletions, above all for the sake of the thereby more clearly apparent line. Several newer versions—typographically, not with respect to content—derive mostly from the later 1920s; they were already then intended for a new edition. Otherwise this early work goes into print materially unchanged: an attempted initial major work, expressive, Baroque, devout, with a central subject matter. Music as it weaves within the shaft of the soul, as Hegel says, yet charged, a "gunpowder" within the subject-object relation. As a whole this principle applies: "The world is untrue, but it wants to return home through man and through truth." Enough about a *Sturm und Drang* book entrenched and carried out by night, against the War, as well as about a first work—built around the *nos ipse*— of a new, utopian kind of philosophy. Its revolutionary Romanticism (as in my monograph on Thomas Münzer) attains measure and definition in *The Principle of Hope* and the books that followed. There, what was specific to *The Spirit of Utopia* became especially definite, something entrusted peculiarly to evil, as to its remedy: revolutionary gnosis.

Reference Matter

Translator's Notes

Objective

1. "Stube" covers a range of meanings in German; here Bloch uses the word pejoratively. Nevertheless it becomes a key word later in the text (cf. 130 and *passim*), to represent a kind of room that is not *bürgerlich*. I have elected to translate it with the not entirely satisfactory "sanctum" as a small room with connotations of refuge or retreat; note that the German *Stube* does not have connotations of sanctity.

2. Bloch uses "Gewissen" in a deliberately archaic sense, consistent with the original Old High German loan translation from the Latin *conscientia* (Greek *syneídesis*): "to know with others." Both *Gewissen* and *conscience* seem to have undergone a similar evolution to mean a private moral awareness. However, only when "conscience" is also understood as collective awareness do formulations such as "conscience of the Absolute" make complete sense; nevertheless, "Gewissen" can simply not be translated as anything but "conscience." Likewise, "böses Gewissen" can only be translated as "guilty conscience," even though in Bloch it seems to mean something here closer to "false consciousness," one assumes deliberately.

Additionally, "Überhaupt" in German is an adverb and only an adverb, which Bloch uses consistently as a noun; it is *not* the usual equivalent for "the Absolute." "Überhaupt" can not only mean "generally" or "as such" or "absolutely," but its derivation is in fact "over-head," i.e., "superindividual." Accordingly, the reader should think of it as meaning "superior to the *Haupt*," another key term in *The Spirit of Utopia* which is sometimes incorrectly translated as "General" or "Master." However, Bloch's use of "Haupt" often alludes clearly to certain biblical passages where "Haupt" means not only one's "head," but the leader of a group, or, more pertinently, the "head of the church." Cf. Colossians 1:15–22; Ephesians 1:16–23; Ephesians 4:10–16; Ephesians 5:21–24.

An Old Pitcher

1. Bloch writes, "Ich bin an mir," which has several possible meanings, all of them significant. The first is "I am *right next to* myself," consistent with the paragraph that follows. The next is, "I am by myself," i.e., "alone," which is consistent not only with the first sentence from the introduction or "Objective," but also with Bloch's assumption that alienation and subjectivation are two sides of the same coin. The next is, "I exist or come into being through or by means of myself," in his dialectal use of "an" to indicate a causal relationship, which is consistent with the methodology of the book, combined equally of phenomenology and Eckhartian introspection, as well as with his reading of the history of art and music (cf. the first sentence of "On the History of Music," p. 34). Finally it corresponds to the American, "It's on you," i.e., "It's all up to you now," corresponding to Bloch's movement within this book: from the "evidence" of the I all the way to the "We." "I am by the pitcher" should then be read as "I am near the pitcher" as well as "I exist through the pitcher."

2. Bloch uses "sich decken" frequently, and it covers a range of meanings from "coincide with," "be congruent to," "equate to," as well as "cover" in the financial sense, i.e., "coverage" or "surety."

3. Possibly an allusion to Eckhart, Quint 20: "A master says that if every medium were removed between myself and a wall, then I would be at the wall but not in it."

4. "Water of life": cf. Revelation 22.

5. "Krug" is "pitcher," but the Grimms' exhaustive dictionary of the German language does not suggest a derivation for "nobis." The Grimms only note that "Nobiskrug" begins to displace "Nobishaus" (house) in the sixteenth century, and designates the inn where the souls of the dead stay overnight on their journey into the afterlife.

6. Urd is the Norn of the past (the Norns are the Nordic equivalent of the Greek fates).

The Production of the Ornament

1. The concept of the "Teppich" or carpet comes from Lukács's *Soul and Form*, where Lukács says of Paul Ernst's tragedies: "Yet there is an order concealed in the world of history, a composition in the confusion of its irregular lines. It is the undefinable order of a carpet or a dance; to interpret its meaning seems impossible, but it is still less possible to give up trying to interpret it. It is as though the whole fabric of fanciful lines were waiting for a single word that is always at the tip of our tongues, yet one which has never yet been spoken by anyone. History appears as a profound symbol of fate—of the regular accidentality of fate, its arbitrariness and tyranny which, in the last analysis, is always

just. Tragedy's fight for history is a great war of conquest against life, an attempt to find the meaning of history (which is immeasurably far from ordinary life) in life, to extract the meaning of history from life as the true, concealed sense of life." Trans. Anna Bostock (Cambridge, MA: MIT, 1971).

2. *Kunstwollen*: Bloch is clearly extending Wilhelm Worringer's use of the term, in his *Abstraction and Empathy*, to connect Expressionism with primitive art. The aesthetic-philosophical use of the term derives ultimately from Alois Riegl. It is conventionally translated as "artistic volition."

3. Bloch actually garbles this passage from dialogue between Parsifal and Gurnemanz in Wagner's *Parsifal*; I have simply translated Bloch's rendering.

4. Theodor Däubler, *Der neue Standpunkt* (1916).

5. From Archimedes' famous words, "Noli turbare circulos meos!" literally, "Don't disturb my circles!"

6. The Sanskrit phrase is common currency in German thanks to Schopenhauer. According to the *Brittanica*: " . . . in Hindu philosophy, the famous expression of the relationship between the individual and the absolute. The statement is frequently repeated in the sixth chapter of the *Chandogya Upanisad* (c. 600 B.C.E.), as the teacher Uddalaka Aruni instructs his son in the nature of the supreme reality."

7. "Frozen" music is an allusion to Schlegel's and Schelling's descriptions of architecture as "frozen music. Cf. p. 148.

8. The "cornerstone" is a reference to a number of biblical passages. Psalms 118:22: "The stone which the builders refused is become the head stone of the corner." Ephesians 2:19–22: "Now therefore ye are no more strangers and foreigners, but fellow-citizens with the saints, and of the household of God; And are built upon the foundation of the apostles and prophets, Jesus Christ himself being the chief corner stone; In whom all the building fitly framed together groweth unto an holy temple in the Lord: In whom ye also are builded together for an habitation of God through the Spirit." 1 Peter 2:4–9: "To whom coming, as unto a living stone, disallowed indeed of men, but chosen of God, and precious, Ye also, as lively stones, are built up a spiritual house, an holy priesthood, to offer up spiritual sacrifices, acceptable to God by Jesus Christ. Wherefore also it is contained in the scripture, Behold, I lay in Sion a chief corner stone, elect, precious: and he that believeth on him shall not be confounded. Unto you therefore which believe he is precious: but unto them which be disobedient, the stone which the builders disallowed, the same is made the head of the corner, And a stone of stumbling, and a rock of offence, even to them which stumble at the word, being disobedient: whereunto also they were appointed." The Egyptian city of Sais is important in both Schiller's "Das Verschleierte Bild zu Sais" [The Veiled Image at Sais] and Novalis' "Die Lehrlinge zu Sais" [The Novices of Sais]. Cf. p. 207 and *passim*.

9. The "macanthropos" is the "Cosmic Man" of Gnostic theology, i.e., the

man whose body corresponds part by part to the entire cosmos. Cf. Bloch's *Atheism in Christianity*. The "morningstar" here is a metaphor for Christ, in Bloch's heterodox understanding; cf. 2 Peter 1:19. Christ is also characterized in this way in Revelation, which is generally the source of the concept of the "seal."

10. "Pointing marks" are a metaphor from marble sculpture: shallow marks in the stone that delineate an area to be chipped away.

11. The reference is to Hofmannsthal's "Reitergeschichte" [A Horseman's Story].

The Philosophy of Music

1. *Human, All Too Human*, vol. 2, pt. 1, "Miscellaneous Opinions and Maxims," no. 171, "Music as every culture's late fruit." My translation.

2. The reference is to Kleist's "Die Heilige Cäcilie oder die Gewalt der Musik" [*Saint Cecilia, or, The Power of Music*].

3. *Soul and Form* 167.

4. Silcher, Friedrich (1789–1860), composer and pedagogue. Important in the development of amateur chorales. Author of numerous artificial folk songs, such as "Ännchen von Tharau" and "Lorelei."

5. Bloch uses the very unusual word "Körperseele," which is more common in occult or alchemical writings than anywhere else, as a German rendering of the Hermetic *anima corporalis*.

6. Bloch is alluding to Bach's *St. Matthew Passion*, BWV 244. The chorus in fact sings "Lass ihn kreuzigen!" based on Matthew 27:22–23.

7. Reference to Klopstock, "Dem Unendlichen" [*To the Infinite*], set to music by Schubert.

8. Piloty, Karl Theodor von (1826–1886), the nineteenth century's foremost German realist painter. He was particularly known for such historicist paintings as "Seni at the Dead Body of Wallenstein," which gained him a professorship in Munich. He would come to head the Munich Academy, and was eventually ennobled by the King of Bavaria.

9. "Unterwegs" as a noun is a key word here, and possibly derives from Meister Eckhart and Nicholas of Cusa.

10. Ibn Tufayl (1109/10–1185/86), Moorish philosopher and physician, best known for certain works of mystical speculation.

11. Bloch is quoting from Friedrich Hebbel's "Ich und Du" [I and Thou], set to music by Hans Pfitzner (1869–1949), op. 11, no. 1, among others.

12. The reference is to "The Devil with the Three Golden Hairs," Grimm no. 29.

13. Grimm no. 36.

14. Franz Rolf Schröder (1893–?), author of the still standard 1934 *Germanische Heldendichtung* [Germanic Heroic Poetry].

15. Bloch misquotes the passage from Mathilde Wesendonck's (1828–1902) "Im Treibhaus" [In the Greenhouse], set to music by Wagner in *Fünf Gedichte für eine Frauenstimme und Klavier*.

16. Cf. Colossians 1:15, *passim*.

17. The title of Hebbel's poem is "Zwei Wandrer" [*Two Wanderers*], and is conventionally held to depict the meeting of a mute Nature with deaf Mankind. Translation mine.

18. Wilhelm Jordan (1819–1904), politician, member of the national assembly, epic poet, theoretician of Social Darwinism. In this context Bloch is alluding to his retelling of the Nibelungen legends, published in 1874. Felix Dahn (1834–1912), author of the hugely popular historical novel *Der Kampf um Rom* [The Battle for Rome]. In this context Bloch is alluding to his 1880 *Odhins Trost* [Odin's Consolation].

19. Meister Eckhart also uses the same image, which in fact comes from 1 Timothy 6:16, about Jesus Christ "who only hath immortality, dwelling in the light which no man can approach unto; whom no man hath seen, nor can see: to whom be honour and power everlasting."

20. An allusion to *Faust*: "Allein der Vortrag macht des Redners Glück."

21. Spoken by an astrologer in *Faust* II, Act 1.

22. See n. 42.

23. Cf. n. 39, the discussion of Schopenhauer.

24. According to the OED, a *logogriph* is "a kind of enigma, in which a certain word, and other words that can be formed out of all or any of its letters, are to be guessed from synonyms of them introduced into a set of verses. Occasionally used for: Any anagram or puzzle involving anagrams."

25. Bloch's source is unknown.

26. Reference to Goethe's *Pandora*.

27. Matthew 24:27 and *passim*: "For as the lightning cometh out of the east, and shineth even unto the west; so shall also the coming [παρουσία] of the Son of man be."

28. A reference to *Faust* II, Act 1: "Am farbigen Abglanz haben wir das Leben."

29. Cf. n. 27.

30. Spoken by Faust in *Faust* I, "Night."

31. Schiller, *Wallensteins* Tod II: 2: "Leicht beieinander wohnen die Gedanken / Doch eng im Raume stoßen sich die Sachen."

32. Bloch often uses "evidence" in the singular, i.e., "*an* evidence," in a fashion I assume comes from phenomenology, and meaning "that which is evident."

33. Note that Bloch uses "Traumwerk," not the Freudian "Traumarbeit"; the former indicates a product, the latter the process.

34. *Merchant of Venice* V:1, Lorenzo to Jessica.

35. "Pious fraud," *pia fraus*, is a phrase from Ovid's *Metamorphoses*.

36. A term from icon painting.

37. Allusion to Book 3, § 52.

38. Not only a biblical allusion, but also an allusion to the Elder Zossima's memoirs in *The Brothers Karamazov*: "Of Masters and Servants, and of whether it is possible for them to be Brothers in the Spirit" (Garnett translation).

39. Here and immediately below, Bloch is quoting very loosely from Schopenhauer's *Welt als Wille und Vorstellung*, Book 3, § 52. My rendering relies on R. B. Haldane and J. Kemp's standard English translation, *The World As Will and Idea*.

40. This text comes from *The World As Will and Idea*, Book IV, § 54, n. 1.

41. The passage is from "Ein sonderlicher Kasus von harten Talern und Waldhorn," in Claudius' *Wandsbecker Bote*.

42. *Kreisleriana*, chapter 6; *Der goldene Topf*, 4th vigil.

43. "Warum vergißt man darüber, daß die Musik freudige und traurige Empfindungen verdoppelt, ja sogar selber erzeugt, daß sie allmächtiger und gewaltsamer als jede Kunst uns zwischen Freude und Schmerz ohne Übergänge in Augenblicken hin und her stürzt—ich sage, warum vergißt man eine höhere Eigentümlichkeit von ihr: ihre Kraft des Heimwehs, nicht ein Heimweh nach einem alten verlassenen Lande, sondern nach einer Zukunft?"

44. "Devachan" is a Vedic word popular in theosophy, meaning "realm of the gods." There the soul sojourns blissfully before being reincarnated. Rudolf Steiner held that we reach it in sleep. It is occasionally represented as a land where everything is music. In any case, Bloch uses "devachan" as another term for the "celestial" as opposed to the "astral" realm.

45. Spoken by Wagner, the "Famulus," in *Faust* I.

46. The image of the sleeper, as well as the passage up to "true," is from Jean Paul Richter's *Titan*, 22. Jobelperiode, 94. Zykel.

The Shape of the Inconstruable Question

1. James 4:17.

2. Revelation 21:5.

3. Bloch often uses the financial terms "Deckung" [*coverage, surety*; more broadly, *equivalence, coincidence, congruence*], "decken" [*to guarantee, to cover*], and "ungedeckt" [both literally and financially, *exposed*].

4. " . . . erst die Religion gründet ihre Aufforderung zur Verneinung des entgegengesetzten falschen Lebens durchaus auf die Bejahung und Kräftigung eines anderen und besseren Lebens, dessen Evolution mit der Involution des schlechten Lebens gleichen Schritt hält."

5. Bloch's source is unknown.

6. Bloch's source is unknown.

7. *Dreams of a Spirit-Seer*, Part 1, Chapter 4.

8. Zendelwald is the conventional German fairy tale hero, in Keller's "The

Virgin As Knight," from his *Sieben Legenden*, who achieves his goal through in-advertence. The tailor is from the story "Clothes Make the Man."

9. The word "Halbunsinn" only appears in Book 12 of *Dichtung und Wahr-heit*, and not in respect of the *Harzreise*, though Bloch seems to be alluding here to Goethe's description of its process of composition in "Campagne in Frank-reich 1792." "Des Chaos wunderlicher Sohn" is Mephistopheles, described so by Faust in *Faust* I, "Study Room" scene. The rest of the passage seems reminiscent of *Faust* II, but is Bloch's.

10. Bloch uses "careers" in a sense almost vanished in American English, to mean course, pathway, progress through life.

11. Reference to Book 9, Chapter 8, *Brothers Karamazov*, in the Pevear/Volokhonsky translation; "babe" in Garnett.

12. "Vergiß das Beste nicht!" is an admonition issued in a number of the Grimms' tales, in particular "The White Bride and the Black Bride" (no. 135).

13. From Yeats' "The Philosophy of Shelley's Poetry."

14. This seems to be the passage preserved only in Hippolytus' *Refutations*, of which the usual translation is, "There was when naught was: nay, even that 'naught' was not aught of things that are. But nakedly, conjecture and mental quibbling apart, there was absolutely not even the one. And when I use the term 'was' I do not mean to say that it was; but merely to give some suggestion of what I wish to indicate, I use the expression 'there was absolutely naught.' Naught was, neither matter, nor substance, nor voidness of substance, nor sim-plicity, nor impossibility of composition, nor inconceptibility, imperceptibility, neither man, nor angel, nor God; in fine, anything at all for which man has ever found a name, nor by any operation which falls within range of his perception or conception." Basilides (ca. 85–150 C.E.) is discussing what existed before cre-ation, which is apparently subject to drastically different translations; this is my rendering of Bloch's rendering.

15. From a sermon now considered spurious (no. 57 in Josef Quint's defini-tive edition; the passage from Augustine is from *De Trinitate* xii, c. 7, n. 10). I am quoting from vol. 1 of M. O'C. Walsh's translation (Shaftesbury, Dorset: El-ement, 1979) 9–10. The sermon is on the Wisdom of Solomon 15:14.

16. Following Eckhart's commentary on John 1:38, Nicholas of Cusa's 1456 "Ubi est qui natus est rex Iudaeorum?" indicates that this sentence need not be taken as a question, but can be read as a statement or declaration, thus: "The king who is born is God who is the place of all things." Jesus is "'where' or 'place' in the absolute sense."

17. Colossians 3:4: "When Christ, who is our life, shall appear, then shall ye also appear with him in glory."

18. "Objective side" is a metaphor from optics, meaning the side of the ap-paratus away from the viewer.

19. " . . . aber das Meer hat keinen Charakter und der Sand hat auch keinen

und abstrakte Verständigkeit auch keinen, denn der Charakter ist eben die In-nerlichkeit." Bloch's source is unknown.

20. "Was nicht der Himmel der Himmel umschloß, / Dies liegt jetzt in Mariae Schoß." This might be Bloch's free reconstruction of a passage from Eckhart, it might refer to a spurious sermon, or even to Nicholas of Cusa's *The Science of Unknowing*.

21. This seems like an extremely loose paraphrase from *The Critique of Pure Reason*, "Transcendental Doctrine of Method," Chapter 2 ("The Canon of Pure Reason"), Section 2 ("The Ideal of the Highest Good, As a Determining Ground of the Ultimate End of Pure Reason").

22. Luther's translation of Exodus 3:14 has: "Ich werde sein, der ich sein werde," i.e., "I will be that I will be." Of course the familiar KJV has "I am that I am."

23. From the text of the Te Deum: "Let me not be damned for eternity."

24. Possibly a reference to Revelation 19:17– 18: "And I saw an angel standing in the sun; and he cried with a loud voice, saying to all the fowls that fly in the midst of heaven, Come and gather yourselves together unto the supper of the great God; That ye may eat the flesh of kings, and the flesh of captains, and the flesh of mighty men, and the flesh of horses, and of them that sit on them, and the flesh of all men, both free and bond, both small and great."

25. The allusion is to Beethoven's *Fidelio*; the minister Fidelio is Florestan's wife, Leonora, who disguises herself as a man in order to rescue her husband.

26. Matthew 19:17. Cf. Mark 10:18 and Luke 18:19.

27. A "resultant" is a term from vector algebra.

28. Cf. Genesis 3:19.

29. From Father Zossima's recollections of the time before he became a monk, in *The Brothers Karamazov*: Here he is feeling remorse at having beaten his orderly, and remembers what his brother had said on his deathbed: "He had said, 'Mother, my little heart, in truth we are each responsible to all for all, it's only that men don't know this. If they knew it, the world would be a paradise at once.'" These are later the words with which Dmitri explains to Alyosha his willingness to go to prison for a murder he did not commit.

30. Isaiah 53:1– : "Who hath believed our report? and to whom is the arm of the LORD revealed? For he shall grow up before him as a tender plant, and as a root out of a dry ground: he hath no form nor comeliness; and when we shall see him, there is no beauty that we should desire him. He is despised and re-jected of men; a man of sorrows, and acquainted with grief: and we hid as it were our faces from him; he was despised, and we esteemed him not. Surely he hath borne our griefs, and carried our sorrows: yet we did esteem him stricken, smitten of God, and afflicted. But he was wounded for our transgressions, he was bruised for our iniquities: the chastisement of our peace was upon him; and with his stripes we are healed. All we like sheep have gone astray; we have

turned every one to his own way; and the LORD hath laid on him the iniquity of us all. He was oppressed, and he was afflicted, yet he opened not his mouth: he is brought as a lamb to the slaughter, and as a sheep before her shearers is dumb, so he openeth not his mouth. He was taken from prison and from judgment: and who shall declare his generation? for he was cut off out of the land of the living: for the transgression of my people was he stricken. And he made his grave with the wicked, and with the rich in his death; because he had done no violence, neither was any deceit in his mouth. Yet it pleased the LORD to bruise him; he hath put him to grief: when thou shalt take his soul an offering for sin, he shall see his seed, he shall prolong his days, and the pleasure of the LORD shall prosper in his hand. He shall see of the travail of his soul, and shall be satisfied: by his knowledge shall my righteous servant justify many; for he shall bear their iniquities. Therefore will I divide him a portion with the great, and he shall divide the spoil with the strong; because he hath poured out his soul unto death: and he was numbered with the transgressors; and he bare the sin of many, and made intercession for the transgressors."

31. Isaiah 66:3.

32. Genesis 22:14: "Und Abraham nannte die Stätte 'Der HERR sieht.' Daher man noch heute sagt: Auf dem Berge, da der HERR sieht," i.e., "where the LORD will see." The NIV has, "So Abraham called that place The LORD Will Provide." And to this day it is said, "On the mountain of the LORD it will be provided." The KJV has, "In the mount of the LORD it shall be seen." Bloch also writes "die drei Schofartöne des oberen Versöhnungsfest," i.e., the highest Day of Atonement.

33. "Der alte Adam" is an allusion to Romans 6:6 ("Knowing this, that our old man is crucified with him, that the body of sin might be destroyed, that henceforth we should not serve sin") and Colossians 3:9–10 ("Lie not one to another, seeing that ye have put off the old man with his deeds; And have put on the new man, which is renewed in knowledge after the image of him that created him"); Luther rendered "old man" as "old Adam." In both German and English, "the old Adam" is an archaic idiom for one's formerly sinful nature.

34. Revelation 21:23.

35. The unnamed Scholastic is in fact Augustine, in a sermon on John 6:9 (Sermon CXXX in the Benedictine edition). Bloch is quoting from St. Gregory of Nyssa's (335–395?) *Great Catechism*, Chapter XXIV, though the image is very widespread.

36. I have translated "Beiwerk" as "accessories" as in the passage from Schopenhauer quoted on p. 152.

37. 1 John 3:2.

38. 1 Corinthians 15; Colossians 3: 3–4.

39. Revelation 21:2: "And I John saw the holy city, new Jerusalem, coming down from God out of heaven, prepared as a bride adorned for her husband."

40. Strindberg, *Ghost Sonata*. The passage in the translation I have is: " . . . greeted by a sun that does not scorch, in a home without dust, by friends without faults, and by a love without flaw."

41. "Zart Gedicht, wie Regenbogen, / Wird nur auf dunklen Grund gezogen; / Darum behagt dem Dichtergenie / Das Element der Melancholie." Goethe: *Gedichte*, Ausgabe letzter Hand, 1827. Cf. *Berliner Ausgabe* I: 447. Schopenhauer quotes it in *Welt als Wille*, vol. 2, book 3, chapter 31.

42. Presumably a reference to Acts 2:1–4, "And when the day of Pentecost was fully come, they were all with one accord in one place. And suddenly there came a sound from heaven as of a rushing mighty wind, and it filled all the house where they were sitting. And there appeared unto them cloven tongues like as of fire, and it sat upon each of them. And they were all filled with the Holy Ghost, and began to speak with other tongues, as the Spirit gave them utterance."

Karl Marx, Death, and the Apocalypse

1. Bloch is exploiting the double meaning of the German "Larve," i.e., both "larva" and "mask." The OED attests both meanings for "larve" in English, which I have elected to use despite its archaism. In the preceding sentence, "Fratze" also means both "deformed face" and "grimace."

2. From a letter to Hegel, November 1815. Niethammer (1766–1848) was a theologian and philosopher, and later played a leading role in the revision of the Bavarian education system, where the conservative Catholic von Weiller was his bitter enemy.

3. Gustav Schwab (1792–1850), best known for his *Sagen des klassischen Altertums* [Legends of Classical Antiquity]. His very popular ballad "Der Reiter und der Bodensee" tells the story of a man who rides unknowingly all the way across the lake in the dark, then dies of fright the next day when he finds out what he has just done.

4. Source unknown: "die Begeisterung für den gleichheitlichen Genuß."

5. Possibly an allusion to Johann Karl August Musäus's (1735–1787) retellings of the Rübezahl stories.

6. Presumably a reference not to the Battle of Cannae (216 B.C.E., during the Second Punic War) itself, where Hannibal's troops defeated the Roman army despite far fewer numbers, but to the German Field Marshal Count Alfred von Schlieffen (1833–1913), chief of the Prussian general staff before World War I, whose book *Cannae* described the Schlieffen plan for fighting on two fronts, with which Germany entered WWI.

7. Augustine, *Soliloquies*, Book I, Chapter 7: "God and the soul, that is what I desire to know. Nothing more? Nothing whatever!"

8. *Faust* I, "Night": "Zu neuen Ufern lockt ein neuer Tag."

9. G. K. Chesterton, *Orthodoxy*.

10. The Seeress of Prevost was famous in the German literary context because of Justinus Kerner's (1786–1862) book about her. She was an international sensation for quite some time: Margret Fuller wrote extensively about her, and she was a touchstone for C. G. Jung and Madame Blavatsky.

11. This section is partly a response to Baron Carl du Prel (1839–1899), philosopher and occultist, who saw himself as a Kantian (arguing conversely that Kant's *Dreams of a Spirit Medium* show him to be a mystic), author of the *Philosophy of Mysticism* (tr. C. C. Massey [London, 1889]). Argued that spiritualistic phenomena furnished empirical evidence of the existence of transcendental beings. He accepted human survival as a proved fact. He was one of the pioneers of psychical research in Germany. He demanded state-appointed commissions for research and insisted on the difference between mediums and conjurors. Cf. Freud's *The Interpretation of Dreams*.

12. *Faust* I, "Night."

13. "Denn freilich werden die Seelen derer, die ganz von zeitlichen Dingen erfüllt sind, gar sehr zusammengehen und sich dem Zustand der Vernichtung nähern; diejenigen aber, die ganz von zeitlichen Dingen erfüllt sind, werden mit dem größten Teil ihres Wesens ewig sein." These words do not appear to be Schelling's, but rather those of John 12:25, "He that loveth his life shall lose it; and he that hateth his life in this world shall keep it unto life eternal."

14. *Huttens letzte Tage* XVI.

15. From *Levana oder Erziehlehre*, 1. Bändchen, 4. Bruckstück, 9. Kapitel, § 74.

16. See Apuleius' *Golden Ass*, Book 11.

17. From Goethe's *West-Östlicher Diwan*, the poem "Selige Sehnsucht" [Blessed Longing].

18. Allusion to the Witch's Kitchen scene of *Faust* I.

19. Matthew 25:1–13: "Then shall the kingdom of heaven be likened unto ten virgins, which took their lamps, and went forth to meet the bridegroom. And five of them were wise, and five were foolish. They that were foolish took their lamps, and took no oil with them: But the wise took oil in their vessels with their lamps. While the bridegroom tarried, they all slumbered and slept. And at midnight there was a cry made, Behold, the bridegroom cometh; go ye out to meet him. Then all those virgins arose, and trimmed their lamps. And the foolish said unto the wise, Give us of your oil; for our lamps are gone out. But the wise answered, saying, Not so; lest there be not enough for us and you: but go ye rather to them that sell, and buy for yourselves. And while they went to buy, the bridegroom came; and they that were ready went in with him to the marriage: and the door was shut. Afterward came also the other virgins, saying, Lord, Lord, open to us. But he answered and said, Verily I say unto you, I know you not. Watch therefore, for ye know neither the day nor the hour wherein the Son of man cometh."

20. Most likely an allusion to Eckhart as well.

21. The goddess who offers Hercules immortality mocks him for wanting to die for honor; from Christoph Martin Wieland's *Die Wahl des Herkules* [Hercules' Decision], a short verse play.

22. Bloch uses the unusual word "Gottgeist" here, which appears only once in the Bible, in Genesis 1:1–2: "In the beginning God created the heaven and the earth. And the earth was without form, and void; and darkness was upon the face of the deep. And the *Spirit of God* moved upon the face of the waters." "Tropic" here in the sense of "trope," i.e., "turn," "tropism" being a keyword in this text (*passim*). "Essenz" could mean either "essence" in the philosophical sense, or simply "distillate," or both. I have chosen to preserve the ambiguity.

23. Revelation 6:14: "And the heaven departed as a scroll when it is rolled together; and every mountain and island were moved out of their places."

24. "Strangle" refers back to the "angel of death," or "Würgengel" in German: "strangling angel." Possibly an allusion to Mark 4:19, "And the cares of this world, and the deceitfulness of riches, and the lusts of other things entering in, choke the word, and it becometh unfruitful." Cf. Matthew 13:22: "He also that received seed among the thorns is he that heareth the word; and the care of this world, and the deceitfulness of riches, choke the word, and he becometh unfruitful."

25. Cf. n. 24.

26. Revelation 6:12: "And I beheld when he had opened the sixth seal, and, lo, there was a great earthquake; and the sun became black as sackcloth of hair, and the moon became as blood."

27. From the text of the Requiem: "Nothing shall remain unpunished." The choir sings this to Gretchen in the "Cathedral" scene of Goethe's *Faust* before she swoons.

28. Apparently from the apocryphal *Revelation of St. John the Theologian*: "And again I said: Lord, is it possible in that world to recognize each other, a brother his brother, or a friend his friend, or a father his own children, or the children their own parents? And I heard a voice saying to me: Hear, John. To the righteous there is recognition, but to the sinners not at all; they cannot in the resurrection recognize each other."

29. Quotations from Constance Garnett's translation, Chapter 4, "Rebellion."

30. "Alleinige Realität" could be simply the kingdom of Spirit, which is the *sole* reality; it could also be "all-einig," all-united.

31. Revelation 3:5.

32. 2 Corinthians 3:18. The NIV has: "And we, who with unveiled faces all reflect [contemplate] the Lord's glory, are being transformed into his likeness with ever-increasing glory, which comes from the Lord, who is the Spirit."

Index of Names

In this index an "f" after a number indicates a separate reference on the next page, and an "ff" indicates separate references on the next two pages. A cluster of references in close but not consecutive sequence is indicated by *passim*.

M E R I D I A N

Crossing Aesthetics

Jacques Derrida, *On the Name*

David Wills, *Prosthesis*

Maurice Blanchot, *The Work of Fire*

Jacques Derrida, *Points ... : Interviews, 1974–1994*

J. Hillis Miller, *Topographies*

Philippe Lacoue-Labarthe, *Musica Ficta (Figures of Wagner)*

Jacques Derrida, *Aporias*

Emmanuel Levinas, *Outside the Subject*

Jean-François Lyotard, *Lessons on the Analytic Sublime*

Peter Fenves, *"Chatter": Language and History in Kierkegaard*

Jean-Luc Nancy, *The Experience of Freedom*

Jean-Joseph Goux, *Oedipus, Philosopher*

Haun Saussy, *The Problem of a Chinese Aesthetic*

Jean-Luc Nancy, *The Birth to Presence*

Library of Congress Cataloging-in-Publication Data

Bloch, Ernst.
  [Geist der Utopie.   English]
  The spirit of Utopia / Ernst Bloch ; translated by Anthony Nassar.
     p.   cm. — (Meridian)
  Includes bibliographical references and index.
ISBN 0-8047-3764-9 (cloth : alk. paper). — ISBN 0-8047-3765-7
(pbk. : alk. paper)
    1. Philosophy.   2. Music—Philosophy and aesthetics.   I. Title.
II. Series : Meridian (Stanford, Calif.)
B3209.B753G4213   2000
193—dc21   99-38497

♾   This book is printed on acid-free, archival quality paper.

Original printing 2000
Last figure below indicates the year of this printing:
09 08 07 06 05 04 03 02 01 00

Typeset by James P. Brommer in 10.9/13 Garamond
and Lithos display